History, Reflection, and Narrative: The Professionalization of Composition, 1963–1983

Perspectives on Writing: Theory, Research, Practice
Kathleen Blake Yancey and Brian Huot, Series Editors

Vol. 1 Assessing Writing Practices Across the Curriculum: Diverse Approaches and Practices
Kathleen Blake Yancey and Brian Huot, editors—1997

Vol. 2 Standing in the Shadow of Giants: Plagiarists, Authors, Collaborators
by Rebecca Moore Howard—1999

Vol. 3 History, Reflection, and Narrative: The Professionalization of Composition, 1963–1983
Mary Rosner, Beth Boehm, and Debra Journet, editors—1999

Vol. 4 The Ethics of Writing Instruction: Issues in Theory and Practice
Michael A. Pemberton, editor—forthcoming

History, Reflection, and Narrative: The Professionalization of Composition, 1963–1983

edited by

Mary Rosner
Beth Boehm
Debra Journet
University of Louisville

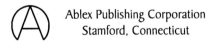

Ablex Publishing Corporation
Stamford, Connecticut

Printed in the United States of America

Library of Congress Cataloging-in-Publication Data

History, reflection, and narrative: the professionalization of composition, 1963–1983 / edited by Mary Rosner, Beth Boehm, Debra Journet.
p. cm. — (Perspectives on writing ; v. 3)
Includes bibliographical references and index.
ISBN 1-56750-397-7 (cloth) — ISBN 1-56750-398-5 (pbk.)
1. English language—Rhetoric—Study and teaching—United States—History—20th century. 2. English teachers—Training of—United States—History—20th century. 3. English language—Composition and exercises. I. Rosner, Mary. II. Boehm, Beth. III. Journet, Debra. IV. Series.
PE1405.U6H56 1999
808'.042'07'073—dc21 99-12960
CIP

Ablex Publishing Corporation
100 Prospect Street
P.O. Box 811
Stamford, CT 06904-0811

P

In order to keep this title in print and available to the academic community, this edition was produced using digital reprint technology in a relatively short print run. This would not have been attainable using traditional methods. Although the cover has been changed from its original appearance, the text remains the same and all materials and methods used still conform to the highest book-making standards.

This book is dedicated to the memory of Dr. Thomas R. Watson, a Louisville physician, banker, and entrepreneur, born August 16, 1935, in Graves County, Kentucky; he died January 15, 1996. He was married to Sylvia Watson and had two daughters, McCall Watson Eng and Emily Watson Ragan.

Dr. Watson was a board-certified gynecologist, active in his profession. In concert with his career in the medical field, he served on civic and charitable boards, including the University of Louisville Board of Overseers, and was involved with Magnolia Bancorp, Commonwealth Bank, Bankers' Mortgage, Health Care Partners, and Celsus, Inc.

In 1995, Dr. Watson gave $1.2 million to the English Department of the University of Louisville to endow a biennial International Conference in Rhetoric and Composition and a Visiting Distinguished Professorship of Rhetoric and Composition. This gift is a mark not only of Dr. Watson's extraordinary generosity, but also of his imaginative and far-sighted vision. It attests to his understanding of the fundamental importance of a literate citizenry, and of the vital task faced by the liberal arts, particularly English studies, in educating students to become critical, active, and engaged readers and writers.

Contents

Acknowledgments

This book is a tribute to the generosity and vision of Dr. Thomas R. Watson. Dr. Watson's gift to the University of Louisville supports a biennial international conference on rhetoric and composition and, in alternate years, a Visiting Distinguished Professorship. This gift has provided remarkable occasions for learning for University of Louisville faculty and students. But it is also an opportunity for writing teachers across the country who will benefit from possibilities for the learning, thinking, and collaborating these conferences will offer. It is, we believe, difficult for us to put a limit on what this far-sighted gift will really mean. Over the years, researchers, teachers, and students will come to the University of Louisville and benefit from Dr. Watson's generosity. They will, in turn, influence other researchers, teachers, and students, spreading the impact of this gift throughout the Commonwealth of Kentucky, the United States, and beyond.

We are also grateful to Mrs. Sylvia Watson for her ongoing encouragement and her support in implementing Dr. Watson's vision.

In addition, we would like to acknowledge the support of many people who helped make the Conference and this book that resulted from it a reality. Most prominently, Dr. Robert H. Miller, former chair of the English Department, helped Dr. Watson shape his exciting vision. Furthermore, in ways too numerous to mention, the English Department owes a debt of gratitude to Dr. Miller, whose leadership and whose commitment to the importance of rhetoric and composition within the Department has provided an intellectual environment always marked by collegiality and respect.

Dr. Brian Huot, the first Thomas R. Watson Conference director, took on the heavy and unfamiliar responsibilities of organizing and running an international conference. The success of the first Conference is in many ways his achievement and that of his assistant directors, Steve Watkins and Annie Brush. We also are grateful to the Watson Conference Faculty Committee (Beth Boehm, Ruth Greenberg, Brian Huot, Hildy Miller, Mary Rosner, Mary Catherine Flannery, Dennis Hall, Debra Journet, and Pamela Takayoshi), and the Watson Conference Graduate

Student Committee (Anthony Baker, Tim Catalano, Mary Jane Cherry, Jane Mathison-Fife, Cassie Mach, Katy Powell, Annie Brush, Randy Cauthen, Mark Crane, Morgan Gresham, Thomas Pace, and Steve Watkins). We also thank Mark Hall, Teresa Kendall, Jack Ramey, and Tony Scott for their editorial assistance in preparing the manuscript.

We also want to thank those who attended and presented papers and who helped make this first conference such an intellectually exciting event. We are particularly grateful for the participation of the featured speakers: David Bartholomae, Patricia Bizzell, Joseph Comprone, Robert Connors, Charles Cooper, Edward P.J. Corbett, Frank D'Angelo, Peter Elbow, Janet Emig, Lester Faigley, Winifred Horner, Jacqueline Jones Royster, James Kinneavy, Richard Larson, Janice Lauer, Richard Lloyd-Jones, Andrea Lunsford, Lee Odell, Richard Ohmann, Sondra Perl, Stephen Witte, and Richard Young. Interviews of most featured speakers are included in this volume.

Finally, we extend our deep thanks to the contributors to this volume, who are responsible for the quality of this work. We also thank them for their patience and responsiveness in helping us prepare the book.

Mary Rosner
Beth Boehm
Debra Journet

Introduction

Debra Journet, Beth Boehm, Mary Rosner
University of Louisville

On October 9-12, 1996, over 400 scholars, researchers, and teachers gathered at the University of Louisville for the first Thomas R. Watson Conference in Rhetoric and Composition. This meeting—and the series that will follow it—were made possible by an endowment from Dr. Thomas R. Watson, a University of Louisville alumnus; this gift established a biennial international thematic conference in rhetoric and composition and, in alternate years, a Visiting Distinguished Professorship of Rhetoric and Composition. Dr. Watson's contribution to the University of Louisville, as well as to the rhetoric and composition community in general, attests not only to his extraordinary generosity, but to his understanding of the importance of critical reading, writing, and thinking skills to an educated democracy.

The Watson Conferences are planned as a series of occasions for scholars and teachers to gather and consider specific and important issues to the discipline. We inaugurated this series by examining the development of composition as a profession and were interested particularly in how the present builds on the past. Twenty-two featured speakers attended the first Watson Conference, all of whom have been prominent in the development of composition as a discipline, as well as over 100 presenters. The topic of the 1998 Watson Conference was "Multiple Literacies for the Twenty-first Century."

For the first Watson Conference, we focused on the period between 1963 and 1983, a time often referred to as the "Birth of Composition" (with a capital "C"). In those 20 years, composition changed in a number of crucial ways, including the development of theoretical warrants and research methodologies, the transformation of pedagogical assumptions and practices, as well a growth in professionalism (such as journals, conferences, and programs). In many ways, what composition is now—and will be in the near future—is the fulfillment of forces put into place during that time.

Now, at the end of this century, we are close enough to benefit from the reflections of many of those most important to the field's development, yet far enough away to view some of these changes with perspective. The 1996 Watson Conference, and this book, written as a result of it, were designed to tap the rich sources of history still available to us and to reflect critically on that history. *History, Reflection, and Narrative* thus combines oral histories and reflections collected from the featured speakers at the Conference—scholars, teachers, and researchers whose work has been among the most influential in composition's development—with critical perspectives on the period from 1963 to 1983 by another generation of scholars, many of whom will play an important role in defining composition's future. We hope this book will thus offer an important contribution to our ongoing understanding of how composition came to be the profession it is, how the present builds on the past, and how the present may challenge the future.

HISTORY, REFLECTION, AND NARRATIVE

This book collects different narratives about the history of composition. All narratives, including histories, are, of course, constructions based on the writer's choices—ideological, epistemological, aesthetic—about what constitutes significance. Some of the chapters in this volume place composition within a larger social perspective (for example, Ohmann, Faigley, Zebroski, Peckham, and Miller), arguing that to understand the way we developed as a profession, we need to understand the economic and political forces that have an impact on the teaching of writing. Others examine internal forces operating within composition studies that influence developments in teaching and research (for example, Connors, Barton, Lloyd-Jones, Perl, Yancey, D'Angelo, and Odell). Still others look at intellectual traditions within composition that shaped the discipline (for example, Phelps, Boardman and Ritchie, Mulderig, Devitt, and Rose). Thus, these chapters together present a complex narrative of composition's multiple histories.

History, Reflection, and Narrative also illustrates a range of different *kinds* of narrative, or different ways of doing history. Because the Watson Conference brought together a number of "veterans," it necessarily privileged, in Lester Faigley's term, "stories on the porch": personal reminiscences and retrospective accounts. Such stories are not only wonderful to listen to (and they were everywhere at the Conference, which one participant said was like being at the Conference on College Composition and Communication [CCCC] in the "old days"), they reveal the complexities and nuances behind the more "official" narratives. These personal stories thread through this volume, in the collected oral histories of featured speakers and in several of the chapters (for example, Lloyd-Jones, Perl, Peckham, and D'Angelo). But *History, Reflection, and Narrative* also includes other kinds of histories, ranging from quantitative analyses and citation studies (Faigley, Zebroski, and Rose) to textual analyses of key documents (Phelps, Barton, Boardman and Ritchie, Mulderig, Devitt, and Rose) to analyses of key forces and events both "inside" and "outside" the profession of composition (Connors, Ohmann, Yancey, Odell, and Miller). This book thus suggests, as well, the different ways in which we may wish to historicize our discipline.

THE PROFESSIONALIZATION OF COMPOSITION

To explore issues concerning the professionalization of composition, we have grouped the chapters in this book into five sections: history and the making of histories; agendas in teaching and research; intellectual influences and disciplinary narratives; the development of a profession; and future possibilities and challenges. These categories are primarily a matter of emphasis, as many of the chapters treat many or all of these topics. This division, however, does have the advantage of highlighting some of the major questions asked by historians of composition.

History and the Making of Histories

The book's opening section collects three chapters that explicitly raise questions about what it means to explore composition's recent history. Robert Connors, in Chapter 1, "Composition History and Disciplinarity," takes up the question "What *does* it mean, what *will* it mean, for us to be a recognizable discipline, as opposed to a group of marginalized enthusiasts coming together for support and sympathy that we were 35 years ago?" The way to understand this question, Connors argues, is to examine it against the background of our past. In response, Connors traces composition's history through the 1990s, in order to examine the positive and negative results of our growing disciplinarity—most worryingly, the "movement away from the human meaning of what we do." The history of composition, Connors argues, shows a field whose primary identity has shifted from teaching and service toward certain kinds of theoretical scholarships. In response, Connors advocates a return to composition's roots, in which "teaching writing and working with writing teachers are and remain the fundamental functions for specialists in composition studies."

In Chapter 2, "Veterans' Stories on the Porch," Lester Faigley looks explicitly at the kinds of histories we can tell, learning from his eighth grade American history teacher two lessons in historiography: everything depends on point of view, and how we understand history depends on the method of writing history. Veterans' stories on the porch, of the kind told at the Watson Conference, offer narratives in which vividly realized people perform important actions, thus emphasizing agency. However, Faigley argues, composition's history can be represented in other ways. In response, he constructs a narrative based on numbers and statistics, one that foregrounds the larger forces that have an impact on writing programs. Both histories, Faigley claims, need to be told: "Big narratives about the demands for increasingly complex multiple literacies and little narratives about why quality education is worth paying for."

Louise Wetherbee Phelps, in the final chapter of this section, argues for the codependence of history, or ideology, and composition/rhetoric's utopian project of working for the common good. Composition's "official" progressive narrative is our representation of the "path taken." Alternate possibilities, glimpsed in the discursive field of 1988—for example, North's *The Making of Knowledge in Composition*; Bazerman's *Shaping Written Knowledge*; Neel's *Plato, Derrida, and Writing*; and Phelps's *Composition as a Human Science*—suggest different ways of framing the field and offer paths to alternate futures.

Agendas in Teaching and Research

The next section of *History, Reflection, and Narrative* recovers some of the complexities and ambiguities behind several of composition's most famous "official" narratives. In Chapter 4, Richard Lloyd-Jones details the political bases of the research with which he was associated in the 1960s and 1970s. He explores the background behind *Research in Written Composition* (1963) and then the book's effects, particularly his own work with the National Assessment of Educational Progress. These projects, Lloyd-Jones argues, demonstrate that while "no research is ever pure...research in composition is inevitably tainted by social purpose."

Sondra Perl, in Chapter 5, "Early Work on Composing: Lessons and Illuminations," also reflects on her earlier work, particularly her seminal study of "Tony." Perl describes the intellectual influences out of which this study arose: most significantly Janet Emig's *Composing Processes of Twelfth Graders* (1971), which offered her a way to observe composing processes directly; Braddock and colleagues' *Research in Written Composi-*

tion (1963), which taught her to control as many variables as she could; and her experience as a writing instructor, which allowed her the opportunity to work with basic writers. To understand the strengths as well as the limitations of this early research, Perl argues, we need to pay attention to the details of that research (vividly represented at the Conference in the tape recording Perl played of Tony composing, transcribed in her chapter) and to the disciplinary matrix out of which that research came.

In Chapter 6, "The Expressivist Menace," James Zebroski critically examines one of composition's accepted narratives: expressivism as a powerful force threatening composition. Zebroski's chapter deconstructs that myth of expressivism's dominance by examining textbook advertisements in the journal *College Composition and Communication* during the period from 1969 to 1990, to show that "in contrast to the increasingly shrill condemnations of a thing called expressivism...the data consistently show that expressivism *never* was a major, persuasive movement in college composition." Zebroski then goes on to explore the reasons for the "rhetoric of menace," finding it explained more by present anxieties (economic conditions, the relation of composition to other disciplines, and the field's stage of development) than past conflicts.

In the concluding chapter of this section, Kathleen Blake Yancey offers "A Brief History of Writing Assessment in the Late Twentieth Century." Yancey's narrative takes into account the more well known stories of assessment, told from the perspective of method—the shift from objective measures to more subjective but valid measures—and the perspective of epistemology—from positivism to constructivisim. Her narrative, however, foregrounds another theme: the positioning and shaping of the self. This narrative reveals a field for which the "writerly self" increasingly becomes the focus of our attention, problematizes our practice, and challenges our plans.

Intellectual Influences and Disciplinary Narratives

The third section of the book explores the ways in which specific influences and disciplinary narratives play out in composition. Kathleen Boardman and Joy Ritchie's chapter, "Rereading Feminism's Absence and Presence in Composition," outlines the multiple narratives of "composition's *connections with* and *disruption* by feminism." Examining various threads in our discursive history, Boardman and Ritchie trace out the ways in which composition has represented its relation with feminism. Absence narratives, for example, assert that composition and feminism were either incommunicado or running on parallel tracks for many years. Narratives of connection, in contrast, look at the ways feminist issues show up in composition or at how women were instrumental in composition's development. Narratives of disruption emphasize neither absence nor connection, but use feminism to reread or reconfigure past experience. These multiple narratives, Boardman and Ritchie argue, suggest that present connections between composition and feminism were not inevitable or automatic, but required "bursts of insight and creative leaps."

Gerald Mulderig, in Chapter 9, considers the relation of rhetorical history to composition's professional identity. In the 1960s, Mulderig argues, the rhetorical tradition provided composition with a source of intellectual content and disciplinary identity. It also created a synergy that revitalized writing instruction. However, that synergy, Mulderig argues, is in jeopardy, because of declining intellectual interest in rhetorical history. Looking at Ph.D. program descriptions and at dissertation topics over the past several years, Mulderig concludes that historical rhetoric has been marginalized in graduate education and thus in present and future scholarship. Such a move, he concludes, represents a significant restriction of composition's disciplinary identity.

Chapter 10, "The Developing Discipline of Composition: From Text Linguistics to Genre Theory," by Amy Devitt, looks at composition's changing relation to linguistics and from this draws conclusions about our maturity as a discipline. In its early years, composition treated *writing* as a noun and borrowed heavily from linguistics, particularly in its description of textual features. More recently, composition defines *writing* as a verb and transforms insights from linguistics to create genre theory useful for its own purposes. Such a process not only reveals a more complex relation between composition and linguistics than is always recognized, but it also demonstrates composition's development as a discipline—one able to form productive connections with other disciplines that go beyond mere borrowing.

In Chapter 11, "Two Disciplinary Narratives for Nonstandard English in the Classroom," Shirley Rose employs citation histories of Shaughnessy's *Errors and Expectations* (1977) and Smitherman's *Talkin' and Testifyin'* (1977), as they are referenced in academic journals, to suggest competing narratives of the use of nonstandard English in composition classrooms. Citation histories of these two texts show that Shaughnessy's narrative of our disciplinary project—her description of "the work we have to do as *teachers* analyzing *student* error"—has been more acceptable to our field than Smitherman's narrative—her description of "what we need to learn about the grammar and rhetoric, the history and politics of black English." Use of citation analysis, Rose notes, can be an important tool in helping us understand how we have constructed ourselves as a knowledge-making community.

The Development of a Profession

This section includes four chapters that offer reflections on how composition moved into a recognizable profession and what some of the implications of this move have been. In Chapter 12, Richard Ohmann discusses the relation between professionalization and politics. In contrast to that of other fields, which tend to disengage from politics as they professionalize, composition's "professional articulation and purposeful disciplinarity," Ohmann argues, "did not damp down political engagement." Rather, composition has established a professional identity built, to some degree, on conflict and politics.

Ellen Barton, in "Evocative Gestures in CCCC Chairs' Addresses" (Chapter 13), looks at this genre as a field's self-representation of its professionalism. These addresses, Barton explains, offer articulations of the importance of teaching and service that have not changed substantially over the past 20 years; representations of research, however, vary widely and reflect much conflict. Thus, these addresses suggest we have consensus in our understanding of the teaching of writing as a complex and important activity. We are divided, however, in our evaluation of research from empirical versus humanistic paradigms, and are still debating issues of disciplinary autonomy versus intradisciplinary fit with respect to English studies.

In the next chapter, "Whispers from the Margin," Irvin Peckham argues that there are multiple narratives of composition's development, and the history told by college teachers is not one often recognized by high school teachers. Moreover, the absence of high school teachers in the canonical stories of our discipline's development reflects a conflict between the two groups that is class-based: "The working class and high school teachers share the same habitus; likewise with the professional/managerial class and professors." Peckham's chapter centers on a narrative of his own professional development—moving from high school to university teaching—but it uses that history to illustrate a larger theme about the way history is constructed to reflect political and ideological values.

Chapter 15, "Professing Rhetoric and Composition," by Frank D'Angelo, also illustrates the value of personal narrative in understanding our discipline's development. D'Angelo's chapter, perhaps more than any included in this volume, is an example of a "veteran's story on the porch." He traces the multiple connections between groups of people as composition developed in the 1970s. Official histories concentrate on the way ideas about the teaching of writing were disseminated through professional meetings and journals; also important, D'Angelo argues, were small groups of individuals meeting informally and interacting to expand knowledge. D'Angelo's social history of composition reveals certain networks of teachers, researchers, and scholars who knew and helped each other during this crucial period in the history of composition.

Future Prospects and Challenges

In this last section, scholars look at the prospects and challenges composition faces in the future. Lee Odell and Christina Lynn Prell, in Chapter 16, talk about new research agendas. They begin by looking back on Odell and Cooper's 1978 book *Research on Composing*, which claimed that "what we have needed for decades and what we must have soon is a period of vigorous research on written discourse and the composing process." Now, going into a new millennium, Odell and Prell say, "What we have needed for at least a decade and what we must have soon is a period of vigorous research on composing. Not just writing. Composing." Specifically, Odell and Prell explain, we need research that focuses on the interanimation of words, visual images, and page (or screen) design. Such research will investigate new concepts of authorship, new choices in composing processes, new meaning-making processes of readers, and new criteria or standards.

Chapter 17, Richard Miller's "Intellectual-Bureaucrats: The Future of Employment in the Twilight of the Professions," examines the radical transformation of the nature of work in the academy, brought upon by such material phenomena as declining revenues, erosion of tenure, and encroachment of quality management and outcomes assessment. These changes in the nature of academic work, Miller argues, usually wholly regretted, may be better understood as emergent opportunities for those committed to improving educational chances of the disenfranchised and meeting the needs of students on the margins of the academy. Accomplishing this means moving beyond "ceaseless cultural critique" and working instead within the "fiscal and bureaucratic constraints that both enable the academic enterprise and limit its scope." By committing oneself to the "seemingly impossible project of becoming a 'good bureaucrat,'" Miller suggests, one may be able to develop a sense of agency.

ORAL HISTORIES

Interspersed among the book's sections are oral histories collected during the first Thomas R. Watson Conference. Interviews of most featured speakers and the chairs of those speakers' panels were conducted by University of Louisville graduate students under the direction of

Professor Pamela Takayoshi. The interviews tended to be open-ended and, for the most part, centered—without the interviewers' prompting—on some aspect of the conference topic. Much of the discussion revolved around issues of disciplinary identity: what was gained and what was lost in the formation of composition as a field. Participants also reflected on where composition seems to be headed, and on what composition should, most profitably, take from its past into the future.

Running through these interviews is the conviction that we have established a disciplinary identity that allows for and facilitates the serious and organized study of writing and the teaching of writing. As a discipline, we have developed genres, professional organizations, and programs of advanced study—all of which have helped to organize and support work in composition. However, these interviews also suggest a sense of the struggle and constraint that characterized the careers of so many rhetoric and composition scholars. Of particular concern was the role of composition within English departments. The fact that composition's disciplinary formation was constructed in terms of the work of English departments raises important questions about how rhetoric and composition is defined within English studies and what institutions are empowered to do the defining.

Often, these discussions acknowledged that the act of defining and (concomitantly) establishing disciplinary boundaries has always been an act fraught with political struggle. Along these lines, when participants talked about where composition is headed (that is, electronic media, cross-disciplinary institutes, studies of rhetoric that lie outside of English, the role of empirical research), it was with a recognition that where we have been colors where we are headed. The struggles that characterized the founding of the discipline are not over in many places, and battles for recognition are still being fought.

STORIES OF COMPOSITION

The stories of composition told in *History, Reflection, and Narrative* are primarily positive—even self-congratulatory. Though conscious of complexity and dissonance, most of the writers in this volume portray a discipline confident of its achievements: stronger relations between teaching and research; improved research methods and more valid results; a greater sense of professionalization and the opportunities building a discipline can bring. There are notable exceptions to this story within the book, and indeed no contributor offers such a completely positive account. Nevertheless, the overall theme is the growth and development of a rich and complex field.

Alongside this sense of achievement is a strong sense of plurality—the story of a discipline that contains within itself multiple goals and agendas. As a field, we are marked by ongoing conversations: How are teaching and research connected in our mission? What are our research and teaching agendas? Where is our disciplinary, or interdisciplinary, identity founded? How do we relate to English departments? What have we gained and lost by our professionalization? Questions such as these have engaged us from the beginning and suggest a discipline still (and perhaps productively) not prepared to offer definitive answers.

Implicit within this story is the assumption that history is important. Not only can we know our history and understand how we developed; that understanding can affect our future. The cause/effect shape of this narrative of progress was, in many ways, determined by the goals and design of the conference itself. Constructing a history that begins in 1963 and proceeds through 1983 almost inevitably produces a story that privileges growth, change, and success. The choice also to listen carefully to the voices of those members of the discipline often perceived as most influential—people who have distinguished themselves as scholars and teachers, particularly of the discipline's next influential generation—also contributes to the largely positive story this volume tells.

However, the story of hierarchy—our conviction that important figures from composition's history can tell us important truths about our discipline—also necessarily means that there are other stories this book ignores. There are, as some contributors note, several missing voices. This book does not highlight the many "unimportant" or obscure figures who helped form composition's disciplinary identity: people in the attic, or, more likely, the basement. Missing from these accounts are the voices of students and of the majority of teachers—particularly adjunct faculty and those in secondary schools and in two-year or junior colleges—who formed composition as a material practice. Nor does this book treat the complicated relation of composition and race in our disciplinary identity.

Because this book primarily offers stories of success, there is not a strong sense of the many incarnations Composition has gone through, for example, tagmemics, sentence-combining, cognitive studies, and so forth. Furthermore, current practitioner lore, the kind of information that was so important in the early days, is largely missing here.

Gaps and omissions are, as we have noted, inevitable results of organizing events of the past into a historical narrative account. And, indeed, our goal has never been to present a comprehensive history of composition in this 20-year period. The value of this book, we believe, lies most powerfully in its immediacy, particularly its ability to bring into conversation figures who helped shape the discipline with contemporary scholars and teachers. These conversations are reflected most vividly, perhaps, in the oral histories that intersperse this book's sections. But we believe these conversations are also implicit in the formal presentations. There is in the chapters and interviews a powerful sense of audience, particularly a sense of talking to and with people who are and have been engaged in important issues over a crucial period of time. Gathering so many teachers and researchers who shaped the past together with those who are shaping the present and will shape the future was a unique opportunity. We hope this book reflects something of the excitement of this endeavor and the genuine collegiality and enthusiasm that characterized the first Thomas R. Watson Conference.

Part I

History and the Making of Histories

chapter 1

Composition History and Disciplinarity

Robert J. Connors
University of New Hampshire

Growing older within any intellectual field has both its pleasures and terrors: The excitement and stress of entry into the Burkean parlor, the whitewater canoe ride of achieving tenure and disciplinary maturity, the (always unexpected) revelation of the extra work that comes with seniority, and, finally, the gradual letting go into younger hands of the work to which one has devoted one's life. This pattern holds for every intellectual discipline, but I suspect that the pleasures and terrors are a bit sharper for those of us who have been working in composition studies since the 1960s. We are so new; most of our Ph.D. programs are less than two decades old. One of our most noted award winners was barely 50 years old when she was named an Exemplar to the field. The very name of our discipline has only been around for 15 years. Those of us who have been active over the past 30 years are aware that we were present at the making of something.

The 1996 Watson Conference at Louisville was in some ways the outward and visible sign of who we have become. The reality of what we have been making is all around us at every Conference on College Composition and Communication, but the Watson Conference was the first meeting I know of that was specifically meant to look at the meanings of our making. What *does* it mean, what *will* it mean, for us to be a recognizable discipline, as opposed to the group of marginalized enthusiasts coming together for support and sympathy that we were 35 years ago?

I'm a historian, so this question presents itself to me—as do most questions—against the background of our past. What it means for us to have become a discipline can only be understood in reference to what we were before. Without an understanding of history, a field of action has no memory, and without memory it cannot measure movement outside the realm of a narrow, incremental present. That is why the developed sciences still retain, as important field information, the archaeologies of their theoretical explorations. Chemists today do not need knowledge of the phlogiston theory nor linguists knowledge of early transformation-based theory except to understand where their fields have been and are not anymore—and why this is. Development of a field is always understood comparatively, which is why I'm bemused by people in the field today who say they don't need to know about rhetorical history or past developments in composition teaching.

HISTORICAL AWARENESS AND DISCIPLINARY ROOTS

Part of the way in which historians have always made meaning, and a method I'd like to adopt here to help make sense of the part of the disciplinary story we are currently traversing, is to look at events as occurring in related "periods." Reductive and simplifying as such periodization can be, it seems an inevitable result of the way our hearts, if not our too-active minds, conceive the past. The "Age of Chivalry," the "Plague Years," the "Ante-Bellum Period," the "Era of Good Feeling"—these terms may not be completely descriptive of everything that was going on during those times, but we respond to them as accurate enough descriptions of what we want to call out for attention. As a historian, I want to call this time in our historical development the "Era of Disciplinarity" in the field of composition studies.

What is it that allows us to use this term? I don't ask the question lightly, because the history of people who teach writing in American colleges is peppered with a number of previous unrequited romances with disciplinarity. What do we have now that we didn't have then?

I hope those who were there, or who have heard these stories, will forgive me for quickly rehearsing them. I do so because our modern relationship with history is implicated in and contemporaneous with our disciplinarity, and it illustrates how gaining a historical sense means gaining a self. American composition-rhetoric before 1850 was still strongly attached to the traditional discipline of rhetoric, and such early American teachers of writing as Edward T. Channing and Henry Day, in addition to their biweekly writing conferences, worked from a deep knowledge of sources ranging from Aristotle to Whately. But then the Germanic scholarly approach to learning, with its overt scientistic disdain for rhetoric, was imported to America after the Civil War. Tradition-based rhetoric came gradually to be despised by the new scholars, who preferred social science, philology, and literary scholarship, and who built the new academic departments around them.

Without a historical component, American composition-rhetoric before 1950 lacked connections to any tradition and was rendered weak and vulnerable. Our first great chance at disciplinarity was lost in the 1890s, when Fred Newton Scott determined to found his pioneering University of Michigan doctoral program on psychological and linguistic bases, while downplaying rhetorical and historical elements. Scott's Ph.D. students, oriented toward modern educational and psychological theory but unwilling or unable to dialogue successfully with literary or classical colleagues, found themselves excluded from academia or trapped in English or speech departments, where they were aliens. Scott's intellectual line of psychological and philosophical composition died out after his retirement in 1927.

Rhetorical history never died, but the bulk of the work done there from the 1920s through the 1940s was the effort of scholars in the relatively new field of speech communication. Unlike compositionists, speech rhetoricians had never severed their ties to the history of rhetoric, and they were thus able to grid historical methodologies onto their work in ways immediately recognizable as scholarly. As a result, speech departments had established the legitimacy of their discipline and were granting their own doctorates a scant decade after declaring the secession of speech teachers from the National Council of Teachers of English in 1914. They were speaking a language the rest of the academy could understand and accredit.

But in English departments there was no reception, and it was some time after the demise of Scott's experiment that the first historians of the rhetoric of teaching writing arose. It's not accidental that these torches in the darkness were also preeminent among the intellectual figures striving to create, out of the oppressed and unmemoried activity of teaching required composition, some sense of what it meant to do so. Porter Perrin's 1936 dissertation, entitled *The Teaching of Rhetoric in the American Colleges Before 1750*, was a history of rhetoric in America during the 18th century, and Perrin went on to become an important voice, demanding self-awareness and seriousness in composition teaching during the late 1930s, 1940s, and 1950s. Perrin is a little-recognized today, because he was active during a time in American educational history not friendly to the possibilities for composition as a developed intellectual field. Only toward the end of his life did he see the stirrings of what would become composition studies—a field that should honor him as a progenitor.

A sense of our own place in history and tradition was a surprisingly late entry on our professional scene, one that began with a realization of lost roots. The Conference on College Composition and Communication was founded in 1949 on principles considered very modern, as part of a nationwide movement to break down what were seen as rigid disciplinary boundaries. As the Harvard Committee on the Objectives of a General Education in a Free Society put it, "Specialization enhances the centrifugal forces in our society.... Our conclusion, then, is that the aim of education should be to prepare an individual to become an expert both in some particular vocation or art and in the general art of the free man and the citizen" (1945, pp. 53–54). The General Education movement and its subset, the Communication movement, wanted to bring together fields that had grown too specialized, and thus courses in writing or in speech were brought together into communication courses, which incorporated the four communication skills of reading, writing, speaking, and listening. But these modern, reformist ideas led, as they often do, to a new realization about history and its centrality. Staffing these courses was a group of teachers who had been raised in English and speech departments, and the result of their meeting was a new dialogue between writing teachers and their speech counterparts—public-speaking teachers, who had kept alive the history and theories of Western rhetoric far more completely than had English. Though the Communication movement did not outlast the mid-1950s except in a few places, its supporters from both speech and English had come into touch with each other around the issue of rhetoric, and an organization had been formed that would allow important disciplinary developments in the future.

The CCCC was a necessary, though not a sufficient, cause for composition's becoming a discipline. The people around whom composition studies would coalesce were becoming active in the early 1950s, but the content of their work was still scattered and noncumulative. Few had much sense of the source their work and ideas had derived from because English department compositionists tended to concentrate on immediate pragmatic issues. But forces were at work, and it was Albert R. Kitzhaber, a graduate student of Porter Perrin's, who wrote the first definitive history of American composition. Our modern history really begins with his 1953 dissertation *Rhetoric in American Colleges, 1850–1900*, a work in which Kitzhaber concentrated on material about the teaching of writing in America that had been almost completely elided in the rhetorical histories done in the field of speech communication. Though Kitzhaber's work was a secret classic, destined to have an immense impact on a group of later historians, it was hardly known to most composition specialists until two decades after its creation.

We had a journal and a conference, but still not much of a sense of our own history, and our second failed attempt at disciplinarity played out during the 1950s around that lack of a center. During that time, many composition teachers were tending to seek disciplinary validity by reaching out and subordinating themselves to more developed or seemingly impressive fields of learning. There was an early 1950s fling with general semantics, then popular. In particular, that time saw an unhappy rekindling of composition's old affair with grammar in the form of structural linguistics, a smooth-talking Lothario that swept us off our feet through the late 1950s and early 1960s. Structural linguists were so confident, so scientific, so sure that their hard-edged analyses would allow composition to become respectable—how could we resist? When Harry Warfel told us that structural linguistics was analogous to atomic physics and that "a widespread familiarity with the principles of structural linguistics will work a similar revolution in the teaching of verbal composition" (1959, p. 212), his claims were forceful. Many writing teachers came to believe that linguistics would give composition a leg-up to disciplinarity, but when the Chomskian revolution swept structural linguistics away after 1963, those who had invested heavily in structural analysis were left wondering and discouraged. It began to appear that affiliation with a language science most people could not at all understand offered no obvious road to any new status for composition.

The New Rhetoric of the 1960s, to which it is easy to trace our primary lines of disciplinarity, was both a blossoming of the promise of the earlier Communication movement and a new social movement coming from within English departments. Elsewhere, I have made comparisons between the New Criticism and the New Rhetoric, not in terms of their theoretical origins, but in terms of their both representing populist movements growing out of the new GI Bill-socioculture of English departments (Connors, 1989). Though a part of the New Rhetoric movement was genuinely interdisciplinary, especially in relation to new connections made with philosophy (and to lesser degrees with linguistics and psychology), its most important effects were felt within English departments and within composition programs. It influenced English courses, its proponents were English teachers, and its literature was read by English department scholars. It was resolutely traditional in its historical and analytical backgrounds, presenting English scholars for the first time with a vision of composition that was based on a classical past, with even deeper roots in Western culture than their own Anglo-Saxon roots.

New Rhetorical scholarship for the first time could hold its own as a literature that argued positions by relying consistently on previous scholarship in a dialectic. It went beyond the narrow presentism that had previously cursed composition journals. Examine an issue of *College Composition and Communication* from 1960 and contrast it to an issue from 1970 and the difference will immediately become apparent to you. I think we can trace the possibility of the field of composition studies from this point; what had been scattered and mostly rootless conversations was evolving into a dialogical and cumulating scholarly literature. The rebirth of classical rhetoric, the development of tagmemic rhetoric, the prewriting movement, sentence combining, the writing-process movement, Christensen rhetoric, and the entire new seriousness of the research strand in composition—with its new journal, *Research in the Teaching of English*—all date to the middle and late 1960s. Disparate as these ideas and movements look to us in retrospect, collectively they were the New Rhetoric, and they represent a huge leap forward for the discourse of the field. We were not yet a discipline, but the conditions were coming together.

TRADITION AND REPRODUCTION

The 1970s, rather than the 1960s, were the founding decade of the disciplinarity of composition studies because two elements coalesced then that had not existed before. The first we have already seen in the beginning of the 1960s (and some would place it even earlier): methods of intellectual tradition in a great burgeoning of journals and books. The 1970s was the first decade since the 1890s to see large numbers of serious-minded scholarly and practical books appearing concerning themselves with the problems and issues of rhetoric and composition. It was also a decade of astounding journal foundings. In addition to new vitality in the NCTE journals *College English*, *College Composition and Communication*, and *Research in the Teaching of English*, we saw the foundings of *Freshman English News*, *Teaching English in the Two-Year College*, *Journal of Basic Writing*, *Rhetoric Society Quarterly*, *Writing Lab Newletter*, and *Writing Program Administration*. The 1960s and 1970s were times of hero-editors who made a literature: Richard Ohmann, Ken Macrorie, Don Gray, Bill Irmscher, Ed Corbett, Gary Tate, Mina Shaughnessy, Muriel Harris, and Richard Braddock.

In addition to a method of tradition, however, a discipline needs a method of scholarly reproduction, and this we had never had before the 1970s. The failure to endure of the first American composition boom—lasting from 1885 to 1905—provides an example of how methods of tradition alone cannot keep a discipline alive without some system that can continue to provide a community of accredited disciplinary authors and informed readers. In practical institutional terms, that means a doctorate.

I have elsewhere discussed reasons why written rhetoric did not evolve a doctoral capacity until almost a century after it began to be institutionally taught (Connors, 1991). Though there existed a strong interest in and dialogue about teaching writing between 1885 and 1905, the great generation of experts from the 1890s—John Genung, Barrett Wendell, and Adams Hill, to name a few—either did not or could not train replacements for themselves. As I've mentioned, the only person who had the will and the resources to try was Fred Newton Scott at Michigan. He fought almost alone for a composition-based Ph.D., but he could not succeed as the only such program in the United States. When he retired in 1927, his doctoral program in rhetoric was folded back into the Michigan English department, and the 23 doctorates in rhetoric he produced between 1898 and 1930, finding no jobs and no support system for their training in the departments that proposed to hire them, gradually drifted into other professions or other parts of English studies. And with the exceptions of those speech-trained rhetoricians like Warren Guthrie, whose interests included the 19th century, and very few English- and education-based students like Porter Perrin and Al Kitzhaber, there were no more composition-oriented doctoral students in American colleges until the late 1960s.

The "first generation" of modern composition specialists, such GI Bill-generation scholars as Kitzhaber, Jix Lloyd-Jones, Priscilla Tyler, Donald Murray, and Ed Corbett, began work in the field between the late 1940s and the early 1960s. They were mainly literary in background and were forced to be rhetorical autodidacts, often in their spare time. Their writings and example helped create the "second generation," which includes such people as Dave Bartholomae, Susan Miller, and Erika Lindemann. Trained in the late 1960s, when there was a literature and a lot of excitement but no possibility of official doctoral recognition, this second generation, too, had to retool as writing specialists after literary doctorates. It was only after 1970 that a groundbreaking change occurred, with the appearance of the first rhetoric doctorates in English departments. I don't know who the "first Ph.D." was, and it's probably not a useful question, but sometime between 1970 and 1975, such universities as Texas, Michigan, Ohio State, USC, and UCSD began to allow their faculty composition specialists to develop and teach graduate courses in rhetoric and composition, and then the freedom to examine students and direct dissertations in these fields.

This new group of students, the "third generation" of modern composition people, was the first generation of fully composition-trained Ph.D.'s in America since the 1920s and Fred Scott. This generation—and I am a member of it—saw its mission clearly: it was to go forth and multiply, establishing doctoral programs almost everywhere it went. As a result of our success, the third generation quickly became leaders within the field as it grew rapidly, and relatively young people, such as Lee Odell, Andrea Lunsford, and Nancy Sommers, have now assumed almost elder statesperson roles within the field.

With both methods of tradition and methods of reproduction burgeoning for composition studies, the decade of the 1980s saw full-blown growth of disciplinarity. We discovered our own history as Kitzhaber's 1953 dissertation began to circulate in microfilm and photocopied *samizdat* form in the 1970s. A copy of it was a *sine qua non* for the new generation of young professors who wanted to know about the past times of composition. This generation of historians—Kate Adams, Jim Berlin, Sharon Crowley, Nan Johnson, Tom Miller, David Russell, and Bill Woods—at first wrote history simply because they were fascinated by it and wanted to explore the trails that Perrin and Kitzhaber as well as other early historians such as Warren Guthrie, Glenn Hess, and Wallace Douglas had blazed. But, half-realized, we were also writing history in order to create ourselves as members of a discipline, and then in order to inform that discipline and try to unify it. We even, rather quickly, had a name: composition studies.[1] The Educational Resources Information Center (ERIC) shows 46 examples of its use between 1983 and 1991, and 46 more between 1992 and 1994. The journal *Freshman English News* became *Composition Studies* in 1992. We began to assume a definable position as a field coequal with other fields within English studies.

THE SOCIOCULTURE OF DISCIPLINE

It is easy to see the positive results of our growing disciplinarity. We now have what we did not have before. We write and publish serious scholarship in journals that are professional and respectable. We have diverse interests, and there are a plethora of positions and theoretical stances with which we can affiliate ourselves. We have our places in the hierarchy of discourse circles—both our own and those outside. Composition scholars are capable of performing conscientious critical analyses of a sort that allows us to hold up our ends in conversations at both MLA and AERA. We are part of a field whose intellectual vitality is still growing, as opposed to some fields that seem exhausted. Locally, we get better salaries and enjoy more respect in the English departments that are still home for most of us. We have in those departments graduate students to mentor, often among the most intelligent and capable of the crop, and the pleasures of reproduction are real ones.

The negative results of our disciplinarity have been less explored in public, if not less considered privately. "An intellectual hatred is the worst," says Yeats, and it seems that one of the inevitable concomitants of disciplinarity is intellectual hatred. If we are more real as a discipline, we are also more hierarchical and exclusive. If the credulous wheel-reinventing of our earlier journal articles was replaced with more rigorous means of testing and discussing writing and its teaching, the supportive good fellowship of earlier composition dialogue was also replaced with something more pointed—and more divided.

Disciplinarity has not been, in this sense, an unmixed blessing. Our understanding of writing has undoubtedly deepened, as doctoral research of many sorts was bent to the psychological and then the social understanding of it, but with the Ph.D. research orientation have come unexpected side effects. Between 1970 and 1990, as we were building composition studies, 4C's ceased being the love-feast of a marginalized minority and came to be marked more and more by a theoretical-camps mentality of inclusion and exclusion. "Special interests" came more and more to the fore, and identity politics of every kind popped up in the program. We have seen the growth of sharp disagreements, simmering dislikes, and warring factions, sometimes within the same city. The skirmish of egotisms that was always one of the least admirable aspects of literary studies has come home to composition over the last 15 years as people have built reputations, staked out turf, and gotten famous. Like every other discipline, we have evolved our own jargon and code terms, which are sometimes part of standard dialogic lore, but use of which (or failure to use which) can also represent ideological purity tests. The Passchendaele sense of entrenched and warring intellectual cliques, with their creation of friend and enemy lists, that so troubled me when I began to go to MLA in the 1970s has become a too-familiar phenomenon even at CCCC. Nearly all of us are familiar, at least tacitly, with the growth of hierarchy in the field—hierarchies of graduate programs, journal placements, and awards.

Within a discipline, the power to critique is also the power to destroy. Since 1970, the power of cumulating criticism within the field has been getting more marked. In the 1970s, critiques of tagmemic rhetoric were enough to cause it to lose momentum, and in the early 1980s we saw the dominating juggernaut of sentence combining brought to a shivering halt by a combined attack from linguistic and expressivist criticism. A little later, expressivism itself was rendered disreputable, at least theoretically, by cultural and ideological critiques. And in the most recent and potent example of a line of research being overthrown, we saw the psychology-based research approach that had marked the early 1980s essentially terminated by criticism from the more theoretical social and cultural-studies approach that has been ascendent since 1987. In the wake of that event, theory wars gradually made their way from literary and cultural studies into composition studies. Our graduate students are now expected to know their Gramsci, Bakhtin, and Foucault as thoroughly as they know their Quintilian and Elbow.

Curiously, as some aspects of the field have been moving closer to those in literary and cultural studies, others are coming to resemble the practices of the "hard" sciences. The critique of individualism underlying much of the current theoretical construction of the field has had both explicit and tacit elements. Explicitly, we see the rise of constructivism, intellectual-property theory, collaborative methodologies, and collaboration-based pedagogies. Tacitly, the concept of author-blind peer review has come to have almost absolute control over our publications and conferences. Peer review has always been dominant in scientific publication, of course, and scientific fields still provide a tacit model for disciplinary maturity. Thus, with social construction of scholarly acceptability as prime desideratum, we have seen the rise of the idea that no individual can or should control the gates of public dialogue. The "hero-editors" who constructed our journals in the heady 1970s and early 1980s have thus disappeared in favor of "facilitator-editors," who solicit blind readings for acceptance of journal articles and even conference papers. The replacement of the more traditional footnoting citation systems in favor either of "new MLA" or APA parenthetical systems in composition journals is another reflection of the social orientation of the field. Parenthetical citation systems, designed for easy reference to previous work in literature survey form, won out over the more individualistic (albeit natural and reader-friendly) footnote and endnote in the social sciences, and their quick acceptance by composition studies (as opposed to literary studies, which is still convulsed by disagreements about "new MLA") indicates where some of our affinities lie. These more communitarian ideas of scholarship have led to more defensible and more replicable research at the same time that they have filtered a certain amount of unpredictability and polemical energy out of many of our journals.

It cannot be a surprise that scholarly communities tend to enforce scholarly norms. If I may speak personally, the most disturbing corollary of our movement into disciplinary status has been a change in our attitude toward our service identity. The growth of our disciplinary literature has, let us admit, been marked by a retreat from pragmatic pedagogical issues more than by any other single phenomenon. The origin of most doctoral programs in English departments left us open to a sort of "theory-pride," and to a resulting reflexive movement away from teaching issues and writing pedagogy as too "ed-school." The Ph.D. licensure in English has for several decades usually meant safety from the danger of having to teach freshman composition on a standard rotation, and it has increasingly come to mean the same thing even in composition studies. New composition doctorates may be asked to teach first-year composition or even basic writing once or twice a year, but usually they are hired primarily to coordinate programs, teach graduate courses, run writing centers, and assist in writing-across-the-curriculum (WAC) programs. It's a rare college that hires a composition doctoral specialist simply to teach undergraduate writing; the tacit feeling on all sides is that such duties would be a waste of valuable training.

As a result, composition studies as a discipline has moved farther and farther from our original teaching duties and the awarenesses that went with them. We have all seen the eclipse of the "Staffroom Interchange" section of *CCC*, and the journal is simply reflecting the reality that most of its readers don't go into the staffroom anymore, except perhaps to post notices or lead meetings. Let me again speak personally; it's 10 years since I taught more than one writing course in a semester, and today I can choose how often I teach composition and what courses I teach. When I go into the staffroom, the lecturers and instructors there see me essentially as no more one of them than is the Shakespeare scholar down the hall from me.

THE EROSION OF A SERVICE IDENTITY

The conformity that intellectual communities unavoidably enforce operates in ways that are powerful while remaining hidden, and composition studies is no more free of such conformity than any other field. To the degree that we have bound ourselves to scientific methods of knowledge construction, more and more of what we do is, in Kuhnian terms, "normal science"—even if it critiques scientism. A field constructs itself, in part, by excluding the alien, and the range of variation of ideas that will be allowed before a person is effectively read out of the community is smaller than it has been. We do not mean to enforce conformity; it's just what communities do. And increasingly, what our community does is marginalize practitioners. In a talk at the 1991 Boston CCCC, Alice Calderonello made the claim—a strong one, and supported strongly—that composition disciplinarity is in part defined by devaluing practitioner knowledge. Donald Murray, who represents practitioner knowledge better than almost anyone, has told me that for over five years he has been unable to get his essays accepted by the major journals. Blind reviewed, his articles come back to him with readers saying they cannot recommend publication because the essay is "too quaint" or, in one case, "too Murrayesque." He has effectively given up on publishing in journals he helped make reputable. We cannot really blame journal editors for this situation, since they must listen to their reviewers. It is the socioculture of composition studies that has changed, out from under Murray and people like him.

The book publishers, too, have lined up on one side or the other, and there has been some movement toward marginalizing those presses that show an overt orientation toward serving teachers rather than scholars. Bob Boynton once told me that during the six years of Richard Larson's editorship of *CCC*, not a single Boynton/Cook book was reviewed in the journal. (That changed, of course, in the last Larson-edited issue, which carried three separate reviews of Knoblauch and Brannon's *Rhetorical Traditions and the Teaching of Writing* [1984].) Even the NCTE Press, which had for years been one of only two serious presses to publish composition material (SIUP being the other), entered a long decline in its reputation during the early 1980s, during which it was thought to be not quite serious enough, not quite scholarly enough—too "teacherly," in other words.

On the other side of the street, we've also seen a strong movement into composition of the specialty presses that had long served the social sciences: Ablex, Sage, Greenwood, Guilford, Erlbaum. These presses are happy to sign a narrow-focus scholarly book that will sell only 600 copies, mostly to libraries. Their economies of scale are much different from those of even university presses, since they typically price their books so high that they can make a profit on a small press run. The only people who lose are graduate students and those other scholars who cannot afford these expensive books. All of us have probably had the experience recently of planning a graduate course and being shocked to find that the five books we've asked students to buy total hundreds of dollars. Specialization and its attendant movement away from large markets for our writings is an inescapable result of disciplinarity.

Of course, the growth of our disciplinary identity is only part of this movement away from a primary identity as teachers of writing. In part, we seem not to believe quite so strongly that our practical work can make a difference. The world has changed around us, and we are far from the heady days of the 1970s when the doors of colleges were thrown wide to anyone who wanted to try and writing teachers plunged into trying to serve this new population. Mina Shaughnessy once told us that the process of coming to teach basic writers began, usually, with the attitude of wanting to "convert the natives." Elitist or wrongheaded though that attitude might have been, it was still determinedly optimistic. Today, however, with Shaughnessy's own City University of New York open-admissions program shut down and with fewer and fewer colleges seeming to care about basic writers, how many new doctorates emerge from their programs with that sort of wrongheaded but idealistic missionary attitude? How many in our newly meritocratic world pine to tackle the problems of seriously underprepared students?

As the teaching and service elements of composition studies attenuate, the theoretical side of our field is, then, coming more and more to the fore. And for many of us, the question is beginning to arise: *Whom* does the theory serve? This is not simply querulous idealism, but a very practical question, because we have historically gained intellectual vitality from teaching and service. If we look at the geneses of the two most recent important theoretical developments in the field, we note that cognitivism grew out of questions that arose while teaching professional writing, and social constructionism originated in questions raised by basic writing. The development of theoretical approaches means that they can come to exist far from their pragmatic roots, as both those approaches often have. But both had deep roots in teaching, and the question still nags: out of service to whom will grow today's theories and tomorrow's? What connections are we forging to our world—to students and their needs—with the work we are doing in our journals and our conferences? From what practical or service question will the new theoretical ideas of tomorrow emerge?

I ask these questions of myself first, because I have seen so much change so quickly in this field, which I had never even heard of before 1975. After I entered it, I pushed as hard as I knew how for the respect that disciplinary status would bring to composition studies—and now I find myself thinking about the problems of answered prayers.

We wanted to escape the endless reinvention of the wheel that had long marked composition, that "what-to-do-Monday-morning" practical pedagogy that got our journals dismissed by literary scholars. We wanted to be a new kind of composition professional, and we are that. But what have we left behind in that staffroom? We sought seriousness in our literature, and we got it, in spades. We watched *CCC* covers turn from multicolored to brown to gray, and many writing teachers thought the contents of the journal followed the cover colors. And although the membership of CCCC has continued to grow, we have no way of knowing how many people who used to be members and who used to read *CCC* have fallen away. I was once shown a rejection letter from a journal stating that acceptable articles should "advance knowledge, not merely use it," and that dictum automatically cuts out a whole segment of the kind of people who formerly *were* the CCCC. In talking to instructors in my own program, I certainly hear that most of what's in the journals is no longer accessible to them, even if they used to read the literature. When Steve North, in his 1987 book *The Making of Knowledge in Composition,* put forward the concept of "practitioners" as differentiated from other people in the field, he was simply being truthful about a hiatus between teachers and scholars in composition that had been growing for more than a decade.

What I'm worried about is that our movement toward disciplinarity may be a movement away from the human meaning of what we do. In many of our specialized scholarly and theoretical books today, you are much more likely to find discussion of "writing" or of "discourse" than you are of "students." In fact, whether the favored theory is poststructuralism or cultural criticism, the tendency in today's professional dialectic is to problematize the student to the point where he or she becomes a theoretical counter on a conceptual board rather than the living, breathing person we formerly saw ourselves—naively, no doubt—as trying to help out. Some of us, indeed, have become so oriented toward doing our "real" work—research, publication, administration, public service—that we are in danger of becoming the sort of intellectual mandarins we once disliked when we met them in literary studies.

Mandarinism seems to me the worst danger attending our move into disciplinary status, because it nearly always means devaluation of service and teaching in favor of scholarship and reputation. We saw it in literary studies nearly a century ago, when literary scholars were determined to do away with the MLA's Pedagogical Section because the MLA was *not*, in the words of its president, James Bright, "a Gild of Barbers...a Teachers' Agency," or a group friendly to the "known class of advocates of 'methods of teachings,'" who were treated by the MLA to a "gentle but unflinching suppression" (1902, pp. xlvii–xlviii). We see the results in today's MLA. Though it is hard to imagine composition studies ever divorcing itself from teaching as thoroughly as the MLA has, our successes are increasingly defining us, and our growing identity as a discipline is endangering our traditional commitment to personally serving students. The American Council of Learned Societies has just admitted the NCTE, dropping its previous objection that our organization was too pedagogical, too little oriented toward research and too much oriented toward teaching students to write. So now we are officially learned. But with all our learning, there may be some simple truths we are in danger of forgetting.

POSSIBLE DISCIPLINARY FUTURES

Every developed discipline has its tacit or explicit ideological dictates, and every disciplinary dictate works in part by effacing some defined Other. The New Rhetoric marginalized what we used to call Current-Traditional Rhetoric. The Writing Process movement worked to erase the old formal correctness-based composition teaching.

Cognitivism had an antipathy for "soft" theories and for politics. Constructivism ravaged empiricism and positivism and ended up all but obliterating cognitivism. Today, poststructuralism and feminism marginalize essentialism and foundationalism. Such intellectual enmities are all too familiar to anyone who has followed the history of literary studies over the past five decades. But composition teaching and the study of it have in the past served other needs and other primary ends. Issues of teaching students to write were once more than a background for the movement of theoretical concepts, more than the profane and quantitative raw material of tenure cases and scholarly fame. Our successes have marked us, and they have changed our world. Will we return to that earlier and more service-based world again, and, can we?

I can only offer a few provisional thoughts. I am a historian, and social history teaches us to watch the demographics, because they undergird many other things. Our disciplinary demographics are shifting, and it may be that those changes will have a more profound impact on where we go from here than any theoretical shifts.

In 1977, there were eight doctoral programs in composition, the pioneering programs that produced most of the members of what I have called the third generation of composition scholars. Based mainly around rhetorical ideas, these programs were the only ones in a position to try to meet the need for composition specialists that resulted from the much-cried-up literacy crises of the late 1970s. New doctoral programs founded by the second and third generations of composition scholars burgeoned between 1977 and 1987, when Gary Tate and David Chapman found that there were 38 Ph.D. programs. But if the rate at which programs were founded went down after 1987, the sheer numbers of programs did not, and when Brown, Meyer, and Enos redid the Chapman and Tate survey in 1993, they found that there were 72 doctoral programs. By now it seems reasonable to assume that there are over 80 programs currently turning out composition Ph.D.'s.

There is a connection here between the growth of our discipline and the market's need for our students. Indeed, it would be a determined idealist who would argue that some large part of our growth into a discipline over the past three decades has not been built on the success our candidates have enjoyed on the otherwise terrible academic job market. We have all heard or experienced stories of composition students getting 15 or 25 job interviews at MLA, being wooed at campus interviews, and having their choice of good tenure-track jobs. At the same time, we have for two decades been watching talented literature candidates scrambling for any sort of position, knowing that their vitas would fall into that stack of 500 other vitas, knowing they were up against competition from elite schools as well as desperate assistant (and even associate) professors looking to improve their lots with a move. The terrific boom in composition jobs created a hothouse atmosphere that forced composition studies into bloom. Graduate students are not fools, and once the job market signals became clear, they responded. The older graduate student attitude (which some of you may remember from the 1970s) that composition-oriented doctoral students were "dupes" or "feebs" who could not compete in literary studies evaporated very quickly. The movement of many good graduate students into composition studies was what really fueled the foundation of the many programs that Brown, Meyer, and Enos found in 1993, when they estimated there were 1,174 students pursuing doctoral work in composition studies.

My point here is that the job market, which for the past two decades had been radically out of balance in favor of the seller, is returning, as markets do, to equilibrium. We owe much of our rapid disciplinarity to the degree to which our doctoral candidates moved directly into good jobs that had to compete for them, but the seller's market we have so long counted on is coming to an end. It is not that good composition jobs are disappearing, but there *are* fewer of them than there used to be in the 1980s. In 1989, 158 of the 1,057 jobs in the October *Job Information List* were entry-level composition positions. We owned 15 percent of a large job market. In October of 1998, we owned almost 16 percent of the listed jobs in the *JIL*—but there were only 875 jobs in total, and only 139 were for our applicants. We are having to live in times of a shrunken market, but the real issue is that we are producing so many more people to fill the fewer jobs that are being advertised. In 1980, there were fewer than 50 people with composition Ph.D.'s; today, there are hundreds. If we assume that there are around 80 doctoral programs turning out Ph.D.'s today, and further assume that each program turns out an average of one finished candidate a year, then there is probably a job for every candidate. There are even some candidates—the very best ones, from the very best programs—who get multiple campus interviews, and even more than one job offer.

But are we now, will we be producing only 80 doctorates a year? With 1,200 doctoral students in the pipeline, even assuming some are on the 8-year plan, it is inescapable that we will soon be producing well over 100 doctorates a year, and perhaps closer to 200. Meanwhile, the boom in program foundations that produced the doctoral rush of the past two decades is easing off; most of the universities that want composition doctoral work in their programs have already built up their faculties in the field, and we are not likely to see huge new demands for ground-floor program creation. The need for good administrators will remain steady in both first-year programs and other writing-based programs such as writing centers and WAC programs, but these jobs are better suited for—and are usually filled by—experienced administrators or department veterans.

It may well be, in other words, that the 20 fat years that have forced our hothouse disciplinarity so quickly are coming to an end. The unbalanced seller's market that fueled our program growth, our journal foundings, and our presses and publishers is slowing, and composition studies will be affected—is already being affected—by its coming more into balance. More of our students will not get tenure-track jobs. Journals will have a harder time attracting enough subscribers to break even. University presses will not sign as many books. And our disciplinarity, for so long nurtured by kindly influences, will once again be shaped by other social effects. "Pull down thy vanity," says Pound in the Cantos, and the next 10 years may well work to bring us down closer to the same earth trod by other English department people.

I want to suggest that the end of the boom may not be a bad thing. During the late 1960s, when the left causes he had always fought for were in something of a vogue, the famous organizer Saul Alinsky said to his younger colleagues, "Don't worry, boys, we'll weather this storm of approval and emerge as hated as ever." Most of us entered the field of composition studies not, God knows, because of careerism or the status the field could bring us, but because we really believed in the work and wanted to be of service to our worlds. The 20 fat years made us, but they also changed some of the ethical dimensions of the work, and not always for the better. I know I am not the only one here who has viewed the growing success and status—what I think of as the "MLA-ization"—of the field with strongly conflicted feelings. We entered composition work out of a deep dissatisfaction with the fatuity of overly specialized and theoretical literary studies—but we brought more baggage from that world than we meant to.

From here, it seems to me, our path of disciplinarity can go in one of two directions. In one model, we can continue to follow the example of literary studies, making theoretical sophistication, specialized expertise, and sheer scholarly output the prime criteria of success in the field. Approval of the approved theorists, mastery of one or two deep, tiny slices of the world of knowledge, and evidence of success in the form of the single-author critical book or the sheaf of articles from respectable journals—these will be our demands of composition scholars, and fulfilling them will be the unwritten law. We will be a modern discipline of the very sort blessed by the ACLS, and it will be natural for us to become more and more interlinked with the interests and professional attitudes of our literary colleagues. Though we'll be asked to run composition programs a little more often than our Americanist or cultural-studies friends, and though such service expectations will be considered one of the tiresome aspects of our choice of field, we won't need to worry about teaching writing ourselves any more than we want to. Under our direction, writing programs will run smoothly, staffed by instructors and graduate students we supervise. We'll teach our graduate courses on theoretical issues that interest us. Composition studies will end up being smaller, and a bit more competitive, but we'll be a completely familiar scholarly subfield of English studies, pursuing our own research in honorable obscurity and bothering no one.

The other possible model for composition studies as a discipline is less clear in outline, more muddled and uncertain. It produces scholars who embrace teaching and service as indispensable parts of the world of their research, and puts scholarly research in the service of action in colleges and universities. It exults in the complex and imperfect bungle of pedagogy and teaching issues as much as in the cool abstractions of research and theory. Doctoral candidates in composition studies are trained in administrative and programming issues as well as in history and theory, spending serious time in writing centers, staffrooms, WAC programs, and cross-curricular outreach as well as in English department classrooms. Publication is still expected for advancement, but it can take many forms—websites, textbooks, software packages, and program guides, as well as the more familiar books and articles. We remain open to many interdisciplinary influences, but with a skeptical enthusiasm rather than the credulous acceptance that marked our past. Most centrally, teaching writing and working with writing teachers are and remain the fundamental functions for specialists in composition studies. In this model, working rhetorically in the world with writers is the continuing key to defining the field.

I don't know which of these models, or what combination of them, we will see. Analogies from the past take us only so far. We have made ourselves a *new* discipline, and despite our uncertainties, I don't think that most of us who helped build this world would choose to go back to a time when we were less self-aware. But real decisions loom up at us about where we will take this thing we have made. Primarily, we are still deciding whom we will serve—our students and our communities, or some more abstract and ideal world of scholarly discovery that is only tangentially attached to our originary roles as writing teachers. I think I have probably sufficiently betrayed my own biases. I am a composition teacher, defining myself as that before anything else. I'm also a scholar, and I hope to continue studying our history, which shows me over and over that whatever problems we have had in the past, the constant commitment of our best people has been to work with their students and serve their society rather than concentrating on narrow career goals or sterile intellectual puzzles. Teaching writing was the path of Ned Channing in 1850, of

Fred Newton Scott and Gertrude Buck in 1900, and of Porter Perrin in 1950. Here, on the doorstep of the millennium, we could do far worse than try to follow in their footsteps.

NOTE

[1] I feel curiously implicated in this naming, since I seem to have been the first to use the term in a journal article, "Composition Studies and Science," in January 1983. But the term was in the air, and though it was not completely accepted for several years—some people liked just "composition," some liked "literacy studies," some wanted to stay with "rhetoric"—the name seemed to stick.

REFERENCES

Bright, J. W. (1902). President's address. *Proceedings of the MLA, 18,* xli– lxii.

Brown, S. C., Meyer, P. R., & Enos, T. (1994). Doctoral programs in rhetoric and composition: A catalog of the profession. *Rhetoric Review, 12,* 240–387.

Calderonello, A. (1991, March). *Professionalization of rhetoric/composition: Consequences and commitment.* Paper presented at the Conference on College Composition and Communication, Boston. (ERIC Document Reproduction Service No. ED333 464)

Chapman, D. W., & Tate, G. (1987). A survey of doctoral programs in rhetoric and composition. *Rhetoric Review, 5,* 124–185.

Connors, R. J. (1983). Composition studies and science. *College English, 45,* 1–20.

Connors, R. J. (1989). Introduction. In R. J. Connors (Ed.), *Selected essays of Edward P. J. Corbett* (pp. xi–xxii). Dallas, TX: Southern Methodist University Press.

Connors, R. J. (1991). Rhetoric in the modern university: The creation of an underclass. In. R. Bullock & J. Trimbur (Eds.), *The politics of writing instruction: Postsecondary* (pp. 55–84). Portsmouth, NH: Boynton/Cook.

Harvard Committee on the Objectives of a General Education in a Free Society. (1945). *General education in a free society.* Cambridge, MA: Harvard University Press.

Kitzhaber, A. R. (1953). *Rhetoric in American colleges, 1850–1900.* Unpublished doctoral dissertation, University of Washington, Seattle.

Knoblauch, C. H., & Brannon, L. (1984). *Rhetorical traditions and the teaching of writing.* Upper Montclair, NJ: Boynton/Cook.

North, S. M. (1987). *The making of knowledge in composition: Portrait of an emerging field.* Upper Montclair, NJ: Boynton/Cook.

Perrin, P. G. (1936). *The teaching of rhetoric in the American colleges before 1750.* Unpublished doctoral dissertation, University of Chicago.

Warfel, H. R. (1959). Structural linguistics and composition. *College English, 20,* 205–212.

chapter 2

Veterans' Stories on the Porch

Lester Faigley
University of Texas at Austin

I grew up in the South during the last years when an oral tradition from the Civil War still survived. The stories I heard, however, were primarily those of a Union soldier, my great grandfather John Faigley, who at age 17 had joined the Union Army and served throughout the war under William Tecumseh Sherman, the man who said "War is hell" and then proceeded to demonstrate it on much of the South. My grandfather, Henry Clay Faigley, told me his father's stories. Henry Clay Faigley was born in 1881 in Lancaster, Ohio, the same hometown of his father and General Sherman. As a boy, he listened to the narratives of his father and the men of his generation, who had gone with Sherman to fight at Shiloh, Vicksburg, Chattanooga, Atlanta, and the March to the Sea. I don't think he ever read anything about the Civil War, but he cultivated an enormous knowledge just from listening to veterans talking on their porches on long summer evenings.

My grandfather didn't have war stories of his own. The Spanish-American War didn't last long enough for mass conscription, and by the time the United States entered World War I, my grandfather, then age 36, was too old to be drafted. So I had to be content to hear his stories of traveling around the country by hopping freight trains and a brief career as a minor league pitcher at the turn of the century.

My great grandfather died at age 98, living long enough to see his grandchildren go off to fight in World War II. One of them was my father, V. V. Faigley. My father served in the Army Signal Corps in

North Africa, Italy, and France as an aerial photographer. He was in combat and was shot down twice over the Mediterranean. Unlike my grandfather, however, I could rarely get my father to tell stories. He had a standard reply for any general questions about World War II: "We built ships, tanks, and planes faster than the Germans could destroy them." Specific questions sometimes could get a bit of information, but to this day the narratives are no more than a half dozen—the best of which is a diverted mission to Cairo that returned with a cargo of steaks and whiskey. I thought for a long time that my father's reticence came from losing his only brother in the final months of the war, but I came to realize that his attitude was typical of many veterans. Paul Fussell (1989) sums up this attitude in his book *Wartime*, when he writes that for the average soldier, World War II was about genocide. When you killed all of them, you could go home.

On my mother's side of the family there were also Civil War veterans. My mother's parents were much younger than my father's, and thus the veterans were their grandfathers and great uncles. My grandparents knew where their grandfathers had fought, but because the war was over so quickly where they lived in what is now West Virginia, there wasn't much to tell. Nonetheless, there was one enticing bit of information. My grandmother was a Jackson, and her grandfather, Nathaniel Muncy Jackson, was born in 1842 at Jackson's Mill, Virginia, near the present Clarksburg, West Virginia. Another Jackson who fought in the Civil War was born at Jackson's Mill 18 years earlier. His name was Thomas Jonathan Jackson. He was an orphan but managed to get to West Point, served in the Mexican War, and became a professor at Virginia Military Institute until the Civil War began. My grandmother, and the men who served under him, called him "Tom," but to the rest of the world he became known as "Stonewall." My grandmother knew very little about Stonewall Jackson because her grandfather had fought for the Union. Her great uncle Shadrach Jackson had fought for the Confederacy under his famous cousin. Shadrach's descendants lived not far from my grandmother, but there was no communication between the branches of the family—some wounds of the Civil War have never healed.

Stonewall Jackson did not become a presence in my life until I entered the eighth grade in 1961 and was taught American history by Mrs. Henley, who was about the same age as my maternal grandparents. Mrs. Henley grew up in Williamsburg in a house that was bought and torn down by John D. Rockefeller in the 1930s to make way for the restoration of Colonial Williamsburg. She was a walking encyclopedia of Virginia history. I discovered quickly that she was an even richer source of narratives than my grandfather, and, best of all, I had never heard the stories before because they were all from Confederate veterans. Even the names of the battles were different. She referred to the battles of Bull Run as First and Second Manassas and Antietam as Sharpsburg. When I told her about my great grandfather at Shiloh, she informed me that even though it had been a Union victory, Confederate veterans were fond of saying, "Remember what we did to the Yankees at Shiloh." It was my first lesson in historiography: *Everything depends on point of view.*

Mrs. Henley was a wonderful teacher throughout the year, but when we got to the Civil War, she had us totally engaged. She used the Centennial of the Civil War as reason enough to expand its place in the curriculum. She wasn't teaching us out of the book. Instead, we heard the stories of the Army of Northern Virginia, under the command of Robert E. Lee. Mrs. Henley narrated each battle in detail, and with her own collection of maps and photographs, she made us familiar with the terrain over which they were fought. Each battle had stories more dramatic than those my grandfather told. All the smaller narratives were part of a larger plot in which Stonewall Jackson became the tragic hero. We studied Jackson's rise to fame at First Manassas, his brilliant campaign in the Shenandoah Valley in 1862, and his victories with Lee in the Peninsular Campaign, Second Manassas, and Fredericksburg.

Lee and Jackson's masterpiece was the battle of Chancellorsville in May 1863. The Union army for the first time had a competent and aggressive general in Joseph Hooker, who promised to exploit the North's huge advantage in numbers and weapons. Faced by the much superior Union army advancing toward him, Lee did the unthinkable by dividing his army in half and sending Jackson on a long march around Hooker's force to attack it from the rear as the soldiers sat down for supper. Hooker's army was taken by surprise and fled in panic. The Confederate advance was stopped only by nightfall. In the darkness, Jackson rode forward to survey the positions of the enemy and was mistakenly shot by his own men. His left arm was amputated and he went into a coma. He died a week later.

In Mrs. Henley's master plot, the Civil War came down to a misunderstood speech act. After the battle of Chancellorsville, Lee and President Jefferson Davis recognized time was running out on the Confederacy. The Union army in the West, under General Ulysses S. Grant, had Vicksburg under siege, and the South was running out of food everywhere. A major victory on Northern soil might end the Union's will to continue the war. Lee marched his army up the Shenandoah Valley into Pennsylvania. Jackson was replaced by one of his division commanders, Richard Ewell, who also had been severely wounded, lost a leg, and returned to battle.

Meanwhile, Abraham Lincoln replaced Joe Hooker with Gordon Meade, a competent but cautious general, who kept the Union Army between Lee's army and Washington. On July 1, 1863, a Confederate infantry division heading toward Gettysburg in search of shoes ran into Union cavalry patrolling the roads outside of town. Both sides sent for help, and the great battle began. On the first day, it was no contest because the Confederates had two-thirds of their army present while the Union had only one fourth of theirs. Lee saw the advantage and sent his army forward, routing the Northern troops and sending them fleeing to the high ground east of Gettysburg. The new Union position was potentially a strong one, but they had to maintain the hills at each end of the defensive line with the few men they had left until the rest of Meade's army could join the battle.

Late in the afternoon, Lee accurately assessed the situation and sent Richard Ewell a politely worded order to take the hills on the Union right "if practicable." Ewell failed to grasp the intent of the courteous order and did nothing more than send out probing attacks. Meade and his soldiers arrived that night, and he quickly recognized the danger on his right flank and rushed divisions to defend the hills. When Ewell finally did attack the next day, he ran into a well-fortified position and the Confederates were turned back. Mrs. Henley didn't have to tell us that if Stonewall Jackson had still been alive, he would have intuitively known Lee's intentions and would have acted immediately. The battle of Gettysburg would have turned out much differently—and perhaps the entire war.

When I got to college and took a course in American history, I didn't expect to get Mrs. Henley's version of the Civil War, but neither did I expect that the battles would be totally elided from the account. After I bought the textbook for the course, I turned to the section on the Civil War. What sufficed for the history of the war itself was a series of graphs showing that there was a remarkable disparity of resources between the North and the South. The North had over twice the population, even counting the nearly 4 million African Americans held in slavery in the South. The North had a 2-to-1 advantage in the number of horses, cows, and railroad miles, a 4-to-1 advantage in wheat production, a 5-to-1 advantage in factories, and over a 10-to-1 advantage in numbers of industrial workers and the value of goods produced. Mrs. Henley had told us about these differences, but in her narrative they served to underscore the heroism of the Confederate soldiers. The graphs in the college textbook coldly made it appear that the South never had any realistic chance of winning the war. It was over before it started. Mrs. Henley had said as much, but what a difference in presentation. It was my second lesson in historiography: *How we understand history depends on the method of writing history.*

The papers delivered at the 1996 Watson Conference at the University of Louisville, which form the basis of this volume, were stacked toward Mrs. Henley's kind of history as a series of narratives. Yet, as much as I like to hear and tell stories, I also have come to appreciate that the story of the rise of composition studies can be told with graphs and that like the victory of the North in the Civil War, it had a high probability of coming into being as a discipline. While it is more pleasurable to tell and listen to stories on the porch, especially at a reunion of veterans, it is also useful to consider how else that history could be represented.

Even by the end of the period that was the focus of the Watson Conference—1963 to 1983—those teaching college writing in the United States recognized that the growth of their discipline was being propelled by the enormous expansion of college enrollment: from 2.7 million in 1949–50, to 3.6 million in 1959–60, to over 8 million in 1969–70, and over 11.5 million in 1979–80 (National Center for Education Statistics, 1995). The increases during the 1960s and 1970s are by far the largest in numbers of students during the history of American higher education.

When the bar graph in Figure 2.1 is read in the context of other graphs, then the development of composition studies seems almost inevitable. The makeup of the workforce in the United States greatly changed between 1950 and 1980. We can see this change clearly in Figure 2.2 by contrasting employment statistics in three industrial sectors: agriculture, manufacturing, and services (Mitchell, 1993). In 1950, 9.2 million people were employed in agriculture, 16.1 in manufacturing, and almost 10 million in services. By 1960, the number of agricultural workers drops in half, while manufacturing and services both add about 3.5 million workers. However, by 1970, growth in manufacturing jobs has leveled off, while almost 7 million jobs have been added in services, bringing its even with manufacturing. During the 1970s, 1 million manufacturing jobs were added, in contrast to 8 million jobs in services, trends that continued in the 1980s.

The service sector of the economy is a mixed bag of highly educated and poorly educated workers, but most of the job growth within the service sector came in business services and in the professional services of health care, education, and social and legal services. Many jobs in these services require highly literate and well educated workers. We do not have good statistics on literacy education in the schools (see Figure 2.3), but there is one valuable snapshot taken by Arthur Applebee and his associates (1981). They found that little writing was being taught in high schools and almost none outside English courses. For example, the percentage of high school homework assignments devoted to producing texts of a paragraph or more was only 3 percent.

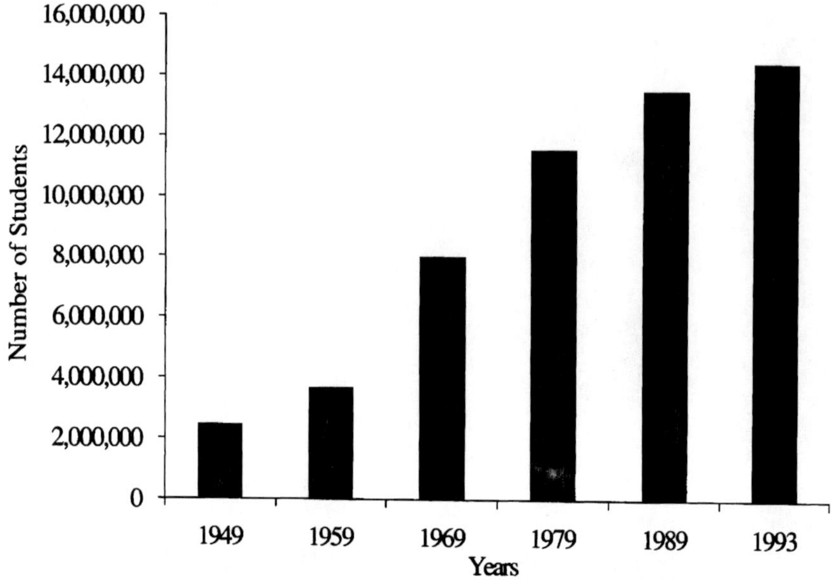

FIGURE 2.1 Total Fall Enrollment in Institutions of Higher Education: 1949 to 1993

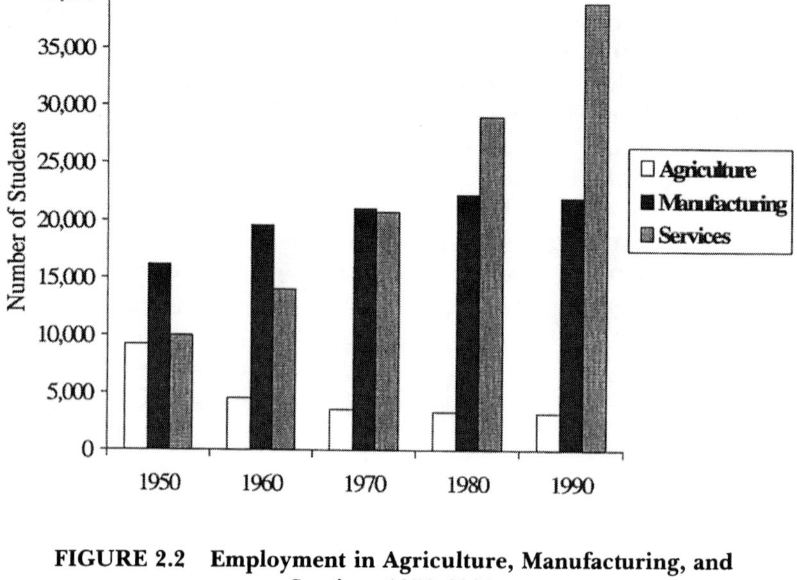

FIGURE 2.2 Employment in Agriculture, Manufacturing, and Services 1950-1990

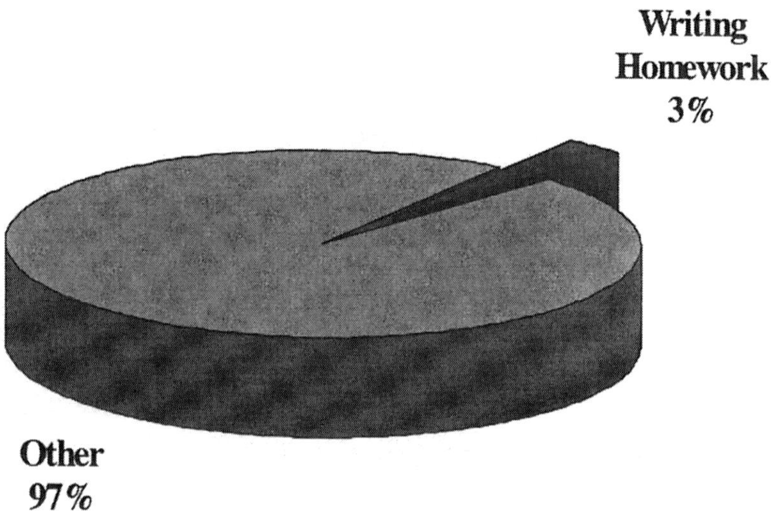

FIGURE 2.3 Percentage of High School Homework Assignments Devoted to Producing Texts of a Paragraph or More

Given the enormous increase in the numbers of students going to college, the demand for highly literate professionals, and the absence of writing instruction in the schools, it is not hard to see why there was a great perceived need for writing instruction in post-secondary education. The "literacy crisis" of the 1970s proclaimed in such articles as "Why Johnny Can't Write" (Sheils, 1975) was real enough, although the culprit was not the decline of standards but the tripling of the number of college students within two decades. In response to pressure from employers and professional schools, colleges and universities augmented the resources available to teach writing, and new sources of external funding from both private foundations and federal agencies helped to launch writing-across-the-curriculum (WAC) programs and other ambitious efforts to place writing instruction at the center of undergraduate education. The scholars present at the Watson Conference certainly made a difference in how composition studies developed and what became emphasized. But I still think that if none of us had been around from 1963 to 1983, the study of composition would have still happened. Though I would like to think that it would not have had the intellectual richness or the broader impact on higher education.

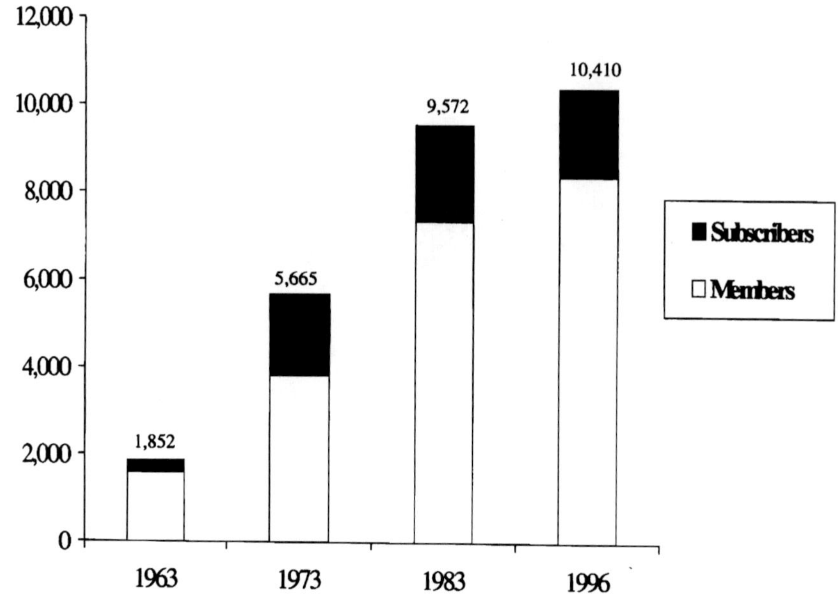

FIGURE 2.4 CCCC Membership and Subscribers: 1963-1996

To look for a moment at what did happen, I turn to the growth of the Conference on College Composition and Communication illustrated in Figure 2.4. In May 1963, the CCCC had 1,573 members and 279 subscribers, for a total of 1,852. In May 1973, that total had grown to 5,665, a 207 percent increase, and in May 1983, the total was 9,572, a 417 percent increase over 1963. In May 1996, the total was 10,410, only a 9 percent increase over 1983 (W. Subick, personal communication, September 30, 1996). In the late 1970s and early 1980s, graduate rhetoric programs began producing specialists in rhetoric and composition and publishing venues for rhetoric and composition multiplied. Between 1978 and 1984, an impressive collection of books were published by the National Council of Teachers of English, Southern Illinois University Press, Oxford University Press, and Boynton/Cook. New journals also appeared (*Journal of Advanced Composition*, *Journal of Basic Writing*, *PRE/TEXT*, *Rhetoric Review*, *The Writing Instructor*, *Written Communication*, and *WPA: Writing Program Administration*). Nevertheless, the growth in graduate programs in rhetoric and composition and in published scholarship through the 1980s and 1990s is not matched by a similar rise in membership.

Clearly, other factors are involved besides the landmarks we point to as proof of our status as a discipline, and I keep recalling my father's comment about World War II that they built ships, tanks, and planes faster than the Germans could destroy them. For several decades, World War II was understood to be about battles, generals, and politicians, and only recently have we come to recognize the importance of factory and transportation workers in the war effort and especially the contributions of women. Similarly, we are only beginning to acknowledge the role of early writing program administrators in the development of composition studies as a discipline. During the 1950s, the institutional contexts of teaching composition were the main concerns of CCCC, and in the meeting reports and the published articles from that decade we find the structure of a large writing program being collectively developed. By the 1970s, institutional issues are seldom found in the articles of *College Composition and Communication*, and their absence eventually led to the founding of the Council of Writing Program Administrators in 1979. When institutional issues become prominent, the situation is almost always a time of local crisis, such as the open-admissions policy at the City University in New York in the early 1970s, detailed in Shaughnessy's *Errors and Expectations* (1977).

Even less discussed are the impacts of bricks-and-mortar higher education initiatives to make college spaces available to the baby-boom generation. Tripling the number of college students in two decades meant building many new campuses and increasing the capacities of existing ones. For example, in the late 1960s and early 1970s, California built 42 new community colleges, 4 state colleges, and 3 new University of California campuses. Another major increase in the number of college-age students is on the immediate horizon (see Figure 2.5 and Figure 2.6). The U.S. Department of Education predicts that the number of college students will rise from an estimated 14.1 million in 1994 to 16.4 million by the year 2006, representing an average annual growth rate of 1.3 percent and a total of 16 percent for the period (Hussar & Gerald, 1995). In the next decade, California alone will add nearly 500,000 students to its public colleges and universities, increasing to 2.2 million in 2005 from 1.7 million in 1994 (Honan, 1996). Furthermore, we know there remains a great demand for highly educated workers, generated by the growth of small businesses, although the jobs they offer are often at longer hours for less pay and less security than those previously offered by large corporations. And while there has not been a follow-up study to Applebee's (1981) important research, anecdotal evidence suggests that the teaching of writing in high schools is at best infrequent outside of English classes, and secondary English teachers continue to struggle to include writing in a packed curriculum.

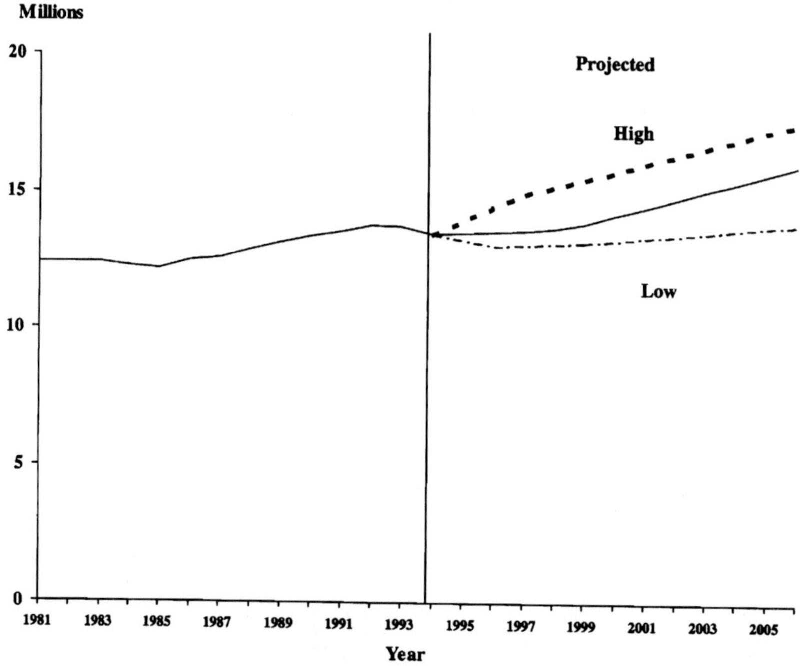

FIGURE 2.5 Enrollment in Institutions of Higher Education, with Alternative Projections: Fall 1981 to Fall 2006

Thus, the surface statistics would indicate a steady state with small growth for composition studies, but we should be skeptical of direct correlations. The MLA *Job Information List* (1996) is one indicator of why we should be skeptical. The number of students enrolled in college rose steadily at 1.3 percent a year from 1988 to 1994, but the number of jobs advertised plummeted almost 50 percent (see Figure 2.7). While the situation was much better for those candidates in composition than those in literature, the figures nevertheless show that there is not a linear relationship between the number of students and the number of jobs; nor should we assume one in the near future. Tuition continues to rise rapidly as state support for colleges and universities continues to decline. If money can be found in the budgets of the states to spend on education, K–12 education stands in line in front of higher education.

We should expect the next decade in higher education to be a highly turbulent one. Attacks on tenure are now prominent in the news, but they may be only harbingers of more sweeping changes to come. Many

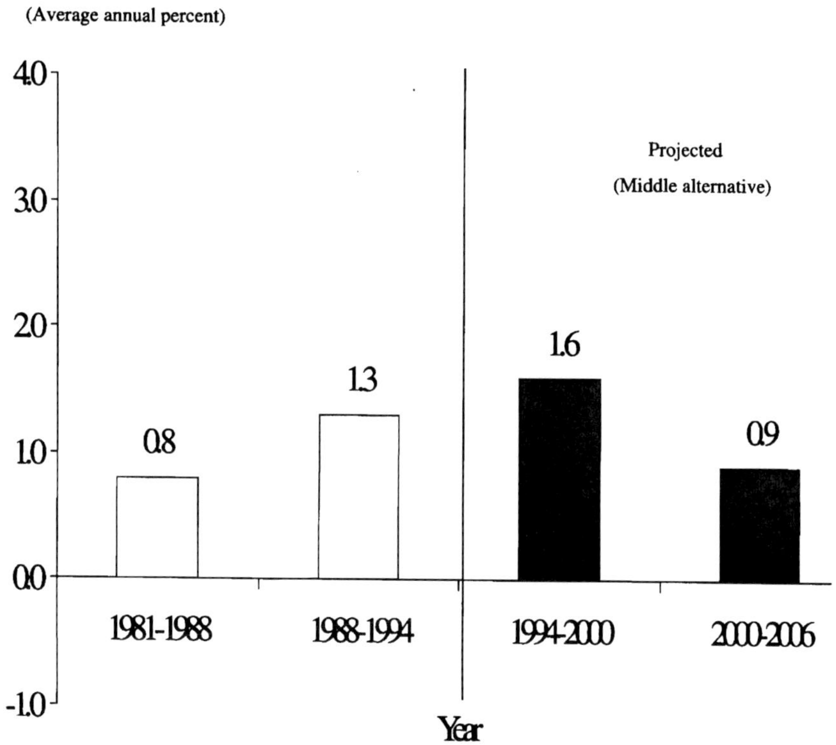

FIGURE 2.6 Average Annual Growth Rates for Total Higher Education Enrollment

powerful voices are calling for change in higher education, and we ignore them at our peril. To give one example, the governors of western states, led by Roy Romer of Colorado and Michael Leavitt of Utah, have launched an ambitious plan to create Western Governors' University, an alternative to higher education. They are planning a virtual university, where credit is given according to demonstrated competencies based on employer-defined standards. The delivery of instruction will be through telecommunications technologies. Courses offered by businesses for their employees will count toward degrees. Leavitt (1996) describes the new initiative as creating a "'virtual learning system' that will deliver traditional university courses, but also vocational/technical skills and job training for corporate and industry needs.... It will be a learning system for a new millennium, one that incorporates the necessity of lifelong

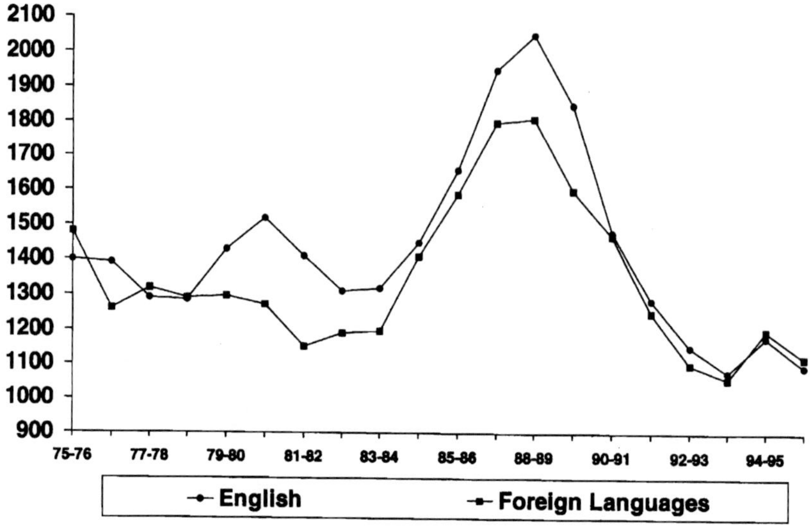

FIGURE 2.7 Number of Positions Advertised in the JIL by Academic Year

learning as the era of the 'knowledge worker' emerges in the new century." In fall 1996, Pete Wilson announced a similar plan for California

Plans for virtual universities should have some shock value for us. When universities are increasingly turning to principles of "value-centered management," where dollars are tied closely to credit hours generated, writing programs always look expensive. If all classes in a writing program are small ones and the costs of supporting a staff are added, instructional budgets of writing programs at major state universities often run over $1 million a year. In tight budgetary times, they become ripe targets for budget raids and for increased pressure to exploit part-timers. The programs that flourish in these times will be ones that can convey the value of all the many things they do for students, other faculty, administrators, and the larger communities that support higher education.

If my argument that we need to be much more aware of the larger forces that impact writing programs in understanding our past and in anticipating the future is convincing, then what good are veterans' stories on the porch? During the long hours I spent in the library researching and writing a tedious dissertation, I took relief by wandering in the stacks. The section on Civil War history was not far from my carrel, and for the first time since junior high, I began reading again about the Civil War. I soon realized that Mrs. Henley had given us chapter and verse, with one important exception, which I will discuss shortly: the myth of the "Lost Cause." The Lost Cause myth took shape in the South soon after the war ended. During the bleak years of Reconstruction, it was easy to convince white Southerners that they had not been defeated, but merely outnumbered and that their struggle still continued. The Lost Cause myth had strong religious overtones. God had really been on the Southern side, but in His mysterious wisdom had elected to force His people to endure a time of woe, much as the early Christians had suffered under the Romans. The Confederate generals who fell in battle, most notably Jackson, became its martyrs.

After Robert E. Lee died in 1870, the myth became the dominant ideology in the South. Lee ended the war as a revered but somewhat controversial figure. He had, after all, commanded the losing army, and there was no shortage of second guessers. Lee's great successes were in his backyard; away from home, he proved to be not only ordinary, but also capable of major blunders like Pickett's Charge at Gettysburg. Thus, to turn him into the central figure, his blunders had to be deflected to someone else. That person turned out to be Lee's second-in-command and close friend, James Longstreet, the man Lee called his "war horse."

Mrs. Henley told us a story her father had told her about witnessing the unveiling of an equestrian statue of Robert E. Lee in Richmond in 1890. Most of the officers and many of the men still living who fought under Lee came to Richmond for the occasion. Lee's nephew, Fitzhugh Lee, led the parade, and the crowd loudly cheered when the generals' carriages passed by. The one detail I remember from her story was that the old soldiers broke ranks and stopped the parade when James Longstreet appeared in order to get close to their old commander. Their action would not have seemed unusual since Longstreet was the highest-ranking Confederate still alive, but Mrs. Henley added that Longstreet was a controversial figure in the South because he had joined the Republican party and had urged reconciliation with the North.

My dissertation-avoiding curiosity turned to James Longstreet to discover why he rejected the Lost Cause myth. I never found the complete answer, in part because Longstreet's diaries and papers were destroyed in a fire. Whatever the reason, Longstreet saw the larger picture much earlier than others in the South. He realized that the South was not going to rise again and urged cooperation with the Republican party. Longstreet was branded a traitor for speaking out, and when he accepted a position under President Ulysses S. Grant in 1869, he became the Judas of the Lost Cause myth. Lee remained a friend of Longstreet and never faulted him for his military or civilian conduct, but when Lee died, Longstreet was made a scapegoat. Although Longstreet's record on the battlefield was one of a hard fighter and shrewd tactician and there was no one whom Lee trusted more, Longstreet began to be blamed for Southern defeats. In the Lost Cause myth, Gettysburg became the decisive battle where the fate of the South was decided, and Longstreet was made its villain. Longstreet was accused of failing to carry out an order to attack at dawn on the second day of Gettysburg, though in fact no such order was ever given (Piston, 1987).

I don't know why Mrs. Henley didn't give us the Lost Cause version of Gettysburg. Perhaps her sympathy with Longstreet came through her father's memory, but I now wonder if her revision of the Lost Cause myth had something to do with her own situation as a teacher who taught for nearly all of her career in segregated schools and suddenly found her students were at least one third African American. Perhaps she could see in Longstreet someone who understood the necessity of responding to change.

Long after the eighth grade, I was still learning historiography from Mrs. Henley. She had taught me not only that the facts don't speak for themselves, but moreover that everything depends on how particular lives encounter particular situations. Longstreet understood the facts far beyond other Confederate leaders, but he did not appreciate the narrative power of the Lost Cause myth and he lacked the rhetorical ability to refute his critics. For his forward thinking, Longstreet suffered greatly, and his reputation to this day has never fully recovered.

Stories on the porch are often ones of pain as well as triumph. The big narratives of composition studies are largely successes, but in the little narratives are many stories of short-sighted actions by administrators and colleagues to dismantle overnight writing programs that have taken years to create. We need both the big and little narratives to understand our history, and we need both big and little narratives to convince others to support what we do—big narratives about the demands for increasingly complex multiple literacies, and little narratives about why quality education is worth paying for.

REFERENCES

Applebee, A. N. (with Auten, A., & Lehr, F.). (1981). *Writing in the secondary school: English and the content areas* (NCTE Research Report No. 21). Urbana, IL: National Council of Teachers of English.

Fussell, P. (1989). *Wartime: Understanding and behavior in the Second World War.* New York: Oxford University Press.

Honan, W. H. (1996, September 25). Without money to build, western colleges innovate to handle more students. *New York Times*, p. B9.

Hussar, W. J., & Gerald, D. E. (1995). *Projections of education statistics to 2006.* Washington, DC: U.S. Department of Education.

Leavitt, M. O. (1996). *Virtual University* [Online]. Available: http://www.das.state.ut.us/ capconn/Mar96/GOVMESS.htm

Mitchell, B. R. (1993). *International historical statistics: The Americas, 1750–1988* (2nd ed.). New York: Stockton.

Modern Language Association. (1996, Summer). 1995–1996 *Job Information List* figures. *MLA Newsletter, 28*, 1.

National Center for Education Statistics. (1995). *Digest of education statistics 1995.* Washington, DC: U.S. Department of Education.

Piston, W. G. (1987). *Lee's tarnished lieutenant: James Longstreet and his place in Southern history.* Athens, GA: University of Georgia Press.

Shaughnessy, M. P. (1977). *Errors and expectations: A guide for the teacher of basic writing.* New York: Oxford University Press.

Sheils, M. (1975, December 8). Why Johnny can't write. *Newsweek*, 58–65.

chapter 3

Paths Not Taken: Recovering History as Alternate Future*

Louise Wetherbee Phelps
Syracuse University

On the one hand, there is no movement towards full humanity which does not go beyond the given; on the other hand, elsewhere leads back to here and now.
Ricoeur, 1979, p. 122

To historians every year is an anniversary. To ordinary people the past is entombed.
Moore, 1996, p. 136

In my 1988 book, *Composition as a Human Science*, I suggested that one feature defining a discipline was "a mission: a moral imperative, social responsibility" (p. ix). At the 4Cs that same year, Connors (1989) claimed that work in composition reflects an "open and almost ingenuous desire *to do some good in the world* with our study and our teaching" (original emphasis, p. 237). However, what I had induced as a feature common to the intellectual and social formations we call disciplines, he saw as a rare if not unique "field moralism" in composition, created by the 20th century history of teaching writing in response to a cultural problem.

*In our panel, "Going beyond the Given," at the Watson Conference, my colleagues represented the codependence of history, or ideology (James Comas, "At the Limit of 'the Political': Rethinking the Act of Criticism as a Compositionist") with utopia (Keith Gilyard, "Higher Learning Composition's Racialized Reflection").

Elsewhere at the convention, Connors remarked that "composition teachers and composition researchers from early on have felt a moral charge that goes far beyond mere aesthetics: instill the literacy, transfer the power, solve the problem" (Octalog, 1988, p. 38). Despite his wry tone, Connors identified with this utopian motive and celebrated it.

Expressions of personal, moral commitment and recognition of the moralism infusing composition/rhetoric are commonplaces of its scholarship and professional identity. Both Connors and I made our remarks in the context of a collective effort to construct the self-understanding of an emergent field. My book defines its purpose as articulating and participating in a communal reflective project, while Connors was one speaker at a symposium answering the question "What Are We Doing as a Research Community?"[1] Connors, explaining his own historical approach, linked the utopian motive of composition directly to history. He presented historical knowledge as a precondition not only for defining the field (self-understanding), but also for making wise choices in our personal actions as writers or teachers and for deciding where the field should go as a research discipline. Historical study, in Connors's view, by "situat[ing] ourselves and our current struggles" (1989, p. 239), enables members of the field to pursue its ethical imperative to envision and work toward a better future for others. Although I am not a historian and (to my regret) overlooked history in enumerating the necessary features of a discipline, implicitly my language also correlated lived history and future possibilities with the writing of histories. I referred to the reflective enterprise as autobiography and the discipline as story; called for composition to write theory with irony "to express its own rhetorical self-understanding and development over time"; and realized that "to 'write' such a narrative is to give personal shape and form to a flux of events; it is to 'reframe' the unfinished story in the minds of participants and by doing so to change its meaning or direction" (Phelps, 1988, p. xi).[2]

In 1988, this suggestive but unelaborated association between moralism and history went unnoticed, nor did it dramatically influence the subsequent development of the field. One might plausibly argue that the two were split instead, or even that a relationship with the future was chosen over a connection with the past. Today, with historical studies burgeoning and the field developing more deeply historicized representations of its own identity, the time is ripe to reconsider the function of history in forming the self-understanding of composition/rhetoric and enabling the pursuit of its utopian goals. The questions raised by these earlier thoughts and by their fate in the discursive field of 1988 provide my starting point for arguing the codependence of history, or ideology, and a utopian project of working for the common good.

My essay treats 1988 semifiguratively, as emblematic of a certain historical moment (which slides into "the late '80s") representing a choice point or branching of paths. This is something like how we have imagined 1963 as a partly historical and partly fictionalized, symbolic point of origin for the modern, professionalized field. I'll begin my analysis by describing the period between 1988 and today in terms of the figure of a "path taken" and its shadow counterpart of unrealized possibilities, or "paths not taken."[3]

THE PATH TAKEN

A certain version of the ongoing development of composition that was composed in the late 1980s became in the 1990s a "given": that which goes without saying, which is taken for granted, which requires no argument. This narrative reinterprets the moral mission of composition or, more precisely, shifts it on the continuum from an ideological motive toward a utopian one. At one pole, composition aims to civilize or empower students through cultural indoctrination in literate traditions. At the other, composition is a critical project using rhetorical analysis and the teaching of writing to foster awareness of social inequities in an unjust society, question its discursive orders, reveal students' own complicity in its ideologies, and enlist them in working toward its transformation.

The tale of that shift is a classic narrative of progress that goes something like this: Composition has developed into a modern field of writing studies through several stages. In the founding moment, it rejected a sterile "current-traditional rhetoric" for the study and teaching of writing as process. As the so-called process "paradigm" or process theory and pedagogy developed, it featured an opposition between Romantic views, or expressivism, and cognitive studies focusing on mental operations, or cognitive rhetoric.[4] While cognitivism won the day for awhile, replacing the initial expressivism of process studies, both were superseded (and to a certain extent themselves modified) by a "social" or "rhetorical" turn, producing what is variously called social-epistemic rhetoric, new rhetoric, or, most often today, "social constructionism." This social paradigm, associated with antifoundationalism and postmodernism, traveled into rhetoric and composition along multiple disciplinary routes, but, it turns out, was most influentially formulated in poststructuralist terms drawn from literary-critical theory and, later, cultural studies. Earlier forms of social constructionism gradually acquired a more overtly political cast from cultural studies and radical pedagogy and in this radicalized version—as the practice of cultural criticism—became the reigning discourse of the 1990s and the assumed point of departure for future inquiry and practice.[5]

In the prevailing account of the path composition has taken, "we"—the good guys, the "progressives"—have essentially triumphed, although rearguard actions continue against a resurgent, defiant expressivism and a cognitivism that is gamely but futilely struggling to incorporate a sociopolitical dimension. This tale, and its variants, may be told from the point of view of the defeated voices; but it remains the same narrative, organized by the same oppositional relations and successions. Despite their differences in emotional tone and attitude, negative and positive versions of "what happened" converge through strategies and tropes of mutual accommodation favoring the dominant position. Proponents of expressivism or cognitivism (accepting the labels) acknowledge respectfully how much postmodern critiques "have taught us" or "revealed"—about the ubiquity of the political, the decentering of the self, the fallacy of objective truth, and so forth—while social constructionists deflect the rhetorical force of opposition by assimilating and historicizing other positions as successive moments in the inevitable march toward an intellectually and morally superior stance.

In this way, though, the story of the "path taken" by composition incorporates resistance without leaving us these positions as future options, because they lie in a past that is understood as "given" in a different sense: already lived through, over and done with, fixed, unchangeable, shaped through convergent choices into the single "path," "mainstream," "paradigm," or (most tellingly) into *the* "system."[6] If the past converges and solidifies into the path taken, what remains today of multiple "paths not taken" becomes invisible. Either they are subsumed and reduced to steps in the progression, or they are simply loose ends, discarded possibilities that don't fit into the narrative and whose presence in the field, if ever noticed, has now been forgotten.

THE DISCURSIVE FIELD OF 1988

Provisionally accepting this telling of our history, without the attached value judgments of any of the specified "sides," let us consider the discursive field of 1988 as the matrix from which it arose.

North's book *The Making of Knowledge in Composition* had appeared in 1987. Bazerman's *Shaping Written Knowledge* as well as my own *Composition as a Human Science* appeared in 1988, along with Neel's *Plato, Derrida, and Writing. Rescuing the Subject* by Miller followed in 1989. These works were preceded by a series of monographs in the National Council of Teachers of English's Studies in Writing and Rhetoric, including Berlin's *Rhetoric and Reality* (1987) and LeFevre's *Invention as a Social Act* (1987). As a group, these were a breakthrough: the first critical mass of single-authored, openly theoretical books in composition, an event made possible by the opening of university presses and other outlets to composition/rhetoric. Two of them (North and Phelps) explicitly set out to describe composition studies as a discipline and to envision a coherent construction of its projects.

Exempting Berlin's (1987) history (for reasons that will appear), I would challenge anyone to locate these books definitively on the path taken. Each frames a theoretical coherence uniquely for the field and offers dissimilar proposals for its future development. Although these are not necessarily incompatible, there are few obvious overlaps among them. With negligible exceptions, the authors do not cite or make use of one another's published work, nor do they draw inspiration from the same interdisciplinary sources. One gets the impression of a group of writers working in parallel and in some degree of mutual isolation to create distinctive visions of composition studies, each out of his or her own partial, idiosyncratic exposure—and resistance—to its fragmented discourse.[7]

Yet none of these works is based on then conventional or shallow notions of process theory, nor do any of them operate exclusively within one of the named paradigms (LeFevre [1987] comes closest). Although they address some of the issues raised by and within process theory, each may also be seen as written implicitly or explicitly to problematize, detour, or surpass it, in part by seeking outside the field itself for new concepts and theoretical languages. Even when portraying the field as it is or was (see, for example, Miller, 1989; North, 1987), these authors ignore much of what was current when they were writing their books to propose an extraordinarily diverse array of questions, terms, taxonomies, and traditions as a basis for consolidating and advancing composition studies and rhetoric.

As far as I can tell, the field never sought to juxtapose these visions critically or to place them directly in dialogue or confrontation with one another. In fact, I suggest that despite praise, criticism, controversy, awards,[8] and subsequent citations of these books, there was little immediate uptake by the field of most of the ideas in them (still excepting Berlin's). As the story was told of "what is happening" and in the telling turned into "what happened," the alternate attitudes and histories in these books, their theoretical terms and concepts, and the questions that these authorized disappeared as such in "mainstream composition" during much of the 1990s, even as oppositional positions or complementary analyses. In the view of history implicit in this narrative, they are unrecoverable.

Instead, I propose, the publication that most definitively heralded and thereby shaped both the image and the reality of the path taken and its culmination in the "political turn" was Berlin's 1988 *College English* article "Rhetoric and Ideology." This article laid out four positions in composition/rhetoric, similar to those Berlin had proposed in earlier articles and books (including *Rhetoric and Reality*, in 1987), but now redescribed in a framework that subsumes rhetoric to ideology, or more precisely to the critique of ideology:

> Ideology is here foregounded and problematized in a way that situates rhetoric within ideology, rather than ideology within rhetoric. In other words, instead of rhetoric acting as the transcendental recorder or arbiter of competing ideological claims, rhetoric is regarded as always already ideological. This position means that any examination of a rhetoric must first consider the ways its very discursive structure can be read so as to favor one version of economic, social, and political arrangements over other versions. (p. 477)

And it subtly arrayed these positions (the now familiar current-traditional rhetoric, cognitive rhetoric, expressionist rhetoric, and social-epistemic rhetoric) in a progressive order so that not only does the social-epistemic position appear to be morally and intellectually superior (by virtue of its self-consciousness of ideology), but it also coopts and assimilates the others as its precursors. Although others foreshadowed or proposed cultural criticism, critique of ideology, or a more political interpretation of social constructionism at about the same time or earlier (see, for example, Bizzell, 1986, 1992a; Chase, 1988; Faigley, 1986), only Berlin actually articulated the field narrative itself, and his particular way of doing it was decisive for the way these ideas were then taken up.

Whatever the reasons (complex and various) for Berlin's success in initiating the political turn and imposing his representation of the field in place of other versions, visions, and histories, I am more interested here in how the rhetoric of his essay became so consequential in our subsequent understanding of composition's history. I have already pointed to several features of his rhetoric. He subtly but effectively transformed what appeared to be a synchronic taxonomy of differences into a chronology, a method that is characteristic of his work. While the overarching conception subsumed rhetoric to ideology, the essay waffled strategically between a neutral and an evaluative concept of ideology (Geertz, 1973), obscuring the degree to which its premise created considerable difficulties in claiming the possibility of escaping ideology through the role of cultural critic. At the same time, under "social-epistemic rhetoric" Berlin conflated the "social" turn in composition, which was by then widely accepted among scholars of various persuasions, with a more politicized interpretation of social construction (holding that "behavior is determined by the ideology which upholds the contemporary class structure and in turn serves to perpetuate that class structure" [Green, 1995, p. 118]). Berlin's (1988) artful ambiguity in using the terms "ideology" and "social-epistemic," along with his narratizing strategy for displacing other positions, displayed what I can only call a rhetorical genius in winning adherents. Berlin's article functioned for the 1990s as did Hairston's 1982 article "The Winds of Change" for the 1980s, to popularize and gather together under a single rubric a variety of dissimilar positions, which actually fall at various points along a continuum between two poles that I will now designate as "ideology" and "utopia." In both cases, these histories and representations were partly self-fulfilling ones, and each in its turn led to certain impasses.

IDEOLOGY AND UTOPIA

Next, I introduce some distinctions from the work of Ricoeur (1976/1979; 1973/1981; see also Taylor, 1986) to explore further the connections between moralism and history. In "Ideology and Utopia as Cultural Imagination" (1976/1979), Ricoeur attempts to theorize ideology and utopia as complementary functions within a process of cultural imagination. Each has a healthy function and an unhealthy or distorted modality. Borrowing from Geertz (1973), Ricoeur describes ideology as having three levels unified by the rhetorical function of symbolizing and thus conserving pattern and social order. Most basically, ideology is a symbolic process that mediates and integrates public understanding of human action. At another level, Ricoeur explains, it legitimates the social organization it symbolizes, while in its pathologic aspect it dissimulates the interest of a dominant group in maintaining this order, overvalues the validity of authority, and associates it with violence.

In contrast, utopian thinking has the function of social subversion and reformation. Utopian fictions or experiments, in imagining alternate social orders and ways of using power, call into question existing ones. (In the case of composition, utopians hypothesize and experiment with alternate orders through their own writing, student writings, and in the semifictional utopian worlds created in the classroom [see, for example, O'Reilly, 1984].) This critique of the ideology of the real is made explicit in the practice of cultural criticism, which unmasks the interests of power structures and analyzes the distortions and dissimulations of ideology in light of a moral ideal (for example, undistorted communication or social justice). In its pathology, the critique of ideology tends, in Ricoeur's (1976/1979) words, to "delineate self-contained schemas of perfection severed from the whole course of the human experience of value" and to schizophrenically develop an escapist

> logic of all or nothing which ignores the labor of time. Hence the preference for spatial schematisms and the projections of the future in frozen models which have to be immediately perfect, as well as the lack of care for the first steps to be taken in the direction of the ideal city. (p. 121)

Ricoeur argues that utopia and ideology need each other as limit-experiences for one another's pathologies, to keep each of them wholesome and in balance. Cultural imagination requires both integrative and inventive, conserving and critical functions.

In a second essay (1973/1981), Ricoeur figures this opposition as "Hermeneutics and the Critique of Ideology," or what I have called history and (a certain version of) composition's moralism. Here, he identifies ideology with the hermeneutical awareness of history, which acknowledges human finitude and values tradition, while utopia is identified with the defiant and distancing attitude of the critical social sciences (p. 63). He used Gadamer and Habermas as representatives of these different stances toward culture and language.

The humanities (including rhetoric and composition in this aspect) "are essentially sciences of culture, concerned with the renewal of cultural heritage in the historical present. They are thus by nature sciences of tradition—of tradition reinterpreted and reinvented in terms of its implications here and now, but of continuous tradition nonetheless" (Ricoeur, 1973/1981, p. 82). The critical social sciences (and our field in this aspect) have as their task emancipation through self-reflection, requiring them to reject the authority of tradition and distance themselves critically from the past. However, Ricoeur finds that each not only depends on the other, but also incorporates the other into its own structure. Specifically, he argues that history, or a hermeneutics of tradition, interpenetrates a critique of ideology (or any utopian moralism) and must inform and enable it in a number of ways. Among other points, it is impossible even to discern and resist givens, much less to envisage novelty, without recourse to the past, which provides a wealth of alternate, unrealized possibilities. When a new path is opened, it always turns out to have a history. As Ricoeur remarks, critique itself is a tradition.

GOING BEYOND THE GIVEN

Initially, Ricoeur's analysis points to the path not taken in 1988 as the hermeneutical one, suggesting that in order to move beyond the given, the field needs to pursue more profoundly both historical studies and a criticism distinct from critique. Furthermore, utopia chastened by history will itself look different, incorporating a richer possibility for "imagining where we could go from here as well as what's wrong with now" (Bizzell, 1992a, p. 29).

But these two motives can no longer be conceptualized chronologically as in the progress narrative, where one position ("current-traditional" pedagogy) is superseded by its oppositional other (the entire path to the present theoretical moment). Instead, ideology and utopia may be thought of variously: as motives, moments, poles, or functions. The recent period is not the end of history (that is, the disciplinary history of composition/rhetoric), but one during which the utopian motive has temporarily dominated. This way of thinking not only calls for us to foreground history and criticism more vigorously as hermeneutical activities, but also for us to connect them with ideological functions inherent in the mission of composition and to examine these working on all three of Geertz's (1973) levels. At the same time, it enables us to analyze how an imbalance between ideology and utopia during the recent period has incurred specific losses and created current impasses. Without the limit-experience of a wholesome ideology function, utopia is susceptible to its own pathologies (and vice versa). From this perspective, a third path (not taken in 1988) is the one that refuses to choose definitively between ideology and utopia.

On a less global level of analysis, "paths not taken" may refer to an indefinite number of alternatives discarded in the past: ideas, methodologies, traditions, and practices that have been forgotten, neglected, misrepresented, or relegated to the margins. But were all these paths actually "not taken"? To continue this heuristic formulation uncritically may perpetuate the claim of a monolithic representation of history. The call for more primary historical research brings to mind the complexity of our actual, historicized experience of composition studies: filled with a myriad of unresolved conflicts, major and minor traditions, ambiguities, and contradictory practices irreducible to the dominant narrative. Even globally, the positive claims of ideology have persisted alongside the critical project seeking social justice—a tension at the heart of composition pedagogy that often manifests itself as ambivalence (for example, about the "service" functions of composition).

Despite poststructuralism, metanarratives should not be dismissed out of hand (and indeed can't be avoided); at best, they are bold simplifications that can provide conceptual insight and exert rhetorical force (as, I think, the concept of "paths not taken" does for this argument or the "classical tradition" served composition positively as a myth of origin). But such interpretations are judged and can be refuted not only in those (historically contingent) terms, but for their continuing adequacy to the actual multiplicity of texts and practices recovered in primary historical research and their ability to capture our evolving sense of the complex, slippery eventfulness of history. Berlin's (1988) account of composition in "Rhetoric and Ideology" fails as history because it is a structuralist analysis (questionable even on its own terms) projected into time, deductive rather than inductive, homogenizing multiple scholarly positions and practices and misrepresenting them in its idealist categories, while acknowledging no need for broad-based empirical evidence of instructional and social practices.[9] This critique resembles that which feminists and other historians have mounted of standard intellectual histories of ancient rhetoric and the subsequent (pedagogical) tradition; of Harvard-based accounts of 19th-century writing instruction; and of conventional wisdom about women's and American minorities' limited public role as rhetoricians.

I began this project with the intention of advocating a return to history itself as a path not taken in 1988, in the double sense of history as a mode of inquiry and as a fruitful relation to tradition and culture (Ricoeur's ideology). My investigation has revised this conception to a more recuperative one, wary of imagining composition as a tree of evolution where all branches die out or converge on a singular present. I could just as easily redescribe the discursive field of 1988 in terms of the historical projects already underway at that time, the debates over historiography, and the hermeneutical themes available in its theoretical works. The books I cited as published around that time all incorporate historical impressions, narratives, or hermeneutical appropriations; some (Berlin, 1987; Miller, 1989) are explicit histories, and two (North, 1987; Phelps, 1988) describe or advocate hermeneutical approaches. Since 1988, intensive work by a small enclave of historians of rhetoric has gradually broadened, increased, and diffused into the field, until now reflection on the past is seen as crucial for envisioning the future...as symbolized by the conference recorded in this volume (see also Bloom, Daiker, & White, 1996; Tobin & Newkirk, 1994).

Vocally impatient with the dichotomies and dead ends afflicting composition, scholars (especially younger ones prepared in the maturing doctoral programs of rhetoric and composition) are seeking alternate strands in the history of ideas and cultural practices and appropriating a much wider range of historical, philosophical, disciplinary, and cultural traditions to go "beyond the given" with fresh questions, topics, and diverse purposes. Some directly confront antinomies, impasses, and givens in contemporary discourse (see, for example, Bawarshi, 1997; Couture, 1993; Crosswhite, 1992); while others pursue independent intellectual agendas reflecting frames of reference outside the metanarrative (e.g., Haswell, 1991; Kaufer & Butler, 1996). Among the more promising trends, in my view, are:

- taking a "philosophical turn" that includes, for example, recuperating American philosophers such as Dewey, Whitehead, Peirce, James, and Langer as pragmatists, realists, process philosophers, constructive postmodernists, or feminists; drawing on more diverse figures and discourses from phenomenology and philosophical hermeneutics to analytic language philosophy and non-Western thought; and questioning the exclusive focus on epistemology over, for example, political philosophy, ontology, or ethics;
- expanding the scope of the field (through a deeper integration of composition studies with rhetoric) beyond the academy's canonical texts, Western rhetorics, academic discourse, textbooks, and freshman writing to encompass ethnic and national rhetorics, instructional traditions, culturally specific literacies, multiple technologies and media, and material practices of writing; and
- engaging more critically, directly, and mutually with the work of other fields, enabled in part by the *Journal of Advanced Composition*'s provocative series of interviews with major figures influencing composition and rhetoric (collected in Olson, 1994; Olson & Gale, 1991; and Olson & Hirsh, 1995).

None of this, of course, has erased the continuing salience of cultural studies and utopian critique or the contentious vitality of many major and minor paths supposedly left behind (for example, so-called expressivism, or the teaching of grammar).

One can also observe a new readiness among some who have led composition on its current path to seek out the complementarities of ideology and utopia. Bizzell (1992a, 1992b, 1995, 1997), self-proclaimed utopian, exemplifies this shift in her thoughtful and candid effort to think through the problems of avowing moral values in a climate of postmodern skepticism. Tellingly, Bizzell turned to history "to rebuild my confidence on firmer scholarly ground, by undertaking projects that would give me a wider grasp of contemporary and premodern rhetoric and composition work" (1992a, p. 25; see also Bizzell & Herzberg, 1990). Now, instead of perceiving Hirsch, quintessential spokesperson for ideology (Hirsch, Kett, & Trefil, 1988), as her antithesis, she unconsciously echoes Ricoeur's conception of the cultural imagination when she characterizes "his role in my imagination as more that of dark double" (1992a, p. 29).

* * *

Rather than exhaustively exemplifying and characterizing work that represents the new prominence of historical and hermeneutical consciousness in composition/rhetoric, I want to invoke tradition as a symbol with a rich history in composition studies and propose that it can serve the field now as a mediating term between ideology and utopia.

References to tradition have played a key role in the (re)formation and professionalization of composition and rhetoric (a mediating function traced in the conjunctive naming of the discipline). For scholars needing to claim a lineage to lend gravitas to a new discipline, tradition served as topos in a long list of titles: *The Rhetorical Tradition* (Bizzell & Herzberg, 1990); *Traditions of Inquiry* (Brereton, 1985); "The Tacit Tradition" (Emig, 1980/1983); *Reinventing the Rhetorical Tradition* (Freedman & Pringle, 1980); *Rhetorical Traditions and the Teaching of Writing* (Knoblauch & Brannon, 1984); and *The Rhetorical Tradition and Modern Writing* (Murphy, 1982), among others. In making its new beginning, composition sought conceptual tools simultaneously in the humanistic tradition of classical rhetoric and in the methodological traditions of the social sciences, cognitive sciences, and education, well aware in each case of the rhetorical functions (and dangers) in these borrowings and associations. More recently, it has made the same dual use of traditions in philosophy and the critical social sciences (strained through the nets of literary and cultural studies in English departments). Emig (1983), in referring to the "inevitability" of a tacit tradition, sought as much to create a broader common interdisciplinary tradition as to identify an existing but invisible one (p. 145). Hers, like most invocations of tradition in composition and rhetoric, was controversial. Knoblauch and Brannon (1984), for example, tried to escape the heritage they attributed to classical rhetoric and created a storm of criticism. Almost any significant debate in composition could be refigured as a battle of traditions.

In 1988, Russell presciently reviewed four books (Berlin, 1984; Brereton, 1985; Coles & Vopat, 1985; and Macrorie, 1984) as signs of a maturing appreciation for the rhetorical uses of history, motivating a broader "search for tradition" that he thought had only become possible in the decade of the 1980s. Russell's specific interest was in how such traditions—including, as in the case of Macrorie and Coles and Vopat, tacit traditions of practice—influence the teaching of writing as an art. He recognized the paucity of then-available histories and the degree to which traditions are "social, political, and personal...as well as intellectual categories" (p. 440).

Russell (1988) anticipated Horner's (1994) analysis of tradition, a brilliant contribution to countering the monolithic understanding of history in the composition narrative of the "path taken" with one that fully incorporates the dynamic of history as event. Following Horner, I see tradition as a generative process as well as a heritage: a material practice of constituting and sustaining the past as alive in the present. In this understanding of tradition, the past cannot be subject to "direct, unproblematic transmission" or simple reproduction (p. 496). In fact, it is necessarily in perpetual tension between repetition (which preserves continuity) and change (which adapts a tradition and therefore keeps it viable). A living language is a tradition in precisely this sense. As Horner argues etymologically, "in carrying out a tradition—that is, in the act of attempting to transmit that tradition...a teacher may also simultaneously enact, constitute, surrender, and betray it" (p. 496). He might say the same of the learner (new practitioner) of a tradition. Horner uses the teaching practices of Coles and Bartholomae to illustrate, first, a resistant tradition (one that continually problematizes its own authority, understands teachers to be reinventing the tradition as they write and teach, and encourages students to do the same); and second, a performative tradition, for which teaching–learning practices and their artifacts are primary evidence. (Varnum, 1996, documents the Amherst teaching tradition that inspired their practice.)

Crosswhite (1992) asks: How can we think and write freely as individuals despite the pressure of history upon us? His defense of individuality describes tradition as a "field of historical possibilities"—a gift. "This gift is an inheritance of possibilities which can be used to gain a certain independence from the possibilities themselves" (p. 100). Like Horner, Crosswhite understands that for this to happen with ourselves or our students as readers and authors, "traditions must be conceived more dynamically and expansively than they sometimes are" (p. 104; compare Miller, 1993; Varnum, 1992). Specifically,

> all discourse traditions—legal-political, ethnic, disciplinary, and so on—need to cultivate their margins. In a world of changing and conflicting discourses, interpreters of canons must not only retrospect, they must conceive retrospection as a way of forecasting, and forecasting as a way of interpreting the past. Cultivating the margins of discourse communities is not only a way of preparing for social change and shaping what forms it may take, it is also a way of identifying the genuine continuing authority of a traditional canon. In their reinterpretation of historical works as participating in a continuing tradition in which new authors are included, the authority of past writing is reexamined and articulated in new contexts.... Without such interaction in the margins, a discourse community, a dis-

> course tradition even, is much less historically capable than it would otherwise be. (p. 104)

The seeds in history of multiple traditions, along with the dynamic process necessary to maintain or recuperate a tradition as a living one, prevent it from fixing the present in the overdetermined way that Linda Shamoon, Robert Schwegler, and others feared in their critique of things that go without saying in composition studies (Shamoon & Wall, 1995; see Note #6). Paraphrasing Raymond Williams, Horner (1994) says that "the ties of tradition to the contemporary and its basis in the historical record are the source of its power but also render it vulnerable to critique. For those ties can be revealed, and exclusions from that record are always subject to re-vision and recovery" (p. 497). In other words, critique is always built into the hermeneutical structure of tradition as a recuperative and not merely a chastening moment. On the other hand, the utopian impulse needs a living tradition to realize the other side of its double-sidedness: it can function as criticism (disappointment in the gap between ideal and real) only in light of hopeful fictions of perfectibility. This analysis suggests that in principle nothing can finally be lost from history as a path to an alternate future. The past is overdetermined in a very different sense that always allows the cultural imagination to go beyond the given: it has so much complexity—so many conflicting elements, multiple causes, and loose ends, while memory and ideology are so selective, that the past is inexhaustible as a source of alternate futures. In this way, history is essential to moralism as a vision of freedom.

NOTES

[1]According to Charles Bazerman, the Research Network was organized in 1987–1988 to encourage dialogue among researchers in writing, amid concerns that competition and misunderstandings were preventing fruitful collaboration in a common disciplinary enterprise ("What Are We Doing?," 1989). It sponsored a preconvention workshop at the 1988 Conference on College Composition and Communication, where Connors was one of five plenary speakers invited to present accounts of their research issues and methods. In a separate panel, he and seven other historians debated views of historiography (Octalog, 1988). The two events emphasized rising perceptions of fragmentation and intensifying conflicts of vision in a field that had seemed unified by its struggle to become a discipline only a few years earlier.

[2]Compare James Murphy's characterization of history as a means of working for the common good of the *polis* (Octalog, 1988); the nature and importance of this relationship is a central issue in that debate.

[3]My method is schematic and conceptual rather than a comprehensively documented account of composition texts or practices. It is of course ironic to make claims about history that are based not on systematic historical research but on "historical impressions," which I define as the observations and inferences made by a participant–observer about a period, then or later, that historicize it. The brevity of this essay has conspired with my purposes to create this irony, which I will escape partly, if not fully, by focusing on the way historical claims or narratives about the development of scholarship in rhetoric and composition, and about related pedagogical theories, have rhetorical force for participants and become self-fulfilling prophecies, or, more accurately, self-fulfilling histories.

[4]Composition has typically used Kuhn's (1970) concept of paradigms shifts to frame descriptions of its own progress (see, for example, Hairston, 1982), generating controversy over the relevance and aptness of its application to composition (see, for example, Connors, 1983), as well as criticisms of the ambiguity of Kuhn's term. It is a useful but protean concept that needs to be defined in a given instance. I use it here in its most common sense in composition, as a matrix of premises, assumptions, values, and practices that authorizes work in one sector or gestalt of the field, but is clearly disputable with others. The term articulates interestingly with my use of "given," which refers to another aspect of the Kuhnian definition, the invisibility of governing paradigms (compare also "status quo" or "the system" in dystopian narratives; see Note #6.) While this sense of Kuhn's term encompasses the notion of successive paradigms, it also acknowledges continuing conflict and dialogue among coexisting, holistic perspectives (on research methods, for example, see Arrington, 1991; Charney, 1996). As such, their premises are not so "given" (tacit) as to be totally incommensurable, that is, mutually unintelligible or unarguable, as Kuhn would suggest. However, each paradigm has its own givens, which internally go without saying and enable its activities. The field develops not only by revealing and contesting such assumptions, but also by demonstrating, as in my argument here, that such givens are operating between as well as within sectors and their paradigms. This is a rhetorical notion that does not require proposing or accepting an all-encompassing explanatory framework, although it may heuristically deploy partial, integrative concepts across paradigms.

[5]A usefully stark statement of this three-stage history is presented by Susan Carlton (1996); though speaking from "within the social-epistemic and cultural studies paradigm," she is troubled by its modernist dismissal of others.

[6]The notion of the past as producing a fixed system was expressed with a negative spin at a recent conference at the University of Rhode Island (Shamoon & Wall, 1995). Calling it "overdeterminism," participants applied it to unmask a set of "things that go without saying in composition studies": givens produced by its past and its situatedness in a dystopian society that requires reformation. (As this argument reveals, a progress narrative that pictures the discipline and its practitioners as becoming transformative agents of utopian critique requires a parallel dystopian narrative of society itself.) Overdeterminism appears to be the interlocking effect of these givens in forming, through the action of history, a closed and seemingly immutable system (the "status quo") that homogenizes complexity and conflict to "produce a recognizable effect" (pp. 281–282). The

dilemma created by this structuralist concept is instructive: though those using it called for and in some cases did historical analyses, they found it hard to imagine either a different outcome in the historical formation of the present or the possibility for change in the future. Yet, as Marjorie Roemer's response (p. 292) pointed out, the conference paradoxically positioned its own participants at the apogee of the familiar progress narrative, as change agents. Linda Shamoon and Robert Schwegler acknowledge this difficulty:

> We...want to confront contradictions in our notion of an overdetermined system, for we share the assumption of most critical theorists that by laying bare the things that go without saying in composition studies we can change our discourse practices rather than contribute to the next adaptation. (cited in Shamoon & Wall, 1995, p. 283)

[7]We are only beginning to fathom the part played in the development of composition studies between the 1960s and 1980s by many scholars' experiences of professional isolation during their early careers. Isolating factors included, for example, their position as outsiders in English departments or elsewhere, diverse backgrounds and paths into the field, the idiosyncratic ways they retooled from other specializations, late starts in academic life or tenure-track positions, the lack of graduate programs or associates to form local intellectual communities, and—extremely important for those geographically or institutionally isolated—severely constrained access to publication channels. Not only were journals few in number, but they limited article length and most were practically oriented, while it was almost impossible to publish a full-length theoretical book in composition in as late as the early 1980s (on the paucity of books, see Neel, 1993; on the development of journals, see Goggin, 1997). Bibliographical sources were nonsystematic (Scott, 1991). As a result, patterns of intellectual interaction were strongly constructed by small clusters of scholars and graduate students in personal contact (see Lauer, 1993 ; see also D'Angelo, Chapter 15 in this volume). Scholars with limited access to these invisible networks were perhaps more driven to discover or create their own coherence in the disciplinary intertext (as is explicit in North, 1987, and Phelps, 1988), while their visions, formed in personal experience and unique mixes of interdisciplinary reading, were likely to diverge significantly from one another's and those of such face-to-face groups. In the early days, these concrete social relations and the cross-fertilizations they created are probably as significant a lineage as research methods or teaching paradigms.

[8]Neel's book, *Plato, Derrida, and Writing* (1988) was a co-winner of the Shaughnessy Prize; Miller's work, *Rescuing the Subject* (1989), won the W. Ross Winterowd Award (established in 1989); Bazerman (1988) and Berlin (1987) received honorable mentions for the 1989 Winterowd and 1988 Shaughnessy honors, respectively.

[9]The success of Berlin's (1988) taxonomy in selling itself as history reflects, I believe, the incomplete appropriation in composition of the concept of "process," which, as I argued in 1988, represented at its most profound the reintro-

duction of time and history, along with context or reference, into structuralist notions of language. Because of the particular extradisciplinary sources that dominated its uptake of poststructuralist and postmodernist thought, composition apparently assimilated the idea of context better than it did time and, specifically, as social construction, ideology, culture, and so on, adopted a structuralist–determinist rather than a dynamic, interactionist, and interanimating concept of context. I have been trying to demonstrate here that the now well-recognized impasses (for example, regarding the subject and agency) encountered in conceiving context as an overdetermined, inescapable system are the same as those in conceiving the past as a given, a perpetual self-fufilling prophecy. As Raymond Williams says regarding a "selective tradition," "It is a version of the past which is intended to connect with and ratify the present. What it offers in practice is a sense of predisposed continuity" (qtd. in Horner, 1994, p. 497).

REFERENCES

Arrington, P. (1991). The agon over what "composition research" means. *Journal of Advanced Composition, 11*, 377–393.

Bawarshi, A. S. (1997). Beyond dichotomy: Toward a theory of divergence in composition studies. *Journal of Advanced Composition, 17*, 69–82.

Bazerman, C. (1988). *Shaping written knowledge: The genre and activity of the experimental article in science.* Madison, WI: University of Wisconsin Press.

Berlin, J. A. (1984). *Writing instruction in nineteenth-century colleges.* Carbondale, IL: Southern Illinois University Press.

Berlin, J. A. (1987). *Rhetoric and reality: Writing instruction in American colleges, 1900–1985.* Carbondale, IL: Southern Illinois University Press.

Berlin, J. A. (1988). Rhetoric and ideology in the writing class. *College English, 50*, 477–494.

Bizzell, P. (1986). Foundationalism and anti-foundationalism in composition studies. *Pre/Text, 7*, 37–56.

Bizzell, P. (1992a). *Academic discourse and critical consciousness.* Pittsburgh, PA: University of Pittsburgh Press.

Bizzell, P. (1992b). The politics of teaching virtue. *ADE Bulletin, 103*, 4–7.

Bizzell, P. (1995). Praising folly: Constructing a postmodern rhetorical authority as a woman. In L. W. Phelps & J. Emig (Eds.), *Feminine principles and women's experience in American composition and rhetoric* (pp. 27–42). Pittsburgh, PA: University of Pittsburgh Press.

Bizzell, P. (1997). The 4th of July and the 22nd of December: The function of cultural archives in persuasion, as shown by Frederick Douglass and William Apess. *College Composition and Communication, 48*, 44–60.

Bizzell, P., & Herzberg, B. (Eds.). (1990). *The rhetorical tradition: Readings from classical times to the present.* Boston: Bedford Books.

Bloom, L. Z., Daiker, D. A., & White, E. M. (Eds.). (1996). *Composition in the twenty-first century: Crisis and change*. Carbondale, IL: Southern Illinois University Press.

Brereton, J. (Ed.). (1985). *Traditions of inquiry.* New York: Oxford University Press.

Carlton, S. B. (1996). *Postmodern agency and the logic of paradigms*. Unpublished manuscript.

Charney, D. (1996). Empiricism is not a four-letter word. *College Composition and Communication, 47*, 567–593.

Chase, G. (1988). Accommodation, resistance and the politics of student writing. *College Composition and Communication, 39*, 13–22.

Coles, W. E., Jr., & Vopat, J. (1985). *What makes writing good: A multiperspective*. Lexington, MA: Heath.

Connors, R. J. (1983). Composition studies and science. *College English, 45*, 1–20.

Connors, R. J. (1989). Rhetorical history as a component of composition studies. Symposium, "What are we doing as a research community?" *Rhetoric Review, 7*, 230–240.

Couture, B. (1993). Against relativism: Restoring truth in writing. *Journal of Advanced Composition, 13*, 111–134.

Crosswhite, J. (1992). Authorship and individuality: Heideggerian angles. *Journal of Advanced Composition, 12*, 91–109.

Emig, J. (1983). The tacit tradition: The inevitability of a multi-disciplinary approach to writing research. In D. Goswami & M. Butler (Eds.), *The web of meaning: Essays on writing, teaching, learning, and thinking* (pp. 146–156). Upper Montclair, NJ: Boynton/Cook. (Original work published 1980)

Faigley, L. (1986). Competing theories of process: A critique and a proposal. *College English, 48*, 527–542.

Freedman, A., & Pringle, I. (Eds.). (1980). *Reinventing the rhetorical tradition*. Conway, AR: L & S Books.

Geertz, C. (1973). *The interpretation of cultures.* New York: Basic Books.

Goggin, M. D. (1997). Composing a discipline: The role of scholarly journals in the disciplinary emergence of rhetoric and composition since 1950. *Rhetoric Review, 15*, 322–348.

Green, K. (1995). *The woman of reason: Feminism, humanism and political thought*. New York: Continuum.

Hairston, M. (1982). The winds of change: Thomas Kuhn and the revolution in the teaching of writing. *College Composition and Communication, 33*, 76–88.

Haswell, R. H. (1991). *Gaining ground in college writing: Tales of development and interpretation*. Dallas, TX: Southern Methodist University Press.

Hirsch, E. D., Jr., Kett, J., & Trefil, J. (1988). *Cultural literacy: What every American needs to know* (2nd ed.). New York: Vintage.

Horner, B. (1994). Resisting traditions in composing composition. *Journal of Advanced Composition, 14*, 495–519.

Kaufer, D. S., & Butler, B. S. (1996). *Rhetoric and the arts of design*. Mahwah, NJ: Lawrence Erlbaum.

Knoblauch, C., & Brannon, L. (1984). *Rhetorical traditions and the teaching of writing*. Upper Montclair, NJ: Boynton/Cook.

Kuhn, T. S. (1970). *The structure of scientific revolutions* (2nd ed.). Chicago: University of Chicago Press.

Lauer, J. (1993). A response to "The history of composition: Reclaiming our lost generations." *Journal of Advanced Composition, 13*, 252–253.

LeFevre, K. B. (1987). *Invention as a social act*. Carbondale, IL: Southern Illinois University Press.

Macrorie, K. (Ed.). (1984). *Twenty teachers*. New York: Oxford University Press.

Miller, S. (1989). *Rescuing the subject: A critical introduction to rhetoric and the writer.* Carbondale, IL: Southern Illinois University Press.

Miller, T. P. (1993). Reinventing rhetorical traditions. In T. Enos (Ed.), *Learning from the histories of rhetoric: Essays in honor of Winifred Bryan Horner* (pp. 26–41). Carbondale, IL: Southern Illinois Press.

Moore, B. (1996). *The statement*. New York: Dutton.

Murphy, J. (Ed.). (1982). *The rhetorical tradition and modern writing*. New York: Modern Language Association.

Neel, J. (1988). *Plato, Derrida, and writing*. Carbondale, IL: Southern Illinois University Press.

Neel, J. (1993). Review of *Fragments of rationality: Postmodernity and the subject of composition* [Book]. *Rhetoric Review, 12*, 198–204.

North, S. M. (1987). *The making of knowledge in composition: Portrait of an emerging field*. Upper Montclair, NJ: Boynton/Cook.

O'Reilly, M. R. (1984). The peacable classroom. *College English, 46*, 103–112.

Octalog. (1988). The politics of historiography. *Rhetoric Review, 7*, 5–49.

Olson, G. A. (Ed.). (1994). *Philosophy, rhetoric, literary criticism: (Inter)views*. Carbondale, IL: Southern Illinois University Press.

Olson, G. A., & Gale, I. (Eds.). (1991). *(Inter)views: Cross-disciplinary perspectives on rhetoric and literacy*. Carbondale, IL: Southern Illinois University Press.

Olson, G. A., & Hirsh, E. (Eds.). (1995). *Women writing culture*. Ithaca, NY: State University of New York Press.

Phelps, L. W. (1988). *Composition as a human science: Contributions to the self-understanding of a discipline*. New York: Oxford University Press.

Ricoeur, P. (1979). Ideology and utopia as cultural imagination. In D. M. Borchert (Ed.), *Being human in a technological age* (pp. 107–126). Athens, OH: Ohio University Press. (Original work published 1976)

Ricoeur, P. (1981). Hermeneutics and the critique of ideology. In J. B. Thompson (Ed.), *Paul Ricoeur: Hermeneutics and the human sciences: Essays on language, action and interpretation* (pp. 63–100). Cambridge, England: Cambridge University Press. (Original work published 1973)

Russell, D. R. (1988). The search for traditions. *College English, 50*, 437–443.

Scott, P. (1991). Bibliographical resources and problems. In E. Lindemann & G. Tate (Eds.), *An introduction to composition studies* (pp. 72–93). New York: Oxford.

Shamoon, L. K., & Wall, B. (1995). The things that go without saying in composition studies: A colloquy. *Journal of Advanced Composition, 15*, 281–320.

Taylor, G. H. (Ed.). (1986). *Paul Ricoeur: Lectures on ideology and utopia*. New York: Columbia University Press.

Tobin, L., & Newkirk, T. (Eds.). (1994). *Taking stock: The writing process movement in the '90s*. Portsmouth, NH: Boynton/Cook Heinemann.

Varnum, R. (1992). The history of composition: Reclaiming our lost generations. *Journal of Advanced Composition, 12*, 39–55.

Varnum, R. (1996). *Fencing with words: A history of writing instruction at Amherst College during the era of Theodore Baird, 1938–1966*. Urbana, IL: National Council of Teachers of English.

What are we doing as a research community? (1989). *Rhetoric Review, 7*, 223–293.

Watson Conference Oral History #1: Research Forums and Agendas in Composition Studies October 1996 Carol Berkenkotter, Lester Faigley, Richard Larson, and Stephen Witte

Bob McEachern and Pamela Takayoshi, interviewers
edited by Pamela Takayoshi

Bob McEachern: When you introduced the panel, Carol, you said that these were three major figures in shaping composition's research agenda. I'd like to start with that: Where do the four of you see your influence in shaping composition's research agenda, either through your research or other roles you've had?

Stephen Witte: I don't know. I knock on the door of my own history and I don't find anybody at home. *[Laughter.]* There was a time in the early 1980s when Lester and I together were influencing the sorts of questions that were being asked. Lester has continued to do that, I think, in a way that I haven't. I feel pretty much outside composition, so, from my point of view, I don't see that I have much influence at all.

Lester Faigley: I don't think the program chair of CCCC does much to shape the profession because the CCCC program is composed proportionately by what comes in, plus the acceptance rate is relatively very high—it's now over 50 percent—so basically what goes on the CCCC program is what the membership decides they want to be on the CCCC program.

Carol Berkenkotter: Although I would say that's true only up to a point, Les. Tom [Huckin] and I did a study of CCCC proposals from '87 through '93 and found that the language that the program chair uses in the requests for proposals does in fact influence the proposals. In terms of looking at the lexical items in successful proposals as opposed to the lexical items in unsuccessful proposals, we saw an intertextuality, a recontextualizing of terms that are in the CCCC program chair's initial statement. Plus, between '87 and '93, the categories in which you could make certain proposals changed. The categories create a kind of a map, and different session chairs did alter those categories, so the map changed as the categories changed.

LF: Yeah, that's right, but I would contrast it to Steve's role as one of the founders and first editor of *Written Communication*, a journal that did come out with a particular point of view, and I think it was addressing a sense that Steve and John Daly had that there were certain issues that were not being dealt with adequately in the field. And I'll get Steve to talk about that. *[Laughter.]*

SW: Well, yeah, we did have that sense, and I think I still have that sense about the journal. We've published things that weren't likely to get published in other places, but we also published things that could get published in other places. In terms of shaping the field, I don't know what role an editor has, even though I've been an editor for 15 years. I think of some of the things we've published over the years, and some of those have been first articles of people in the field who have turned out to publish a great deal more in subsequent years, but the role of editor is relatively minor. You can help an author shape a piece, but in point of fact, you can never turn a sow's ear into a silk purse, so what you can publish is altogether contingent on what is submitted to you. There are potentially good things that, with the Editorial Board's help and the editorial process, can be shaped into something publishable. But if you don't get something to work with initially, you have no impact at all. Fortunately, we've gotten enough quality submissions over the years that the journal has been good. That doesn't have anything to do with the editors; it has to do with the people in the field.

Richard Larson: I can echo that—the editor can't do anything if the manuscripts don't come in. One thing the editor can do is print articles that he finds interesting and to that extent encourage intellectual conversation. Potential contributors look at what appears in a journal and say, "Well, I could respond to some of this or I could pick up on some of these issues."

One of the major shortcomings of *CCC* and *CE* as they are now being edited is the neglect of research in what they publish. When I do searches for bibliographies for *RTE,* I can almost never find anything that represents research in *CCC* or *CE*. At least research as defined for the purposes of the bibliography. If you look for a data-centered piece in *CE* or *CCC*, you won't find it. You find it in *WC*, you'll find it in *RTE*, but you don't find it in the major journals of the National Council of Teachers of English.

CB: That seems to be symptomatic of something. Do you have any feelings about what that's symptomatic of?

LF: I think that journals were developed to take particular points of view. To me, this gets back to what Bob Connors described as the "hero editors." When Dick took over as editor at *CCC*, he took the journal in particular directions. One of the ways he did this was by allowing longer articles, which is one of the most significant changes that happened in the history of the journal. It made it possible to submit certain kinds of articles that just wouldn't have been possible before because of the strict page limit the journal had had up to that time.

RL: One of the first issues that I did as editor of *CCC* contained a long article by Linda Flower. That may have set the tone for future submissions in that it said to people, "It's now possible to submit research essays to *CCC* and have a chance at getting them published." *[To Steve]* Much of what you sent me was research material—

SW: And Lester the same way—

RL: Right. When I read these articles, I thought, these are making contributions to the field, these are making contributions to knowledge, these are the kind of articles we want to print. My perception is that the journals in our field, at least as far as writing is concerned, are far more concerned with politics and ethnicity than with advancing the field.

CB: Are there larger issues here? I think you're quite right about the local-level observing phenomenon, but it seems to me there's larger issues of methodology and epistemology that relate to centrifugal and centripetal profession pressures as new fields and young fields begin to get a sense of what it is that constitutes the agendas and the issues of their discipline. It seems to me that like the Democratic party in the United States, we are intensely pluralistic because we have many different constituencies with many different issues. I think it's fair to say that we're developed enough now as a discipline that different constituencies have different agendas and have conversations about those agendas in different disciplinary forums. Now we've had a proliferation of forums that make it possible for differentiation between those constituencies. If we look at the macro level and ask what's happening here in terms of disciplinary development, I don't think it's so much that empirical research is being rejected per se, but rather that people who have particular kinds of questions that use a particular kind of methodology are going to publish within a particular forum. I think particularly of people who do interdisciplinary work—people in applied linguistics, social psychology, or anthropological linguistics, for example. We're becoming quite polyphonic and heteroglossic as a discipline and I don't think that's necessarily a bad thing.

RL: No, it's certainly not a bad thing to be polyphonic and heteroglossic, but what one misses, or at least what I miss, is a sense that having finished this article, I know more about the field than I knew when I began the article—that this is an argument for a kind of knowledge about the field which I find well-sustained by examination of data. That doesn't mean necessarily quantitative data, I'm not wedded to quantitative data, but *data-based*—it can be ethnographic, or an insightful narrative that adds to knowledge.

The feeling I had when I was reading your articles [Lester and Steve's] is that I knew more about discourse, I knew more about writing. I knew more about how language worked as a result of having read your article than I did when I picked it up. I knew more about the way composing processes worked as a result of having read that manuscript than I knew before. I don't have that feeling about very many articles that I see in journals having to do with writing.

LF: To defend those journals, first of all, *CE* is the journal of the college section and it's broadly concerned with English studies. That's a lot of turf to cover. With *CCC*, again the editor certainly has a great deal of influence; nonetheless, after having done the CCCC program, my sense is that what's being published is what the membership is doing. I don't know that the journals are doing more than simply reflecting what is going on in the field right now.

RL: Very probably so.

CB: Except that I think the editor is a gatekeeper certainly and a power broker as well, as I suggested yesterday. Let me give you some examples. The '81 issue of *CCC* that Dick edited had three articles in it. It started with Flower and Hayes's cognitive process model of writing, then my article on audience awareness, and then your article on analyzing revision. The presence of those three articles together, plus Dick's editorial statement, set forth an agenda. Similarly, I think Joseph Harris has made particular kinds of choices. The reason I say that is you wonder, if there are a number of books on genre coming out, and we suggest that there should be a review essay on genre because there have been six or seven collections and single-authored books in the last two to three years, and then there is an essay review but it really has to do with issues in cultural studies, then I think it's fair to say that that particular editor has made a choice and a decision about what the agenda is going to be for that journal. I don't think that's necessarily a bad thing, Les, I think that's simply the function and the role of a journal editor. I don't think it's dirty politics or anything like that, simply because there are enough journals around in which to publish.

But I think editors do have a stake in the development of the discipline, and I don't think you can ignore that.

SW: But I think Lester's right. There's more of the kind of thing represented in *CCC* going on in composition now than there is the kind of stuff that *WC* is interested in publishing. We're not seen as an outlet of the kind of stuff that Harris wants to publish, and, moreover, I don't think much of the stuff Harris publishes would get reviewed very favorably by our Editorial Board.

CB: I guess the question on the table might then be: When we think of the field that we loosely call "composition studies," do *CCC* and *CE* represent composition studies? We're thinking about a field that is an aggregate of many different kinds of individuals with many disciplinary and institutional locations, epistemologies, methodologies, ideologies (because we can't get away from ideology once we get into the question of methodology). Where do the boundaries lie?

SW: I think the problem in composition is that the organization of composition, the enterprise of composition, is too damn big. I also think that there are certain power structures that come into play, where voices get marginalized by the major journals in the field...or the organization. There is a dominant discourse now from which some people are excluded.

CB: I agree with you, Steve, although I see a slightly different picture. There was a period of protean possibility in the 1980s when Dick was editing. Methods from other disciplines were being incorporated into composition studies. Now I think there has been a—if you will—a regression toward the mean and that regression toward the mean has meant a narrow definition of disciplinarity with boundaries being very firmly drawn in a way that they weren't drawn in the 1980s when there was inclusivity. What we're really talking about in this conversation is discursive formations and orders, where they're drawn and how they're reflected in the journals.

RL: This echoes something I said this morning, and I'll say it again. I think the progress and needs of students are being neglected in the journals having to do with writing. I think that this profession as a whole, broadly speaking, is about how we can help young human beings develop in one respect, maybe more than one respect. That is an area imminently open to significant kinds of research. I don't see the teaching and learning process for students being the subject of real inquiry in the way that I wish it were. What I was trying to do as editor was to see to it that things that spoke of progress and learning and the teaching of English got in front of the profession so the profession could think about it.

Pamela Takayoshi: This makes me wonder, at the end of this conference, if there are parts of the history that weren't represented. We talked about the different ways composition is segmenting or becoming heterogenous—

SW: Well, yeah, all the articles that didn't get accepted for publication. I think there are incredibly good stories in some of those, and I don't know how to tell them. For a long time, I saved manuscripts and reviews for everything I got at *WC*, thinking at one time that I wanted to go back and look at them in a systematic way, but then I was cautioned by the publisher that there were all kinds of rights of privacy issues that would be violated in doing that. Quite frankly, I didn't have the time to write another 3,000 letters to get the necessary permissions. So, yeah, there are untold stories that need to be told. And many are stories of disappointments, if not failures. What this conference has glorified are the successes, I think. We have to be conscious of our failures as well as our successes.

LF: I would say that there's a whole segment of writing teachers that we are vaguely aware of and gradually becoming more aware of. A great many of these teachers don't go to professional meetings, don't read the journals, and are largely unaware of the people who were here. I think you could give a quiz and they might have heard of Peter Elbow, but they've probably not heard of the rest of us, and I don't think we've looked very closely at that huge group of teachers out there (except maybe through textbook sales)—there's a lot we don't know about and we probably should know a lot more about.

CB: There's a story here, too, I think, that has to do with textbook sales, the nature of textbooks, and the changes in textbooks in the last 20 and 25 years—the function of textbooks in the professionalization of a discipline. There's a strong pedagogical base operating in some institutions where people are rewarded for pedagogical work, while in other institutions, the production of knowledge is defined as research and theory but not pedagogical knowledge.

SW: Would you say that the textbooks of the field represent pedagogical knowledge?

CB: Would I? No. They don't, in fact. I mean, for the most part.

SW: Well, yeah, the good ones are gonna maybe fill up two hands at most, and out of the probably 500 books to choose from.

CB: That's an interesting question itself. Textbooks are designed for markets by publishers who want to make money, which turns your teacher into a consumer and possibly a colonized one, too, because she can't use what she produces and she doesn't make what she uses.

RL: The production of textbooks is one of the few business-related fields that I am aware of where the purchase decision is not made by the consumer. If you're buying a car, you're buying your own car, usually; if you're buying a dress, you're buying a dress for yourself; but the person who buys the textbook and puts it into the bookstore is not the person who is ultimately going to pay for it. Let me go back to a question that you were asking a few minutes ago: What wasn't represented in this conference? I might be slighting a session that I should have been aware of, but I wonder if enough attention has been given to developments in the *teaching* of writing over the past 15 or 20 years. Is there, for example, and this is a researchable question I suppose, more reliance on peer editing of draft manuscripts in 1996 than there was in 1976? Is there more reliance on what might be called "student-centered instruction," having the student take over the course, having students run the course the way they'd want to? Is there more reliance on that type of teaching than there was in 1976? Is there more reliance on drills and prewriting in 1996 than there was in 1976? Did the program have much in it having to do with developments in the use of computers in the teaching of writing? Computer-assisted instruction, networking [for example].

LF: Computer-assisted instruction largely wasn't possible in the period of focus. The first personal computer was assembled in 1977. In the early 1980s, Steve and I were collaborating extensively using a mainframe computer. We were sending text back and forth, but we were using a 300-baud modem. If you used a full screen editor, every time you made a change it took 64 seconds for the screen to reload, so we used this program called TECO, which basically was editing blind. We would start by marking on printed copies and then we would make changes online, but after you'd made a few changes, you would lose track of what had happened, so eventually you were just editing this thing blind and you had no idea where the changes were going to show up. Then we would run down to the university line printer, pick up a copy, go back home, and then get on the phone again. We'd sometimes call each other up beforehand and try to get straight where we were. It was pretty wild composing.

PT: It was interesting how many times people throughout the conference talked about computers. Although it was never an explicit panel or presentation, it was mentioned often throughout the conference, which is interesting, given that the conference is about the professionalization of composition.

CB: Many perspectives come to bear on teaching. I think back on the Bartholomae, Ohmann, and Bizzell session, for example. In all of those presentations, the technique that each presenter used to make the particular rhetorical point that he or she was going to make had an enormous amount to do with the teaching of writing. They were bringing different perspectives to bear. I think of Connors's statement last night and how his perspective had come to bear on his own teaching to the point that it had led him to a particular decision and dramatic career change. So I think it's there, maybe not in the direct form that we hear it at AERA, with those endless classroom narratives of this is what we did in my classroom and this is how I studied it. I don't think we see that particular kind of account, but I think we heard some very rich accounts by teacher–exemplars.

Part II

Agendas in Teaching and in Research

Chapter 4

Composition Research Agendas in the 1960s and 1970s

Richard Lloyd-Jones
University of Iowa

The research I was associated with during the 1960s and 1970s had political bases. Maybe, because new formulations of knowledge have social consequences, all research is political. Maybe no research is ever "pure," but research in composition is inevitably tainted by social purpose, for rhetoric in the classical sense is a practical art. When we talk of composition rather than of rhetoric, we are especially emphasizing teaching, dissemination, and mastery of craft, and that even more implies political effects.

THE ORIGINS

Let me develop this thesis by giving some background for *Research in Written Composition*, strictly a review of research, published by the National Council of Teachers of English (Braddock, Lloyd-Jones, & Schoer, 1963). After the Basic Issues Conference of 1959, composition acquired status as the third leg of a tripod describing English curricula, along with linguistics and literature. To be sure, the older designation of English language and literature implied composition, and rhetoric had had an honored place in American schools as well as in ancient and medieval learning, but in this century, prestigious scholars fled to *belle lettres*, a cut-down version of rhetoric left when the rationalists stole the parts relating to practicality. It took the pressure of serving a new class of postwar students in the late 1940s to remind some faculties of English that they still had social responsibilities, although even then they cleverly assigned the work to lesser breeds without the law.

Be that as it may, the NCTE was thus stimulated to create a committee to examine the state of knowledge about composition a decade after the founding of CCCC, to assemble summaries of what had been suitably researched. Richard Braddock was co-chair, and he and his committee and consultants—about three dozen prominent scholars—found over 500 titles that seemed relevant. They practically limited their empiricism to "objective," "quantitative," or "comparative" studies, then favored by schools of education, but the list was still too long to review in any systematic way by a committee scattered all over the nation. Fortunately, for a few years the Office of Education was funding disciplinary research—even had a regular "consultant" for English—and Braddock applied for and won a grant. He sought out two University of Iowa colleagues to help him. Lowell Schoer, from the College of Education, was to supply background on research design, and I, who was at that time directing a program in technical writing for the College of Engineering, was to offer background in rhetorical and linguistic theory.

THE PROCEDURES

For nine months or so, we met twice weekly to compare notes on our reading, mostly on microfilm, for the largest part of material came to us as dissertations, and rarely did the names of the authors appear again, for once into that kind of research was enough. Probably too much, for few studies showed any sign of theoretical background, many had sloppy controls, and few reported completely enough that we could be sure of their data. Some of the work may have been better than we knew, but the reports were incomplete. Comparisons and word or error counts were the most common studies, but often the items compared were not significant or defined, and the items counted showed little about the ability to compose. Our list was strictly limited and did not suggest the qualitative empirical research that goes on now. Some significant and more nearly theoretical scholarship we knew about, but it didn't really fit the definitions imposed by the original committee, and since we were swamped with what we had, we did not wish to revise the definition. We didn't imagine that we were creating a landmark; we were just trying to make a small clearing in the woods. On the whole, we found it depressing that so many people had worked so hard to produce so little.

Although we really did consider redefining "research" to include more theoretical studies and some status reports. I recall that Albert Kitzhaber's 1963 survey of freshman English courses especially drew us (and Kitzhaber and David Russell reviewed our manuscript), but there were also early studies in semiotics and sociolinguistics that seemed useful. But we could not see that we would ever finish that job, so we stayed with the more modest task, figuring that it would be useful, and others could deal with larger questions. We had an immediate need to show that composition was a subject needing research, so we hoped to use some promising studies as guides for design and reporting. We wanted to comment on the preparation of various kinds of controlled studies, to suggest procedures for rating papers in mass testing and for controlling variables, and to improve reporting. We wanted to be useful, but we also wanted to demonstrate that here was a "field" that deserved status in colleges and universities. Braddock later used our general strictures as a guide in establishing the journal *Research in the Teaching of English (RTE)*, and I took the material on testing into later discussions with the National Assessment of Educational Progress (NAEP).

THE RESULTS

The political effect of the book was to suggest that we had very little ground for claiming professional status on the basis of controlled research. Indeed, Braddock contributed a metaphor that has frequently been cited to report our judgment. He said research in composition, in comparison with research in the physical sciences, was just emerging from the age of alchemy. That probably is fair if one accepts the limits of our review, and the 24 questions for future research we supplied mostly dealt with such limited studies, although some questions dealt with broad issues of rhetorical situations and the nature of writing itself. I believe that we were much too optimistic about what could be discovered by the methods we critiqued, and little is to be gained now from dealing with the studies themselves, but the book did serve to regulate what was reported about studies of composition and highlighted the need for other kinds of study. We helped create a political assumption that research was possible, and not everyone who writes is automatically an authority on composition.

For Braddock, our reviews led to his creation of *RTE*; for me, they led to my being appointed to the newly-formed NCTE Commission on Composition. Although I had entered the door to composition through the collegiate concerns of CCCC, work on the review pushed me more fully into the whole range of English studies implied by the NCTE. The

Commission was supposed to monitor Council publications to make sure we avoided egregious error about composition and to suggest new areas for study. Several of the members had been part of Braddock's original committee, and all of us were essentially self-taught in matters of rhetoric, so we made ourselves a wonderful seminar. In those days, the commissions met on their own for a couple of days in the spring, as well as at the NCTE convention, so whatever we accomplished for the Council, we learned a lot about our own field from each other. It is another example of the essentially oral quality of composition studies in the 1950s, 1960s, and even the 1970s.

THE NATIONAL WRITING ASSESSMENT

The first big political issue we addressed came as a result of the publication of the initial results from the National Assessment. I can summarize them, without distorting too much, by saying that the NAEP found that some students wrote better than others. Sister Mary Philippa Coogan, chair of the Commission, wrote a hostile review, as did Braddock for *RTE*, and we were ready to offer a resolution of dismay at the annual NCTE meeting. The NAEP people wanted to avoid that, so at the Las Vegas convention we held off on the Resolution, in favor of a promise from them to fund a joint meeting to improve their methods of designing exercises and rating papers.

The meeting was indeed held the next spring in Denver, with five people from the Council (Robert Gorrell, William Irmscher, Louis Milic, Donald Seybold, and I), two psychometrists (Ellis Page and William Coffman), some of the NAEP staff, and a representative of the Educational Testing Service (ETS), which had conducted the first round of assessment. For the first two days we went around in circles, simply not communicating with each other, partly because (in order to keep us free from bias) our hosts didn't let us see any of the raw material. We talked only in high abstractions, until frustration levels made it clear we had to have more detail.

Discovering that they had used exercises that no one would want to respond to, we argued for the need to have tasks with some rhetorical purpose, some kind of implicit reason for writing at all. The NAEP couldn't even depend on students' secondary fear of a grade, for the papers were anonymous and without practical effect for the writers. Furthermore, we said, one should judge discourse on the basis of whether it accomplishes its goal, whether it does something, not whether it conforms to someone's sense of propriety. We should score (or describe) papers in terms of what features of language were drawn upon in order to fit a situation, and since situations differed in what they required, we would have to create scoring guides specific for each stimulus, a response to the primary "trait." The word is misleading. We actually meant the primary movement, or rhetorical thrust, that related to the purpose implied in the situation, but, in the heat of discussion, "trait" became the slogan word and has since sent people looking for countable details. Not what we meant at all, not it at all. But in the context of that conference, the phrase was enough to convince NAEP officials that we needed to be involved in creating exercises and scoring guides, so the word did its political work.

As it happened, an exercise-creating meeting was scheduled two weeks later in Chicago, and I was the only one of the five NCTE people who could go. We all agreed that someone from the complaining group had to be present, even though most of the people scheduled to appear on the exercise panel were also NCTE members, including the chair, Walker Gibson. At that meeting, we were expected to guide the NAEP people in how to score exercises already created and to add new ones to the pool. We proved to be quite troublesome, however, because we didn't observe those limits. We didn't like many of the tasks the NAEP counted on to provide longitudinal data from one cycle of testing to the next. We kept revising what they said we couldn't change, and we were rather slow in agreeing on new stimuli. By the end of the conference, there *were* some new exercises to be field-tested, but not much in the line of scoring guides, and the ETS people were a bit irked because we implied that their system of holistic scoring was inadequate for research purposes. To a large extent, we had simply followed the guidelines for testing implied in *Research in Written Composition* (1963), by that time already considered a politically correct guide.

CREATING SCORING GUIDES

The Education Commission of the States (ECS) decided to reclaim much of what they had contracted to ETS, and they authorized a contract for creating guides. Carl Klaus, who had done work for them on the literature assessment, and I (both at the University of Iowa) were asked to do the work under contract to the Westinghouse Learning Corporation in Iowa City. With their help, we assembled three teams, two mostly from Iowa and one (led by Don Seybold) mostly from Indiana University, to create guides for five or six exercises each. Klaus and I designed a crude descriptive system, based on an ancient rhetorical model and blending in modifications implied by the likes of James Kinneavy, James Britton, Wayne Booth, M. L. Abrams, Roman Jakobson, and others. That is, we argued that each task should especially show a writer's special competence in dealing with one of three variables in a rhetorical situation—self, audience, information—even as we granted that all writing implied all three. We designated the primary concerns as self-expression, persuasion, and explanation, again admitting that in any particular situation all would be present, but governed by a dominant purpose that could be revealed in various linguistic and discursive forms.

(You'll note that we ignored the language variable as such—literary language—because we did not imagine it would be an issue in 20-minute extemporaneous writings and we didn't want to complicate issues more than we already had. We accepted the political reality that the NAEP could not pay for longer samples nor for any revision exercises beyond what could be done in 10 or 15 minutes immediately after drafting. We did make an abortive try to test student writers' ability to write humorously because in one serious persuasive task, high school students had chosen to be funny, but when we specifically encouraged writers to be funny, they chose to be quite serious, as though they were used to school exercises that encouraged them to be solemn in responding to absurdity. We gave up, but we noted to ourselves that these young people were capable of far more sophistication than we were able to evoke.)

Armed with this theoretical construct, we could assign a rhetorical purpose to each exercise and discover aims inadequately represented in the entire batch. We could rephrase directions to evoke situations inviting different kinds of writing. Since the exercises we accepted as written already had been field-tested, and the new exercises we created were promptly tested, we had sample papers to work with both to refine our descriptions of effectiveness and to illustrate our points.

SOURCES OF ERROR

Had we been perfect critics, we might have been able to write descriptive scoring guides simply on the basis of what we knew of how purpose is revealed in language, but it is heartening to report that always some children—even 9-year-olds—discovered strategies we didn't think of. We also were reminded of the effect of even very minor rephrasing had on what students actually produced. (That makes one extremely critical of how political poll takers phrase their questions. It's the same principle.) We noted how easy it is to create unintended bias. We allowed for unisex names—such as Chris or Pat—but we didn't quite figure out how to neutralize cultural preferences in naming. We noted that field tested papers from high socioeconomic areas often were nonresponsive—"smart-alecky," if you wish—but papers from schools sometimes described as depressed usually were earnestly done. And an exercise that dealt with an unpaid bill apparently cut too close to the bone for some respondents—a clear class bias. The specifics are not important for the moment, but they remind us that all testing is a sampling, and samples can easily be skewed. Indeed, they are always skewed; the best we can hope for is to recognize the bias and report it.

It took most of the summer to produce a dozen and a half guides. Each had a rationale, a descriptive scoring guide, sample papers with some commentary about why they were scored as they were, and some secondary descriptors, mostly to satisfy formalists who wanted to correlate various features of language with scores. Most of the guides were 20 to 30 pages long, an issue when it came to training scorers. Partly, the people who were hired didn't read the guides, especially people who came with preconceived notions about what good writing is. (They couldn't ignore handwriting or spelling.) Partly, the conscientious scorers couldn't remember so much material consistently; and partly, I suspect, the trainers did not want to spend the necessary time checking whether scorers understood what they were doing. Still, by most measures used in such situations, the paired readers were consistent, and there were data to report, so the NAEP was relatively happy.

I still worry about the reductiveness of their reporting systems, though. The ECS administered the tests and contracted to have the papers scored. By law they could only report the data as collected by the announced system, so they invited outside scholars to comment interpretively on the score data, although the scholars actually read few of the papers as written. The oral comments of the visitors were written up by a staff member and attached to published summaries of data. The ECS public relations machine made further summaries of the entire report for the press. Some press people were actually competent to read the reports, but most seemed merely to condense the press releases and tie them to some local situation. In some sense, each reduction may have been "fair" to the previous report, but the cumulative selecting out for each condensation rarely gives one the sense of what the actual papers are like. I believe that they undervalue what can be produced extemporaneously in 20 to 30 minutes on a new topic in an unfamiliar situation, and often fully misrepresent something that might be called general writing ability.

Lest I have implied too much and said too little about the motivations and effects of these efforts, I now emphasize that the most careful efforts to measure fairly offer an astonishing number of places for error. My psychometrist friends assure me that errors cancel out in reporting on a mass of papers; we may misjudge Antonio or Hualing, yes, but we rate the class-as-a-class fairly. I am not convinced. Unless we add that the class is at least as good as the most negative formulation and is probably much better, we support a base for creating poor public policy. Politically, people who want to beat on the schools and teachers don't hear any qualifiers. They want a really hard number. Also, most researchers in pursuit of correlations of writing skills with parental education, economic status, race, or occupation want hard numbers. Even deans evaluating faculty production want hard numbers. And all of the above want the hard numbers to be derived cheaply, so they are willing to take shortcuts. The little knowledge we obtain in refining the methods for rating writing is a dangerous thing, but the economics of mass education provides us with little choice but to try to discover more persuasive methods.

DIALECT AND SOCIAL BIAS

We are, of course, still in the midst of major battles about measurement, but before I reprise my theme of the political basis for research in composition let me add another chapter to my own involvement in the 1960s and 1970s. I was one of the editors of the CCCC position statement, entitled *The Students' Right to Their Own Language* (1974). The document was created in the midst of civil rights marches and even became part of discussions on the Vietnam War. On the face of it, the text is mostly political and does not in itself report much new research. Certainly, the supporting document exhibits more signs of political compromise than of research objectivity, even though the tone is calm. I won't deny that in fashioning the final document, we wanted a version that all committee members would agree to sign and might sustain a vote at the annual CCCC meeting, even if that meant suppressing some details and including material not strictly relevant, but we also wanted to emphasize newer studies of language and discourse, especially in relation to dialect and style.

Hiding behind many textbooks even yet is an assumption that English has a perfect Platonic form, and users—especially those from the unenlightened social classes—fall short of realizing the form in practice. I supposes it goes back to assumptions that God's language preceded the mess at Babel, and if we are good enough in imitating classical languages we will get closer to God's language. But I don't know of any modern linguist who would hold such a view, despite its popularity among people who have merely had English courses in school. (An academic mystery is how the eclectic English professors, who borrow theories readily from other fields, are unable to drop them when the original theory is displaced, as, for example, retaining faculty psychology in rhetoric or Freudianism in LitCrit. Overall, we still seem to prefer 18th-century religious philology to modern linguistics.) Our point in the document was that linguistic features not only represent some *thing* in the world, but our *valuing* of that thing and our *associations with others* who use English. The "correct" form is the one that relates writer and reader as the writer intends. That formulation allows for dialect and all sorts of stylistic variation, and it implies that many of the choices represent social allegiances. One might have such an allegiance to the *apparently* uncommitted language of the academy, or to the somewhat more elastic language of the economic establishment, or to the special jargon of an occupational class (say, computer programmers), or to a dialect more conventionally labeled. Black English Vernacular is a good example.

In a broad sense, this CCCC policy statement, like the 1963 NCTE book, is really a summary of research, but cast in the form of political statement, however restrained. Many of the objections to the research then and now are essentially claims by a socially "superior" and economically dominant class that their language is God's language, that their purposes are the only good ones. In a gentler way, many people in departments of English felt that their sense of verbal tradition and excellence was being rejected. They heard a claim of "anything goes." They heard condemnation of their workbooks and their red pencils. They emitted cries parallel to those now heard in English departments, as senior faculty cling to the old canonical texts and formalistic methodologies. Just as the young literary critics now emphasize different values for literary study, we found social needs required us to make different emphases in our study of language. I might have wished we could have expressed this reality in the neutral discourse of the academy, but even the theory explains why this was impossible. Language comes heavily laden with statements of value.

LANGUAGE IS POLITICAL

Let me end where I began. The study of language, particularly the study of writing, cannot be separated from social needs because language is inherently social. The second half of this century has been a period of dramatic and widespread social change. Research in the biological sciences especially, but in the social and physical sciences as well, has forced us to reconsider how people use language to form themselves into groups and to cope with the environment outside of themselves; it is still unnerving for most of us to think of ourselves as electrochemical reactors. Our own kinds of research probably have not kept up with the other changes, yet in that decade from 1963 to 1973, we did see signs of what had to be done, and I like to believe that in the last quarter of the century, as composition/rhetoric has more or less been accepted as a plausible field for academic study, more progress has been made.

We have not yet found the voice that will make a new formulation dominant, even within departments of English. As a practical matter, many of our texts still treat the 18th-century formulations as final. Research has limited validity until it is persuasive to other contemporary researchers and scholars, so the rising generation still has work to do at home and abroad. Some years ago, I asked a mathematician how he defined a mathematical proof. He said, "It is a series of statements persuasive to another mathematician." We do rather well among composition/rhetoric people, but we are obliged to talk to a wider public as well, so we must find a series of statements persuasive to regular users of our language. We must discover a series of statements persuasive to our fellow citizens.

REFERENCES

Braddock, R., Lloyd-Jones, R., & Schoer, L. (1963). *Research in written composition*. Urbana, IL: National Council of Teachers of English.

Conference on College Composition and Communication. (1974). The students' right to their own language. *College Composition and Communication, 25*(3), 1–32.

Kitzhaber, A. (1963). *Themes, theories, and therapy. The teaching of writing in college*. New York: McGraw-Hill.

chapter 5

Early Work on Composing: Lessons and Illuminations

Sondra Perl
City University of New York

CONTEXTUALIZING THE EARLY WORK: A PERSONAL STORY

As we enter the 21st century, it seems fitting to take stock of our field, one that has emerged from its tentative beginnings in the early 1960s. In the 30 years since studies of composing have been undertaken, our understanding of research has been broadened, the designs and methods of the early work critiqued. How have we become so sophisticated? What might we learn by returning to our origins? Let me begin to answer these questions by describing the context in which my own work took shape.

In 1970, the City University of New York created a policy that guaranteed a seat to any New York City resident with a high school diploma, thereby opening its doors to unprecedented numbers of nontraditional students. At the same time, the City's Board of Higher Education created several community colleges to handle the influx of this largely underprepared student body. In 1972, having recently completed my master's degree, I found myself among the faculty at Eugenio Maria de Hostos Community College in the south section of the Bronx. Our task was to develop a writing program.

In 1972, Hostos was only 2 years old and its English department, with six full-time faculty, was small. Even though I was a beginning instructor, I was included in the discussions of how best to meet the needs of our students, who all seemed to be struggling to read and write. Even the more experienced faculty were perplexed. Most of them, with doctorates in literature, had never encountered writing that was, as Shaughnessy (1977) eloquently pointed out a few years later, "so stunningly unskilled" (p. vii). Most had no idea what to do.

To address the needs of these students, and in particular the writing problems they brought with them, my colleagues and I followed college policy and invented a series of "modules," accompanied by lists of "performance objectives"; we designed placement tests and established prerequisites. We created an interdisciplinary set of courses. But no matter how innovative our programs, our approaches were traditional. Most taught the way we had been taught: by isolating and correcting errors, assigning workbook exercises, working on topic sentences and paragraph development. Since I had "placed out" of freshman composition when I was an undergraduate, I had never actually been "taught" to write at all. Having no firsthand experience of freshman composition, I turned to the only models available: those presented in textbooks. Along with my more experienced colleagues, I assigned five-paragraph essays, following the instructions presented in the text selected by the department, which was Troyka and Nudelman's popular *Steps in Composition* (1972).

At the same time, though, I was enrolled in a Ph.D. program at New York University. I selected courses that focused on theories of language acquisition and human development. My interest, I discovered, lay in understanding the relationship between language and thought. Slowly, I began to consider whether the theories I was encountering might explain what I was seeing in the classroom. I thought about Chomsky's (1965) notion of "deep structure," Bruner's (1960) idea of "scaffolding," and Vygotsky's (1962) description of the "zone of proximal development," and I wondered how such notions might help me reconsider the way I was teaching students to write. Once I finished my coursework, practically everything I read suggested a dissertation topic. While reading Piaget (1959), for example, I began to wonder whether the better writers in my class might also be the students who were more cognitively advanced. For a month, I began thinking about ways to administer Piagetian tasks to my students in order to measure their levels of cognitive development. It seemed perfectly reasonable to assume that the more abstract one's level of reasoning, the better one's writing would be. However, as I thought about this, I concluded that even if I could show some correlation between cognitive functioning and writing ability, eventually I would have learned a great deal about cognition but not much about writing or ways to teach it more effectively.

I engaged in the same sort of thinking process many times. For a while, the notion of writing apprehension interested me and again I conceived of a study in which I could measure the level of my students' writing apprehension and then examine that score against their written work to determine if the more apprehensive writers were also the least skilled. I considered examining the ways in which attitudes toward writing might correlate with skill. But with each inquiry, I reached the same conclusion: I would learn about attitudes and apprehension and scales and surveys, but such knowledge would not necessarily teach me about writing.

One afternoon, I raised these concerns with Gordon Pradl, my advisor at NYU. He listened as he always did, smiled, and suggested a new list of books to read. Perhaps Gordon knew all along that at some point something would catch my attention, would stand out and say, "Of course, this is the approach." Perhaps he was advising me to do what I later learned ethnographers are trained to do when beginning a new study, to cast a wide net, for Gordon's constant suggestions for reading ultimately provided me with what I needed.

In January 1975, I was on an airplane traveling to Florida. Among the books I took with me was Emig's *The Composing Processes of Twelfth Graders* (1971). I needed only to read a few sentences to become excited. Emig, I soon realized, was the first person to look directly at a central preoccupation of our field: writing processes. She didn't import theories from cognitive psychology; she didn't try to establish a correlation with a related aspect of writing. Instead, she found a way to observe as directly as she could writing processes as they unfold. Sitting in that seat on the plane, I sensed the rightness in this approach. It said to me, "If you want to understand how something happens, then pay close attention: watch it unfold." I was also aware that while Emig observed 12th graders, no one had yet observed the kinds of writers I was working with at CUNY: not just college students, but those whose writing marked them as deficient. By the time I walked off the plane, I knew I had found the question I considered worth pursuing, one that took writers and their writing and placed them at the center of an inquiry, and one that would, if I were at all fortunate, lead me directly into the heart of what I most cared about: writing and the teaching of writing.

THE FIELD IN THE 1970s

Looking back, I can see that Emig's work gave me one piece. My work as an instructor in a writing classroom gave me another. The excitement, turmoil, and confusion about approaches to basic writing at CUNY added a third. But something else was in the air in the early 1970s, when doctoral students like me began to design research projects. Composition, as a field of inquiry, was still in its infancy, still attempting to make itself respectable by modeling its research methods on those of the experimental or physical sciences. To that end, the field and those faculty in it who were advising students on ways of conducting research based their suggestions on what was considered to be at that time the best possible advice: the 1963 publication, *Research in Written Composition*. "The Braddock book," as it was commonly called, informed beginning researchers that previous work in composition was suspect precisely because it had ignored certain variables. Because researchers had not controlled topics, writing samples could not be compared. Because researchers did not control the amount of time allotted to writing, not very much could be claimed about what they had discovered. If writers wrote in different settings or at different times of the day, then there would be no way to compare what they had done. In other words, in order to make research in composition respectable, we were instructed to control as many variables as we could.

Today, I would argue that there are many other ways to collect data and to form an understanding of how writing occurs in different settings, but I want to underscore that in the early 1970s, there were no alternatives available. Anthropological approaches had not yet entered our discussions of methodology. Mishler (1979) had not yet written about context-stripping procedures. In fact, as startling as it may seem, even within a case study approach, which as a method seeks to understand the particularities and highlight the idiosyncrasies of individual experiences, researchers were still advised to control as many variables as possible.

Looking back, some of what we did may seem naive. Certainly today I would design my research differently. And North (1987) is not entirely misguided when he describes the early studies of composing as employing "an impure method birthing a bastard knowledge" (p. 206). But North's critique ignores any sense of history or any awareness of the governing research paradigms and contextual factors he claims are so important. Critiquing work completed in the 1970s for not taking into account the concerns and understandings that only emerged a decade or so later is, in fact, to perform a sleight of hand, to confuse ends with means. In the early to mid-1970s, the best advice available was to control as many variables as one could and to report one's findings as if one had little to do with creating them.

The truism that all research is a reflection of the ideas and questions that arise in particular moments of history is worth observing here. The early work on composing arose from an overriding urge among scholars in the field to turn composition study into a respectable and scientific endeavor. Along the way, we borrowed paradigms and procedures that fit the natural sciences better than they fit the human ones. But putting this critique aside, I think it is useful to remark that to its credit, the early work also embodied values and perspectives that are still important, namely a deep respect for individual writers and the desire to understand how writing unfolds from within their frames of reference.

STUDYING COMPOSING PROCESSES IN A COMMUNITY COLLEGE

In September 1975, I introduced my research plans to the students in my freshman composition class. I explained that for my doctoral dissertation, I was interested in discovering what happened as they wrote, that as a writing teacher, I knew a lot about their written products, but not nearly as much about their writing processes. In fact, I told them, in order to understand what happens as they write, I'd like to observe them several times outside of class. Then I asked for volunteers, and all 15 students wrote me notes expressing their interest. Ultimately, I selected five who represented the range of backgrounds and abilities I had come to associate with open admissions students.

I designed the study, as I had been instructed, by adhering to strict controls. I met with each of the students individually in a soundproof room in the college library at the same time each week. I gave them the same writing tasks to do, and I sat off to one side, out of their line of sight. Following Emig (1971), I also asked my students to compose aloud, to say whatever crossed their minds while they were writing. Composing aloud, of course, cannot be construed to be the same as composing silently. But, for my students at least, it seemed to be a skill they could develop without a lot of forethought or difficulty. And I was willing to venture that it was the closest I could get to gaining access to what they were thinking while they were actually in the midst of composing.

Readers seeking a detailed description of this work may wish to consult the articles that grew out of this study, particularly "The Composing Processes of Unskilled College Writers," which appeared in the journal *Research in the Teaching of English* in 1979. Tony, the case study student whose work I described in that article, has in fact become almost as well known as Emig's (1971) Lynn. Case study subjects, it seems, take on lives of their own. At conferences, colleagues refer to them; in classes, graduate students call them by name. But how often, I wonder, do we go back and examine the data from which their portraits emerged? What might we learn upon revisiting the original data to see what they reveal to us today?[1]

To understand how Tony became emblematic of a basic writer in our field, I will present below a partial transcript of one of his composing-aloud sessions, a transcript that, until now, was buried in the appendix of my dissertation.

Picture, first of all, a 20-year-old ex-Marine, a Hispanic man who grew up in New York, who, although he speaks Spanish at home, considers English his native language. He has a son and a wife, from whom he is separated. This is his first semester of college, and the second time we are meeting outside of class to conduct the research. Since Tony and all of the other students in my class are enrolled together in a social science course I attend with them, I am able to create a writing assignment based on the concepts they are studying and the vocabulary they are using in this course.[2] As Tony and I sit down, I explain once more about the tape recorder and my desire to have him "think out loud." I hand him the directions and the topic typed on a piece of paper (see Figure 5.1 in the Appendix). He begins by reading the topic aloud[3]:

> [*Reading*] "Topic: Society and Culture. Directions: During this session, you are being asked to write on your personal thoughts and feelings about a particular American belief. You may handle the topic in any way you like, but remember that you are being asked to relate the topic to your personal experience. Statement: All societies have ide-logical beliefs. One of the ide-log, idelogilies of American society is that all men are created equal. If this is true, then you and the members of your family are equal—equal to everyone else in America. Describe your personal reaction to this last statement and define what being equal means—to you."
>
> Okay, I'm going to read this over. I understood the direction part—relate something that happened to me, so I'm going to read the statement over, then I'm going to read the whole thing over, make sure.
>
> [*Reading*] "During this session, you are being asked to write on your personal thoughts and feelings about a particular American belief. [*Tapping on the desk with his pen.*] You may handle the topic in any way you like, but remember that you are being asked to relate the topic to your personal experience."
>
> Okay. Relate it to me. Now I'm going to read over the other part I didn't understand too good—the statement.
>
> [*Reading*] "All societies have idelogical beliefs. One of the idelogilies of American society is that all men are created equal. If this is true, then you and the members of your family are equal to

everyone else in America. Describe your personal reaction to the last statement and define what being equal means to you."

[*Ten-second pause*]

"Means to you."

Tony: Okay. Can I ask you a question? Do they want you to give a past experience, something that happened to you? Or just define what equal means to you?

Sondra: Whichever way you are more comfortable with—whichever you want to write about.

Tony: Cause, um, I have a good example of what unequal is that has happened to me. I could write a story on that, would be quick. Or I could write what equal means to me.

Sondra: Um, whichever you are more comfortable with—

Tony: Okay.

Sondra: You can do either.

Tony: Heh, I shouldn't have even asked you, heh, heh, heh. All right, I'm going to read it over again.

[*Reading*] "All societies have ideol.... [*reading quickly*] If this is true.... Describe...being equals means to you."

Okay, first I'm going to say what being equal, I'm going to write about what being equal means to me, then I'm going to give a past experience, something about the American belief, that relates to me in the first paragraph, so I'm going to answer, like, both questions. Okay. Let me see. I'm going to write by starting off....

[*Composing aloud*] *Being equal means to me, to me, being equal means to me.* Now I'm going to say what it means to me, *No matter what color, race, and religion you are,*

Uh, again, I'm going to write down most of my ideas here, then rewrite it on the next paper, and then rewrite it on the next paper—to get some of the grammar done on the second paper, to get all the grammar done on the next paper. To get my ideas more together on the second paper and get my grammar completed, completed completely on the third paper.

Uh. [*Reading*] "No matter what color, race and religion you are," pause, "you are"—"Being equal means to me no matter what color, race and religion you are," [*Composing aloud*] *no body*—"Being equal means to me that..."

I'm going to change that—[*Sounds of crossing out*]

"Being equal means to me that... " *no one thinks he is better than another person, better than another person, being he white, black, Spanish, or any different religion.*

[*Reading*] "Being equal means to me that no one thinks he is better than another"—

I'm reading it over, see what my idea—what I got down here, see if anything else come to my head that I could add to what being equal means to me.

[*Reading*] "Being equal means to me that no one thinks he is better than another person being he white black Spanish or of a different religion."

[*Eight-second pause*]

Okay. Now I'm trying to think what to say or how to, uh, connect it together with, uh, a personal thing that happened to me, an experience. I'm trying to think, is there anything I could add to this or how to connect it together in my head? All right.

"Being equal means to me—"

I'm reading it over—see if anything pops into my head.

"Being equal means to me that no one thinks he is better than another person being he white, black, Spanish, or of a different religion." [*Pause.*]

[*Composing aloud*] *No matter what we are, different religion, no matter what we are—*

All right, I think I have something that I could end this off with and connect it with my personal experience.

"Spanish or different religion"

No persons, no matter what they are, will have an equal chance to do or finish anything...with a fair chance.

It's hard to think and say it at the same time.

"Spanish or different religion"

"Being he white, black, Spanish, or of a different religion"

[*Composing aloud*] *That we all be able to start and finish things with an equal opportunity.*

Okay, *That we all be able to start and finish things with an equal opportunity.*

Okay. That there I'm going to finish, uh, what being equal means to me, go on to a new paragraph and start off, uh, with my personal experience. This experience happened when I was in the military, the last day I was in the military...

[*Ten-second pause*]

"that we all be able to start and finish things with an equal opportunity."

Okay, start by saying

[*Composing aloud*] *I recall an incident when I was in the service. It happened*, all right, this here I'm going to write and change it around a little bit on my next paper, just get my main thoughts here.

"I recall an incident when I was in the service." *It happened on my EAS—that's my last day of service.*

Service. Cause when I was in the service—my last day of service.

I served three years, three years, and only got into trouble, cross out, *got into, minor diff*—cross out, I'm trying to think how to say, how to express something here, I can't figure out the right words.

I served three years and only had three article 15s. And on the last day, I was expecting a complete honorable discharge. But the CO gave me a general, but the CO gave me a general, but the CO gave me a general, because he said I had two article 15s too recent. And on the same day there was another marine two ranks lower than me and he just got out of the brig a month ago, a month before he got his discharge, and he also had five articles 15 and the CO gave him a complete honorable. I believe that the CO did this because he was prejudice.

Now I'm going to read this here and see how it sounds, then I'm going to rewrite it, rewrite it on the second piece of paper, get some grammar together and get the words better together. Then I'm going to rewrite it over again to hand it into the teacher and have it perfect.

[*Reading the first draft*] "Being equal means to me that no one thinks he is better than another person. Being equal means to me, being equal means to me, that no one thinks he is better than another person."

Okay. That's one sentence there. That sounds pretty good to me.

"Being he, being he, being that he is, being he white black Spanish or of a different religion."

Okay. That sounds a little mixed up there so I'm going to see if I can correct anything in here before I rewrite it.

[*Revising*] "Being that (add that) he is white comma black comma Spanish comma or of a different religion period." I'm going to read that now, see how it sounds.

"Being that he is white, black, Spanish, or of a different religion."

Okay. Let me read it all together—see how it sounds.

"Being equal means to me that no one thinks he is better than—that no one would think, that no one should think he is—" All right, let me see something, "Being equal means to me that no one thinks he is better than another person being that he is white, black, Spanish"

Let me see how it sounds like this. "He is better than—it doesn't matter if he is—"

Let me leave it at that for now—I'll mess with it on the last paper.

DRAWING CONCLUSIONS ABOUT TONY'S COMPOSING PROCESS

What can one learn from studying this partial transcript of Tony composing aloud? It seems clear that Tony's writing process exhibits the recursiveness that has become a governing idea in composing research. Tony reads and rereads, going back, again and again, to the topic, to his own words, to the ideas and associations the topic and the statement evoke in him. Yet, in addition to his reliance on rereading and rethinking, other issues intrude. In the midst of composing his second sentence, for example, Tony is already conscious of error, already making plans to rewrite his paper a second time and then a third so that he can get the "grammar completed completely."

It is also clear that Tony revises during composing—crossing out, substituting words, worrying about word choice and about appropriateness. One can begin to sense, I suggest, that Tony actually knows something about the way composing occurs, that, for instance, rereading may lead him to a new idea, that one can, in my words, "go back to go forward." Tony also shows that he has the kinds of composing concerns many skilled writers have: he thinks about his choices, about transitions, about ways to "connect" his first paragraph with his second, his whole paper with the topic given to him. Tony also listens to the sound of his words and attempts to use his ear as a guide. He struggles, rereading: "no one thinks...no one would think...no one should think" and, unable to make a decision, decides instead to "mess with this on the last paper."

Tony repeats the composing behaviors visible in this transcript in the other three composing sessions as well. And each time he composes during the study, it becomes clear that what goes wrong in his writing process can be attributed both to an overriding and premature concern with correctness, a concern so strong that it preoccupies him even in the midst of creating a new idea, and to his not having at his disposal a fully formed set of rules to guide him when he does attempt to make grammatical or stylistic decisions. In fact, if one tracks the changes Tony makes from the first draft to the third draft, it also becomes clear that the early promise of his piece is not sustained. Rather than improving his product, his elaborate system of working on each sentence and then copying it over ends up producing an increasingly flawed piece of writing (see Figures 5.2, 5.3, and 5.4 in the Appendix for copies of these drafts).

Despite Tony's difficulties, it is nonetheless possible to conclude that he does have a composing process. He exhibits what I called "consistent behaviors" both within and across sessions. Having observed and documented the writing processes of four other writers and having seen that they, too, engaged in consistent kinds of behaviors, some similar to Tony's, others unique, I was able to suggest that the composing processes of even the most unskilled writers seem to be predictable and steady. This conclusion, alone, made it possible for faculty to see their basic writers in a new light. No longer did we need to assume that basic writers did not necessarily know how to write, that their written work indicated merely haphazard or sloppy or inattentive composing processes. Instead, I suggested, we can now look to find ways to help these writers understand their own composing processes and what characteristically gets in their way as they write.

DRAWING CONCLUSIONS ABOUT RESEARCH ON COMPOSING

In hindsight, I agree that there are problems with the design of this study; I agree that isolating Tony and his peers and attempting to control so many variables of the composing situation is contrived and artificial. Certainly, composing aloud is not a common practice for writers. And the purpose of the composing sessions were, after all, driven by my needs as a researcher and my students' interests in pleasing me. Nonetheless, I want to suggest that the findings still carry some import.

Today, I would no longer proceed in a manner that disregards the contexts in which writers live and learn and grow, or the ways the researcher has an impact on what is said and studied; nevertheless, I want to consider, what, if anything, still makes sense here? Twenty years later, what can we distinguish as valuable?

First, and most important, is the obvious fact that Tony and his fellow students served as the center of the inquiry. They were not merely subjects used to test a theory or to prove a point. I had questions that intrigued me: How do students write and what happens while they are writing? Consequently, what my students said, did, and wrote became the focus of my attention. The lesson here, I suggest, is that in any study of composing, writers and what they do must remain at the center of the inquiry. To place them here, I want to argue, is to grant human action central in importance and to enact the belief that looking closely at what people are doing can be a primary starting point for understanding them and their worlds.

Second, the composing tapes of my five case study students, 20 in all, provided me with a body of data in which I could become immersed. Today, I would want the students to listen to the tapes with me, to comment on what they hear, what they think is happening, and what sense they make of their own composing. But even without their perspectives, I want to argue for the value of paying close attention to the data we collect, of finding ways to go over it, again and again, so that it begins to speak to us. I devised a method that allowed me to code what I heard on each tape. Ultimately it was not the code that was important. Rather, the code enabled me to get inside this body of data. I came to know the data intimately and eventually was able to know what was missing and what the code could not detect, particularly in the silent moments that eluded all coding and led me then to a deepened questioning of what I was observing. Some of what came from this inquiry I articulated in the 1971 article "Understanding Composing"; more recently, I have written about it in Graves and Brand's book, *The Presence of Mind: Writing and the Domain Beyond the Cognitive* (1994). But the point is that my understanding of composing processes and of ways to guide students through them grew directly out of the hundreds of hours I spent studying what Tony and his fellow students said and did.

Third, if I were to design a composing study today, it is unlikely that I would isolate my students from the worlds in which they write. Instead, I would look to join them in some way, to ask them to tell me how they see things, and what they experience and think, so that I could immerse myself as well in the contexts that constitute living and learning for them. Since those I am attempting to understand are not me, but become what is currently often referred to as "the other," my understanding of their worlds always entails an imaginative leap, one we too often ignore in our current research and writing.

The early work on composing embodied much that was right. We cannot go too far astray in our understanding of students, classrooms, and literacy if we pay close attention to phenomena, document what we are seeing, and check if our perceptions have some accuracy to them. But it is also crucial to ask who is this "we"? Who are the documenters and how do we account for ourselves, our biases, our prejudices, our desires, and our blindnesses in the research we report? The early work on composing told us to stand aside, to report our findings as if we had little to do with creating them, all of which presupposes that knowledge arises independently of any creator.

I would now argue that we cannot set ourselves apart. One of our misconceptions was to assume that we were not creating our own knowledge, not fashioning it imaginatively no matter how many variables we controlled. Looking back on what the early work has taught us, I would say that researchers need to show more of themselves at work, share more of the data they collect, make tapes, videos, and transcripts available at research seminars and conferences, and through online networks, to let all interested parties in on the ground level. In this way, I suggest, participants in the research community can make imaginative leaps along with the researchers.

This is a call for the creation of stronger collegial and dialogic relationships in the construction of research findings. Such projects need to include the voices of those we study and teach; in them as well need to be our own voices; and all through them I can imagine the responses of those who want to understand the research, who want to make sense of it and to use it.

It is equally important to recognize that whatever sense we make of the data we collect, of the lived experience of our subjects and ourselves, it is still sense that we created, sense that we fashioned out of all we lived during the study. As a result, I think we constantly need to remind ourselves that findings from our research studies should be viewed not as the truths of laboratory science, but as particular and varying versions of what we have come to see and hear and observe. Such an understanding makes room, then, for a vast array of forms for reporting research. In the future, I hope that stories, tales, portraits, and narrative accounts will continue to supplant the more traditional formats, so that in the endeavor to understand who and what we are, our research accounts will reveal rather than reduce what Irmscher (1987) has called "the fullness of experience" (p. 197).

Reflecting on the work we have accomplished brings me to one last point: The questions that excited me when I began to study composing processes grew out of what I was seeking to do in the classroom when I was a beginning instructor. The method I found to study these questions brought me to observe what was occurring before me. If the findings from this early work still speak to us, then I know of no better guide for researchers in our field as we enter the 21st century than to keep the students in our classrooms, their needs and struggles, and our own questions of how to help and guide them, before our eyes. After all, remaining close to the classroom and close to the students, in conversation with them and with one another, honors the impulse and the commitments that brought so many of us here so many years ago.

APPENDIX

Topic: Society and Culture

Directions: During this session, you are being asked to write on your personal thoughts and feelings about a particular American belief. You may handle the topic in any way you like, but remember that you are being asked to relate the topic to your personal experience.
Statement: All societies have ideological beliefs. One of the ideologies of American society is that all men are created equal. If this is true, then you and the members of your family are equal to everyone else in America.

Describe your personal reaction to this last statement and define what being equal means to you.

FIGURE 5.1. Topic given to Tony for Session 2.

Being equal means to me. ~~No matter wahat color race and religion you are, no body~~ that no one thinks he is better than another person. Being that he is white, black, spanish, or ~~and~~ of a different religion. That we all beable to start and finish things with an equal opportunity.
~~I recall an insient when I was in the service.~~ It happen on ~~th~~ my eas that my last day of serice. I severd three years and ~~on go got inot tro minor d~~ only had 3 article 15s. And on the last I was expecting a complete homable dischare. But the CO gave a General. Because he say I had two articule to recent. And the same their was another Marine two ranks lower than me and he just got of the brig ~~a~~ mouth be he got his discharige and he also 5 articles 15s and the Co gave him a complete honable. I believe that the C.O. did this because he was prejuidice.

FIGURE 5.2. Tony's first draft for Session 2.

Being equal means to me that no one thinks he is better than another person. ~~Being that~~ he It dosen't /manner if he is black, white, spanish or of a different religion. I blieve that ~~we~~ all of us should be able to start and finish things with an equal oppoitunity.

For example I had a personal eiperiance, that denied ~~b~~ me from having ~~my~~ and equal opputunity in finishing my military career. This took place on my eas which means your last day of service. I served 3 years with only article 15s. Thier was /also a fellow white marine with the /same eas. as me. This marine here ~~had~~ 5 /was two ranks article 15's and was release from the just a mon t h earlier. And yet the Co. Found to his disc—to give him a complete honorable and to give me a general under ~~unde~~ honable condition. Which I felt was very unjust. And believe thier could not be no other reason for this happening but mere prejudicism.

FIGURE 5.3. Tony's second draft for Session 2.

Being equal means to me. That no one thinks he is better than another person. It dosen't manner if he is white, black, spanish, or of a different religion. I ~~beliver~~ believe that all of us should be able to start and finish things with an equal opperitunity.

For example I had a personal eiperence That denied me from haveing an equal opperetunity in finishing my military career. This took place on my ~~last day of service~~ eas which means your last day of service. I served three years with only ~~3~~ three article 15. There was a fellow white ~~m~~ Marine with the same EAS as me. This marine was two ranks below me, had five arlicle 15, and was release from the brig a mouth eariler. And yet the company commander found to his discretion to give him a complete honorable dischaige, and gave me a general under honable conditions. Which I felt was very unjust. ~~An~~ I believe that there could not be no other reason for this happening but mere prejudicism on behave of the company commander.

FIGURE Figure 5.4. Tony's final draft for Session 2.

NOTES

[1]In the original version of this chapter, presented at the Watson Conference on Rhetoric and Composition at the University of Louisville in October 1996, I

played a tape in which Tony composes aloud. My goal was to provide conference participants with the opportunity to hear Tony composing and to draw their own conclusions directly from the data. The transcript that is included in this chapter is, then, already one step removed from the original data.

[2]I would no longer word a statement in what appears now as the sexist way I did then, another indication of what neither Gordon Pradl nor I was aware of in our use of language when we designed and discussed the topics for the composing sessions.

[3]I have indicated Tony's various composing strategies by using brackets and different type styles. Tony's reading out loud of the topic or his own written text is indicated by quotation marks; Tony's composing aloud is presented in italics; and his comments on the composing process appear in standard typeface. At the Watson Conference, the audience drew many of the conclusions I present following the transcript.

REFERENCES

Braddock, R., Lloyd-Jones, R., & Schoer, L. (1963). *Research in written composition.* Urbana, IL: National Council of Teachers of English.

Bruner, J. (1960). *The process of education.* Cambridge, MA: Harvard University Press.

Chomsky, N. (1965). *Aspects of the theory of syntax.* Cambridge, MA: MIT Press.

Emig, J. (1971). *The composing processes of twelfth graders.* Urbana, IL: National Council of Teachers of English.

Irmscher, W. (1987). Finding a comfortable identity. In S. Perl (Ed.), *Landmark essays on writing process* (pp. 191–197). Mahwah, NJ: Lawrence Erlbaum.

Mishler, E. (1979). Meaning in context: Is there any other kind? *Harvard Educational Review, 39,* 1–19.

North, S. (1987). *The making of knowledge in composition: Portrait of an emerging field.* Upper Montclair, NJ: Boynton/Cook.

Perl, S. (1979). The composing processes of unskilled college writers. *Research in the Teaching of English, 13,* 317–336.

Perl, S. (1980). Understanding composing. *College Composition and Communication, 31,* 363–369.

Perl, S. (1994). A writer's way of knowing. In A. Brand & R. Graves (Eds.), *Writing and the domain beyond the cognitive* (pp. 77–87). Portsmouth, NH: Boynton/Cook.

Piaget, J. (1959). *Language and thought of the child.* London: Clarendon Press.

Shaughnessy, M. (1977). *Errors and expectations.* New York: Oxford University Press.

Troyka, L., & Nudelman, J. (1972). *Steps in composition.* Englewood Cliffs, NJ: Prentice-Hall.

Vygotsky, L. (1962). *Thought and language.* Cambridge, MA: MIT Press.

chapter 6

The Expressivist Menace

James Thomas Zebroski
Syracuse University

RETROJECTED HISTORIES, MYTHIC ORIGINS

Despite the inclusion of empirical data, this essay is a theoretical exploration. Karl Marx, in his book *Capital* (1990), shows how the so- called empirical fact can function theoretically. Similarly, I have constructed an empirical pilot study to begin the larger project of theorizing the function that the concept of expressivism serves in contemporary discussions of composition history (Zebroski, forthcoming, a). Previous histories of college composition have not so much been wrong as they have been *limited* by a) a lack of a comprehensive theoretical framework needed to suggest, order, synthesize, and integrate information regarding what constitutes professional and disciplinary identity; and b) a lack of explicitness about the location of that narrative within the historical stream. Certainly studies like Berlin's (1987) or Strain's (1993) are fully aware and upfront about their bill of theoretical and political goods. Jim Berlin was always clear that his categories were the result of a dialectic between Marxist theory and the so-called historical facts. But such histories of composition do not pay enough attention to where the *field and discipline* is at the moment of production of these texts, and how that larger context composes motives, concepts, figures, tropes, and narrative lines. It makes a great deal of difference when and where historians/histories are produced, since a historical narrative emerges from the dialectic between present and past. For example, a historical narrative written in 1980 will necessarily see the events of the "founding" of 4Cs in 1949 differently from a narrative constructed in 1997 about the same events. Great historians (for example, Duberman, 1972) have realized this and factored this "subjective" dimension into their texts.

Our early studies also use, understandably enough, a narrow band of evidence. We need then to construct a theoretical frame to expand the sort of materials that we consider. Thus, any fair representation of the field of college composition must attend to at least six constitutive practices.

Writing Practices

These are difficult to get at, especially if one is 25 to 30 years removed in time. We do have early process accounts of writers, but most of these involve either creative writers or academics or professionals. Heath (1983) and Radway (1991) provide examples of studies we need in composition to get at common everyday writing practices and their actual rather than purported ideology. Motz's (1987) enlightening scholarship and the work of Bunkers and Huff (1996) demonstrate the historical value of journals and self-sponsored writing for a broader historical understanding of writing.

We also need to investigate popular representations of writing in the early 1970s. Campus bestsellers like Haley's *The Autobiography of Malcolm X* (1965/1981), Jackson's *Soledad Brother* (1970), and Vonnegut's *Slaughterhouse-Five* (1969) show how writing/writers are represented in this period. If we begin to examine these popular representations, we discover far more political than expressivist practice.

Teaching Practices

Traditionally, textbooks have been the means for getting at teaching practices of an historical period. Although relying too heavily on textbook analysis for this purpose can misrepresent teaching, there is a class bias in discounting textbooks as suggestive of teaching, especially at large, TA-driven state universities. In cases where textbooks seem closely related to teaching practices, it makes sense to examine the revisions of textbook exercises across editions. But also teachers' oral histories and course documents—syllabi, handouts, assignment sheets, and teacher commentary on student papers—are key, as are student recollections.

I have begun five oral histories of former freshman composition students who took the course at four universities very different from one other (Zebroski, forthcoming, d). The first oral history is of a freshman student in 1967; the second, in 1970; the third, in 1974; the fourth, in

1977; and the fifth, in 1982. All of this evidence so far has been extremely consistent. All courses were current-traditional rhetoric courses. The only element of any of these composition courses that could possibly be seen as expressivist was the use of literature, and even this tended to devolve into New Critical analysis. Many of these informants still have their textbooks from the course or could give names of them. Two of the five are nonacademics and finished their education with a bachelor's degree. Such studies start to factor in the students' perceptions of our composition courses, something all the academic and professional histories have so far left out.

Curricular Practices

These mostly departmental practices often produce policy documents, so we at least get an official version of the writing course and composition curricula. But I have also turned to textbook advertisements as material tracers for the curricular practice of departmental adoption. The evidence from textbook advertisements of this period, presented below, is that expressivism never was a persuasive influence on curricular practices.

Disciplinary Practices

Berlin's history (1987) is really a history of disciplinary practices, at least in Chapter 7, which examines expressivism. Reading through page after page of explication of Rohman and Wlecke, Stewart, Hayakawa, Blanchard, Simonson, Macrorie, Kelly, Dixon, Wolf, Deemer, Hamalian, Paul and Kligerman, Lutz, Gibson, Coles, Murray, and Elbow, one would get the impression that "expressionism" was the rising tide of the historical moment. But Berlin is always pretty careful about his claims. He says that expressionism was the most pervasive form of subjective rhetoric and was especially prominent during the 1960s and 1970s, which seems true enough. And yet nearly all of these sources come from two journals, *College Composition and Communication* and *College English*, and do not address dissertations, research projects (with the exception of Rohman and Wlecke), or other forms and forums for disciplinary practices, let alone actual classrooms or writing programs beyond their representation in an occasional textbook.

I have yet to discover a single error in Berlin's (1987) facts or in his careful claims, but I have done my own survey of a sample of February issues of *CCC* from 1969 to 1990, and the impression that these journals were mouthpieces of expressivism is wrong (Zebroski, forthcoming, b). The tables of contents indicate overwhelmingly that even in these journals, expressivism was *not* a force to be reckoned with in college composition. The majority of articles and essays in *CCC* in this period were not expressivist. In my sample, they dealt with (largest to smallest):

1) teaching methods—clearly the predominant article at 15, few of which seem predominantly expressivist;
2) grammar, language and style, and rhetoric tie with 8 articles each;
3) social and political issues in composition, 6 articles;
4) writing-across-the-curriculum (WAC), 5;
5) professional history, literature, professional issues, and cognitive process tie, 4 articles each; and
6) expressivist articles *last*, at 3 articles.

A recent study (Phillips, Greenberg, & Gibson, 1993) of *CCC* citations supports my analysis and shows that expressivist disciplinary practices were a bit more prevalent, though not in the 1960s and 1970s, as conventional wisdom would have it, but from 1980 through 1993. So there is a strong tension between disciplinary practices and curricular practices in the period from 1980 through 1993. That is, while the number of expressivist references increased in the journal articles, they declined and barely rebounded in textbook advertisments in this period.

Disciplinary practices were not mostly expressivist, especially during the early 1970s, though in the late 1980s attention to expressivist perspectives did slightly increase in the journals.

Professional Practices

Official documents reflect professional practice and sometimes professional consensus. The CCCC article "Students' Right to Their Own Language" (1974) tells us as much about the profession as it does about student language. The annual CCCC program during the years 1968–1974 included teaching workshops, which were written up in the journal *CCC*. These reports show that politics is everywhere and teaching is receiving increasing attention, undergoing its own quiet renaissance. A bit later, Jasper Neel (1978) collected 18 descriptions of writing programs, written by administrators, which, at best, shows that perhaps 2 of these 18 diverse programs have expressivist leanings. Most of these reports describe the most traditional of current-traditional programs.

Theorizing Practices

Like writing practices, theorizing practices are difficult to get at retroactively. Starting by examination of self-labeled theory books, such as

Abrams (1953), Berthoff (1971), Britton (1970), D'Angelo (1975), Kinneavy (1971), Moffett (1968), and Young, Becker, and Pike (1970), and the underlying theorizing practices, we are struck by the fact that, in contrast to literary studies, there is a good deal of theory coming out in composition in the late 1960s and early 1970s. But the predominant theorizing practice is still formalism, applied to student prose or to the components of the rhetorical situation or to the composing process.

TEXTBOOK ADVERTISEMENTS IN *COLLEGE COMPOSITION AND COMMUNICATION*: 1969–1990

Although my broader claim about expressivism within college composition depends on the coordination of evidence pertaining to all of these practices, I focus on advertisements in February textbook review issues of *CCC*. These ads show a large turnover, especially in reading anthologies ("readers"), though even the "rhetorics" appeared in new editions on a regular basis. Connors (1981) and Faigley (1992), for example, analyzed the nine-edition run of McCrimmon's *Writing With a Purpose*, which started in 1950. Aycock (1985) studied Brooks and Warren's 1949 textbook *Modern Rhetoric*, which had reached its fourth edition by 1979. While the analysis of textbooks can only begin to suggest teaching practices, textbook advertisements do give us a piece of the puzzle geared to the key curricular practice of textbook adoption.

Advertisements also tell us what textbook publishers wanted to sell *and* what they expected would sell. Advertisements, like the choice of the new titles to be promoted each year, tell us much about the publishers' guesses about where the field was and where it was likely to go. Their guesses represent a savvy reading of the futures market in composition, what has reaped profits in the recent past and what most likely will continue to do so, and what new prospects might pull in front of the pack, grabbing market shares in the future. Textbook advertisements are capital investments as well as persuasive appeals. For the most part, you only try to persuade readers to adopt textbooks that have a chance of increasing your profits. Like any investment portfolio, you diversify and assume that what counts is increasing your profit in the long run. So textbook advertisements are good material tracers of composition futures, what the going ideas of the time were, and whether a particular idea as embodied in a textbook is likely to be bullish and bearish down the line.

Given enrollments across the nation in freshman composition, I think it is reasonable to assume that freshman composition texts corner perhaps 10 percent of the higher education market. According to recent figures ("Industry Sales Rose," 1996), the higher education market went up 6.8 percent to $2.3 billion in 1995, significantly better than the overall industry increase (5.3 percent). Higher education accounts for nearly 11.7 percent of total sales, so big money is involved.

It is true that departmental adoptions tend to be conservative and to lag behind disciplinary practices. But they also tend to be good indicators of the consensus among those in charge. New TA's use departmental adoptions, while experienced instructors have more freedom. Textbook advertisements reflect this, splitting layout between old reliables (that is, candidates for department adoption) versus the newfangled (that is, candidates for the experienced).

Textbook publishers are extremely adept at moving fast on a current fad. These quick adjustments are more visible in the composition "readers" than the "rhetorics," but they too change relatively fast. For example, in the 1980s, the rhetorics largely changed within five years, which considering how long term a project book publishing is, is rather quick. So we get a fairly good running commentary on the immediate interests, concerns, and obsessions of the field by looking at the readers, while we get more of a sense of paradigm shifts by examining the rhetorics. When they sensed an opening in a potential market, whether "process," "expressivist," or whole language, publishers wasted no time producing textbooks to appeal to those consumers.

In examining the February issues of *CCC* to discover what sort of books and textbooks were advertised, I found that the categories of "reader" (devoted mostly to either literature, essays [i.e., "traditional"], politics [i.e., "nontraditional"], or media), "rhetoric," "basic writing" texts, "handbook," and "other" worked well. I wanted a total to which I could compare the number of designated expressivist textbooks. I tried to rate advertisements as simply and as conservatively as I could. If the book being advertised was written by one of Berlin's designated expressivists, I immediately tagged it expressivist, regardless of what it seemed to be. I also developed a list of code words. If these words showed up in the description and/or title, I put the textbook into the expressivist camp. Books and textbooks devoted to certain "creative" topics, such as film, media, or experimental genres, I counted as expressivist. Even a partial commitment to expressivist principles made an advertisement expressivist in my count. Finally, I tallied every listing of every advertisement, so it was not unusual in some ads to have dozens of textbooks listed, and just a few played up in white space. (Significantly, mostly basic writing texts were relegated early in this period to the listings.) The data for the analyses of advertisement content is presented in Table 6.1.

TABLE 6.1. Content Analysis of Textbook Advertisements in *College Compsition and Communication*

Date		READERS			RHETS	BW	HB	OTHER		Total	TOTAL %
Feb.	Literature	Trad.	Non-T	Media					Express		
CCC											
1969	21	7	3	0	12	11	1	13	3	68	4.4%
1971	72	9	37	3	21	14	2	18	10	318	3.1%
1975	29	13	14	2	36	13	5	24	5	136	3.7%
1978	20	12	2	1	20	50	14	27	4	146	2.7%
1980	5	14	2	0	27	47	14	17	2	126	1.6%
1981	13	12	0	0	28	44	7	16	5	120	4.1%
1985	12	13	6	0	21	17	15	17	7	101	6.9%
1990	9	13	19	0	20	15	11	32	6	119	5%

Thus, the total number of advertisements in the February *CCC* that I studied was 1,134. The total number of expressivist textbooks advertised in these same issues was 49, or 4 percent of the total.

THE SPECTRE OF "EXPRESSIVISM"

"Spectre" conjures the image from the Cold War of the 1950s and the red menace. "Better red than dead" was one of the phrases of that time. The only thing that went without saying is that "we"—whoever we were—had to take a stand against Communism and that all evil ultimately could be traced back to the "evil empire." So if black people were protesting in front of the Lincoln Memorial in Washington in August 1963, that could hardly have anything to do with their civil rights; rather, there must be Communist infiltrators, duping Martin Luther King and protestors. Then, too, if riots broke out in the spring of 1970 on the Ohio State campus, there must be a close knit group of outside agitators traveling from campus to campus to stir up trouble. I arrived the summer after the riots at Ohio State for freshman orientation and was greeted by a campus with two or three official identification checkpoints, a campus that, after the spring of death at Kent and Jackson State, was literally being fenced off to keep those supposed outside agitators out. One of the first moves of the university that summer was to erect an 8-foot wire-mesh fence of the finest quality around the campus perimeter. The rhetoric of spectre always shows us more about the collective and individual unconscious than about the enemy being demonized. The rhetoric of menace reveals our collective shadow, that is, that part of our collective identity furthest removed from our conscious images of our self.

In contrast to the increasingly shrill condemnations of a thing called expressivism (Shamoon & Wall, 1995), the data consistently show that expressivism *never* was a major, persuasive movement in college composition. I find very little evidence to suggest there even was anything one could title an expressivist movement. If the textbook advertisements indicate anything, it is not that expressivist rhetoric was a hot item; rather, it would be more accurate to talk about the literature movement in teaching composition or the basic writing movement or the recurring movements to politicize composition. These were the hot items of the late 1960s and early 1970s in composition.

How, then, can we account for the rhetoric of menace, which retrojects an expressivist movement fully staffed and operational?

I view this rhetoric of menace as being an indicator of present anxieties, rather than past conflicts. Volosinov (1986) says "the word is the most sensitive index of social changes, and what is more, of changes still in the process of growth" (p. 19). The accents we hear intersecting in the word *expressivism* provide us one such index. What then are the material forces that can begin to account for this? There are at least three.

First, the last five years rival 1973–1974 for bad economic conditions in academe. If you can remember back to 1973 and 1974, when the U.S. entered into a recession and the bottom fell out of the academic job market in English, there were folktales about Ph.D.'s driving taxicabs for a living. In fact, it was largely because of the tailspin in the demand for literature doctorates, matched with the continued commitment to open admissions, that a specialization in composition, especially basic writing, became a big selling point in English departments. As the following writer testifies, the depression of 1974 came as a big shock:

> We used to assume that although our position was "marginal," it was temporary; when we got our Ph.D.'s, or when a tenure-track line opened, we would move out of the *composition ghetto* and take on the more challenging—and professionally rewarding—literary work. Early in the 1970s, however, we began to find the upward ladder blocked by funding problems in higher education, and by an attendant pervasive loss of morale. Our most prestigious professional organization, the Modern Language Association, could not respond to our plight, other than to give cold comfort to job-seekers and to warn undergraduates away from doctoral study. We began to feel that we had little stake in the institutional goals of the English department, including the composition course's questionable "service." But we also saw that *if we were to find any security for ourselves in the academy*, we were going to have to find ways to make professionally rewarding the field in which we were remaining. (emphasis added, Bizzell, 1992, pp. 107–108)

Like Bizzell in the late 1970s, we have been experiencing a similar economic depression in academe, overproducing numerous, extremely qualified Ph.D.'s in English, while simultaneously, the administration cuts existing tenure lines. So what do these people do? If they keep the faith and don't simply convert to the business world in order, understandably enough, to get on with their lives, they take part-time positions at several local colleges and continue to publish scholarship in the hopes that when that position does come through, they will be well prepared not only to take their position, but to establish an extensive publication list for tenure. We are talking about large numbers of prospects without full-time positions who are better published than many of the established full and associate professors that are nonetheless making life and death decisions about hiring and tenure. Many times the established faculty would never survive the standards and criteria that they so routinely apply to interviewees or tenure candidates. So I think a good deal of this anxiety experienced by new scholars is deflected as an unconscious projection to other distant and relatively harmless sources. The expressivists demonized aren't likely to hold any power; they can't hurt you—but the established faculty who make life and death decisions about hiring, tenure, and promotion, may.

A second material force, disciplinary economies, also contributes to the rhetoric of menace. The primary function of the university in capitalist society is to produce officially sanctioned sorts of knowledge through the apparatus of disciplines. Capitalism needs innovative, specialized knowledge, which can only be produced through at least some "free inquiry." But such "freedom" is dangerous and must be constrained. To accomplish these seemingly contradictory functions, an entire underground economy of exchanges, bargains, barters, social contract obligations, disciplinary rights, and values among and between disciplines exists. These exchanges are especially easy to see when disciplinary formations begin. In composition, the disciplinary economies are multiple and diverse, for a whole host of reasons. From its start, however, composition has drawn on primarily two disciplinary formations that have always been in tension. English education has funneled a worldview from the social sciences into composition, while English and rhetoric has funneled the worldview of the humanities. From the late 1960s, emerging compositionists have agreed to be tolerant and to not press the obvious differences entailed by these two opposing disciplinary formations. In fact, from the start, there has been an unspoken, sometimes unconscious, agreement in effect in our disciplinary economies.

English education folk, who had been interested in composition for decades, were ascendant in the late 1950s and early 1960s, when education colleges exploded in size to meet the increasing needs of public schools experiencing enrollment surges due to the baby boomers. But the English education field also preceded English literature in the decline of academic positions. There were at this time, however, always many positions in composition programs within English departments. Then, in 1973–1974, the great depression also hit Ph.D.'s in English literature. The basic writing movement was one of the few boom segments of the academic economy in this period. Thus, it made good economic and intellectual sense for English education folk trained in the study of writing, with a long tradition of research on writing already established, to join forces with both the rhetoricians in English who had always been marginalized within the department since the excommunication of speech, and the new Ph.D.'s—like Patricia Bizzell—trained in literature, but concerned to get some kind of position in academe.

In this unspoken deal, English education folk refrained from undercutting new Ph.D.'s by not saying that these English graduates didn't really know much about writing, while the English folk refrained from focusing on those doctoral degrees from colleges of education when English education candidates came to apply for English positions in composition. A symbiotic exchange thus went into effect between disciplines under the new scholarly label of "composition."

However, with the establishment of doctoral programs in composition in the 1980s mostly *within* English departments, with the failure of cognitive process to take over the field of composition in the mid-1980s due to the labors of Patricia Bizzell and David Bartholomae, and with the retirement in the early 1990s of the generation who made this unspoken social contract, all bets are off. New English Ph.D.'s now are free to critique the education element in composition, with little fear of reprisal. Established compositionists, some of whom were always closet literature scholars, can now advocate the abolition of the field or simply move into literary positions vacated by retiring literati. And the increasing popularity of Foucault, a failed social scientist it must be remembered, provides a perfect machine for mounting the critique and beginning the purge. The long repressed conflict in composition between English education and English, between the social sciences and the humanities, now rises to the surface but takes on distorted, reconfigured shapes. Critiques of "expressivism," "process," even "composition" are then a transference and projection of this basic, unresolved, repressed conflict, rather than solely philosophical differences.

A third material source of the rhetoric of menace comes from the field's stage of development. Social formations have life cycles. The processes by which they develop have been studied in sociology, lifespan developmental psychology, and New Testament text scholarship. Braungart (1984) has noted that one of the ways that a generation revolts against its elders is first to deauthorize their ideas and identity. Much of the rhetoric of menace not only deployed against expressivism, but now also expanding against anything labeled process theory, is about the second generation revolting against, deauthorizing, the preceding generation and in this process recomposing the identity of the social formation as a whole.

A sociohistoricist theoretical approach (Berthoff, 1991, 1992, 1996; Zebroski, 1994; forthcoming, b; forthcoming, c; forthcoming, d) might describe a social formation, in this case, composition studies, as moving through four zones of identity formation. In brief:

Zone 1. Proto-Community. This is the long historical moment when individuals as individuals are unconsciously developing a felt sense that existing social formations and identities are increasingly failing to address new needs and that the individuals need to begin to articulate this.

Much of the work of the 1950s and 1960s that was viewed then, either as rhetoric within English departments or as English education within colleges of education, takes place during this phase. For example, the very phrase "from product to process" was circulating years before it was widely printed and took on the tone of a political slogan. For one, Bateman (1963) wrote: "Many current studies related to the general topic of composition have investigated certain characteristics of the product, but have said little about the composing process itself" (p. 1). He goes on:

> But supposing that the elimination of errors is not our major, or at least, our only concern. Perhaps we are also interested in thoughtfulness, coherence, sentence variety, modification, subordination, and creativity. In other words, would we be willing to shift our attention from product to process? It is the reader who examines the product, the writer who is concerned with the process, and perhaps the composition teacher should shift perspective from reader to writer. (p. 2)

Now I don't think Bateman then thought of himself as a compositionist, and yet it is the important work of many people of this period who may not have identified or affiliated with composition that provided the vocabulary, the key words if you will, that began to make it possible for later compositionists to think of themselves as compositionists.

Zone 2. The Mythic First Generation. An event occurs that serves to crystallize the processes of social formation. Out of this event, itself retrojected as mythic origin, come individuals in community authoring texts, which provide further materials for the composition of identity. Identity, while still amorphous and plural, begins to take shape, as teachers and scholars begin to see themselves as compositionists.

We still have several proposed mythic origins, which indicate that our social formation has not yet gotten to the point where one fragment is hegemonic and can declare the other fragments heretics and erase their narratives. North (1987) argued for the 1963 4Cs conference as origin, but then added a personal note by tapping the 1976 Carl Klaus presentation at 4Cs as speaking to his generation of composition. Nystrand, Green, and Wiemelt (1993) posit a much later date, at least the late 1970s. Although I would not reduce composition to disciplinary practices as do Nystrand and colleagues, I do see many of the other practices that make up composition as reaching a critical mass at about the same time that the disciplinary community of Nystrand and colleagues takes shape. However, I would say that my textbook advertisement data suggest an even later date than the Nystrand, Green, and Wiemelt, the year 1980 perhaps being the earliest. The first ads in *CCC* for disciplinary volumes, and not mixtures of professional or teaching materials, came from Boynton Cook in 1981 and 1982. So I would argue that we are an even younger field and discipline than we think.

Zone 3. The Revolt of the Second Generation. The professional identity composed by the first generation itself reaches a crisis point, and is rewritten according to the antithetical needs of the new generation of scholars and teachers. At this moment, retrojection of mythic histories onto the past occurs, as professionals, trying to establish themselves and their authority in the field, argue against what they take to be the essential character of first generation thought and identity. It is typical for new formations in this zone to find their roots far back in the past, to convince both their opponents and themselves that they are legitimate. Such histories also provide a language and a series of role models and foils in which to form identity.

I believe we are right smack dab in the middle of this phase and that the expressivist menace, as well as the current process menace, are part of a deauthorization move. And our futures?

The model is recursive and spirals back to earlier zones.

Zone 4. Third Generation Consolidation and Thereafter. The social formation either a) fragments and the subcommunities establish independent identities; b) one social fragment in the formation predominates, rewriting the history of the field in its image while erasing alternative histories; or c) new work forges new categories and identities that can incorporate first and second generation work in a consolidated identity in which, however, ideas and practices are more explicitly owned and authored by schools of thought and their individual leaders. Possible forerunners of the third way is new work by Gale (1996), Miller (1996), and Sirc (1997). Although these writers are composing innovative new ways of reconceptualizing our work and our identity, we cannot go home. Within the formation, boundaries of authorship and authority are now in place and policed. But in these ends, we find our beginnings.

REFERENCES

Abrams, M.E. (1953). *The mirror and the lamp*. New York: Oxford University Press.

Aycock, C. (1985). *New critical rhetoric and composition*. Unpublished doctoral dissertation, University of Southern California, Los Angeles.

Bateman, D. (1963, November). The psychology of composition: (I) Suitable conditions for composing. *Center for School Experimentation Bulletin, 1*, 1–15.

Berlin, J. (1987). *Rhetoric and reality: Writing instruction in American colleges*. Carbondale, IL: Southern Illinois University Press.

Berthoff, A. E. (1991). Rhetoric as hermeneutic. *CCC, 42*(3), 279–287.

Berthoff, A. E. (1992). Semiotics and Edward Sapir. In T. Sebeok (Ed.), *Recent developments in theory and history: The semiotic web* (pp. 47–60). New York: Mouton.

Berthoff, A. E. (1996). Problem dissolving by triadic means. *College English, 58*(1), 9–21.

Bizzell, P. (1992). College composition: Initiation into the academic discourse community. In *Academic discourse and critical consciousness* (pp. 105–128). Pittsburgh, PA: University of Pittsburgh Press.

Braungart, R. (1984, Spring). Historical generations and generation units: A global pattern of youth movements. *Journal of Political and Military Sociology, 12,* 113–135.

Britton, J. (1970). *Language and learning*. New York: Penguin.

Brooks, C., & Warren, R. (1949). *Modern rhetoric*. New York: Harcourt Brace.

Bunkers, S., & Huff, C. (Eds.). (1996). *Inscribing the daily: Critical essays on women's diaries*. Amherst, MA: University of Massachusetts Press.

Conference on College Composition and Communication. (1974). Students' right to their own language. *College Composition and Communication, 25*(3), 1–32.

Connors, R. (1981). Current-traditional rhetoric: Thirty years of *Writing with a purpose*. *Rhetorical Society Quarterly, 4,* 208–221.

D'Angelo, F. (1975). *A conceptual theory of rhetoric*. Cambridge, MA: Winthrop.

Duberman, M. (1972). *Black mountain: An exploration of community*. New York: Norton.

Faigley, L. (1992). Coherent contradictions: The conflicting rhetoric of writing textbooks. In *Fragments of rationality: Postmodernity and the subject of composition* (pp. 132–162). Pittsburgh, PA: University of Pittsburgh Press.

Gale, X. (1996). *Teachers, discourses, and authority in the postmodern composition classroom*. Albany, NY: State University of New York Press.

Haley, A., & X, M. (1981). *The autobiography of Malcolm X*. New York: Ballantine. (Original work published 1965)

Heath, S. (1983). *Ways with words*. New York: Cambridge University Press.

Industry sales rose 5% in 1995, to 19.8 billion; Kids PB best. (1996, March 18). *Publishers Weekly, 243*(12), 13.

Jackson, G. (1970). *Soledad brother*. New York: Bantam.

Kinneavy, J. (1971). *A theory of discourse*. New York: Norton.

Marx, K. (1990). *Capital: A critique of political economy* (Vol. 1). New York: Penguin.

McCrimmon, J. (1950). *Writing with a purpose*. Boston: Houghton Mifflin.

Miller, R. (1996). The nervous system. *College English, 58,* 265–286.

Moffett, J. (1968). *Teaching the universe of discourse*. Boston: Houghton Mifflin.

Motz, M. (1987). Folk expression of time and place: Nineteenth-century Midwestern rural diaries. *Journal of American Folklore, 100,* 131–147.

Neel, J. (Ed.). (1978). *Options for the teaching of English: Freshman composition*. New York: Modern Language Association.

North, S. (1987). *The making of knowledge in composition: Portrait of an emerging field*. Upper Montclair, NJ: Boynton Cook.

Nystrand, M., Greene, S., & Wiemelt, J. (Eds.). (1993). Where did composition studies come from? An intellectual history. *Written Communication, 10*(3), 267–333.

Phillips, D., Greenberg, R., & Gibson, S. (1993). College composition and communication: Chronicling a discipline's growth. *College Composition and Ccommunication, 44*(4), 443–465.

Radway, J. (1991). *Reading the romance: Women, patriarchy, and popular literature* (2nd ed.). Chapel Hill, NC: University of North Carolina Press.

Shamoon, L., & Wall, B. (1995). The things that go without saying in composition studies: A colloquy including Robert Swegleer, Nedra Reynolds, Linda Shamoon, Marjorie Roemer, Beverly Wall, Linda Petersen, Lynn Z. Bloom, Roxanne Mountford, John Trimbur, Judith Goleman, Robert Connors. *Journal of Advanced Composition, 15*(2), 281–320.

Sirc, G. (1997). Never mind the tagmemics, where's the sex pistols? *College Composition and Communication, 48*(1), 9–29.

Strain, M. (1993). Toward a hermeneutic model of composition history: Robert Carlsen's "The state of the profession 1961–1962." *Journal of Advanced Composition, 13*(1), 217–240.

Vonnegut, K. (1969). *Slaughterhouse-five*. New York: Dell.

Volosinov, V. (1986). *Marxism and the philosophy of language*. Cambridge, MA: Harvard University Press.

Young, R., Becker, A., & Pike, K. (1970). *Rhetoric: Discovery and change*. New York: Harcourt, Brace, Jovanovich.

Zebroski, J. (1994). *Thinking through theory: Vygotskian perspectives on the teaching of writing*. Portsmouth, NH: Boynton Cook.

Zebroski, J. (forthcoming, a). Toward a theory of theory for composition studies. In C. Farris & C. Anson (Eds.), *Composition research as critical practice*. Logan, UT: Utah State University Press.

Zebroski, J. (forthcoming, b). How textbook advertisements compose composition. In X. L. Gale (Ed.), *Composition textbooks and postmodernity: Theory, pedagogy, and praxis*. Albany, NY: State University of New York Press.

Zebroski, J. (forthcoming, c). Intellectual property, authority, and social formation: Sociohistoricist perspectives on the author function. In A. Roy & L. Buranen (Eds.), *Perspectives on plagiarism: Intellectual property in a postmodern world*. Albany, NY: State University of New York Press.

Zebroski, J. (forthcoming, d). A theory of social formation. In *Writing class: The working class struggle for composition and rhetoric*. Portsmouth, NY: Boynton Cook/Heinemann.

chapter 7

A Brief History of Writing Assessment in the Late Twentieth Century: The Writer Comes Center Stage

Kathleen Blake Yancey
Clemson University

During the last three decades, writing assessment has shifted ground dramatically. It's commonplace, for instance, to talk about such shifts in terms of method: from objective measures like multiple guess tests to more "subjective" and yet more valid measures like essay tests and portfolios. It's commonplace to talk about recent developments in writing assessment in terms of epistemology: from positivism to constructivism. In this essay, I'll call on both these shifts in my efforts to gloss writing assessment's recent history, that is, the history as marked by the shifts that we've seen in the last 30 years. But in detailing the particulars of this history, I'd like as well to thematize it, to emphasize another, more unacknowledged dimension of writing assessment: its positioning and its shaping of the self.

As Faigley (1989) has pointed out in his article "Judging Writing, Judging Selves," the writer him/herself has increasingly become the locus of attention in our evaluative schemes as well as in our classroom practice. Allowing the self to take center stage problematizes assessment, I agree, and I'll examine the difficulties such centering provokes, especially those raised by portfolio assessment and its reflective components.

But it's not a one-sided proposition: figuring the self in writing assessment practice and theory also allows us to bring an ethical dimension to writing assessment heretofore absent, and as such it works toward writing assessment serving humane ends.

My thesis, then: In the recent practices of writing assessment, the more self, the worse; but also, the more self, the better.

WRITING ASSESSMENT: THE TEST

Twenty-five years ago, as scholars in writing assessment have documented well, writing ability was measured by way of a test, a positivistic and indirect measure—typically, a multiple choice test of grammar and usage given under lablike conditions and predicated on a single, universal norm for all writers. Put in a way more consonant with my theme, such a measure predicated a singular, unvarying writer as the ideal: reading each test item the same way; choosing each same right answer; embodying the same text—embodying both literally and figuratively. To the extent that writers could correctly identify the items representing Standard Edited American English, they were assumed to write well.

Ironically, positivism—which depends on an external reality as its litmus test—relied as much on its (hidden) assumptions as on empirical evidence. The measures of writing based in positivism assume as their ideal a single right (and usually white, and usually male) writer that the myriad of writers taking this test must replicate if they are to succeed. Put in terms of the test intersecting with the self, we have as an underlying deterministic construct *the single predictable self*. In rewarding this single model of a writer, as Hanson's (1993) work suggests, such tests shape all our writers into this single variety. It's a case of universalized discourse run amuck.

WRITING ASSESSMENT: THE EVALUATION

Ten years later, as Greenberg (1992) and White (1993) have detailed, our test of writing changed, in three significant ways:

1) it became an evaluation of writing;
2) through asking for essays, it required writing; and
3) it was holistically scored.

As a direct measure, an essay test's face validity made it an obvious preference for teachers of writing. But the move to an essay test from the ubiquitous set of multiple-choice questions was motivated by more than its face validity, by more than its congruence with what it was we were trying to measure. For one thing, as Perl (1994) makes clear in her *Landmark Essays* collection—researched and articulated by Emig, Perl, Sommers, and Flowers and Hayes, among others—process-based methods of composing seemed at odds with the tasks set for writers in objective measures. Essay tests, like classroom tasks, were *writing tasks*, not editing tasks or guessing tasks. For another thing, objective measures seemed at odds with process-based teaching. It wasn't only that we had learned about composing processes; it was that we were learning about *teaching those composing processes*—and in each case, the more we learned, the odder it seemed to be giving a grammatical or editing test as a measure of what we were teaching.

And more than odd. It was, as White (1993) explains, wrong: wrong and unethical to use these measures to *pre-empt* students' education: as White puts it, to "grade, label, place and screen out students [who] seemed then (as now) to demean education in general and writing in particular" (p. 84), which, he says, was the purpose of much large scale assessment. During the late 1970s and into the 1980s, then, writing assessment began to be seen less like testing and more like writing, a writing assessment-as-social-act, one with an accompanying, explicit ideology from which it could not be separated and with accompanying ethical consequences that were likewise to be considered.

As a social act, writing assessment-qua-holistic scoring would do more than sort; it too would shape students. "To the atomization of education," White (1993) says, holistic scoring

> brought a sense of connection, unity, wholeness; to the bureaucratic machinery of fill-in-the-bubble testing, it brought human writers and human readers; to a true–false world of memorized answers to simplified questions, it brought the possibility of complexity; to socially biased correctness, it brought critical thinking. (p. 88)

Writing assessment isn't, in these terms, an afterthought to the teaching of writing: it is a central, shaping activity. And more specifically, the shift to holistic scoring humanized education precisely *because* it allowed the self in.

At the same time, however, the self that was allowed in took pretty narrow forms. In multiple-choice tests, admittedly, the self is merely a passive, forced-choice response to an expert's understanding of language conventions. Agency is neither desired nor allowed. In a holistically scored essay, the self is a producer of text, an agent who creates text. Still, the text that is created is conventionally and substantively determined—some might say overdetermined—by an other, an expert, who creates the prompt, who designs the scoring guide used to evaluate the text, who trains the readers that do the scoring. The authorship of such a text, accordingly, is likely to be a weak, static, single-voiced, single-pointed self who anticipates and fulfills the expert's expectations, whose successful views and textual forms can be forecast. At best, agency is limited. In sum, holistic scoring permits a self-in-writing, but it is a very limited self, with very circumscribed agency.

In part, such limitations are a function of the test itself, as White (1993) acknowledges: first, essay tests measure only products; second, and perhaps more important, the products they measure bear small correspondence to the kind of writing we see outside of an assessment context. "While it is true that students producing text during a test are doing a kind of writing," White explains, "its 'reality' is of a peculiar kind: first draft (usually), pressured, driven by external motivation rather than an internal need to say something, designed to meet someone else's topic and grading criteria" (p. 90). The context of (real) writing, to understate, is not quite the context of holistic scoring, and the difference in such contexts matters. And a third factor: the essay is read a-rhetorically, without any context other than the context invoked by the testing mechanism itself: that is, the directions, the stack of responses, the scoring criteria. Without any other context—that is, without the multiple contexts that more typically embed writing-as-social-act—the power of the idealized, forecasted text both dominates and determines. Such a model of text—text as correct answer—does not admit alternative discourses conceptually or pragmatically. As important, of course, it does not admit multiple selves.

Holistic scoring, then, made explicit several of the assumptions that were previously masked. For one, any writing assessment is an ideological act: it assumes an *answer*—possibly, many answers—and as important, an *answerer*, not the test-taker, but the test-owner, the person who brokers the power relations among *those who test, those who implement tests,* and *those who take tests*. When holistic scoring became the writing assessment vehicle of choice, it did more than make evaluation congruent with research and practice; it brought the teacher self as well as the student self into the mix (Murphy, 1997). In the old "test" model, the test designers and the test implementers were one and the same people; the students were the recipients of the exercise; and the teachers were the invisible and silent members of this dynamic. Presumed to deliver the instruction on which the students were tested, faculty were nonetheless not presumed to be sophisticated enough to conduct the evaluation that mattered (Williamson, 1994). As outlined in White's *Teaching and Assessing Writing* (1985), holistic assessment of writing mounted a direct challenge to this assumption. It invited the teachers into the process, even if that invitation was limited (Elbow & Yancey, 1994). As in the past, teachers could continue to help students prepare for the essay evaluation, but now they also could—if properly trained—score the essays. In fact, a benefit of essay evaluation was precisely this implied linkage: the trained teacher could in turn train her students. Again, however, the selfhood permitted, in this case for the teacher, is severely restricted.

WRITING ASSESSMENT: THE WRITERLY SELF

Today, the writing assessment vehicle of choice is the portfolio: for placement, for exit, for classroom grading, for collaborative inquiry among faculty. The portfolio of writing—a set of multiple kinds of texts contextualized and/or interpreted by the composer in a discourse called reflection (Yancey, 1992)—likewise assumes a kind of writer, one who functions in community. As Greene and Ackerman (1995) explain, "Readers and writers engage in efforts after meaning because of a sense of place, a sense of belonging and of participating in a community—even if that engagement and participation leads to miscommunication" (p. 410). The *place* of writing—typically but not always the classroom or the school--intersects with the place of assessment, the portfolio, so that the assessment context thus becomes more authentic and more naturalistic as well as genuinely social.

Theoretically, this explicit connecting—of instruction to assessment—has been newly conceptualized in assessment theory. Camp (1993), Lucas (1988), and Moss (1994) have all argued that measure of the validity of any writing assessment is related to its exercising beneficent influence on the teaching/learning context. Such validity is known, alternatively, as ecological validity and systemic validity. Portfolios purport to provide that linkage, to enact that validity.

In part, they make such a link because they draw on texts composed in the classroom; in part, they make this link because they can do what cannot be done in an essay test, that is, represent process; and, most importantly, they make this link because by means of a reflection, students are asked to locate their own work—through contextualizing it, for example, or interpreting it. Reflection is thought to enhance such validity because it requires that students narrate, analyze, and evaluate their own learning and their own texts. Thus is a direct link made to student learning.

As a vehicle, portfolios have themselves encouraged the self to step center stage in two ways. First, as is obvious, reading multiple texts is a different activity than reading a single text (Burnham, 1986; Yancey,

1994). When readers look for something to stabilize their reading of divergent texts, they often turn to the writer: who is the writer of these texts, they ask as they move from one to the next (Schuster, 1994; Sommers, Black, Daiker, & Stygall, 1993). Second, turning to the writer is itself encouraged by the reflection, which many classroom teachers and faculty assign as a personal-essay-of-sorts. In the Miami University program *(The Best of Miami University's Portfolios*, 1992), for instance, students are told the following:

> his [reflective, introductory] letter, addressed to Miami University writing teachers, introduces you and your portfolio. It may describe the process used in creating any one portfolio piece, discuss important choices in creating the portfolio, explain the place of writing in your life, chronicle your development as a writer, assess the strengths and weaknesses of your writing, or combine these approaches. Your letter should provide readers with a clearer understanding of *who you are as a writer and a person*. (emphasis added; p. 113)

Likewise, a handout from the now lapsed University of Michigan program, which requires portfolios of all entering students, says in part,

> In order to read your portfolio accurately, we need some background information about each of the pieces. We need to know what the occasion for the writing was, and who the audience for the piece was. We would like to hear anything you would like to tell us about the process you used in writing each piece, what you learned from writing these pieces, what you like about these pieces, and why you selected them for your portfolio. We are interested in learning about your development *as a writer* over time. (emphasis added)

With directions like these informing what is often the first piece of writing in a portfolio, it is no wonder that readers find a self in the writing.

Better, in theory at least: The readers will find multiple selves. In portfolios, as Belanoff (1994) and Berlin (1994) have suggested, we see writers anew, as multi-selved experts of their own knowledge and their own texts, through an agency only made possible through textual diversity and multiple communities. Berlin talks about the writer as assuming multiple subject positions, Belanoff about multivocality; both are talking about a writer who can compose to different purposes on different occasions for different audiences in different genres. Within the portfolio, writing—like the self—is social, situated, and appropriately postmodern. Seen through this lens, writing assessment in the last 30 years has moved from what Gergen (1991) calls a "totalizing" discourse to full expression: In "contrast to the narrow range of options and the oppressive restraints favored by totalizing systems of understanding, postmodernism opens the way to the full expression of all discourses, to a free play of discourses" (p. 247). This, at least, is the hope.

The hope, to continue the postmodern metaphor here, is under erasure in several ways, three of which I'd like to highlight. The first of these concerns is our tendency to create a master narrative of progress, one that fails to account for "the other," that fails to critique. The second is the role that reflection currently plays in the assessment process; when we critique this role, we begin to raise the kinds of questions that can inform theory and enhance practice. Finally, however, moving the self to center stage suggests a more integral link between the ways we assess and the kinds of ethical behavior our assessment practices entail.

MASTER NARRATIVES AS TOTALIZING DISCOURSE

When we review the history of writing assessment, we see a plot of progress, of movement from the "bad" days of standardized measures to the "humanizing" days of holistic scoring to the days of "multiply discoursed," "multivocal" salvation that portfolios have wrought. (To some extent, of course, I've just sounded this narrative myself here.) To note this tendency to celebrate improvement is not, however, to call such progress into question. Certainly asking students to write—if what we care about is writing—and asking them to write multiple kinds of texts is a sensible move, a decided improvement from asking them to edit another's prose, even from asking them to write a single text. Still, the claims made typically surpass the realities encountered. Portfolios, for instance, are too often mere (and redundant) collections of holistically scored essays—not quite the free play of discourse celebrated above. As important, the narratives of writing assessment progress have worked against our observing contradictions, against our seeing discontinuities, against our critique—until, of course, the next seemingly paradigm-displacing shift occurs. And yet such critique is crucial if we are to understand our own practice, if we are to enhance it, even if we are to change it.

REFLECTION IN PORTFOLIOS: A CRITIQUE

The most impressive critique of portfolio practice to date is provided by Schuster (1994). He details four problems with portfolios when they are used for large-scale assessment: 1) students' using in-course portfolios texts written elsewhere; 2) teachers' overcollaborating with their students; 3) teachers' fictionalizing students, made possible by the reflective letter; and 4) teachers' mediating differences among the kinds of writing in the portfolio.

Three of these concerns, while legitimate from Schuster's (1994) perspective, speak more to alternate models of assessment than to objections to portfolio assessment per se. Alternate models—and it's a sign of multiple discourses that we currently have multiple models—make equally persuasive albeit different assumptions about writing and writers. Let me comment briefly on one of Schuster's concerns as illustrative of this axiom. Schuster wants the texts in the portfolios to be produced in the course for which the students are receiving a passing grade: fair enough. But there are other analogous models that are predicated on another, equally persuasive way of seeing writing assessment: through *the writer as a product of all related writing experiences*. In such a case, the institutional setting (not to mention the curricular setting) is less important than the level of performance in multiple rhetorical situations demonstrated in the portfolio. Students seeking to exempt a WAC course at George Mason University, for example, can include writing from work contexts, as can students at Eckerd College fulfilling a writing proficiency portfolio graduation requirement. Students at Washington State University, to cite another well-known example, commonly include texts from other schools to meet their rising-junior requirement; this is especially useful for the large number of transfer students who enroll there. So the appropriate role that "writing-outside"—that is, the writing completed outside a specific curricular or institutional context—will play in any assessment enterprise is an open question, and a good one. But a question more than a concern.

Fictionalizing the self, however, is another matter, and too it's directly related to our theme of student taking center stage. If Schuster (1994) is correct in his observations, we have some serious rethinking to do. Briefly, he suggests that fictionalizing is particularly invited in the reflective text, since it identifies the *writer* (not just the writing), personalizing and particularizing him or her, often as a function of the kinds of directions given to the student. More to the point, when faced with that text, he says, we have a "strong tendency to create a portrait of the writer" (p. 319), a practice at odds with the (nonfictionalized) purpose of assessment:

> In effect, fictionalizing student authors moves readers away from normed criteria, replacing careful evaluation with reader response.... Presumptions concerning personality, intention, behavior and the like skew readings or turn assessment into novel reading.... Such fictionalizing serves a useful purpose within a classroom; by doing so, instructors individualize

> and humanize their students, or at the very least, create narrative explanations and justifications for student work. Writing assessment, however, demands that we exclusively evaluate what the student has produced on the page in the portfolio. Fictionalizing in this context can only obscure judgment. (p. 319)

Schuster's point here is well taken; it provides a keen point of departure for considering our own practice, particularly in light of what we know about reading practices and about student learning as well as about writing assessment.

But first: a few caveats. Fictionalizing, as Schuster (1994) himself suggests, can play a useful role: in the classroom, it is through the power of fictionalizing ourselves into roles otherwise foreign that we become that which we might not. Students become writers, in part, precisely because they can fictionalize and imagine and rehearse their way into such a role, just as prospective teachers imagine themselves into a faculty role. So the fictionalizing that is useful in the classroom takes multiple forms, for both teachers and students. As Schuster suggests, then, fictionalizing per se isn't the problem: it's when and where it occurs.

The assumption here, however, seems to be that we don't fictionalize when we read single texts. I'd respectfully suggest that texts routinely invite us to create a portrait of a writer. That in fact was the point of Faigley's (1989) indictment in "Judging Writing, Judging Selves": that what faculty were praising was the very ethos *they* were creating in their reading process. Of course, as Schuster (1994) quite rightly suggests, portfolios *don't* present an exception to this observation--and worse (from his perspective) there is some evidence beyond that on his own campus for the portfolio reflective text *qua* text inviting such fictionalizing. For instance, the Miami University researchers concur, but they take another stance: that it is this inclusion of the personal in the portfolio that readers respond to favorably, and that this *enhances* the reading process (Sommers, Black, Daiker, & Stygall, 1993). Researchers at the University of Cincinnati have found similar results; their work suggests that readers create not only a persona of the author, but also the classroom context in which he or she works. But they see this "narrativizing tendency" on the part of readers as inevitable:

> This narrativizing tendency constitutes one of our primary ways of understanding, one of our primary ways of making sense of the world, and is an essential strategy in comprehension. As far as portfolio evaluation is concerned, rather than say that narrativizing is right or wrong, perhaps we should start by admitting its inevitability, and by advising teachers to be aware of this tendency and not overvalue the stories we create. (Schultz, Durst, & Roemer, in press)

The question, then, seems not to be so much how to eliminate fictionalizing from the assessment process, if indeed this tendency is inevitable, but rather to consider how our reading and our judgment are affected by the inclusion of the personal.

And a final thought: The inclusion of the personal in these models of portfolio assessment is, if anything, heightened by three factors that themselves could be adjusted. In the first place, the reflective texts discussed here come first in the packet. As an item in a set of texts (portfolio), the reflective text exerts a disproportionate influence on the reading of the portfolio. So, if fictionalizing is a concern, perhaps placing the reflective text elsewhere in the packet, at the conclusion, for instance, might diminish its effects. In the second place, we might ask that the reflection take a form other than a letter. For most students, the letter is a personal genre, and given the open directions that seem all-too-characteristic for reflective texts, student writers quite correctly see this text as intentionally personal. What would happen if we asked for a "reflective essay" rather than letter? How might that change both our texts and our readings? (Yancey, 1996). In the third place, we could think a little more precisely about what purposes we want the reflection to serve and could sculpt our directions toward those ends. The directions that we've looked at tend to welcome virtually all observations and to assume that all responses are equally valuable. But of course all responses aren't equal; we do privilege some more than others. As well-intended as such freedom may be, it seems also at odds with any sense of the task that we want the reflection to perform. Are we interested in students' judgments about their own work and how they arrived at those? Are we interested in their understanding and application of writing process? Are we interested in the relationship between their judgments and our judgments about their texts? Once we have these answers, and once we have them provided to students, what kinds of texts will students produce, how will we read them, and how will they influence our evaluation?

More generally, how much of the writer do we want in an assessment context? Clearly, the agentless writer of the multiple-choice test is too little, as is the single-voiced and often-scripted writer of the essay test. But can the portfolio invite too much? What is appropriate, and why?

WRITING ASSESSMENT AS ETHICAL ACTIVITY

The second factor influencing current theory and practice in writing assessment is a variation on the theme of systemic validity. As we think about writers and what we ask of them in an assessment exercise, we return to writing-assessment-as-social-act. Such a conception necessarily entails a set of conventions and ethics. It too complicates and problematizes assessment.

Hilgers (1996) provides us with a good example of such a case. As director of the Manoa Writing Program, he is concerned about what he calls the "appropriate use" dimension of portfolios. He explains his concern by reference to the CCCC Position Statement on Writing Assessment (CCCC Committee on Assessment, 1994), which constructs writing as a social act and which recommends the use of multiple texts of the kind we see in portfolios:

> Clearly, among the prime benefits of portfolio-based assessment is the learning that occurs when teacher-assessors talk about the portfolios before them. Another benefit, less documented, has to do with the work students do when they compose, assemble, and reflectively assess their portfolio. A third benefit is the real wealth of information that each individual portfolio can provide, for example, a student and her advisor as they work together to plot course choices and the like for the next semester or year.
>
> My emerging question, then, is something like this. Is there any benefit to requiring students to develop portfolios when a primary concern (imposed or implied) of those who set the requirement is to achieve a unidimensional decision in the quickest time at the least cost?
>
> This is becoming a very real concern on this campus as we revisit our own five-hour, two essay placement exam for incoming freshmen in light of the CCCC policy statement on the assessment of writing. Some of us see that portfolios of high school work are the only vehicle which would allow us to really conform with those principles. Others, however, wonder about the legitimacy of asking high-school students and their teachers to work on the portfolio-development project when all we will give it is ten minutes of attention for a relatively low-stakes decision: whether the student will have to take a remedial writing course at a community college or will be placed into one of our mainstream introductory writing courses (which happens to about 95% of the 2,000 students we test each year).
>
> Our current exam takes most of the day in an incoming student's life. It does require that students write two different types of essays and it gives them ample time to revise them. Each essay is read by at least two faculty members (paid about $17 per hour). Our accuracy, at least as measured by teachers' subsequent efforts to place students differently, is probably 98%. Nonetheless, our exam falls far short of following the principles set forth by CCCC.
>
> As much as I might like to require portfolios from all incoming students, I am not sure that doing so would be consistent with the whole ideology of

> portfolio-based development and assessment (or perhaps even ethical) if our use of them will be no more broadly based than is our current use of our placement examination. I have read and heard very little discussion of this "appropriate use" dimension of portfolio use.

A couple of points here, at least, are worth making. First, writing assessment is constructed here as an exercise that should give something back to the writer; if it cannot give back in proportional measure, it should change what it requires. Second, there is an implied assumption here that for the effort required to produce multiple texts and to compose a portfolio, students should receive more than a cursory reading. Third, the readers' needs should be considered as well: assessment should aspire to embody humane conditions for *all its participants*. In a word, this way of conceptualizing writing assessment is humane. Again, it's also problematic, but only because Hilgers (1996) has gone to the trouble of articulating the assumptions underlying the choices. Such articulation, such consideration of options and their consequences, move all of us toward a more humane, more ethical writing assessment. In this case, then, Hilgers models for us the kinds of questions we should be asking of all writing assessment exercises.

CONCLUSION

In this brief history of writing assessment in the years 1965 to 1995, we see a modern self coming center stage and becoming postmodern. We see other shifts as well:

- a shift from a focus on choosing among others' copy-editing options, for instance, to creating a single text, then to producing multiple texts and accompanying them with metanarrative;
- a shift from text to text-qua-context;
- a shift from a-rhetorical to social; and
- a shift from text(s) to writer.

As we have navigated these shifts, our theoretical questions have changed: from how we can improve scoring agreement among essay raters, for instance, to how much writing is appropriate in an assessment exercise and to how we can assure that writing assessment serves ethical ends. As a rhetorical act, writing assessment itself is seen differently: as its own agent with responsibilities to all its participants. As a narrative of progress, writing assessment is beginning to be more reflective about its own practice, to uncover assumptions we bring to texts and that we create as we read texts, to see what we do in light of what others do, to understand that what we do is social and thus entails both ideological and ethical dimensions that themselves are increasingly very much a part of both theory and practice.

As Schuster (1994) says, the "struggle of portfolio assessment may well be to retain the fundamental value of helping students construct a writerly self through the authoring of a portfolio while simultaneously finding ways to deemphasize and contextualize its evaluative consequences" (p. 323). The recent history of writing assessment suggests that the writerly self will continue to focus our attention, to problematize our practice, to challenge our best-laid plans.

Such a focus also ensures that we keep our writing assessments targeted on the places they belong: on our students and on ways to help them.

REFERENCES

Belanoff, P. (1994). Portfolios and literacy. In L. Black, D. Daiker, J. Sommers, & G. Stygall (Eds.), *New directions in portfolio assessment: Reflective practice, critical theory, and large-scale scoring* (pp. 13–24). Portsmouth, NH: Boynton/Cook Heinemann.

Berlin, J. (1994). The subversions of the portfolio. In L. Black, D. Daiker, J. Sommers, & G. Stygall (Eds.), *New directions in portfolio assessment: Reflective practice, critical theory, and large-scale scoring* (pp. 56–67). Portsmouth, NH: Boynton/Cook Heinemann.

The best of Miami University's portfolios. (1992). Oxford, OH: Miami University.

Burnham, C. (1986). Portfolio evaluation: Room to breathe and grow. In C. Bridges (Ed.), *Training the new teacher of composition* (pp. 125–138). Urbana, IL: National Council of Teachers of English.

CCCC Committee on Assessment. (1994). Writing assessment: A position statement. *College Composition and Communication, 46*, 430–437.

Camp, R. (1993). Changing the model for the direct assessment of writing. In M. Williamson & B. Huot (Eds.), *Validating holistic scoring for writing assessment* (pp. 45–79). Cresskill, NJ: Hampton.

Elbow, P., & Yancey, K. B. (1994). On the nature of holistic scoring and reading: An inquiry composed on email. *Assessing Writing, 1*, 91–109.

Faigley, L. (1989). Judging writing, judging selves. *College Composition and Communication, 40*, 395–412.

Gergen, K. (1991). *The saturated self.* New York: Basic Books.

Greenberg, K. (1992). Validity and reliability: Issues in the direct assessment of writing. *WPA: Writing Program Administration, 16*, 7–22.

Greene, S., & Ackerman, J. (1995). Expanding the constructivist metaphor: A rhetorical perspective on literacy research and practice. *Review of Educational Research, 65*, 383–420.

Hanson, F. A. (1993). *Testing testing*. Berkeley, CA: University of California Press.

Hilgers, T. (1996, October). *WPA-L* [Online]. Available: kyancey@clemson.edu

Lucas, C. (1988). Toward ecological evaluation: Recontextualizing literacy assessment. *The Quarterly, 10*, 4–17.

Moss, P. (1994) Can there be validity without reliability? *Educational researcher, 23*, 5–12.

Murphy, S. (1997). Teachers and students: Reclaiming assessment via portfolios. In K. B. Yancey & I. Weiser (Eds.), *Situating portfolios: Four perspectives* (pp. 72–89). Logan, UT: Utah State University Press.

Perl, S. (1994). *Landmark essays on writing process*. Davis, CA: Hermagoras Press.

Schultz, L., Durst, R., & Roemer, M. (1999). Stories of reading: Inside and outside the texts of portfolios. *Assessing Writing, 4*(2), 121–133.

Schuster, C. (1994). Climbing the slippery slope of writing assessment: The programmatic use of writing portfolios. In L. Black, D. Daiker, J. Sommers, & G. Stygall (Eds.), *New directions in portfolio assessment: Reflective practice, critical theory, and large-scale scoring* (pp. 314–325). Portsmouth, NH: Boynton/Cook Heinemann.

Sommers, J., Black, L., Daiker, D. A., & Stygall, G. (1993). The challenges of reading portfolios. *WPA: Writing Program Administration, 17*, 7–31.

White, E. (1985). *Teaching and assessing writing*. San Francisco: Jossey-Bass.

White, E. (1993). Holistic scoring: Past triumphs, future challenges. In M. Williamson & B. Huot (Eds.), *Validating holistic scoring for writing assessment* (pp. 79–108). Cresskill, NJ: Hampton.

Williamson, M. (1994). The worship of efficiency: Untangling practical and theoretical considerations in writing assessment. *Assessing Writing, 1*, 147–174.

Yancey, K. B. (1992). Portfolios in the writing classroom: A final reflection. In K. B. Yancey (Ed.), *Portfolios in the writing classroom: An introduction* (pp. 102–117). Urbana, IL: National Council of Teachers of English.

Yancey, K. B. (1994). Make haste slowly. In L. Black, D. Daiker, J. Sommers, & G. Stygall (Eds.), *New directions in portfolio assessment: Reflective practice, critical theory, and large-scale scoring* (pp. 210–219). Portsmouth, NH: Boynton/Cook Heinemann.

Yancey, K. B. (1996). Portfolio as genre, rhetoric as reflection: Situating selves, literacies, and knowledge. *WPA: Writing Program Administration, 20*, 55–70.

Watson Conference Oral History #2: Process Theory and the Shape of Composition Studies October 1996 Deborah Brandt, Janet Emig, and Sondra Perl

Bob McEachern, interviewer
edited by Pamela Takayoshi

Bob McEachern: Is process research still around now? In what form?

Janet Emig: A few years ago, I was checking the bibliography on a chapter June Bierbaum and I are doing on case study, and I think there were well over 500 dissertations on process, if the titles give us an indication of what's going on.

Deborah Brandt: I notice that process has remained central in much of the research on writing and learning. It is very much focused on students' interpretive processes, using think aloud protocols, and it is augmented by more contextualized observation, more long term natural study.

Sondra Perl: When I was putting together *Landmark Essays on Writing Processes*, I was tracing the evolution of research on writing processes. It seemed to me that the kind of work we once did is no longer appearing. The way we did our research has come under criticism in terms of being too controlled. What I was seeing were much larger projects where composing as an activity was still important, but people were looking much more closely at context. Examples are the kind of work being done by Anne Dyson, Mike Rose, and Glynda Hull. People are looking at composing as one aspect of literate activity. They are less likely to place students in laboratories and ask them to compose; rather, they are studying the places where writers work.

JE: With the exception probably being Anne Dyson, and it is interesting to see where her work has appeared in recent years. Anne has appeared most regularly in whatever has replaced *Elementary English*. But her work doesn't appear in *CCC*. It occasionally appears, I think, in *RTE* and she's doing very complex work of the contextualized sort that Sondra is describing.

SP: Deborah, you worked with this to some extent with your study on literacy, didn't you?

DB: Well, I don't think I would characterize the most recent stuff in that way. I'm hoping eventually to get back to individual processes with a much more cultural and historical understanding. That's my aim. In my work, we're talking about people's memories of how they encountered literacy across their lifetimes, and I think that is far from the immediate actions of composing. But I hope to get back there with this wider perspective.

SP: I think process research and the questions we raised in research still inform my teaching. After I completed my studies on composing, I did some ethnographic studies of teachers teaching. It was very much the same sort of inquiry: wanting to understand processes by immersing myself within them. Limited time right now prevents me from doing a larger study, but my interest has not disappeared. I think I probably have some graduate students who are beginning to think along the lines of documenting literacy practices in context which, to me, is what grew out of composing research.

BM: I just got a copy of Joseph Harris's book, *Teaching Subject: Composition Since 1966*, and in a chapter on process, he argues that one of the failures of process was that it really didn't affect college classrooms much. At least, it didn't change the way people began teaching.

JE: Well, yeah. The greater effect was in the schools. I cannot speak to the college because I know much more about what happens in schools. That is simply not true where schools are concerned, when you think of the number of National Writing Projects and the number of classrooms in which process is used. There are literally millions and millions of schoolchildren who are now authoring and making their own books and having a totally different experience of composition from what they would have had in the '50s.

DB: Workshop, I think, is the norm in college writing classrooms and that derives from making the activity of writing, the work of writing, the center of concern in the classroom. Collaborative groups, drafting, revising—I think they all descended from the early work of Emig, Perl, and others.

SP: I don't know how widespread it is at the college level. Even on my own campus, there are people who have been teaching writing for years and their classrooms don't resemble mine at all. So although I do not know what Harris is looking at, I think I would probably agree with him that there's been less of an impact on college campuses, except in certain important centers—perhaps places that have Ph.D. programs and places where TA training is very much in line with current theory. In the session I was just in, there were people who have been in classrooms with "process teachers" who have not found it particularly liberating. They saw abuses in it, but you can see abuses in all pedagogy. I agree with Janet that teachers who came to writing projects, attended summer institutes, and took writing seriously returned to their classrooms with a very clear idea of what they wanted to do, including giving students freedom and access to writing, to a choice of topics, to writing drafts, to working in small groups and celebrating the kinds of work they could do. Much of this did not exist before the writing projects came on the scene.

JE: It might have been a characteristic of the sessions I have been in, but I haven't heard sufficient talk from my point of view of the power and effect of the National Writing Project upon changing classroom practice. We have stunning data that demonstrates that it has made a difference to how children fare on tests, how their attitudes change toward literacy, and we can cite these. A session I wish were present at this meeting is one that acknowledges the role of the writing projects in the professionalization of the field. My concern is that the implication is it happened all at the college level, and this an inaccurate, incomplete portrait of the period. One needs to know who we were, the nonprograms in which we found ourselves, and the level of hostility to what we were doing from both sides. This is not literary study and this is not social science; it's a hybrid. So there we were. It might have changed its nature later, but we had many, many audiences to bow to, particularly if we were going to continue living in academe.

BM: How did cognitive studies pick up on process studies?

JE: I was quite startled to see what we thought was a fairly complex and somewhat inchoate process in flow charts. I found some of the work prematurely reapplied. I do want to say, though, that Linda Flower was a pioneer and what she did, she did first. For me to be critical is just as unwarranted as his [Harris's] being critical of us. Linda Flower, as Lisa Ede pointed out, is very active in literacy movements and she was crucial in the Center for Writing.

SP: I have a similar response which I'll frame a little differently. My understanding of Linda's approach is that she took a methodology from work being conducted in problem solving and applied it to writing. For instance, if you're solving a problem in mathematics, you can ask people to think out loud and you can follow how they arrive at their answer. Linda took this approach and said, "Let's define writing as a rhetorical problem and watch how people solve it." I had difficulty with the notion that you could take the protocols she had produced and assume that they described writing processes. My argument is that writing is much more of a bodily experience. Without thinking of cognition more broadly, we will never get at the more deeply embedded processes by which human beings make meaning, which, as Janet said earlier, leads to a philosophical inquiry about the nature of meaning and the nature of language. What was unfortunate, I think, is that all process studies came under the label of cognition. It isn't that writing is not a cognitive process, but that this is not all it is. It is much richer and far more difficult to articulate because there are, in fact, unspoken pieces of it—the groping and grasping that we all go through. I always felt that the label or rubric of cognition, particularly the cognition that came out of information processing and problem solving, was too narrow to reflect the richness of composing.

DB: I'll defend Linda Flower a little bit. Probably she was under the same kinds of pressures that you talked about. When you borrow theory from other places, you have some constraints that come with it. Her best work, in my view, has always been pedagogically driven. First of all, she has had a tremendous impact on the field. That was a very heady time, when she was spreading the idea of process. The expert/novice contrast, which has its problems and has been made more complex, still was a powerful move in pedagogy. The move wasn't to try to imitate the text—"Here is a well-crafted text, imitate it." She asked instead, what are the actual moves that experienced writers, effective writers, are using? How are they handling themselves? Those comparative studies, while problematic, enriched pedagogy, and they changed my mind about what I was trying to help students do.

SP: In those early days, we all thought we were contributing to the development of knowledge in this field. Both Nancy Sommers and I followed the prescriptions of social science research by conducting controlled studies. As Janet said, the specific methodology is not as important now as the fact that it focused on students and gave writing a central place in our work.

JE: Some recent descriptions of us make us sound as if we were doing these madly manipulative kinds of acts. What we thought we were doing, and we may not have been doing what we thought—we often aren't—was to illuminate what students actually did as they wrote, to make a more humane classroom possible and to persuade teachers that the only way to understand what was going on was if they themselves became writers. In other words, writing as a human activity became the center of the lives of not only students, but of those teaching them. Because, without what Polyani calls "personal knowledge," it is not possible to teach. You read the earlier accounts and you really wonder, for example, if McCrimmon ever wrote a poem.

DB: I think process has been so absorbed into the orientation of the field that it is forgotten—it is invisible. That is the tribute to it. I don't think we could have gotten anyplace else without that. I think of both Janet's study and Sondra's study: I always read them as extremely social. They were all about the positionality of the writers. Those questions were all there in the beginning. I never thought the social perspective needed to turn away from individual writers. I think it was just opening up and following through on latent questions that were in those early studies. I don't want to make process sound rosy, but it's just a very powerful idea. It was so powerful that it got absorbed and is so much a part of normal thinking that you can't tease it out.

BM: How do you answer criticisms of process studies?

SP: I think, certainly, one criticism was that it was apolitical. It was seen as too expressivist or individualistic. It began to seem bland to people. It didn't have an edge, at least the way people began to read it. We could probably argue that it was highly political to take students, particularly unskilled students, and put them at the center of an inquiry. Our work gave students room to compose their own ways to understanding and to teach us.

JE: I still happen to believe—as I've said too often—that the writing citizen is the most crucial part of any society and the person who is going to change and reform the society. I clearly believe in the power of certain kinds of writing to change systems. I think we have fairly good evidence from Marx and others like Thomas Paine that that is possible.

SP: For many years, actually just as I finished my dissertation, I was funded with my colleague, Richard Sterling, to direct the New York City

Writing Project. For 10 years, I thought of almost nothing else besides my own classroom and the work of other teachers in urban settings—

JE: And since I lived across the river, I can make some statements that she may be too modest to make about the effect that the Writing Project had upon the curriculum not only in New York City schools, but in the state of New York.

SP: They were very exciting years and it was wonderful to get to understand teaching from the way teachers in the schools see it, to be part of a national network. Again, not all projects were alike. But, by and large, there seemed to be a commitment to writing, to what writing meant in the lives of individual teachers and then what they would do with that in their classrooms. At the college level, there seems to be a different kind of conversation and a lack of opportunity to discuss teaching. We have done a disservice to ourselves in not foregrounding our pedagogies.

BM: What was your reaction to Bob Connors's discussion of the direction composition studies might take—the MLA-ization where it becomes very into theory and devaluative of practice versus a focus on practice in teaching?

JE: Whenever I predict the future, the only emotion I have is surprise, but I must say what I want to happen, and that is that we start being far more open and generous and get out of our departments. I am very critical of English departments—which are departments of cultural theory in too many cases, in my opinion—because I deliberately chose to live elsewhere. We need to get into the larger roles and not be over critical of what goes on in social sciences and misrepresent it.

DB: I think Connors was saying we have to stay connected to freshman composition. If we lose our connection to the course, we lose our connection to our history, and then we lose our discipline.

SP: I was struck by the man in the audience [at Connors's keynote] who said that while teaching may have been lost as a focus at big institutions with Ph.D. programs, the focus has not been lost in community colleges, where people are teaching five courses. Connors was describing a trend and a possibility, but one that may be true only in certain places. Ultimately, we're teaching writing, which focuses what we do, how we do it, who we are. It seems to me, if anything has been left out of our training, it is how to be reflective about what we do. Why don't we ask ourselves questions more often? For instance, how do I know what is happening here? How do I find out what is happening here? Who am I in this? What am I asking for? What do my students have the right to ask me for? What I want to privilege in our work is the act of teaching and what it means. Going into the classroom and closing the door is the most isolating move we make and it allows for abuse and too much silence. I would want to see a future that honors and makes public the daily work of the classroom at the university.

DB: I hope the field can continue to do all of this. But I am a bit bothered by Connors's critique of the critics in our field, people who do cultural studies or critical theory, because they play an essential role. I am dedicated to my teaching, but I am interested in understanding writing as a cultural and economic activity as it runs through history, and what I discover doesn't always translate into implications for teaching freshman composition. I would hope that I would have a place in composition, too. I don't know why people who are doing things that seem like literary criticism or lean toward literary theory should be considered traitors to composition. I don't understand that.

BM: If you could change something in the history of our discipline, what would it be?

JE: I would assure that anyone who is required or asked to teach would be given training in how to teach and that methods would not be regarded as some kind of rinky-dink activity, but rather a matter of developing a theory about a field and knowing the importance of enacting it with students. Much, much more attention to teaching than many departments of English are giving it. It is extraordinarily important and it is not a matter of those three to five days before a semester or quarter begins.

SP: From writing projects, I learned how important it is to have teachers of writing write often and not only in a professional voice. A life's work in my mind has to provide pleasure so that work is not only toil, but brings some kind of human joy with it. I don't mean that joy and pleasure are without critique or challenge or questions—just that often such qualities are lacking in our work.

DB: I wonder sometimes if Mina Shaughnessy had lived, that commitment to inclusion and diversity would have stayed stronger through the '80s. In the Reagan era, it just became easier for a lot of people to do work in comfortable places and to forget issues of diversity, inclusion, and justice. I think the field is suffering and higher education is suffering and too many people are suffering from that neglect. There was a lot of lost time.

JE: As I said, we were so late. We have always been. Where is the diversity in our community? It isn't here. It is terribly worrisome. We are not at all representative demographically of who our students are and who they will be.

SP: Do you think that is a result of how English departments treat students? Sometimes I try to determine what draws someone into our profession. What is it that gets us here? And I wonder if the exclusion starts much earlier on.

JE: I think it starts extremely early in American schools.

DB: I do, too.

Part III

Intellectual Influences and Disciplinary Narratives

chapter 8

Rereading Feminism's Absence and Presence in Composition

Kathleen Boardman
University of Nevada, Reno

Joy Ritchie
University of Nebraska-Lincoln

The complex history of composition's relationship to feminism cannot be told in a tidy, linear narrative. What we read, tell, and hear is a series of overlapping, parallel, and often contradictory stories. Some emphasize feminism as theory and composition as discipline, others focus on classroom practice in both feminism and composition, while still others elide those theory-practice and research-teaching boundaries. In rereading and retelling composition's past from a feminist viewpoint, many of us are trying to reclaim our own past, and, ironically, that is only partly possible. We have to reread in terms of our vision of the present. Our words about the past now are infused with our postmodern sensibilities about what words mean. Individual, self, voice: words like these we thought of as connections between revisionist teaching in composition and feminist practice in the 1970s. Now, seen through feminist theories of the 1990s, these terms are problematic. The current interest in feminist theory and methodology in composition also alerts us to the absence of explicit and systematic theorizing about gender in the professional and scholarly documents of the discipline in the 1970s and early 1980s. Yet, while the hindsight provided by feminist theory allows us to note these absences, it also enables narratives of composition's *connections with* and *disruption by* feminism.

Our own experience as feminist teachers also moves us to examine our intuitive understanding of the connections between feminism and composition that informed our practice. Both of us began teaching high school English in 1970, moved into college writing instruction in the late 1970s and 1980s, and did graduate work in composition in the 1980s. We were feminists, members of NOW and subscribers to *Ms.* magazine, advocates of the work of women writers, both student and professional. We experienced a revitalized, highly visible second-wave feminist movement and an energetic, emerging field in English: composition. Looking back, we cannot imagine a teaching practice that was not informed in some way by feminist principles; we want to tell a story of unarticulated but fundamental connections between the two. Yet neither of us can point to a time in the 1970s when we made explicit, systematic connections between the ideas of feminist theorists and compositionists; we did not see a space to discuss the gendered nature of writing. To evoke that time, we would also have to tell how these gaps in our own thinking about feminism reflected the relationship of feminism and composition.

Our interest in narratives that articulate the feminist absences, connections, and disruptions in the history of composition has led us to two sets of professional documents in English studies from the early 1970s. Reading for both feminist presence and absence in 1970s composition journals and in later accounts, we have teased out several overlapping narratives, including stories of absence or avoidance, stories about parallel tracks (one composition, one feminist), consciousness-raising stories, narratives that construct composition's leaders as "foremothers," and accounts of the feminization of composition. These narratives are "true" and "useful" in understanding the relationship of feminism to composition, but they are also problematic and partial. And, of course, in retelling and interweaving these stories, we are constructing yet another historical narrative.

FEMINIST ABSENCE AND PARALLEL TRACKS

One way to read the early 1970s is to highlight the absence of feminist perspectives from composition. Flynn (1988), for example, has seen composition and feminist theory before 1988 as largely incommunicado: "For the most part, the fields of feminist studies and composition studies have not engaged each other in a serious way" (p. 425). Sullivan (1992) argues that until the 1990s, there had been little systematic attention to gender difference and thus little feminism in composition studies. While the 1970s brought a flowering of feminist perspectives in the academy, composition's official, published discussions were indeed silent on issues of gender. This is particularly striking because in English departments, the work of composition as an emerging discipline was occurring right next door to, down the hall from, or in the basement under the work of feminist linguists and literary scholars. The irony of this apparent detachment has not yet been explored by feminist commentators of the 1990s, who pass quickly over the history of feminism-composition association as they move on to theorize about the present and the future.

Another version of the absence narrative is the assertion that composition and feminist theory followed parallel tracks. In their introduction to *Teaching Writing: Pedagogy, Gender, and Equity* (1987), Caywood and Overing declare that they have found little "scholarship on the relationships between feminist theory and the teaching of writing" and thus need to ask, "At what point did our parallel interest in feminism and revisionist writing theory converge?" (p. xi). While highlighting an absence of attention to gender, they also posit a more complicated reading of this absence by pointing to the parallel, or nearly parallel, lives of composition and feminist theory. According to this story, the two have run for years at about the same speed, in the same direction, along close lines. All that is needed, then, is for someone on one train to notice the other, heading to the same destination, and to make the necessary connections.

A review of the journal *College Composition and Communication* in the years 1970 to 1972 supports narratives of feminist absence in composition, while a reading of two special issues of *College English* in 1971 and 1972, the more general NCTE journal, dramatizes a parallel track of feminist thinking in English studies that might have been—and probably was—useful to feminists in composition. The February 1970 issue of *CCC* contains articles by Donald Murray and by William Coles, articulating many of the crucial progressive assumptions emerging in composition: the value of individual students' writing as an articulation of agency and selfhood rather than merely as an object of diagnosis and correction. Essays like these attest to the profession's increasing attempts in the 1970s to redefine writing and writing instruction. The *CCC* journals also contain several proposals for alternative freshman English courses for minority students, and the October 1972 issue contains the CCCC Executive Committee's Resolution, "The Student's Right to His Own Language," which promoted anguished debate in subsequent journals, but not over the use of the masculine singular pronoun. (For the 1974 special issue of *CCC*, the title became "Students' Right to Their Own Language.")

Even with disciplinary calls for cultural diversity in the curriculum and for students' rights to their own language, no space in *CCC* was available to theorize a gendered subject of writing, to open a discursive space for women to speak as women writers and teachers, or to consider the implications of Coles's (1970) goal for writing "to allow the student to put himself together" (p. 34). No one raised the question: What difference might it make if the student is female? In most of the essays, the student, if referred to, is either "he" or is not identified by gender at all. The absence of feminist perspectives in *CCC* may be contrasted with their presence in *College English*, notably in 1971 and 1972 special issues on women, which report on the newly formed MLA Commission on the Status of Women in the profession and document courses designed by feminists in English to reshape the curriculum from the standpoint of women students. Howe's (1971b) impassioned essay reports the inequities she uncovered as chair of the MLA commission. In addition to these first attempts to address the low status of women in the profession, Howe (1971a) and Showalter (1971) both illustrate their efforts to revise the curriculum with women students in mind. Showalter describes her newly organized course, "The Educated Woman in Literature," and Howe presents a writing course she designed to help women alter their self-image "from centuries of belief in their inferiority, as well as from male-dominated and controlled institutions" (p. 870). Howe's goals for her course were parallel to Coles's and to the "writing process" courses Murray and others were describing at the time. But Howe's goal was more overtly political than theirs and perhaps might be said to anticipate cultural studies courses of the 1990s: she wanted to allow students to examine the cultural contexts, including gender, that shaped their ideas about writing and their consciousness as writers. A second special issue of *College English*, in October 1972, is devoted to another group of essays presented at the MLA Women's Forum of the Commission on the Status of Women. This volume contains landmark essays concerning gender and the discipline of English, among them Olsen's "Women Who Are Writers in Our Century: One Out of Twelve" (1972) and Rich's "When We Dead Awaken: Writing as Re-vision" (1972). Both essays finesse the boundary between literature (reading/consumption) and composition (writing/production).

The *College English* essays demonstrate that, in contrast to the silence surrounding gender in college composition research, the wider discipline was constructing a discursive space for thinking, writing, and reading as women. They articulate the potential for student and teacher subjectivities that are not neutral or universal, but uniquely influenced by the textual, social, and political context of gender. Here were women trained as literary scholars and (most of them) experienced in writing instruction, thinking about textuality, evaluating how gendered discursive practices had shaped their own identities and those of their students, and linking their theoretical analysis to the pedagogical implications of such understandings.

Our sense of the absence of feminist perspectives in composition and at the same time a strong feminist presence in a parallel track of the discipline may be experienced as a lack of articulation, a failure to connect. Compositionists writing for *CCC* were not necessarily throwing up boundaries against feminist influence; nor was English studies in general wholeheartedly embracing feminist theories and issues: in the early 1970s, *College English* contained its own feminist discussions within the bounds of special issues on women. Many recent narratives emphasize the absence of feminist theorizing in the past as a stark backdrop for the energetic activity that is now filling the gap, making the connection at last. Teacher-researcher Ruth Ray (1993) takes a progressive view of the new "heightened interest in feminist studies" in composition, predicting that "the merging of these two fields...will undoubtedly be one of the richest subjects of inquiry for compositionists in the next few years" (p. 29). In narratives like these, the burgeoning of feminist theories and research in the past 10 years represents an intellectual coming of age—a new world opening as the feminism-composition connection has finally been made. These same years have witnessed not only a new majority of women among students studying for the Ph.D. in composition and rhetoric (Enos, 1996), but also a backlash against feminism in popular culture.

INTUITIVE CONNECTIONS AND PERMEABLE BOUNDARIES

Yet to insist only on a story of absence is to negate the work of many female and male teachers who tried to promote feminist principles and goals. It is also to ignore our own sense, as practitioners in the 1970s, that boundaries between feminism and composition were permeable and sometimes marked by unarticulated overlaps and crossovers. Among the *College English* authors we have just cited, Howe taught composition and wrote about how her course focused on women, and Rich taught writing with Shaughnessy at the City College of New York. Later, in the article "Taking Women Students Seriously" (1979), Rich described how the questions she learned to ask as a writing instructor about her minority students' experiences of education in a racist society took a gender turn when she moved to Douglass College and saw the stunning parallel questions she needed to ask about women students: "How does a woman gain a sense of her self in a system which devalues work done by women, denies the importance of female experience and is physically violent toward women?... How do we, as women, teach women students a canon of literature which has consistently excluded or depreciated female experience?" (p. 237).

Some gestures toward connecting composition with feminist language research appeared in the late 1970s in articles explaining, applying, and investigating claims made by Lakoff in *Language and Woman's Place* (1975): that women, by using a ladylike middle-class language, contributed to their own oppression. Lakoff's argument reflected the "dominance" approach to women's language use that was prominent among feminists of the 1970s: attributing gender differences in language mainly to social oppression of women. Bolker's *College English* article "Teaching Griselda to Write" (1979) is a composition practitioner's account of the struggle with the absence of voice and authority in the work of "good-girl" student writers. The many citations of this short article suggest that it has resonated with feminists in composition. Two articles examining women's "different" style appeared in *CCC*. In "The Feminine Style: Theory and Fact" (1978), Hiatt discusses her study of the stylistic features of women's and men's writing. She reports "clear evidence of a feminine [written] style...[that] is in fact rather different from the common assumptions about it" (p. 226). Contrary to Lakoff's generalizations about women's oral language, women's written style, according to Hiatt, has "no excesses of length or complexity or emotion" (p. 226). In "Women in a Double-Bind: Hazards of the Argumentative Edge" (1978), Taylor draws composition instructors' attention to the "invisible, though real, disadvantage" that women students face in writing courses because "both the methods and the goals of such classes are alien to them" (p. 385). More specifically, she argues that the competitive, impersonal style of traditional argument alienates women; she urges instructors to validate "conversational tone, dramatic technique, and intimate reader involvement...[as] legitimate tactics for the essayist" (p. 389).

Bolker and Taylor (writing as practitioners) and Hiatt (writing as a researcher) respond in different ways to the idea that women students must have special problems because a feminine style represents deficiency. Taylor (1978) uses language of victimization to describe the woman student: "She must feel that something is wrong with her, a self-destructive disapproval common enough in women.... Of course, much of the damage has been done by the time our students reach us. They have been taught a special language" (p. 385). But she quotes extensively from Virginia Woolf to support her contention that a feminine style of argument is only "deficient" because society has refused to validate it. Bolker (1979) believes that with more self-esteem and voice, the good girl can be a contender in the arena of the dominant discourse. In contrast, Hiatt (1978) implies that readers need to be more discerning about the gender differences they think they see. All the authors refer to literary work by and about women, but only Hiatt performs any empirical study. None of these fairly short articles is heavily theorized; with the possible exception of Hiatt's, we can say that they arise from and return directly to practice.

It is possible, then, to say that it was not feminism but only feminist theory that was lacking in composition; but this is to draw a dangerous line between theory and practice in both fields. Caywood and Overing (1987), for example, say that, despite the absence of explicit, systematic discussion, they had an "intuitive understanding" as practitioners of a "fundamental connection" between feminism and revisionist writing theory. We would like now to tease out a few of the stories of feminist presence in composition: first those stories that emphasize connection and continuity, then those that foreground disruption.

Various factors account for the intuitive sense of connection that many of us have felt. First, emerging pedagogical theories spoke a language that resonated with feminism's concerns of the time: coming to voice and consciousness, illuminating experience and its relationship to individual identity, playing the believing game rather than the doubting game, collaborating rather than competing, subverting hierarchy in the classroom. These watchwords characterized composition's link to liberal, progressive, political and social agendas shared by feminist scholars in other disciplines and aimed at challenging established traditions, epistemologies, and practices of the academy. Many feminist composition instructors, coming from other areas of specialization, continued reading in their fields and appropriating whatever feminist approaches seemed useful—much as compositionists of the1980s and 1990s have appropriated the work of Belenky, Clinchy, Goldberger, and Tarule (l986). Rich's "When We Dead Awaken" (1972) is still quoted in articles by feminist composition scholars, researchers, and practitioners.

In addition, composition was and still is constructed as women's work and the majority of workers were women. The material conditions surrounding us have contributed to a felt sense of the feminist connections to our work: many of us teaching composition or working on composition degrees during the 1970s were newly arrived from secondary teaching. Surrounded by colleagues with similar career patterns, we entered conversations that enacted an interplay between our lives and our professional work. The drawbacks of this feminization of the field were only theorized several years later.

Finally, as the field developed in the 1970s, although journal editors and the professional hierarchy were primarily male, the names of women were also moving into prominent places: Janet Emig, Ann Berthoff, Sondra Perl, Mina Shaughnessy, Lillian Bridwell-Bowles, and others were writing many of the important articles and books we studied. Many feminists refer with appreciation to the "foremothers," first for their presence as models, and second for their ideas that, though not articulated in terms of gender, are often read as consistent with feminist practice. In many cases, these ideas have to do with nurturing, collaboration, and decentering. Some retrospective accounts use theory to make the composition-feminism connections less intuitive, more explicit. Turning from foremothers to "midwives" (Belenky et al., 1986), Hill (1990) uses feminist theory to read composition history through the gendering of practices, of theories, and of the field itself. She reads the label "midwives" back onto male composition theorists active in the 1960s and early 1970s: Peter Elbow, Ken Macrorie, William Coles, Jr., and John Schultz. Without necessarily claiming them as feminists, she does, with the aid of postmodern theory, gender their approach as feminine and place their work into a certain feminist context: they helped "birth" the experiential self. The expressivist-nurturing feminist connection has often been made in passing, but Hill's label "midwives" claims these key composition figures for feminist theorizing—and also marginalizes them. In the 1990s, Hill argues, these four "expressivist" figures have indeed been pushed to the edge of a newly theorized and professionalized field; their gender-blindness and humanistic model of the autonomous self have had to make way for gender-difference and shifting subject positions—powerful constructs for feminist analysis. Hill sees in the compartmentalization—rather than dynamic rereading—of the four men's so-called expressivism a parallel with the "othering" of "woman," the "othering" of feminism, that continues to occur.

The rereading of "foremothers"—or even "midwives"—as feminist precursors may be problematic if it ignores context and complexity—as we see from a few examples of foremothers who resist labeling. Berthoff (1991) roundly rejected the gendering of nonpropositional logic and the either/or-ism of all discussions of women's ways of knowing. In the early 1990s, Sommers (1994), whose early work on revision and recursiveness might be read as tacitly feminist, wrote that although she was "probably obsessed with the subject of revision since graduate school," she had "always treated revising as an academic subject, not a personal one" (p. 220). Still, the foremother figures can both exemplify and disrupt the notion of the feminization of the field. As fore*mothers* they are both marginalized and typically characterized as nurturers. But insofar as they are envisioned as *fore*mothers—as founders—they are not feminized, but rather constructed in a traditionally masculine position.

These narratives of connection and continuity between feminism and composition allow us to claim a tradition, along with a series of "foremothers." Yet they also elide certain distinctions and disruptions that need to be recognized. They point to composition's intellectual investment in enlightenment conceptions of autonomous selfhood uncomplicated by postmodern readings of discourse and power. They also highlight the need for explicit systematic theorizing about gender and the implications for women students' and teachers' material lives.

FEMINIST DISRUPTIONS

Composition also has many narratives of feminist disruption, which emphasize neither absence nor intuitive connection, but rather represent some form of feminism (newly experienced or theorized) reaching back to reread or even reconfigure past experience and practice. The explicit recognition of the lack of attention in composition to women's material lives has led women in anger, frustration, and recognition to tell the stories of their coming to awareness. A classic feminist narrative, coming out of the early 1970s, is the story of a "good girl," silenced by her compulsion to please, whose recognition of her oppression releases an anger strong enough to overcome politeness and fear; thus, she finds both her voice and an agenda for change. The consciousness-raising sessions of the late 1960s and early 1970s provided a model for this narrative. So did some of the essays in the two special issues of *College English* focusing on women. In "When We Dead Awaken" (1972), Rich told her own story of silent frustration at the demands that she be good at all the roles women were supposed to play. In her 1971 MLA report on the status of women in English, Howe inserted her own autobiographical section explaining how she had wryly but uncomplainingly accepted years of inequitable treatment. She wrote, "Eighteen months as commission Chairwoman have eroded that wry smile. I feel now a growing anger as I come to realize that I am not alone in my state" (1971b, p. 849).

Many of today's feminist accounts of the 1960s and 1970s follow a similar pattern. Bloom's essay, "Teaching College English as a Woman" (1992) is a scathing look at the days when a woman in the field—whether student or teacher—would be exploited if she did not speak up. Bloom recalls a conversion experience when, as a part-time composition instructor, she finally was able to obtain office space: in a basement room full of desks, on the floor under the stairs, next to the kitty litter. Surveying these wretched conditions, she told herself, "If I ever do this again, I deserve what I get" (p. 821). Separated by more than 20 years, Bloom's and Howe's angry accounts nevertheless make it clear that the writing classroom was a place where women felt professionally challenged and where they put feminist theories and principles into practice. Although both were active literary scholars, they would also have been considered practitioners in composition.

Other women who are currently doing feminist work in composition studies have written similar stories of naive compliance, oppressed silence, and angry voice: Bishop (1990), Bridwell-Bowles (1995), and Sommers (1994) are just a few. Enos's work, *Gender Roles and Faculty Lives in Rhetoric and Composition* (1996), contains a number of anonymous stories from women in composition, along with her narrative of her own experience as an "academically battered woman" (p. ix). That we have so many such narratives may mean that women in composition are now in a position to claim the authority of the autobiographical; it may also mean that, largely due to feminist efforts, the conventions of scholarly discourse have expanded to allow and value the personal narrative as a way of situating oneself in one's scholarship. As Enos says, her book's "most powerful use of 'data' is the narrative, in the stories that help us define our places in academia so that we can better trace our future" (p. 1). These stories are disruptive because they exemplify "the pattern of well-rewarded, male supervision of under-rewarded, female workers" that has existed in composition and "is entrenched in our whole culture" (p. vii). The disruption that is so central to the consciousness-raising narrative itself also highlights gaps in our reading of our past and of business as usual. Rereading these consciousness-raising essays, which have recurred in composition over the past 25 years, gives us a further sense of the sites where women were silent (though not *absent*) and where they now want to rupture that silence. These accounts also show the "revisioning" that feminist thinking has enabled women to do.

While Bloom's (1992) account emphasizes how she decided to fight the chilly climate of academia, a retrospective article by McCracken, Green, and Greenwood (1993) tells how they acquiesced as researchers to a field characterized by "a persistent silence on the subject of gender" in the "landmark research studies on writing development and writing processes" (p. 352). Their version of the consciousness-raising account is also a striking example of the recursiveness and revisioning of feminist research in composition. They return to studies of teacher responses to student writing that they had published earlier (and separately), now reinterpreting those studies in terms of gender differences. These authors emphasize that until the late 1980s, the climate in composition studies had made it difficult to notice or report gender differences in empirical studies: "None of us went looking for gender differences," they write. "When the data began to speak of gender, we dared not listen" (p. 356). McCracken, Green, and Greenwood recall being worried about accusations of biological determinism, about seeming to exclude men, about being seen as unprofessional, and about calling attention to themselves as women. "Having begun our careers in the 1970s, we had learned to achieve in the academy by persistently ignoring frequent and irrelevant references to the fact that we are women" (p. 356). These researchers use the language of personal narratives such as Bloom's (1992) when they say, "All women know firsthand what it is to be rendered voiceless when trying to speak" (p. 370), but theirs is not a story of breaking silence by themselves. Instead, the current "research environment in which it is both important and safe to study the interplay between students' gender and their development as writers" (p. 354) has made it possible to revise their findings. Their story is not about singular heroism but about collaboration in a network of mutual support; not about going solo against a hostile discipline, but about rereading the field and their own complicity. This reading disrupts, among other things, their own research, by requiring that they *return* to and *revise* it.

McCracken, Green, and Greenwood's (1993) story also highlights another disruptive reading of the past, particularly when it is placed alongside the earlier reports of Lakoff (1975), Hiatt (1978), Taylor (1978), and Bolker (1979). An emphasis on gender difference did not mean the same thing in the 1970s that it means now. Feminists in that decade generally drew on an oppression model that stressed the exclusion of women and viewed differences in terms of dominance—male dominance over females in a patriarchal culture. Thus, any differences in women's speech and writing would be read as both causes and results of the oppression of women. In contrast is the discourse model that informs much of the current feminist theoretical work in composition: seeing gender and difference as embedded in discourses that construct teacher and student subjectivities as well as the discipline of composition itself. The linguists' argument that we are situated by our own use of language, in tension with composition's early emphasis on the voice and autonomy of the writer, were troubling for feminists who used the "finding a voice" narrative. The "different voice" was problematic until it could be theorized as something other than deficiency. But now, when we retell the past, oppression and discourse versions and dominance and difference slants often appear together in our multiple, disruptive accounts.

In a final example of disruptive feminist rereadings, postmodern theories are used to reread the feminization of composition as problematic. The preponderance of women in composition does not lead inevitably to the triumph of feminist interests and values in the field. For example, Miller (1991b) describes feminization as the "female coding" of the "ideologically constructed identity for the teacher of composition" (p. 123); it involves constructing (and devaluing) composition as "*women's* work." Feminization refers to the gendering of the entire field of composition and of various activities that have taken place within it (nonhierarchical pedagogy, the writing process movement, "romantic" philosophies, nurturing of writers). For Miller, feminization points to the *subordination* of the composition instructor, and of composition to literature, throughout the history of the field. Feminization accounts of composition's past powerfully critique the father–mother or husband–wife relationship between scholarship and teaching, between literature and composition studies. They may be construed as a feminist call to political action, a wake-up call for the discipline of composition, or as a way to reread and flatten the struggles of the 1970s as a "natural," or at least expectable, outgrowth of the presence of many women in the field. Feminization accounts work well when we wish to examine disciplinary issues, and especially when we discuss the evolution of composition's status as a professional field. They seem less illuminating when we want to examine our evolving views of writing, consider the complexities of the student's status as writer, or even talk about gender at the site of writing. And ironically, they may tend to re-silence the practitioner *as* practitioner. Feminization narratives work disruptively in two directions: their analysis foregrounds the political position of composition within institutional structures, and they highlight tensions within women's roles and interests in composition.

USING FEMINIST NARRATIVES TODAY

These different but oddly converging stories of feminism's absences from, connections with, and disruptions of composition suggest something about the contradictory institutional and philosophical forces at work in the emerging discipline as it attempted to define and legitimize itself in the 1970s and 1980s. These stories should help us examine the assumptions shaping the discipline at present, and their implications for the future of composition.

When we begin to look at composition's history from a feminist perspective, it becomes clear that composition's progressive, sometimes revolutionary ethos of the 1970s existed alongside an equally compelling drive for legitimacy. Flynn (1991) attributes the absence of feminist perspectives in composition to the institutional structures, politics, and philosophical dependencies of our field. She contrasts composition to literary studies, where critiques of the male-dominated canon arose naturally from critiques of patriarchal culture and where feminist work in literature could easily be adapted to the traditional work of literary scholarship. Composition was struggling to claim power for itself as a legitimate area of study in the academy with little disciplinary support. By the late 1970s, although important women held leadership positions in composition, their energies were largely occupied with asserting and defending composition's status as a viable discipline worthy of a room of its own. Ede (1994) notes that this active attempt to professionalize composition was also occurring in a reactive context—as composition attempted to respond to the "literacy crisis" of the early 1970s.

In addition, while feminist literary scholars had a tradition of research on which to build in recovering lost foremothers and rereading traditional male texts, composition had no single tradition of research and scholarship from which to work. Grounded as it was in pedagogy, the task of composition was to develop an identifiable body of theory and research on which to base claims for disciplinarity. In this quest, composition teachers turned to various traditions—linguistics, cognitive psychology, rhetoric—whose androcentric assumptions have been well documented. Instead of recovering its lost foremothers, composition in the 1970s was occupied with reclaiming its forefathers, who would restore its legitimacy. (A landmark example is Berlin's history of writing instruction, *Rhetoric and Reality* [1987], which places composition within a 2,500-year-old rhetorical tradition, with Plato, Aristotle, Campbell, Burke, and others as its forefathers.) A discipline struggling for recognition would hardly be likely to spotlight its foremothers, female majority, or feminist inclinations.

Other factors may have delayed (and for a time suppressed) the gender turn in composition. The goals proposed by some feminist theories demanded ways of thinking that were antithetical to basic philosophical assumptions in composition, and other feminist goals conflicted with composition's need for legitimacy. Feminism also presented composition with conflicting assumptions about the structure of knowledge and about what might be considered legitimate methodologies for the production of knowledge. Jarratt (1991) argues, for example, that one of the early feminism-composition connections is problematic. Specifically, she argues that expressivism's tendency to suppress conflict and to promote consensus in composition fails to arm women students and teachers with the tools to analyze and fight against the power relations inherent in their positions. It is true that some early practitioners in composition did embrace a feminist approach that views argument as agonistic and masculinist, but other feminisms were, at the same time, encouraging women to storm the battlements. It may say a great deal about the white, middle-class "good girl" status of composition that the field was most comfortable with a feminism that emphasized women's nurturing nature—a feminism most often expressed in classroom practice. Even today, this distinction is made. Try substituting "compositionist" for "student" in Rosenthal's (1995) commentary on the 1990s:

> Few, if any students [compositionists] ever resist feminist pedagogy. Shared decision making, collaboration, and validation of the personal do not often find resistance.... Feminist content and theory, on the other hand, often lead to...discomfort and dismay, and understandably so. (p. 152)

Some forms of feminism in the 1970s were simply too dangerous for the emerging field to embrace wholeheartedly. Radical and Marxist-socialist feminist goals demanded ways of thinking antithetical to composition's philosophical assumptions and also to its goal of disciplinary legitimization. These feminists were not merely seeking to gain equality for women; they were attempting to analyze the constitution of gender relations, the economic and political sources of women's inferior status, and the material effects of male domination on women's lives. Unlike the liberals, they wished to make gender visible, not irrelevant. These feminist theorists were already making the social constructionist and anthropological turn, documenting women's histories, examining the details of gendered lives as workers, mothers, and lovers within the culture. We see this even in the examples we have discussed from *College English*. Radical feminists were positing an essential difference between men and women, one that to be sure, we have come to problematize, but one that may have seemed too negative in its emphasis on male domination and female victimhood, too strident or too potentially polarizing in the academy and the wider culture for a fragile emerging discipline like composition. Radical feminism also began to posit revision of gender and social relationships, ending male domination by reshaping male–female relationships, allowing women to take charge of and foreground their sexuality, bringing lesbians out of the closet and, in some instances, proposing separatism. These views sparked consternation in the culture generally, but they may also have seemed remote from the concerns of a discipline still focused on writing skills, struggling to define a writing process, and only beginning to consider how writing might be implicated in the construction of the writer's subjectivity.

To complicate the situation further, composition's link to liberal, progressive political agendas may have worked to silence feminism. In its less alarming liberal forms, feminism had argued for over a century for equal rights for women, for women's fundamental equality with men. Without diminishing the positive work of liberal feminism, one might say that its assumptions—like the progressive, liberal assumptions of composition—rested on conceptions of equality and individualism. This parallel may have contributed to composition's silence on the subject of gender difference; it may also explain why we hear stories of both the absence and the presence of feminism in composition in the 1970s. If composition was attempting to encourage expressions of autonomous selfhood and voice, it surely should make no difference if those voices were male or female. The acknowledgment of women's equality meant that women's humanity was assumed, their sameness to men was a given. But their womanness could not be the subject of investigation (nor could maleness, or gayness). In this way, a liberal feminist perspective could easily be acknowledged and then just as easily erased.

Also in conflict with composition's need for institutional legitimacy at this time was the fundamental feminist goal to disrupt rather than extend the tradition of patriarchal discourses and their assumptions about knowledge. Feminists began to reread and challenge the rational, linear epistemologies responsible for constituting and maintaining women's inferior position. Composition was challenging current-traditional conceptions of language and learning as it introduced new writing pedagogies, and it was a disruptive impulse within English as it attempted to challenge the existing hierarchy in relation to literature studies. We can read these activities as parallel with the feminist activity of the time. Yet there was also a difference in the ways composition and feminism positioned themselves that illuminates the contradictions present in the discipline: Composition identified itself with established patriarchal tradition and sought to prove its legitimate position in a long line of rational humanist discourse; at the same time, feminism drew on interdisciplinarity, adapting and merging theories in order to arrive at an explanation for women's lives. This multiplicity may have undermined feminism's usefulness and accessibility for composition: While feminist theorists were challenging traditional notions of a singular universal concept of truth, composition sought a single theory of the writing process.

In order to claim status for its emerging theories and methodologies, composition also needed the trappings of scientific objectivity and neutrality, as those have conventionally been understood. Although researchers such as Emig and Perl were beginning to take the anthropological turn that feminism and other academic disciplines were taking—beginning to examine the social, material, and political contexts of students' and teachers' lives—these developments moved slowly because legitimacy still rested on positivistic forms of knowledge. Still suspect were the ethnographic methodologies that might have helped composition consider the gendered conditions surrounding writers and teachers. This allegiance to traditional epistemologies also led to the compartmentalization that professionalization imposes on members of a discipline. In order to professionalize, one must define herself apart from others, drawing lines to create separations and distinctions. The drive to professionalize not only forced composition to defend its territory and assert its independence from literary studies, but, as McCracken, Green, and Greenwood (1993) attest, it also forced researchers to narrow the scope of their questions. For that reason they did not immediately ask: What difference does it make if the writer is a woman?

As we look at the institutional and philosophical strictures that have led to these interwoven histories of feminism's absence and presence in composition, what questions do they prompt us to ask about the present and future for feminism in composition? We are pretty sure of its presence in composition today. Many respected scholars in our discipline have announced the flowering of feminist research. But is it possible that 21st-century historians of our field might look at the 1990s and tell stories of absence, of parallel, nonconvergent tracks? Although feminists like Holbrook (1990), Miller (1991a), and many others have now examined from a feminist perspective the status of women in composition and the feminized status of composition within English studies, many women still teach composition in the "basement." Although Phelps (1995), Connors (1996), and others have considered how gender may shape their pedagogical efforts, and although a body of metacommentary on feminist writing and research methodologies is emerging, we have not thoroughly explored the implications of students' or teachers' gendered position in the academy. Kirsch (1995) and others have highlighted the gender blindness of liberatory and critical pedagogies, but we have not thoroughly considered how such theories and pedagogies stop short of realizing their goals where women students and gay and lesbian students are concerned. While feminists in composition are reclaiming our lost foremothers in rhetoric and composition and are looking for parallels to feminism in composition, we have only begun to reread the master narratives of our discipline. Elbow's work has been reconsidered by Worsham (1991), and Sullivan (1992) has reread North's *The Making of Knowledge in Composition* (1987) from a feminist perspective. But composition has no serious rereadings of Vygotsky, Britton, Moffett, or Corbett. And how might feminist perspectives amplify Harris's (1997) recent account of how the teaching of college writing has been theorized? Feminist perspectives should continue to prompt us to pose disruptive questions about our disciplinary and institutional narratives.

In composition, feminist stories emphasize recovery and difference, and they remain ambivalent about the connections that should be made between theory and practice. At first glance, the recovery or "writing women into" the history of composition has been easy—compared to writing women into the history of rhetoric—because our field is young and our foremothers visible. But this ease tempts us to ignore some questions of redefinition that have energized feminist rhetoricians. Who *is* in composition? Part-time instructors? Scholars in other fields who teach and write about writing? Writers who reflect on their work? Can the field and its history be shaped to be inclusive? Drawing tight disciplinary lines around composition may give status but may lose useful overlaps with literature and linguistics and mask historical connections with feminist thinkers in those fields. Composition's divorce from literature, appealing in light of some recent "feminization" rereadings, leaves figures like Howe and Rich out of our history. Feminist scholars in composition have only begun to explore the implications of African American, post-colonial, and other non-Western feminist theories for our work. What other perspectives are also unexamined?

One important function of a feminist rereading of composition's history is to help us understand the recent attention to feminist theory in the field and to negotiate its relationship with feminist practice in composition. How will our valuation of feminist teaching practice, both past and present, be altered as feminist research in composition becomes more visible and valorized? It doesn't necessarily follow that feminist composition research will validate all kinds of feminist classroom practice. Furthermore, and once again, there is the question of status. "Composition, until the recent paradigm shift to postmodernism, has been inextricably linked to teaching, and teaching to nurturing" (Graham & Goubil-Gambrell, 1995, p. 105). To what extent does this shift represent "a struggle to eradicate the mother voice of pedagogy and emulate the father-voice of scholarship" (p. 104)? As postmodern feminist theories have begun to influence composition, we speak more about global disciplinary issues, less about the site of writing in the classroom. This postmodern move can be read as a welcome release, particularly for individual scholars who understandably wish to be free of the insistence on immediate practical applications. But it is problematic to read or tell our professional history as a gradual or sudden separation from the demands of pedagogical practice—as if it were a reprieve from housework—or in our theorizing to ignore the female and male students that we teach.

With the history of gendered subject positions in mind, feminists aptly point out that the professionalization of composition does not necessarily benefit the actual women teaching in the field. In a critique of Schuster's metaphor of the composition wife caring for the student-children, Reichert (1996) says, "It is only when composition studies is understood as an abstract concept, and not as real people engaged in real activities, that this metaphor can play itself out. Many in the field simply would not recognize themselves in this passage" (p. 148). Those of us feminists who are rereading a past in which we participated as composition practitioners would like to recognize ourselves somewhere in the family history, as active participants, not as bystanders waiting to be theorized. Our feminist rereadings should also prompt us to make sure that the overwhelming numbers of actual women teaching in the field—especially women in nontenure-track positions—are included in our narratives and our theorizing.

The history of feminism in composition is written in interruptions, silences, anachronisms, and resistances. These narratives show that connections between composition and feminism were not inevitable—an outgrowth of the presence of so many women in the field. Integrating feminist goals and practices with certain aims and disciplinary practices of composition was not automatic, but required bursts of insight and creative leaps. This way of reading our history emphasizes the importance of keeping channels open between research and practice, between literary and composition studies, and between teaching and everything, as our professionalized field of composition draws its boundaries more and more clearly.

REFERENCES

Belenky, M., Clinchy, B., Goldberger, N., & Tarule, J. (1986). *Women's ways of knowing: The development of self, voice, and mind.* New York: Basic Books.

Berlin, J. (1987). *Rhetoric and reality: Writing instruction in American colleges, 1900–1985.* Carbondale, IL: Southern Illinois University Press.

Berthoff, A. (1991). Rhetoric as hermeneutic. *College Composition and Communication, 42,* 279–287.

Bishop, W. (1990). Learning our own ways to situate composition and feminist studies in the English department. *Journal of Advanced Composition, 10,* 339–355.

Bloom, L. (1992). Teaching college English as a woman. *College English, 54,* 818–825.

Bolker, J. (1979). Teaching Griselda to write. *College English, 40,* 906–908.

Bridwell-Bowles, L. (1995). Freedom, form, function: Varieties of academic discourse. *College Composition and Communication, 46,* 46–61.

Caywood, C. & Overing, G. (1987). *Teaching writing: Pedagogy, gender, and equity.* Albany, NY: State University of New York Press.

Coles, W., Jr. (1970). The sense of nonsense as a design for sequential writing assignments. *College Composition and Communication, 21,* 27–34.

Conference on College Composition and Communication. (1972). The student's right to his own language. *College Composition and Communication, 23,* 325.

Conference on College Composition and Communication. (1974). Students' right to their own language. *College Composition and Communication, 25*(3), 1–32.

Connors, R. (1996). Teaching & learning as a man. *College English, 58,* 137–157.

Ede, L. (1994). Reading the writing process. In L. Tobin & T. Newkirk (Eds.), *Taking stock: The writing process movement in the 90's* (pp. 331–343). Portsmouth, NH: Boynton/Cook, Heinemann.

Enos, T. (1996). *Gender roles and faculty lives in rhetoric and composition.* Carbondale, IL: Southern Illinois University Press.

Flynn, E. (1988). Composing as a woman. *College Composition and Communication, 39,* 423–435.

Flynn, E. (1991). Composition from a feminist perspective. In R. Bullock & J. Trimbur (Eds.), *The politics of writing instruction: Postsecondary* (pp. 137–154). Portsmouth, NH: Boynton/Cook, Heinemann.

Graham, M. B., & Goubil-Gambrell, P. (1995). Hearing voices in English studies. *Journal of Advanced Composition, 15,* 103–119.

Harris, J. (1997). *A teaching subject: Composition since l966.* New York: Prentice-Hall.

Hiatt, M. P. (1978). The feminine style: Theory and fact. *College Composition and Communication, 29,* 222–226.

Hill, C. (1990). *Writing from the margins: Power and pedagogy for teachers of composition.* New York: Oxford.

Holbrook, S. (1990). Women's work: The feminizing of composition. *Rhetoric Review, 9,* 201–219.

Howe, F. (1971a). Identity and expression: A writing course for women. *College English, 32,* 863–871.

Howe, F. (1971b). A report on women and the profession. *College English, 32,* 847–854.

Jarratt, S. (1991). Feminism and composition: The case for conflict. In P. Harkin & J. Schilb (Eds.), *Contending with words: Composition and rhetoric in a postmodern age* (pp.105–123). New York: Modern Language Association.

Kirsch, G. (1995) Feminist critical pedagogy and composition. *College English, 57,* 723–729.

Lakoff, R. (1975). *Language and woman's place.* New York: Harper & Row.

McCracken, N., Green, L., & Greenwood, C. (1993). Gender in composition research: A strange silence. In S. Fontaine & S. Hunter (Eds.), *Writing ourselves into the story: Unheard voices from composition studies* (pp. 352–373). Carbondale, IL: Southern Illinois University Press.

Miller, S. (1991a). The feminization of composition. In R. Bullock & J. Trimbur (Eds.), *The politics of writing instruction: Postsecondary* (pp. 39–53). Portsmouth, NH: Boynton/Cook, Heinemann.

Miller, S. (1991b). *Textual carnivals: The politics of composition.* Carbondale, IL: Southern Illinois University Press.

Murray, D. (l970). The interior view: One writer's philosophy of composition. *College Composition and Communication, 21,* 21–27.

Olsen, T. (1972). Women who are writers in our century: One out of twelve. *College English, 34,* 6–17.

Phelps, L. (1995). Becoming a warrior: Lessons of the feminist workplace. In L. Phelps & J. Emig (Eds.), *Feminine principles and women's experience in American composition and rhetoric* (pp. 289–339). Pittsburgh, PA: University of Pittsburgh Press.

Ray, R. (1993). *The practice of theory: Teacher research in composition*. Urbana, IL: National Council of Teachers of English.

Reichert, P. (1996). A contributing listener and other composition wives: Reading and writing the feminine metaphors in composition studies. *Journal of Advanced Composition, 16*, 141–158.

Rich, A. (1972). When we dead awaken: Writing as re-vision. *College English, 34*, 18–25.

Rich, A. (1979). Taking women students seriously. In *On lies secrets, and silence* (pp. 237–245). New York: Norton.

Rosenthal, R. (1995). Feminists in action: How to practice what we teach. In K. Fitts & A. France (Eds.), *Left margins: Cultural studies and composition pedagogy* (pp. 139–156). Albany, NY: State University of New York Press.

Showalter, E. (1971). Women and the literary curriculum. *College English, 32*, 855–862.

Sommers, N. (1994). Between the drafts. In S. Perl (Ed.), *Landmark essays on writing process* (pp. 217–224). Davis, CA: Hermagoras.

Sullivan, P. (1992). Feminism and methodology. In G. Kirsch & P. Sullivan (Eds.), *Methods and methodology in composition research* (pp. 37–61). Carbondale, IL: Southern Illinois University Press.

Taylor, S. (1978). Women in a double-bind: Hazards of the argumentative edge. *College Composition and Communication, 29*, 385–389.

Worsham, L. (1991). Writing against writing: The predicament of écriture feminine in composition studies. In P. Harkin & J. Schilb (Eds.), *Contending with words: Composition and rhetoric in a postmodern age* (pp. 82–104). New York: Modern Language Association

chapter 9

Is There Still a Place for Rhetorical History in Composition Studies?

Gerald P. Mulderig
DePaul University

At the height of the so-called rhetoric revival in English departments 30 years ago, Corbett (1967) paused to characterize the movement in a *College Composition and Communication* article, its title posing the question "What is Being Revived?" The prominence that rhetoric had achieved in English studies by this time is suggested by Corbett's ability to invoke the term in his title without actually using it, yet the newness of rhetoric as a concept in English departments during the 1960s is revealed by his observation that he is addressing his article to teachers of English who have encountered the word "in the titles of new college textbooks, in journal articles, and in panel sessions at regional and national conventions," but who remain "understandably bewildered" by its precise meaning (p. 166). Corbett responds to this puzzlement by deftly tracing the history of rhetoric from Aristotle, Cicero, and Quintilian to Young, Becker, and Pike, focusing on the point that rhetoric throughout history has been "an art governing the choice of strategies that a speaker or writer must make in order to communicate most effectively with an audience" (p. 166). By defining rhetoric in explicitly historical terms and stressing its enduring connection with the art of effective communication, Corbett affirms the great commonplace of the rhetoric revival in English studies—the conviction that rhetorical history offered teachers of writing a valuable theoretical foundation for understanding what they were doing and a fund of ideas for doing it better.

The intersections of rhetorical history and composition pedagogy have been even more explicitly asserted in writing textbooks such as those by Corbett (1965), Crowley (1994), and Horner (1988). Nonetheless, in recent years, a gulf has been forming between rhetoric and composition, between rhetoricians and compositionists. The newly problematic nature of the connection between these terms is reflected, for example, in Gage's (1991) observation that "anyone who presumes to assert what the relationship [between rhetoric and composition] *really* is or ought to be is looking for trouble" (p. 15). I intend to heed this sensible warning and avoid any such pronouncements, but I wish to explore the signs and implications of what I believe is an accelerating shift in the profession today away from the synergy between rhetorical history and composition pedagogy that characterized the rhetoric revival in the 1960s and helped to shape the field that we have for several decades referred to as rhetoric and composition.

REDISCOVERING THE "NEGLECTED ART" OF RHETORIC IN THE 1960S

Until the rhetoric revival, of course, there was no such field. Indeed, even after the establishment of the Conference on College Composition and Communication in 1949 and the founding of its journal in 1950, teachers of writing remained acutely aware of their lack of agreement about the objectives and design of first-year college writing courses. The inchoate nature of the profession is evident throughout the early issues of *CCC,* where laments about underprepared students, accounts of idiosyncratic classroom experiments in teaching writing, and tedious reports on the content of first-year composition courses around the country suggest nothing so much as the desperate search for an identity and purpose. In 1963, as the incoming president of the National Council of Teachers of English, Albert Kitzhaber described this situation at length in a *CCC* article in which he bluntly charged that in its 15 years of existence, CCCC had done little to improve the condition of writing instruction in America. It was time, he said, for teachers of English to "start asking fundamental questions about the act of writing, and [to ask] them in a way that will make it possible to get answers based on more than hunches and personal theories and long-established custom" (p. 133).

One can readily understand how, in such a climate, the 2,500-year history of rhetorical theory and practice seemed to promise an intellectual foundation upon which a new conception of writing instruction might be built. Its beginnings in English departments, though, were slow and uncertain. In a helpful note to us here at the century's end, Burke wrote in 1965 that future historians of composition studies should date the rediscovery of rhetoric to 1958, when the CCCC program included three workshops devoted to rhetorical issues, if not to the history of rhetoric itself. Two years passed without another appearance of rhetoric at CCCC. Then, in 1961, came a CCCC workshop with the title "Rhetoric—The Neglected Art," the published report on which reveals how little agreement existed about the meaning of this new concept among teachers of writing. "If rhetoric is being neglected in composition/communication courses," it began, "the members of the workshop needed to reach some common understanding of what was being neglected" (1991, p. 177). The report hints at the difficulty of this task: for some participants, *rhetoric* referred to the work of Aristotle, I. A. Richards, or Porter Perrin; for others, it meant ensuring that every paragraph in an essay is controlled by a clearly stated topic sentence. Not until the 1963 convention in Los Angeles can rhetoric really be said to have established a toehold in English departments. That conference featured seven speakers on rhetoric, including Booth (1963) on the rhetorical stance, Christensen (1963) on generative rhetoric, and Corbett (1963) on the usefulness of classical rhetoric. With the reprinting of their presentations in the October issue of *CCC* that year, the rhetoric revival was under way.[1]

The rediscovery of the rhetorical tradition that occurred in departments of English in the 1960s played an indisputably central role in creating the field of rhetoric and composition that we recognize today. I have no desire to perpetuate the notion that composition is the weak and insubstantial area of study and rhetoric the strong and true one, but it is clear that teachers of writing during the 1960s widely viewed the rhetorical tradition as a potential source of intellectual content and disciplinary integrity for a field previously characterized by randomness and incoherence. Writing at the start of the rhetoric revival, Burke (1965) argued that "there is chaos today in the teaching of composition because since the turn of the century composition has lacked an informing discipline" (p. 5). Without such a disciplinary foundation, she proposed, all of the pedagogical decisions made by teachers of writing were ultimately arbitrary and indefensible. Burke looked forward to the possibility that a 20th-century adaptation of the rhetorical tradition would reduce this intellectual chaos by spurring research in the teaching of writing that would improve textbooks, teacher training, and course and program design. The establishment of rhetoric as the informing discipline of composition, she wrote, would encourage graduate students "to respect composition as a teaching field" and would produce a "salutary revision of our own view of our professional responsibilities" (p. 7). The contribution that rhetorical history could make to a modern discipline of composition was a frequently echoed theme in the years after Burke wrote, and by the 1970s rhetoric was so well established in English departments that Gorrell (1972) could comfortably contrast the modern teaching of writing as a true discipline founded on rhetoric with an earlier time of aimless experiments in writing pedagogy, "most of [which] assumed that there was something to be taught about writing—if only we could figure out what" (p. 265).

To whatever extent the rhetorical tradition helped composition studies develop a new disciplinary identity, it did so because teachers of writing in the 1960s and 1970s wholeheartedly embraced the idea that a connection existed between the history of rhetorical theory and the contemporary business of teaching composition. As early as 1963, in his *CCC* article entitled "The Usefulness of Classical Rhetoric," Corbett was proselytizing for the classroom applications of key principles from ancient rhetorical theory—a theme that he would develop much more fully two years later in the first edition of his incomparably influential textbook, *Classical Rhetoric for the Modern Student.* Other early *CCC* articles—by Hughes (1965) on the pedagogical value of Aristotle's stress on audience and invention; by Kinneavy (1969) on the aims of discourse; by Winterowd (1971) on *dispositio*; by Corbett (1971) on the tradition of imitation; by McCarron (1975) on the need for formal training of writing teachers in the precepts of classical rhetoric; by Zappen (1975) on the relation of Bacon's rhetoric of science to contemporary technical writing; and by Lauer (1976) on the needed "theoretical base" (p. 342) that rhetoric had provided to teachers of writing—all give evidence of the pervasive feeling during this period that the history of rhetoric had more than merely symbolic value for instructors of writing, that it offered, instead, a route to sounder thinking about writing and to more effective teaching.

NEGLECTING THE REDISCOVERED ART OF RHETORIC IN THE 1990S

For most of the two decades after the rediscovery of rhetoric in English departments, this link between the rhetorical tradition and composition pedagogy was unquestioned, and, as recently as the 1980s, it was still being resoundingly affirmed. In his introduction to *The Rhetorical Tradition and Modern Writing*, for example, Murphy (1982) called for a broad approach to literacy in college teaching inspired by the rhetorical curriculum of Quintilian. Two years later, in the opening chapter of *Essays on Classical Rhetoric and Modern Discourse*, Connors, Ede, and Lunsford (1984) applauded the fact that composition research was no longer exclusively pedagogical, as it had been in the past. The revival of rhetoric and the development of graduate programs in composition and rhetoric, they noted appreciatively, had given impetus to important new theoretical and historical research in the field. At the same time, Schilb (1986) noted that "composition studies is now marked by a strong interest in historical research" (p. 12) and asserted precisely the connection between rhetorical history and composition pedagogy that had fueled the rhetoric revival two decades earlier:

> Today, we have more historians of rhetoric because we have more people anxious to legitimize the teaching of writing as a serious affair, and therefore anxious to persuade all writing teachers to think about the contingent nature of their pedagogies so they can revise them for better. (p. 12)

In the 1990s, however, a number of signs seem to be pointing away from this integration of rhetorical history and writing pedagogy—indeed, away from a scholarly interest in the history of rhetoric altogether among teachers and researchers in the field of composition studies. One indication that such a shift is in progress may be found in the research being undertaken by new Ph.D.'s in rhetoric and composition. Between 1990–91 and 1993–94, my department mounted eight national searches for faculty in rhetoric and composition, in response to which we received a total of 527 applications. I cannot claim, of course, that this pool included an application from every candidate on the job market during these four years, but I think it offers a reasonable snapshot of the research interests of the rising professionals in our field today and a rather troubling indication of the direction in which we are heading. Among the 218 applicants in our pool who were specializing in some aspect of rhetoric and composition studies (rather than in literary fields) and who received their degrees between 1990 and 1994, there were far more dissertations on pedagogical subjects than in any other subfield of rhetoric and composition (see Figure 9.1).

Despite the fact that our advertisements specifically invited applications in a broad range of specializations, including the history of rhetoric, historical projects in our pool of applications represented a very small category of research, with a total of only 20 dissertations during this four-year period. Only two candidates presented dissertations on 18th-century rhetoric, and no one at all was working in medieval rhetoric. Renaissance, 19th-century, and ancient rhetoric were marginally more popular areas for research, but with only seven, six, and four dissertations, respectively.[2]

Let me pause to state as clearly as I can some of the arguments that I am *not* trying to make here: I am not suggesting that research in peda-

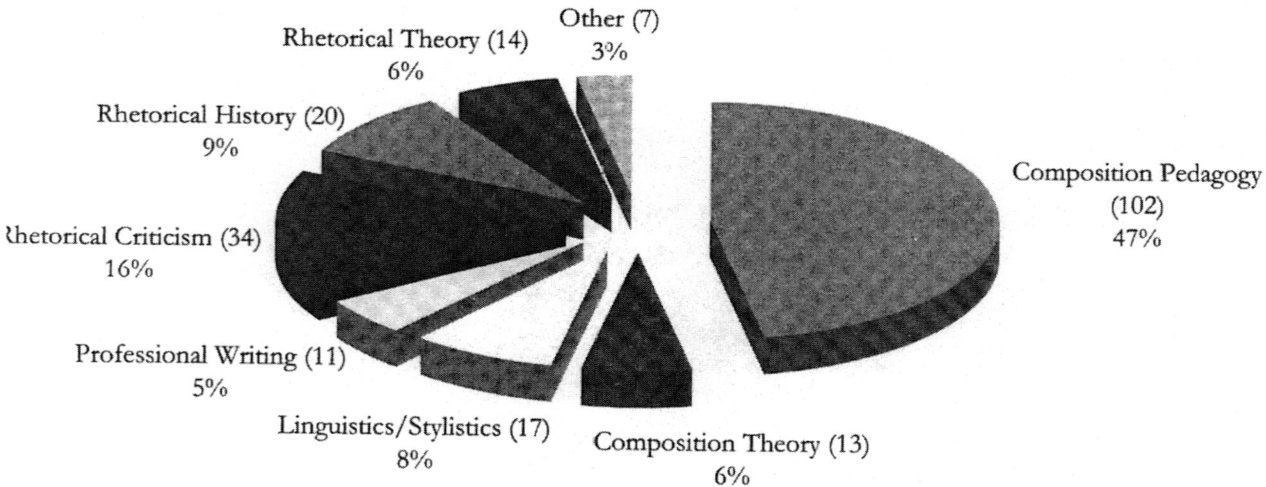

FIGURE 9.1. Dissertation subjects in rhetoric and composition, 1990-94. Data drawn from 218 applications submitted for eight advertised faculty positions in rhetoric and composition at DePaul University.

gogy is unimportant; I am not suggesting that there is no valuable scholarship in historical rhetoric being done today; and I am certainly not suggesting that we should lament the apparent decline of interest in rhetorical history because rhetoric is somehow a richer or more legitimate academic pursuit than composition. Rather, it's the synergy that has existed between rhetoric and composition that I fear is in jeopardy. If on the one hand rhetoric offered composition studies in the 1960s a new and revitalizing intellectual framework, it was composition teaching that provided a route for rhetoric back into English departments and English curricula. Like many other English departments, mine today offers graduate and undergraduate courses in rhetorical history, theory, and practice that probably would not exist in our curriculum had the teaching of composition not been among the department's traditional functions. But when we look at the research interests of this group of new scholars in the discipline that we have known as rhetoric and composition, scholars whose work will help to shape the field in the next century, we can see clear indications of a shift away from the synergistic balance between historical rhetoric and composition pedagogy of the past 30 years, as well as an apparent return to an earlier time when composition pedagogy dominated the field.

If I am correct in interpreting these data as an erosion of the place of rhetorical history in composition studies and in English departments today—even though it is an erosion whose full effects may not be felt for another decade or more—then one cannot help but ask what forces are leading us to retreat from the celebrated integration of rhetoric and composition that occurred during the 1960s and 1970s. I do not claim to have definitive answers to this question, but I believe that this intellectual shift stems at least in part from the fact that those of us with professional interests in rhetoric and composition are increasingly allowing ourselves to be defined by our English department colleagues primarily as specialists in pedagogy rather than as faculty who can also enrich an English curriculum with courses in rhetorical history, theory, and criticism. In 1987, North cynically suggested that writing specialists were calling themselves rhetoricians simply because rhetoric, with its centuries-long tradition, "sells" better as a "legitimate intellectual enterprise" in English departments than does composition, with its narrower suggestions of "'mere' practice" (pp. 64–65). But a decade later, the MLA *Job Information List* suggests that just the opposite may now be the case—that "mere practice" has become the essential enterprise of rhetoric and composition. In the October 1996 *Job List,* of the 70 advertisements for specialists in composition and/or rhetoric that offered some description of the position to be filled, 93 percent explicitly described the available job in terms of undergraduate composition teaching and/or writing program administration. Only 5 of these 70 advertisements even mentioned rhetorical history as a qualification for applicants or as a possible area of teaching. The figures in 1995 were similar: Ninety percent of the rhetoric and composition openings with descriptions in the October *Job List* were in composition teaching and/or writing program administration, and only four advertisements mentioned rhetorical history. And so, while teachers of literature in our departments are being recruited as specialists in literature, teachers of rhetoric and composition are recruited as specialists in teaching. If those of us with credibility and stature in our departments permit our colleagues to define us and our work in purely pedagogical terms, we will be providing ample reason for graduate students who want a job in this field to devote themselves primarily to pedagogical research and to look skeptically on the value of research in the history of rhetorical theory.

We cannot blame English departments or the job market for our profession's declining interest in rhetorical history without also looking critically at the Conference on College Composition and Communication itself. Just as our predecessors in 1914 willingly permitted teachers of public speaking to secede from the NCTE, taking with them a tradition of research in rhetoric that would disappear from English departments for more than 50 years, the members and leadership of CCCC have increasingly surrendered rhetoric to the Rhetoric Society of America and have chosen instead to focus much of the annual CCCC convention on issues of composition pedagogy. Of the 502 sessions listed in the program for the 1997 conference, for example, only 13—a little more than 2 percent—dealt at least in part with the history of rhetoric before the 20th century. The statistics were about the same for the 1996 program, where only 8 of 429 sessions (under 2 percent) featured presentations on the history of rhetoric. No one who attends CCCC—certainly no graduate student contemplating the choice of a dissertation subject—can fail to recognize the professional priorities suggested by these figures and implicitly endorsed by the organization.

The marginalization of historical rhetoric is also apparent in graduate education in rhetoric and composition throughout the country, according to a recent survey of the 72 North American Ph.D. programs in rhetoric and composition by Brown, Meyer, and Enos (1994). Among the surprising facts that may be found in the data from this survey are these: one third of the Ph.D. programs in rhetoric and composition include no faculty who list the history of rhetoric among their areas of specialization, and fully one half of these programs do not have any courses[3] in the history of rhetoric among their core or required courses. In a sense, the future without rhetorical history that I have been describing is already here, at least for the graduate students enrolled in these Ph.D. programs.

DEFINING THE ROLE OF RHETORIC IN ENGLISH STUDIES FOR THE 21ST CENTURY

If the history of rhetoric and composition teaches us anything, it teaches that we must welcome change and embrace the theoretical, empirical, pedagogical, and technological research that helps us more fully understand writing and makes us more responsive to the conditions of our culture that affect our teaching of writing today. Given the expanding body of scholarship in these areas, it may be true that composition no longer needs rhetorical history to provide the disciplinary identity that it offered in the 1960s. But the accelerating valorization of pedagogical research at the expense of historical study portends a shift in and a narrowing of the field that has not been widely recognized or discussed. Goggin (1995) is one of the few who have expressed the concern that a professional focus on composition pedagogy divorced from the intellectual framework of rhetorical study threatens to impoverish the field and to lead us back to our unsatisfactory past. "Restricting our disciplinary enterprise to the composition classroom," she writes, "severely restricts the kinds of problems, questions, and objects of study that we validate for study, and thus severely restricts the shape of the discipline" (p. 43).

As I have tried to suggest above, the issue is not only what rhetorical history offers composition studies, but what specialists in the history and theory of rhetoric bring to the larger field of English studies. Reintroduced into English departments 30 years ago for the limited purpose of invigorating the teaching of writing, rhetoric now finds itself at the nexus of composition studies, literary study, critical theory, and discourse analysis in these departments. In fact, Clark (1995) has argued that a rhetorical epistemology is the very foundation of English studies, for "what English departments know and teach are the language arts of rhetorical practice: reading and writing, interpretation and argument" (p. 249). Indeed, the growing prominence in English studies of texts that are outside the traditional genres of fiction, poetry, and drama—biography and autobiography, diaries and letters, captivity and slave narratives, scientific and historical writing, the discourse of political and cultural movements—has focused new attention on rhetoric's potential for illuminating "the ways speakers and listeners meet or fail to meet in *all* kinds of texts, spoken and written" (Booth, 1981, p. 3). "Rhetoric has a history and the history of rhetoric opens up English studies," writes

Clark, for it "is not narrowly attached to the history of print technologies, of national literatures, or of limited genres" (p. 250).

How ironic that the place of rhetorical history in composition studies seems to be shrinking just as rhetoric's role in English studies is so rapidly expanding. Before we allow the book to be closed on the relevance of the rhetorical tradition to the teaching of writing, we should at least openly discuss the potential value of ensuring that the history of rhetoric remains a vital element in composition studies and an integral part of English departments. What teachers of English lost when the NCTE turned away from the rhetorical tradition nearly a century ago is abundantly clear. Whether we will take deliberate measures to avoid reenacting our past in the new century ahead remains for us to decide.

NOTES

[1]In one sense, of course, it was and is absurd for English teachers to talk about a revival of rhetoric in the 1960s, for at the very time that many teachers of English were pondering what meaning could lie behind a CCCC program title like "Rhetoric—The Neglected Art," research in the history and theory of rhetoric was in fact thriving in departments of speech across the nation. Indeed, from articles in just a dozen or so issues of the *Quarterly Journal of Speech* published during the 1960s, one could have constructed an entire syllabus of secondary works on the history of rhetoric from the ancient world to the present. Between 1963 and 1969, for example, *QJS* published articles on dialectic in Plato's *Phaedrus;* Aristotle and Horace on rhetoric and poetics; theories of delivery from Homer to Quintilian; Aristotle's and Cicero's rhetorical theory in the Middle Ages; the rhetoric of medieval preaching and letter writing; invention in English rhetoric from 1600 to 1800; Locke and rhetoric; British and American Puritan rhetoric; John Quincy Adams's *Lectures on Rhetoric and Oratory;* Boswell on rhetoric and belles lettres; Campbell and the classical tradition; argumentation in Whatley's rhetoric; Alexander Bain and the organic paragraph; the elocutionary movement at Harvard in the 19th century; the Boylston Professorship of Rhetoric and Oratory; Chaim Perelman; and Stephen Toulmin, not to mention a host of articles on rhetoric and philosophy, logic, film, television, politics, and literature.

The circumstances that had taken such scholarly work out of English departments and had left most English faculty blithely ignorant of its existence for nearly half a century are well known. Teachers of public speaking, most of whom found themselves in departments of English at the start of this century and who therefore joined the NCTE when it was founded in 1911, petitioned the council in 1912 for the opportunity to organize a meeting of speech professionals as part of the NCTE annual program. English faculty in the NCTE, refusing to recognize a distinction between oral and written communication, moved to block the proposal, and the battle lines were drawn. For two years, relations between teachers of English and teachers of speech deteriorated as the NCTE refused to yield; finally, during the 1914 NCTE meeting in Chicago, 17 speech faculty voted to leave the council and found their own organization, which eventually became the Speech Association of America—and the home of virtually all of the serious scholarly work done on rhetorical history and theory for more than 50 years (Gray, 1964; Jeffrey, 1964).

[2]In addition to the 218 applications represented in Figure 9.1, the complete pool of 527 applications included those from candidates in literary fields, those from candidates in rhetoric and composition who completed their dissertations before 1990, duplicate applications from the same candidates during this four-year period, and a handful of applications that did not refer to the candidate's dissertation project at all.

The amount of detail that applicants provided about their dissertations varied: most provided a paragraph-length description of the dissertation in the application letter or the *vita*; some included a one- or two-page dissertation abstract; a few offered only the dissertation title. The eight categories in Figure 9.1 represent my best effort to collect the dissertations into groups of similar projects based on the information available. Below are fuller descriptions of these categories and the titles of some representative dissertations in each:

A. **Composition pedagogy.** Projects that focused largely on classroom practices, including studies of student writers, composition textbooks, course design, writing assessment, and teacher training. Representative titles include "Context and Cognition in the Composing Processes of Two Deaf Student Writers," "Critical Pedagogy and the Student-Centered Classroom: Multicultural Approaches to Writing Courses," and "Discourse Community and the Evaluation of Student Writing."
B. **Composition theory.** Projects that appeared to focus primarily on theoretical issues rather than on classroom practices, including critiques of theorists in the field and discussions of composition studies as a discipline since 1950. Representative titles include "Dialogism in Composition: Toward a Comprehensive Theory," "A Phenomenological Critique of Protocol Analysis in Composing Process Research," and "Mapping Disciplinary Territory in Academic Journals: Rhetoric and Composition in the 1970s."
C. **Rhetorical theory.** Studies of modern rhetorical theory and theorists; studies of links between rhetoric and other disciplines, including critical theory and philosophy. Representative titles include "Agreement, Disagreement, and Rhetorical Invention," "Kenneth Burke's Theory of Comedy," and "Religious Dialectics of Pain and Imagination: Postmodern and Liberation Rhetorics."
D. **Rhetorical history.** Studies in the history of rhetoric and writing before the 20th century, including contemporary applications of principles from the history of rhetoric. Representative titles include "Power, Pedagogy, Possession: Classical Rhetoric and the Origin of Teacherly Power," "Imitation in Renaissance Rhetoric and Contemporary Composition," and "Re-membering Rhetorical History: The Elocutionary Movement and Bodily Decorum."
E. **Rhetorical criticism.** Rhetorical studies of literary and nonliterary texts. Representative titles include "Burke, Campbell, Johnson, and Priestly: A Rhetorical Analysis of Four British Pamphlets of the American Revolution,"

"Situated Knowledge and the Teaching of Writing: A Rhetorical Analysis of the Professional Writing of Women's Studies Scholars," and "The Rhetoric of Identification in Business Discourse."

F. **Linguistics/stylistics.** Studies in linguistic theory; linguistic and stylistic analyses of literary and nonliterary texts. Representative titles include "An Inference-Based Account of Restrictive Relative Constructions," "Repetition and Coherence in Alzheimer Discourse: An Interactional and Contextual Study," and "What Attracted His Attention Lying: Discourse, Style, and *Ulysses*."

G. **Professional writing.** Studies of writers and writing outside the academy. Representative titles include "Writing an Environmental Policy in a Corporation: A Study" and "Discourse and Community: Rhetoric and Relationships at a Social Service Agency."

H. **Other.** A small but eclectic set of dissertations that did not seem to fit into any of the categories above. Examples include "Mentoring Recomposed: A Study of Gender, History, and the Discourses of Education" (on the mentoring of women in higher education), "A Comparative Study of Chinese and English Academic Discourse" (on traditions of citation in academic writing), and "Rhetoric, Ideology, and the Possibility of Justice" (no description provided).

[3]The profession's contemporary emphasis on pedagogy is reflected in graduate programs like the one at Miami University in Ohio, where, according to this survey, the core or required courses are "Studies in Composition Research and Pedagogy," "Theory and Practice of Teaching Composition," "Studies in Composition Theory," "Studies in Rhetoric," "Issues in Composition Pedagogy," "Research Methods in Composition," and "Linguistics and Writing" (Brown, Meyer, & Enos, 1994, p. 301).

REFERENCES

Booth, W. C. (1963). The rhetorical stance. *College Composition and Communication, 14,* 139–154.

Booth, W. C. (1981). The common aims that divide us; or, is there a "Profession 1981"? *ADE Bulletin, 69,* 1–5.

Brown, S. C., Meyer, P. R., & Enos, T. (Eds.). (1994). Doctoral programs in rhetoric and composition [Special issue]. *Rhetoric Review, 12.*

Burke, V. M. (1965). The composition-rhetoric pyramid. *College Composition and Communication, 16,* 3–7.

Christensen, F. (1963). A generative rhetoric of the sentence. *College Composition and Communication, 14,* 155–161.

Clark, S. (1995). The future of rhetoric in English department Ph.D. programs. *Rhetoric Society Quarterly, 25,* 249–251.

Connors, R. J., Ede, L. S., & Lunsford, A. A. (Eds.). (1984). *Essays on classical rhetoric and modern discourse.* Carbondale, IL: Southern Illinois University Press.

Corbett, E. P. J. (1963). The usefulness of classical rhetoric. *College Composition and Communication, 14,* 162–164.

Corbett, E. P. J. (1965). *Classical rhetoric for the modern student.* New York: Oxford University Press.

Corbett, E. P. J. (1967). What is being revived? *College Composition and Communication, 18,* 166–172.

Corbett, E. P. J. (1971). The theory and practice of imitation in classical rhetoric. *College Composition and Communication, 22,* 243–250.

Crowley, S. (1994). *Ancient rhetorics for contemporary students.* New York: Macmillan.

Gage, J. T. (1991). On "rhetoric" and "composition." In E. Lindemann & G. Tate (Eds.), *An introduction to composition studies* (pp. 15–32). New York: Oxford University Press.

Goggin, M. D. (1995). The disciplinary instability of composition. In J. Petraglia (Ed.), *Reconceiving writing, rethinking writing instruction* (pp. 27–48). Mahwah, NJ: Lawrence Erlbaum.

Gorrell, R. M. (1972). The traditional course: When is old hat new. *College Composition and Communication, 23,* 264–270.

Gray, G. W. (1964). The founding of the Speech Association of America: Happy birthday. *Quarterly Journal of Speech, 50,* 342–345.

Horner, W. B. (1988). *Rhetoric in the classical tradition.* New York: St. Martin's Press.

Hughes, R. E. (1965). The contemporaneity of classical rhetoric. *College Composition and Communication, 16,* 157–159.

Jeffrey, R. C. (1964). A history of the Speech Association of America, 1914–1964. *Quarterly Journal of Speech, 50,* 432–444.

Kinneavy, J. E. (1969). The basic aims of discourse. *College Composition and Communication, 20,* 297–304.

Kitzhaber, A. R. (1963). 4C, freshman English, and the future. *College Composition and Communication, 14,* 129–138.

Lauer, J. M. (1976). The teacher of writing. *College Composition and Communication, 27,* 341–343.

McCarron, W. E. (1975). Are teachers "uptaught" on classical rhetoric? *College Composition and Communication, 26,* 253–257.

Murphy, J. J. (1982). (Ed.). *The rhetorical tradition and modern writing.* New York: Modern Language Association.

North, S. M. (1987). *The making of knowledge in composition: Portrait of an emerging field.* Upper Montclair, NJ: Boynton/Cook.

Rhetoric--The neglected art. (1961). *College Composition and Communication, 12,* 177–178.

Schilb, J. (1986). The history of rhetoric and the rhetoric of history. *PRE/TEXT, 7,* 11–34.

Winterowd, W. R. (1971). Dispositio: The concept of form in discourse. *College Composition and Communication, 22,* 39–45.

Zappen, J. P. (1975). Francis Bacon and the rhetoric of science. *College Composition and Communication, 26,* 244–247.

chapter 10

The Developing Discipline of Composition: From Text Linguistics to Genre Theory

Amy J. Devitt
University of Kansas

In 1977, I began my graduate work in English and simultaneously discovered two exciting fields of study: linguistics and composition. The big books in the program in composition that year were Halliday and Hasan's *Cohesion in English* (1976), Hirsch's *The Philosophy of Composition* (1977), and Shaughnessy's *Errors and Expectations* (1977). Shaughnessy's book considered the psychology of underprepared students, but it emphasized the textual features of "basic writers." Hirsch's tome reflected his literary background, but it was most notable for importing psychological research on reading and the concept of grapholect. Halliday and Hasan's book was a linguistic analysis of cohesion in texts, identifying and categorizing the textual creators of cohesion. In other words, all three books examined composition as textual features, a largely linguistic approach to the study of writing.

More than 20 years later, the "big books" in composition are more likely to deal with student diversity, cultural contexts, and social constructionism than with features of texts. Composition pedagogy, too, has changed: Today, teachers more likely stress portfolios and multicultural classrooms rather than 1977's pedagogy of "generative" rhetoric and sentence combining. Although sentence combining has not completely disappeared from the classroom today, it certainly does not appear frequently in our research on pedagogy. From such appearances, one might conclude that the linguistic study of texts—the study of the language used in writing—has vanished from composition, but I argue that that appearance is misleading. Rather, composition's use of linguistics has become more sophisticated and less visible. As it has gained intellectual focus over the past 20 years, composition has learned how to incorporate linguistic schema and insights within its own field of study to serve its own purposes. This change in how composition uses linguistics is exemplified by the shift from text linguistics of the 1970s to genre theory of the 1990s.

LINGUISTIC BORROWING

Composition's early days of trying to understand writing required trying to understand writing as a noun, as written text. Although linguistics had largely concentrated on understanding spoken language, compositionists applied language theory and studies of speech directly to writing. The linguistic heyday of the 1950s, when compositionists eagerly applied and taught structural linguistics, was squelched by Chomsky's bomb of transformational-generative grammar in the 1960s, but compositionists still did not abandon linguistics. The 1960s and 1970s saw composition's incorporation of this new "generative" linguistics and, in the late 1960s and into the 1970s, the addition of the new linguistic perspective of sociolinguistics. But in this fledgling era through the 1970s, each new linguistic theory was translated directly into composition research and the composition classroom. Hence, writing teachers taught transformational grammar, sentence combining became the rage, and "Black English Vernacular" was endorsed for formal classroom writing.

Not all of composition's use of linguistics came from the study of speech. Some areas of linguistics had examined written language specifically, especially some parts of discourse analysis and what is usually called text linguistics. Text linguistics, too, however, was simply applied directly to student texts—hence, Hirsch's (1977) use of grapholect and compositionists' use of cohesion analysis. Composition's use of cohesion analysis at the time illustrates the direct application of linguistic theory for composition's ends. Halliday and Hasan (1976) meticulously detailed every conceivable kind of linguistic device that added cohesiveness to a text, including repetition of key words, use of pronouns, and development of cohesive chains, among many others. In attempting to help students improve the coherence and cohesiveness of their writing, compositionists often reduced Halliday and Hasan's complex and detailed descriptions to a list of common cohesive devices that students should look for in their texts and work to increase. Textbooks and articles in our journals advised students and teachers to mark the key words, pronouns, and cohesive chains in their texts, see that they were insufficient, and add more. Of course, teachers taught cohesion with more complexity than my simplification, and they examined what kinds of effects were achieved with different kinds of ties and how they operated in individual students' texts. But, in practice, too often we applied the linguistic discovery too literally: If these devices mark cohesiveness, as linguistics tells us, and our students' texts are not very cohesive, as our experience tells us, then we need to teach students to add more cohesive markers. We seemed not to consider that increasing the number of markers might not actually increase cohesion or coherence, just increase the number of cohesive markers. Learning what is contained in the forms of finished professional texts might not tell us much about how to help students improve the forms of their own texts.

That realization, of course, is part of what led us to shift from the so-called product emphasis to a process emphasis in composition. With that shift to treating writing as a verb, however, composition at first rejected anything connected with writing as a noun, including linguistics. When linguistics considered writing at all, rather than speech, it considered the textual form of writing. That textual form was the writing product and hence rejected by the new process approach. At first, written products were still studied, but only to see what they revealed about writing processes. Faigley and Witte (1982), for example, wrote a thoughtful article about the process of revision, entitled "Analyzing Revision," in which they examined the changes made in student texts. However, examining processes through the product came, in time, to be so thoroughly dismissed that even such carefully conducted research was criticized. Faigley (1986) himself later criticized that article for assigning meaning to the text apart from its individual readers and writers. The careful description of text came to be seen as an essentially flawed approach, an approach essentially linguistic in kind and now seen as inadequate.

In rejecting the overemphasis on product, compositionists tended to reject all linguistic-based analysis as being too centered on the product and all linguistic systems as too noncognitive and rigid. Advances in text linguistics and discourse analysis were now largely ignored within composition in favor of advances within psychology and cognitive science, disciplines more concerned with composition's new interest in human behavior and mental processes. Since textual description no longer served the aims of composition study, the study of language, the medium of texts, also no longer served composition.

Now some claim that composition has moved "post-process," breaking down the dichotomy and attempting to reintegrate process and product within broader concerns and more situated contexts. As a field, we are developing a fuller, contextualized understanding of writing, one that enables compositionists to reintegrate linguistic study within composition study as well. Now we are returning to linguistics, but on our own terms. So, from one current composition perspective, language is not just a formal medium, a product, but a social construct, a cultural fact to be used or resisted (see, for example, the work on *ecriture feminine*, such as that by Worsham [1991]). From another emphasis, texts are sociorhetorical creations within cultural contexts, and their forms are to be interpreted critically as well as rhetorically (as in, for example, so much of the recent work on academic discourse, such as that by Bizzell [1992] or Brodkey [1987]). Textual forms themselves are no longer merely described, prescribed, or ignored, but rather their cultural significance is critiqued. As language has been complicated within composition studies, so has composition complicated its use of linguistics.

GENERIC INTEGRATION

Rather than applying linguistics literally or ignoring its discoveries, we now integrate linguistics within our own understanding of the complexity of language and writing, an integration illustrated by the development of genre theory. The study of genres, of course, has been around since Aristotle and has been a significant part of what rhetoricians study. Rhetorical analyses of sermons, inaugural speeches, and other genres have formed a vertebra in the backbone of traditional rhetorical analysis. In contrast, though, composition in the past—especially current-traditional composition study and teaching—has attended to genre only in the form of the modes and school genres (the definition paper, comparison/contrast, and research paper, for example). Until recently, composition rarely dealt with genre as a subject worthy of research, perhaps because of composition's heavy dependence on linguistics and literary study in the past. Since linguistics rarely dealt with text type, composition—which had depended heavily on linguistics for its textual description—rarely dealt with genre. Literary study, on the other hand, had dealt with genre, but it had reserved the term for either the highest literary genres (tragedy, comedy, sonnet, lyric) or derogatory "genre writing" (mystery, romance, western, science fiction). The texts studied by compositionists, then, either didn't deserve the name "genre" or would be degraded by being called "genre writing." (Literary study's split personality on the issue of genre would be an intriguing topic for a later essay.)

Thus, research and practice in composition has largely ignored genre. For example, Christensen and Christensen's (1978) generative rhetoric did not at first even notice (or at least acknowledge) that its examples emphasized fiction. Sentence combining exercises did not vary the amount or kind of sentence combining for different kinds of writing. Cohesion analysis did not distinguish markers of cohesion in scholarly articles *versus* letters to the editor. Later scholars in process theory recognized that there were multiple writing processes rather than a single process, yet they still rarely dealt substantially with the fact that there might be different processes for different genres. We didn't even notice.

Today, however, composition has developed a substantial body of work in genre theory and is coming to recognize the significance of genre in many aspects of writing, for writing as both the noun and the verb. Books by Berkenkotter and Huckin (1995), Freedman and Medway (1994a, 1994b), Reid (1987), Swales (1990), and others profess the new perspectives on genre, along with articles in *CCC*, *JAC*, and other professional journals (see, for example, articles by Bawarshi [1997], Russell [1997], and Smith [1997]). The new genre, though, is not the genre of literary scholars—high literary forms or rigid conventions—nor is it the simplistic text categories of early text linguistics. The new genre is a dynamic social construct, a changing cultural artifact with rhetorical and social functionality. Developing in response to recurring rhetorical situations, the new genre has forms and conventions that are rhetorically and socially meaningful. The organization of a lab report, for example, helps writers transform the research process into a neater product and helps readers scan quickly for desired information. The conventions of the lab report, like other genres, fulfill its rhetorical and social purposes. Developing within groups of users, the new genres are also fluid categories that reflect and reify the ideology and values of their users. The conventions of lab reports define accepted methodologies and stances toward research, which have changed over time (see Bazerman [1988] for more detail). The new genre, in other words, develops from composition's current understandings of writing rather than from its current understanding of another discipline. The new genre is distinctly composition's genre.

With composition's genre, we can come closer to achieving our field's goals, rather than those of linguistics, literary study, or psychology. Composition's genre helps us to better understand how, what, and why people write. Once we see genres as dynamic and rhetorical, we see that the processes of writing must vary with different genres. Once we see genres as evolving from users' needs, we see that issues of new technologies also involve issues of emerging genres. Once we see how group ideologies translate into generic constraints, we see how the academic essay can restrict intellectual expression. Once we understand composition's genre, we understand better composition's subject matter: writing. When we learn best how to apply such new knowledge of composition's genre, we should also be more effective teachers of writing, more effectively helping students both to fulfill readers' expectations and critique those expectations.

Composition studies has developed its own conception of genre to serve its own purposes—to help us better understand how and what people write. But it has not done so by rejecting completely the insights of other disciplines, as it did with linguistics in the 1980s. Remaining as productively interdisciplinary as ever, compositionists have developed their ideas of genre using the works of literary scholars, rhetoricians, anthropologists, and linguists (for example, Bakhtin [1986], Bitzer [1968], Halliday [1978], Halliday & Hasan [1989], and Todorov [1978]).

In a nice twist for my purposes, one of the major influences on current genre theory is Halliday, the same linguist who co-wrote *Cohesion in English* (1976). Halliday's functional linguistics has been a starting ground for many genre theorists, for he develops the insight that language serves social functions and that different functions are associated with different language. He defines different situations according to their field, mode, and tenor, and he concentrates on the different registers, or language styles, that develop in those different situations. Our use of Halliday today, however, marks the difference in how composition uses linguistic theories today *versus* the 1970s. Following the model of how we taught cohesion, in the 1970s compositionists' discovery of Halliday's functional linguistics might have led to teaching students about the concepts of field, mode, and tenor and showing them the textual markers of register. We might have developed lists of formal markers of particular registers, and students might have been taught to write in different registers by putting those register markers into their texts. In fact, linguists like Biber (1988) have developed such lists of register markers based on research, with productive results for the linguistic description of textual variation.

Compositionists today, however, have not taken such lists of markers and transferred them to textbooks. We have not taught students tenor, field, and mode, nor have we shown students which textual markers to insert into their texts in order to write in a legal, business, or academic register. Rather, we have transformed the linguistic concept of register within our own concept of genre, and we have resisted premature translation into teaching—with the exception, perhaps, of some Australian linguists and educationists (working with Halliday himself), who have designed public school curricula to teach the textual features of different genres. In fact, the reaction to those curricular moves in Australia may prove the point, for the Australian school's direct transfer from

Hallidayan linguistics to the writing class has received a great deal of explicit discussion—and not a little criticism—especially among North American compositionists (see especially the discussions in Freedman [1993] and Reid [1987]). To use discoveries or theories from linguistics in composition teaching or research today requires considerable debate and modification of those discoveries for composition's purposes, as composition has developed into a distinct discipline with purposes distinct from those of linguistics or any other discipline.

Composition's new genre theory has developed out of composition's distinct purposes: to understand the texts students and professionals write and how they write them. But understanding texts no longer means, for composition, describing merely form, but also how texts function and operate in their worlds and how people use texts for creation, for communication, and for power. Genre theory, therefore, seeks to understand genre forms, functions, and operations. Such understanding requires knowledge about language, human behavior, and society. From our initial recognition that genres matter in actual writing, we have sought a theory that will acknowledge that importance without overly systematizing or trivializing it. We have not found that theory in linguistics, literary theory, psychology, nor in sociology, though we have learned from functional linguistics, dialogic theory, schema theory, and structuration theory. We have developed genre theory out of our own merging, blending, adapting, and discovery of new conceptions that accomplish our goals. Compared to prior uses of linguistics, we have developed our own genre theory in composition not as a preexisting linguistic system that we need merely adopt, nor as a rigid system that we need reject, but rather as a dynamic and flexible theory that we ourselves created by integrating and adapting multiple linguistic theories with other theories to do what we need done. Davis (listserv communication, May 2, 1997) quotes Freire as saying, when asked about the application of his work in the United States, "One cannot and should not attempt to 'apply' my work in an American context. You must re-invent me for yourselves, not apply me." As composition has developed as a discipline, it has moved from applying other fields to reinventing them for itself.

BOUNDARY CROSSING

In the 1990s, composition has developed a genuine, unique, intellectual context that is rich enough to support the development of new ideas. What was true for linguistics is true for other fields as well, including the fields of psychology, philosophy, education, and rhetoric: composition has moved or is moving from wholesale adoption, to wholesale rejection, to reinvention of each of these fields for its own distinct purposes. Along with composition's ability to purposefully incorporate other fields within its own intellectual context has come improved status as a discipline and the ability to maintain its boundaries in the face of other, more established disciplines.

Yet our ability to maintain our focus and our boundaries may have solidified just when those disciplinary boundaries are—or should be—breaking down. Genre theory is a perspective that takes from literature, linguistics, psychology, and rhetoric and that has something to give to all of those fields as well. Composition's genre theory can now contribute to an understanding of literary as well as nonliterary texts, of spoken as well as written discourse, and of individual behavior as well as textual and social constructs. Rather than waiting for each of those fields to modify genre theory for its own purposes, scholars in genre theory would do better to expand their range to encompass issues and research from all disciplines, to make genre theory—and composition studies—genuinely interdisciplinary. Twenty years from now, composition will perhaps be sufficiently intellectually complex and independently grounded as a discipline so that the big books for composition will be hard to distinguish from the big books for literary theory, or psychology, or, even, linguistics, as scholars in all those fields pursue common topics like genre from multiple perspectives. At that point, composition will perhaps have developed furthest as a discipline.

REFERENCES

Bakhtin, M. M. (1986). The problem of speech genres. In C. Emerson & M. Holquist (Eds.) & V. W. McGee (Trans.), *Speech genres and other late essays* (pp. 60–102). Austin, TX: University of Texas Press.

Bawarshi, A. (1997). Beyond dichotomy: Toward a theory of divergence in composition studies. *JAC: A Journal of Composition Theory, 17*, 69–82.

Bazerman, C. (1988). *Shaping written knowledge: The genre and activity of the experimental article in science*. Madison, WI: University of Wisconsin Press.

Berkenkotter, C., & Huckin, T. N. (1995). *Genre knowledge in disciplinary communication: Cognition/culture/power.* Hillsdale, NJ: Lawrence Erlbaum.

Biber, D. (1988). *Variation across speech and writing*. New York: Cambridge University Press.

Bitzer, L. (1968). The rhetorical situation. *Philosophy and Rhetoric, 1*, 1–14.

Bizzell, P. (1992). *Academic discourse and critical consciousness*. Pittsburgh, PA: University of Pittsburgh Press.

Brodkey, L. (1987). *Academic writing as social practice*. Philadelphia: Temple University Press.

Christensen, F., & Christensen, B. (1978). *Notes toward a new rhetoric: Nine essays for teachers* (2nd ed.). New York: Harper & Row.

Faigley, L. (1986). Competing theories of process: A critique and a proposal. *College English, 48*, 527–542.

Faigley, L., & Witte, S. (1982). Analyzing revision. *College Composition and Communication, 32*, 400–414.

Freedman, A. (1993). Show and tell? The role of explicit teaching in the learning of new genres. *Research in the Teaching of English, 27*, 222–251.

Freedman, A., & Medway, P. (Eds.). (1994a). *Genre and the new rhetoric*. Bristol, PA: Taylor & Francis.

Freedman, A., & Medway, P. (Eds.). (1994b). *Learning and teaching genre*. Portsmouth, NH: Boynton/Cook-Heinemann.

Halliday, M. A. K. (1978). *Language as social semiotic: The social interpretation of language and meaning*. London: Edward Arnold.

Halliday, M. A. K., & Hasan, R. (1976). *Cohesion in English*. London: Longman.

Halliday, M. A. K., & Hasan, R. (1989). *Language, context, and text: Aspects of language in a social-semiotic perspective* (2nd ed.). Oxford, England: Oxford University Press.

Hirsch, E. D. (1977). *The philosophy of composition*. Chicago: University of Chicago Press.

Reid, I. (Ed.). (1987). *The place of genre in learning: Current debates*. Deakin University, Centre for Studies in Literary Education, Geelong, Victoria, Australia.

Russell, D. R. (1997). Rethinking genre in school and society: An activity theory analysis. *Written Communication, 14*, 504–554.

Shaughnessy, M. P. (1977). *Errors and expectations: A guide for the teacher of basic writing*. New York: Oxford University Press.

Smith, S. (1997). The genre of the end comment: Conventions in teacher responses to student writing. *College Composition and Communication, 48*, 249–268.

Swales, J. (1990). *Genre analysis: English in academic and research settings*. Cambridge and New York: Cambridge University Press.

Todorov, T. (1990). *Genres in discourse* (C. Porter, Trans.). Cambridge and New York: Cambridge University Press. (Original work published 1978)

Worsham, L. (1991). Writing against writing: The predicament of *ecriture feminine* in composition studies. In P. Harkin & J. Schilb (Eds.), *Contending with words: Composition and rhetoric in a postmodern age* (pp. 82–104). New York: Modern Language Association.

chapter 11

Two Disciplinary Narratives for Nonstandard English in the Classroom: Citation Histories of Shaughnessy's *Errors and Expectations* and Smitherman's *Talkin' and Testifyin'* in Rhetoric and Composition Studies*

Shirley K Rose
Purdue University

INTRODUCTION

Scholarly disciplines, knowledge-making professions, are discursively constructed systems that make their knowledge discursively. Scholarly citation practice contributes to this construction of knowledge and the knowledge-making community. Because composition studies are characterized by shared scholarly and practical interest in discourse,

*Special thanks to Elisa Lurkis and Laura Bonner for their assistance in locating and analyzing documents examined in this study.

attempts to understand how we use citations in our own scholarly discourse are of special significance to us.

In this essay, I will demonstrate a methodology for examining the means by which citations contribute to the discursive construction of knowledge and knowledge-making communities. I examine the disciplinary narratives constructed in the citation histories of Shaughnessy's *Errors and Expectations* (1977) and Smitherman's *Talkin' and Testifyin': The Language of Black America* (1977), as these two books are referenced in academic journals. In order to examine the citations of these works from the time of their publication in 1977 through 1992, I use an approach grounded in Burke's (1945/1969, 1950/1969) rhetoric of identification. Arguing that scholarly citations are one means by which a disciplinary community discourse is made coherent, I view the rhetorical histories of *Errors and Expectations* (from now on referred to as *E&E*) and *Talkin' and Testifyin'* (*T&T*) as representative anecdotes of the ways in which scholarly citations construct and legitimate narratives of disciplinary projects. Specifically, I demonstrate that the citation histories of these two works suggest competing narratives of the uses of nonstandard English in composition classrooms.

THEORETICAL GROUND AND METHODOLOGY

Most of the scholarly work on citation practices has been contributed by the disciplines of library science and social studies of science. When computerized citation indexing became possible, scholars in these disciplines used these databases to aid document retrieval and to evaluate the contributions of individual scholars. (See Ferber, 1986, for a review of these studies.) Other scholars have used counts of citations made possible by citation index databases to identify core journals in a field and relationships between those journals. (See, for example, Summers, 1984.) While there is a large and growing body of scholarship in citation studies, most of this work has used these bibliometric approaches. (For a description of bibliometric approaches to citation studies, see White and McCain, 1989.) Recently, citation scholars have become more interested in identifying citer motivations and analyzing citation contexts, having realized that counting is not enough. The field's attention has turned to work that has attempted to develop a rhetoric of citation practice, including work by Bazerman (1988), Berkenkotter and Huckin (1993), Cozzens (1988a, 1988b), Gilbert (1972), Latour (1987), Small (1978), Swales (1986, 1987).

Gilbert's (1972) early work on the rhetoric of citations viewed the practice of scholarly citation as *persuasion*, describing the scholar's practice as an effort to present the best argument or case to his/her reader and the citation as a persuasive tool. (As Gottschalk, 1950, has pointed out, the several denotations of the word *citation* suggest the ways in which the footnote might be viewed as a summons to a witness in a court of law.)

In *Shaping Written Knowledge* (1988), Bazerman argues that citation practices are cues to the "cognitive structure" of knowledge in a discipline. He examines the ways citations in scientific articles refer to, invoke, or respond to the existing literature of a field to establish a relationship with that literature. In Bazerman's cognitive rhetoric of citations, the length of a literature review, the specificity of summaries of earlier work, evaluations of connections between the current work and previous work, and the distribution of references throughout a scientific article are all indicators of the size, structure, and maturity of the discipline of which it is a part. (See also Cronin, 1984; Griffith, 1977.)

Arguing here, as I have elsewhere (Rose, 1993, 1996), for what might be characterized as a social rhetoric of citations, I will use conceptual terms suggested by Burke's rhetoric of identification. With the help of Burke's terminology for examining human motives (1945/1969, 1950/1969), I have developed a methodology for citation analysis that employs three analytical stages for examining citations of a particular scholarly work: a "grammar of citations," which looks at the *types* of relationships citing texts construct with cited texts; a "rhetoric of citations," which identifies the arguments these constructions of relationship implicitly make for incorporating a particular text into the collective knowledge-making and knowledge-circulating processes of a discipline; and a "symbolic of citations," which explores the values assigned to a particular text within a scholarly community. Using this analytical approach, it is possible to identify a discipline's narratives as they are represented in its scholarly discourse.

As a grammar, citations are an obvious means by which writers name relationships between texts. My analytical framework for examining this grammar is adapted from Winterowd's (1970) "grammar of coherence," which I've extended from analysis of relationships within a text to relationships among texts[1] in order to highlight *how* a particular work is integrated into community discourse. Briefly, these relationships can be identified by the use or logical appropriateness of particular words we recognize as "transitions": "and" is implicit in the *coordinate* relationship, "but" in the *opposite* relationship, "for" in the *generative*, "so" in the *consequential*, "or" in the *apposite*, "for example" in the *exemplary*, and temporal order ("first," "second," and so forth) in the *sequential relationship*. The *iterative* relationship is invoked by the repetition of words or ideas in the form of summary, paraphrase, or direct quotation.[2] These relationships are created between texts when citing authors reference other texts within their own texts. (For the sake of stylistic simplicity, I refer to "citing authors," though I acknowledge that these authors have not acted autonomously when their texts have been significantly mediated by editors and reviewers by the time they reach published form.)

A *coordinate* relationship is created when a citing author mentions two or more texts together. In the following citation, for example, Fox (1992) creates a *coordinative* relationship between *T&T* and Labov's *Language in the Inner City* (1972):

> Literacy issues for African Americans have been obscured, unfortunately, by a focus on a narrowly understood black English, despite the efforts of Labov, Smitherman, and others to place the language of African Americans in a more fully understood social and historical context. (p. 219)

By placing a particular text in a group of texts, a citing author does more than recognize some relevant similarity between it and the other texts named; the author establishes that similarity by creating a category or class to which all mentioned texts belong.

An *opposite* relationship between citing text and cited text is created when a citing author identifies a disagreement between his own work and the cited work or between two cited works. In the following example, Ney (1986) criticizes some of the categories Shaughnessy (1977) used for her error analysis in *Errors and Expectations*:

> Another of the problems with the work of Shaughnessy lies in the impressionistic kinds of language that she uses to categorize and classify groups of errors. For instance, one of her categories is *blurred patterns*. This category is little better than the category *awkward*, which has been used in freshman handbooks for years. (p. 26)

An oppositive citation, though implicitly a negative evaluation of the cited text because presumably two people who disagree can't both be right (although both could be wrong), constructs a role for texts in the collective knowledge-making activity of the discipline. Thus, it is better to be cited for being wrong than not to be cited at all.

A *generative* relationship, one cited text identified as cause and other text(s) as effects, is suggested when a work is named as a basis of later research. The following citation by Neuleib (1992) constructs such a role for *E&E*:

> Fifteen years ago Shaughnessy began the quest to know why many students read and write so differently from the academic community of their

> teachers. Her theories about the nature of error have since informed the work of nearly all basic-writing researchers and theorists. (p. 240)

The other cause–effect relationship, the *consequential* relationship, is created when the citer asserts that the cited text is an effect or result of one or more other texts, as Nystrand (1993) does in the following example:

> These developments toward a social theory of language use—especially Labov's insights about the logic of nonstandard English, Hymes' concept of *speech community*, and the more general reorientation of analyses by Searle and others from syntax (form) to discourse (function)—found considerable influence among composition scholars in the late 1970s and 1980s. These include, for example, (a) Shaughnessy's (1977) discussion of the logic of error in the writing of "nontraditional" student populations. (pp. 287–288)

A citer's assertion of a *sequential* relationship can be especially significant because it suggests a particular narrative of the community's history. Ordering texts chronologically makes very specific claims about their significance to the orderly development of a discipline, as the following citation of *E&E* suggests:

> From Shaughnessy's marathon study of thousands of students' papers, the focus has steadily narrowed to concentrated study of a few individual readers and writers at work processing and producing text (Hull and Rose, McCarthy, Selfe). Recent research and theory suggest that.... (Neuleib, 1992, p. 240)

An *apposite* relationship, the "or" relationship between one cited text and another or between the cited text and the citing text, is asserted when a significant difference between the texts is identified without implying that either is in error—for example, differences in focus or membership in different categories of a particular classification scheme, as the following example illustrates:

> Freeman (1979, p. 143) sees the error analysis of E. D. Hirsch Jr. as deductive but the error analysis of Shaughnessy as inductive. (Ney, 1986, p. 17)

The *exemplary* relationship between texts is created when the cited text is posited as an example of a type. In the following citation, Gilyard (1990) uses *T&T* as an:

> Consider the oft-debated notion of African survivals, in this instance the conception that cultural practices in Africa can account for certain forms literature by African-Americans has taken. A concise treatment of this idea can be found in Geneva Smitherman's *Talkin' and Testifyin'*. (p. 777)

Assigning the status of "exemplar" to a work makes the strongest of claims for the significance of its contribution to the discourse community.

An *iterative* relationship is established when a text repeats a unit of the cited text, whether by repeating a term, quoting or paraphrasing a passage, or by summarizing the whole or a part of the cited text. In the following example, Nembhard (1983) iterates *E&E* by both paraphrasing and quoting:

> These teachers, according to Shaughnessy, point out that conventions vary from dialect to dialect and, therefore, are not obligatory, "not at least in those situations where variant forms can be understood by a reader or where the imposition of new forms undermines the writer's pride or confidence in his native language or vernacular" [qtd. from p. 9]. (p. 76)

Most citing texts create a web of connections between their own texts and the texts they cite by asserting several of these relationships. This "grammar of coherence" describes a set of possible relationships that members of a scholarly community can posit between texts (their own or others) for which they wish to claim a place in disciplinary discourse.

The grammar provides a formal groundwork for the next level of analysis, the rhetoric of citations. Whereas the grammar predicts and describes the relationships constructed between texts, the rhetoric explains the effects of this construction. Citing authors write in order to negotiate and maintain a role in the discourse community, arguing for a particular construction of that community as they shape its collective narrative.

Small (1978) has suggested that scholars cite works that are symbolic of ideas they are discussing. Citation of these works is a shorthand way of including large sets of information and complex ideas. Small observes that cited documents serve as symbols for concepts or ideas the citing author wishes to express or discuss. Using Small's notion of the frequently cited document as a standard symbol for the whole community, we can examine the ways in which citing authors who use these symbols participate in a discipline's collective process of creating knowledge.

Every time a scholar presents a review of the literature in her area of inquiry, or writes a bibliographical essay, or incorporates another writer's words or ideas to advance her own thesis, she maps the field of her discipline. She draws the boundaries, circumscribes the territory of her field of discourse, and determines who is within and who is without. Thus, what Burke (1945/1969, 1950/1969) has described as a rhetorical process of identification and division takes place in the practices of citation in scholarly writing as the author identifies her own work with what counts as shared knowledge and divides it from what is refuted or rejected as knowledge.

An analytical approach that examines the grammar, rhetoric, and symbolic of scholarly citations has several research applications for composition studies and writing in the disciplines. Examining citation practices at each of these levels of analysis will help us to understand the role of citations in scholarly discourse. Comparative analyses of citation practices in different disciplines or within multidisciplinary areas of study can help in identifying the shared values of these scholarly communities—for example, what does composition studies cite from linguistics and what does it ignore? When we study the citation practice of an individual author in a particular text, we can see how that text first enters the community discourse. And of course this analytical approach can be used to understand and evaluate a particular cited text's contribution to a discipline's processes of making knowledge.

ANALYSIS OF FOCUS TEXTS

The following discussion of the citation histories of *Errors and Expectations* and *Talkin' and Testifyin'* is a demonstration of the claims I've been making. I've chosen these two texts for several reasons: first, they share a historical context—both were published in 1977 (the institutional context of open admissions policies and the professional context of the CCCC statement, "Students' Right to Their Own Language," do not need to be rehearsed here); second, they share a topical focus: Both address the ways teachers might understand the writing of students who were not fluent in Standard American English; both draw on Labov's (1972) work on Black English Vernacular (BEV); and both call for changes in pedagogical practices, which would demand a reeducation and reorientation for teachers of writing.

Explanation of Procedures for Identifying Citations

Citations were identified by using the *Arts and Humanities Citation Index* and *Social Sciences Citation Index*. In addition to these indexes, since they do not include many important composition studies journals, I physically inspected the footnotes and lists of works cited for references to *E&E* and *T&T* in nine composition studies journals. (The increasing

TABLE 11.1. Citations of Shaughnessy's *Errors and Expectations* from 1978 to 1992

	1978	1979	1980	1981	1982	1983	1984	1985	1986	1987	1988	1989	1990	1991	1992	Total
CE	3	3	11	0	1	3	3	2	0	2	0	2	2	2	0	34
CCC	0	0	3	0	5	4	7	7	3	4	5	3	0	1	4	46
RTE	2	4	3	0	0	0	0	2	3	2	2	2	0	0	1	21
JBW	2	2	3	6	NP	NP	4	4	2	5	0	5	1	6	4	44
JAC	NP	NP	NP	0	0	0	1	0	0	0	0	2	0	1	0	4
TWI	NP	NP	NP	1	1	1	2	0	4	0	0	1	0	0	1	11
JTW	NP	NP	NP	0	0	0	3	0	1	1	1	2	1	0	3	12
RR	NP	NP	NP	1	1	1	0	1	2	0	0	1	0	2	1	10
WC	NP	NP	NP	NP	NP	NP	0	3	3	2	5	1	1	0	2	17
Comp totals	7	9	20	8	8	9	20	19	18	16	13	19	5	12	16	199
Idx Non-comp	6	5	6	10	16	10	5	9	10	22	4	6	14	5	2	130
Totals	13	14	26	18	24	19	25	28	28	38	17	25	19	17	18	329

Notes: NP = Not published.
Idx Non-comp = Citations listed in *A&HCI* or *SSCI*

availability of electronic journals and online versions of journals will eventually make citation searches easier.)

I have examined and analyzed all identified citations of both texts that appeared from 1977 to 1992, with the exception of articles that were not available from the San Diego State University library, the Purdue University libraries, or Interlibrary loan, as well as articles that were not written in English.

Analysis of Citations of *Errors and Expectations*

I have examined a total of 329 citations of Shaughnessy's *Errors and Expectations* (1977), which appeared in scholarly journals from 1978 through 1992; 199 of these citations appeared in composition studies journals; the balance appeared in indexed journals in other areas of study. (See Table 11.1.)

I won't go into the specific numbers of each type of citation here, except to note that coordinate and exemplary citations overwhelmingly outnumber appositional and oppositional citations and that generative citations far outnumber consequential citations. In other words, more citing authors cite Shaughnessy as an authority to support their own work than challenge her; and more authors identify Shaughnessy as an influence on other work than identify influences on Shaughnessy. In order to provide readers with some sense of the kind of data I am working with, I will briefly summarize and review the exemplary, coordinate, and iterative citations of *E&E*. In this analysis, I have not made special note of texts that are extended evaluations, critiques, or reconsiderations of *T&T* or *E&E* because I have been more interested in looking at the ways these two works have been generally used or constructed in academic discourse. Shaughnessy's book is cited as an exemplar of all of the following (these phrases are actual quotations from citing authors):

- a large-scale study of college freshman writing;
- a formal study based on a hermeneutic approach to student writing;
- discussions of effects of open admissions;
- a most impressive error taxonomy for written language;
- a composition work on the phenomenology of error;
- the importance of affective elements in teaching writing;
- practical investigator at work;
- a humanistic account of teaching basic composition;
- a book that presents a particular teacher's philosophy;
- a middle ground in controversy over conventions and social issues; and
- an influential member of the composition community urging contextual research on the composing process.

Citing authors coordinate *E&E* with other research on student writing, other analyses of error in student writing, and other discussions of student writers' composing processes.

Most frequently iterated is Shaughnessy's explanation of basic writers' errors as patterned or logical; her claim that basic writers' errors reflect the influence of their spoken language; her discussions of basic writers' fear of or obsession with error to the point of being unable to compose fluently; and her concept of an economics of energy for explaining readers' difficulty with error.

Analysis of Citations of *Talkin' and Testifyin'*

I have examined a total of 50 citations of Smitherman's *Talkin' and Testifyin'* (1977), which appeared in scholarly journals. Of these, 11 appeared in composition studies journals, while 39 citations appeared in indexed journals in other areas of study. (See Table 11.2.)

There are so few citations of *T&T* in composition studies journals that it is difficult to generalize about the way it has been characterized and represented in our profession. Two of the 11 citations of *T&T* in composition journals are self- citations by Smitherman, which, while they are valuable for their presumed accuracy of representation, are less useful as indicators of how the work might be integrated into the community discourse. The only unquestionable generalization is that *T&T* was relatively ignored by composition studies in the first 15 years after publication.

However, we can look at the ways journals in other disciplines and areas of study have represented *T&T* and speculate about whether composition studies' ignorance is significant. *Talkin' and Testifyin'* has been characterized as an exemplar of the following:

- research on Black English rhetorical and semantic strategies;
- a work on Black English that discusses the role of folklore;
- researchers who have addressed test bias;
- sociolinguists who have shown BEV is a different, not a deficient, dialect;
- scholars on significance of rhetorical skill in African American communities;
- a work on Black English that has had an impact on the education of children; and
- scholarship on the influence of African culture on African American literature.

TABLE 11.2. Citations of Smitherman's *Talkin' and Testifyin'* from 1978 to 1992

	1978	1979	1980	1981	1982	1983	1984	1985	1986	1987	1988	1989	1990	1991	1992	Total
CE	0	0	1	0	0	0	0	0	0	1	0	0	1	0	0	3
CCC	0	0	0	0	0	0	0	0	0	0	0	0	0	0	0	0
RTE	0	0	0	1	0	0	0	0	2	0	0	0	0	0	0	3
JBW	0	0	0	0	NP	NP	1	0	0	0	0	0	0	0	0	1
JAC	NP	NP	NP	0	0	0	0	0	0	NP	NP	0	0	0	1	1
TWI	NP	NP	NP	0	1	0	0	0	0	0	0	0	0	1	0	2
JTW	NP	NP	NP	NP	0	0	0	0	0	0	0	0	1	0	0	1
RR	NP	NP	NP	NP	0	0	0	0	0	0	0	0	0	0	0	0
WC	NP	NP	NP	NP	NP	NP	0	0	0	0	0	0	0	0	0	0
Comp totals	0	0	1	1	1	0	1	0	2	1	0	0	2	1	1	11
Idx Non-comp	0	1	2	7	2	8	3	3	1	3	1	4	2	2	0	39
Totals	0	1	3	8	3	8	4	3	3	4	1	4	4	3	1	50

Notes: NP = Not published.
Idx Non-comp = Citations listed in *A&HCI* or *SSCI*

Coordinating citations identify Smitherman's work with other scholars and researchers' work on particular subjects, for example:

- other research on syntactic patterns in BEV;
- other scholars explaining the concept of signification in African American discourse;
- other scholars who discuss tropes in African American discourse;
- other researchers who support the cultural differences (versus cultural deficit) hypothesis;
- other researchers on black children's communicative competence in their own language;
- other scholars who provide a comprehensive survey of the history, syntax, phonology, and semantics of Black English;
- other scholars who discuss the role of figurative language in Black English rhetorical strategies;
- other researchers who have shown that African Americans are less influenced by school literacy than white children;
- other work on the historical prominence of storytellers in the African American community; and
- others who have made efforts to place the language of African Americans in a social and historical context.

Authors who iterate portions of Smitherman's book mention specific explanations of lexical, syntactic, stylistic, and rhetorical features of Black English, such as:

- forms of "to be" in BEV;
- definition of "rap" in BEV;
- explanation of "big momma" in BEV;
- indirection in black speech;
- her discussion of "tonal semantics" and "talk singing"; and
- her description of black adult concrete narrative style;

or they iterate Smitherman's discussion of cultural and political issues, such as her explanation of

- the "push–pull" dynamics;
- her claim that the segregation effect keeps Black English alive; and
- her claims that bidialectism causes schism.

These topics can be organized into three general categories: 1) descriptions of Black English (including phonology, syntactic features, stylistic and rhetorical strategies, and lexical and semantic characteristics); 2) discussions of the cultural traditions of Black English (including history in general, role of folklore, and influence of African worldview); and 3) discussions of the politics of Black English (including discussions of test bias, national public educational policy, and the difference versus deficit hypotheses).

These are all matters appropriate to the concerns and interests of composition teachers and scholars. Yet, among the 50 citations of *T&T* over the period from 1978 to 1992, of the 25 that referred to Smitherman's research on Black English, only 2 appeared in composition journals; of the 14 that referred to Smitherman's scholarship on the cultural traditions of Black English, only 3 appeared in composition journals; and of the 11 that explicitly mentioned Smitherman's discussions of the politics of Black English, only 2 appeared in composition studies journals.

This comparative lack of discussion of *T&T* by the composition studies community suggests that we have neither wanted to know nor wanted to reiterate for ourselves the history and characteristics of Black English Vernacular or the communication traditions of African Americans in our discussions of the uses of nonstandard English in the classroom.

Comparison of Competing Narratives

To give another example of what more the composition studies profession might learn about ourselves by comparing the citation histories of these two works, I have reviewed citations of *Errors and Expectations* and divided them into three categories. The first category is citations of *E&E* where citation of *T&T* would have been inappropriate—for example, mentions of Shaughnessy's discussions of basic writers' composing processes, discussions of Shaughnessy's methodology, or iterations of terms credited to Shaughnessy or quotations of particular turns of phrase. I have placed 77 of the total of 329 citations in this category.

The second category is citations of *E&E* where citation of *T&T* would, I believe, have been not only appropriate but called for—for example, discussions of the influences of spoken language on nontraditional students' writing, descriptions of the pattern or logic of basic writers' deviations from Standard American English, and discussions of rhetorical strategies of basic writers. In this category, I've identified 37 citations of *E&E* that could have included or substituted *T&T*.

In the third category, I've placed citations of *E&E* related to cultural and political issues that *T&T* addresses. These are citations where reference to *T&T* would have been relevant, such as those mentioning basic writers' fear of or obsession with error, basic writers' apparent lack of audience awareness, the importance of affective elements in writing, and the importance of meaningful content in the curriculum. The balance of the E&E citations, which total 225, fall into this category.

To put this simply, we've preferred iterating Shaughnessy's concept of a logic of error or pattern of error to iterating Smitherman's description of the grammar of BEV. We've chosen to iterate Shaughnessy's description of the work we have to do as *teachers* analyzing *student* error to Smitherman's description of what we need to learn about the grammar and rhetoric, the history and politics of Black English. These citation histories suggest that Shaughnessy's narrative of our disciplinary project has been more acceptable to the profession of composition studies. Perhaps Shaughnessy's discursive construction of our work as a response to student need has appealed to us because this narrative simultaneously constructs a need for our work and serves to perpetuate us professionally.

In his historical inquiry into the professional functioning of the footnote in classical studies, Nimis (1984) points out that footnotes are "intimately bound up with authority" (p. 106)—not just in the sense of providing an "argument from authority" but also in the professional sense of being an exercise of the "ability to impose symbols" (p. 106).

Nimis cites Toulmin's (1972) distinction between the disciplinary and professional "faces" of any rational enterprise: a *discipline* comprises a "communal tradition of procedures and techniques for dealing with theoretical or practical problems"; a *profession* comprises "the organized set of institutions, roles, and [persons] whose task it is to apply or improve these procedures and techniques" (1984, p. 114). By distinguishing between disciplinary authority and professional authority, it is possible to see the strategies by which appeals to the professional face are "masked" as appeals to its disciplinary face (p. 114). An examination of our citation practices reveals that composition studies is a discourse that reproduces itself.

USES OF CITATION ANALYSIS IN COMPOSITION STUDIES

By allowing us to look at how a text's meaning for the discourse community of composition studies has changed over time, citation analysis helps us understand who we are. By showing us how we construct ourselves as a knowledge-making community, citation analysis helps us understand how we maintain ourselves as a professional community.

One of the chief drawbacks to the method of citation analysis I have used in this project is that identifying and retrieving the citing documents can be a laborious, and sometimes tedious, process. However, the improved access to the *Arts and Humanities Citation Index* and the *Social*

Sciences Citation Index databases in their CD-ROM versions and the increasing availability of electronic journals and electronic versions of major journals will eventually make thorough citation searches simpler, making increased attention to content analysis possible.

As a research methodology, citation analysis is appropriate to rhetoric and composition studies because it requires us to be self-conscious about the means of our discursive construction of disciplinary status. By using rhetorical analysis—tools of the discipline—to study the discipline, citation analysis can make a contribution to understanding our history as a discipline and as a professional community.

NOTES

[1]In his essay entitled "The Grammar of Coherence," Winterowd (1970) identified seven "structural relationships" that contributed to creating a coherence between parts of a text. Winterowd demonstrated that these relationships exist between sentences in a text, and claimed that they existed between larger units of a text, such as paragraphs or even chapters of a book, as well. I have extended this grammar of coherence to identify the relationships created between discrete texts through the use of citations. I have substituted my own, slightly less jargonistic, terms for Winterowd's original seven: coordinativity (coordinate), obversativity (opposite), causativity (generative), conclusivity (consequential), alternativity (apposite), inclusivity (exemplary), and sequentiality (sequential).

[2]*Iterative* is my own word for describing relationships based on repetition (quotation, summary, and paraphrase). Winterowd (1970) may have considered iteration an element of lexical coherence or semantic rather than syntactic relationship.

REFERENCES

Bazerman, C. (1988). *Shaping written knowledge: The genre and activity of the experimental article in science*. Madison, WI: University of Wisconsin Press.

Berkenkotter, C., & Huckin, T. N. (1993). You are what you cite. In N. R. Blyer & C. Thralls (Eds.), *Professional communication: The social perspective* (pp. 109–127). Newbury Park, CA: Sage.

Burke, K. (1969). *A grammar of motives*. Berkeley, CA: University of California Press. (Original work published 1949)

Burke, K. (1969). *A rhetoric of motives*. Berkeley, CA: University of California Press. (Original work published 1950)

Conference on College Composition and Communication. (1974). Students' right to their own language. *College Composition and Communication, 25*(3), 1–32.

Cozzens, S. E. (1988a). *Social control and multiple discovery in science: The opiate receptor case*. Albany, NY: State University of New York Press.
Cozzens, S. E. (1988b). What do citations count? The rhetoric-first model. *Scientometrics, 15*, 437–447.
Cronin, B. (1984). *The citation process: The role and significance of citations in scientific communication*. London: Taylor Graham.
Ferber, M. A. (1986). Citations: Are they an objective measure of scholarly merit? *Signs: Journal of Women in Culture and Society, 11*, 381–389.
Fox, T. (1992). Repositioning the profession: Teaching writing to African American students. *Journal of Advanced Composition, 12*, 291–303.
Gilbert, G. N. (1972). Referencing as persuasion. *Social Studies of Science, 7*, 113–122.
Gilyard, K. (1990). Genopsycholinguisticide and the language theme in African-American fiction. *College English, 52*, 776–786.
Gottschalk, L. (1950). *Understanding history: A primer of historical method*. New York: Knopf.
Griffith, B. C. (1977). On the use of citation in studying scientific achievement and communication. *Society for the Social Studies of Science Newsletter, 2*, 9–13.
Labov, W. (1972). *Language in the inner city: Studies in the Black English Vernacular.* Philadelphia: University of Pennsylvania Press.
Latour, B. (1987). *Science in action: How to follow scientists and engineers through society.* Cambridge, MA: Harvard U Press.
Nembhard, J. P. (1983). A perspective on teaching Black Dialect students to write Standard English. *Journal of Negro Education, 52*, 755–782.
Neuleib, J. (1992). The friendly stranger: Twenty-five years as "Other." *College Composition and Communication, 43*, 231–243.
Ney, J. W. (1986). Error analysis, theories of language, and the teaching of writing. *Written Communication, 3*, 15–29.
Nimis, S. (1984). Fussnoten: Das fundament der wissenschaft. *Arethusa, 17*(2), 105–134.
Nystrand, M. (1993). Where did composition studies come from? An intellectual history. *Written Communication, 10*, 267–333.
Rose, S. K. (1993). Citation rituals in academic cultures. *Issues in Writing, 6*, 24–37.
Rose, S. K. (1996). What's love got to do with it? Scholarly citation practices as courtship rituals. *Journal of Language and Learning Across the Disciplines, 1(3)*, 34–48.
Shaughnessy, M. P. (1977). *Errors and expectations: A guide for the teacher of basic writing*. New York: Oxford University Press.
Small, H. G. (1978). Cited documents as concept symbols. *Social Studies of Science, 8*, 327–340.
Smitherman, G. (1977). *Talkin' and testifyin': The language of black America*. Boston: Houghton Mifflin.
Summers, E. G. (1984). A review and application of citation analysis methodology to reading research journal literature. *Journal of the American Society for Information Science, 35*, 332–343.
Swales, J. (1986). Citation analysis and discourse analysis. *Applied Linguistics, 7*, 39†56.

Swales, J. (1987). Utilizing the literature in teaching the research paper. *TESOL Quarterly, 21*(1), 41–68.
Toulmin, S. (1972). *Human understanding*. Princeton, NJ: Princeton University Press.
White, H. D., & McCain, K. W. (1989). Bibliometrics. *Annual Review of Information Science and Technology, 24*, 119–186.
Winterowd, W. R. (1970). A grammar of coherence. *College English, 31*, 828–835.

Watson Conference Oral History #3: The Breadth of Composition Studies: Professionalization and Interdisciplinarity October 1996 Joseph Comprone, Lisa Ede, Peter Elbow, Janice Lauer, Andrea Lunsford, and Richard Young

Randy Cauthen, interviewer
edited by Pamela Takayoshi

Randy Cauthen: I would like to start by asking you all to finish the sentence: If I knew then what I do now...

Joseph Comprone: One of the motives behind rhetoric and composition has always been not so much professionalization, but how to cope with a kind of antiprofessional stance on some things. I worked hard to try to help the profession become professional and at the same time I have always recognized that my motives going into the field in 1969 were actually motives that were opposed to the professional motives within the graduate program I was in. I'm a first generation college graduate, so I had no clear ideas about profession when I graduated from college. What I looked at was what would be exciting and useful. What was exciting and useful for me when I started to get involved in composition was seeing it as an area in the university that was open to a larger universe of students. It was also an area that many of my mentors thought I was crazy to be involved in at the time. When I look back on that time now, I realize that I wanted a different definition of profession.

Andrea Lunsford: I would like to hear what this group has to say in response to the attacks on professionalization that are going on right now in the academy, especially within the humanities—the arguments that what's wrong with Ph.D. programs in humanities is that they've become too "professional." What Joe's been talking about is related to arguments which single out women and composition as instrumental to the death of literature. When you hook up the sense of professionalism that Joe was being encouraged to embody with the notion of a *work* as being the repository of meaning, you get a kind of confluence that attaches the work we do to a commodified object, usually a literary text. And the discipline of composition, to be legitimized, or "professionalized," needed to define an area of "work" that could similarly be commodified. My sense right now is that the notion of text as a *work* which is objectifiable and commodifiable is being radically challenged. If we in composition can't use that concept of work, which is attached to the construct of "writer" as a single kind of autonomous intelligence, what is our work going to be? The big question for us in the 21st century is not only going to be how to redefine *a* work, but also how to link *our* work in composition with whatever that work turns out to be.

JC: That is a much more articulate way of putting what I was talking about when I look back at the transition I was trying to go through in '69 and '70. I didn't have the language to name it, but that was definitely a presence at the time, and it was certainly one of the reasons that I did what I ended up doing.

Janice Lauer: When you look into the attacks on professionalism, what often is at stake is definition—how a discipline or profession is defined. We in rhetoric and composition have from the beginning wanted to have a field that could authorize a serious study of writing, but our concept of discipline differed from the narrow view being criticized today. The things we wanted to study were so complex that we couldn't confine ourselves to one mode of study—we had to have multiple modes. Traditional notions of disciplinarity often define a field by a single mode of inquiry, which ends up excluding so many important questions that the people in the discipline are stifled. But it is possible to redefine what is meant by "a discipline" or by "a profession" or refuse to fit into a preconceived notion of discipline.

AL: I'm talking, too, about the arguments that we ought not to be helping students publish, we ought not to be doing mock interviews, we ought not to be doing any job-related workshops because that is "professionalism" and that is bad. Instead, we ought to give graduate students their carrels and let them think deep thoughts about something so they can come forward years later with the products of that thought. So again, this particular attack on professionalizing English departments is a backhanded way of critiquing what compositionists are doing because, in the English department, it's mostly the compositionists who are at the forefront of trying to help graduate students become professionals.

RC: For those who work in the field in that way, the professionalization disrupts the purity of the discipline.

Richard Young: As we have been talking, I have been thinking back over my own experiences and by and large I wouldn't change or at least make any major changes in the way I have lived out my career—with one exception. When I went to Carnegie Mellon, the dean offered me the option of building a rhetoric program inside or outside the English Department. I chose to build it in the Department. Looking back over the almost 20 years in the English Department, I find it has been a constant uphill battle, and we in rhetorical studies have never quite been able to shake ourselves loose from the definitions that have been imposed upon us. What's the discipline of English? What's our place in the discipline? If you look at the history of rhetoric in the MLA, what you see is a contest over whose definition of the enterprise is going to be the one that is institutionalized and that drives professional practice. We, that is, rhetoricians around the country, might have grown in a more desirable way and the shape of our discipline might be less problematic today had we been able to step outside the English Department, which I have found to be constraining in all kinds of ways. For example, rhetoric is still designed by many around the country chiefly in terms of the freshman course. That definition is responsible for a lot of the ills that we're facing today, such as the growing overproduction of Ph.D.'s. The minute you tie a doctoral program to the freshmen course, you are going to overproduce Ph.D.'s. You will need more people to teach that course than are needed subsequently in the field, at least in tenure-track positions. So we have this problem: Are we rhetoricians? Are we compositionists? Compositionists tend to define themselves with reference to the freshman course. Had we taken another direction and developed outside English departments, we might have done better, since we might well have begun with a larger definition of the discipline. And look at the problems we have by staying in English. For example, over the last generation, there has been an extraordinary proliferation of knowledge about how writing and the teaching of writing and about languaging in the world. But how do you teach classical rhetoric or any other sophisticated rhetoric in a 15-week course? Current-traditional rhetoric worked, but largely because it was so simplistic. We have a kind o knowledge now that does not fit well within the institutional framework, which is extremely difficult to change.

Peter Elbow: It is a burden and an impossible task faced not just by the English department. The idea is that we gave you the 15 weeks, and you still didn't solve all of your students' problems. Nevertheless, I think it is very intellectually fertile trying to teach everybody to write.

JL: I have an ambivalence about being in the English department. I must say that our program at Purdue has flourished in the English Department...but not without an enormous amount of work and effort. We will never know what would have happened had we taken another direction. One of the trickiest problems has been the recognition of our types of research when it comes down to the reward system. It has taken a great deal of "rhetoric" to educate the faculty in literature who make personnel decisions about younger colleagues. On the other hand, one could say, "Well, the effort to remain in English departments has helped change the field of English." Because I have seen a lot of change in the attitudes and understanding of literature faculty toward rhetoric and composition scholarship, including empirical research and work on pedagogy, I am ambivalent on this matter.

Lisa Ede: We certainly professionalized ourselves if you look at the development of composition studies from the perspective of studies of professionalization and expectations within the humanities. We have done exactly what is required of disciplines in the humanities, whether they are multimodal or not—we have developed journals, conferences, and awards. I would put forward a kind of both/and paradox in terms of professionalization.

AL: I do think we are at a crucial historical moment right now, especially given what Lester Faigley was saying about virtual universities. London has made an incredible foray in trying to become the world's university. They are trying to arrive at a virtual university which draws its student body not just from the British Isles, but from around the world. We are going to see more and more of that. I wouldn't have made the decision to move outside the traditional department structure 20 years ago. I wouldn't have had the wit or the courage. But, right now, I really think that traditional disciplinarity is crumbling all around us. That's one reason we see institutes and centers springing up everywhere. At this historical moment, composition seems perfectly poised for such an interdisciplinary enterprise than almost anybody else in traditional fields, through our work with texts and information providers and consumers. What we need to find is a site—and increasingly, I don't think it is going to be the English department.

RC: Could you relate that to a larger mission of literacy across culture?

AL: Across cultures, across national boundaries, across age groups—we have always been interested in the way people write, from the time that they can pick up a crayon or a pencil until the time that they die. So, again, we are not so focused on that 18-year-old population, and we really never have been.

LE: The kind of institute that Andrea suggests could provide a new model for professionalization.

RY: Take Lee Odell's talk yesterday, where he delineated a growing edge in rhetorical studies. My own observations of departments around the country suggest that it would be difficult to tenure someone in an English department working in the areas Odell is describing. They are so alien to the focus of attention and the values that have characterized traditional English faculties.

LE: You started by asking us to complete the sentence "If I knew then what I know now..." I didn't have an answer when you asked the question, but as we've been talking I've realized that I have a much clearer and more acute sense of the kind of ethical and political issues that any effort to work within the academy inevitably raises than I did when I first entered the profession. The 1970s was a tremendously exciting time in composition studies—heady, really—and it was very easy to imagine that "progress" in research would inevitably benefit the field at large. But it's not that simple, as Jackie [Royster] said today. We are always operating and extending in more ways than we think, and it's very tempting in a disciplinary context to focus on those aspects of our situation that confirm our sense of identity and mission. It was easy—too easy—for scholars to imagine that our research would directly and immediately benefit the classroom teachers whom we saw as our audience. I now have a much more complicated (and tension-filled) understanding of my rhetorical and material situation in the academy.

JC: You know, there is a distinction, I think, between the Ph.D.'s in literature and the PhDs in composition. Maybe that's because I just came from the conference session on the rhetoric program at University of Louisville. The training that the Ph.D.'s at Louisville got was far broader than I have ever experienced in almost every other discipline I have worked with as a dean, a chair, whatever. The profession does have a tradition of broadness. As I think about it, that's really what I was looking for back in '69—a chance to move out. And today's graduate students don't just teach—they often serve in administrative positions within writing programs, they go to conferences earlier.

RY: One of the things that led me into rhetoric in the first place was a kind of Deweyan preference for reasoned action in the world. There is a deep current of Platonism that runs through literary education that places value on dissociating oneself from the world. Being a good Midwestern boy from a rural community in the 1930s, I had trouble with that. Rhetoric, though, offered a way of hanging on to the values that led me into the literary studies and at the same time let me see connections between what I was doing intellectually and what was going on in the world.

JL: I saw working with writing as having a lot of possibilities for making changes. Instead of viewing composition teaching as something apart from social action, I felt that through teaching, and especially through teaching writing, I could ground my concern for others.

JC: It would be interesting to hear somebody like Jim Berlin on that kind of question. He was so committed to composition as a broadening-out of the narrower kind of perspective on the world. Jim was the kind of theoretician who would argue with businessmen on the corner. There must be something in composition that has to do with people having motives like that.

PE: That makes me think of my father, who was a machinist. I would try to study literature very seriously, and when he would ask me what I was doing and I would tell him, I would see his eyes glaze as I would talk. While I was talking to him about a writing program, that was different. That had a kind of functional, real thing. You know, it was partly...I had to get my hands on something.

JL: One of the reasons for working toward professionalization for the next generation of people was the motivation that we had for ourselves—to provide the possibility for doing serious, rigorous research on writing and therefore to help others to learn to write well. We wanted to create a space within departments of English, so that the endeavor of writing would be taken seriously.

PE: To pick it up on what Janice was saying...I guess I hear the echoes of that reading this morning. The people we're now educating in graduate school really need to be encouraged to take advantage of the potential for breadth in rhetoric and composition.

JL: Bob Connors argued at the beginning of the conference that graduates are moving away from teaching. He argued that composition specialists are becoming researchers and getting away from the classroom, but I question this conclusion and think it should be carefully researched. My impression from talking with our graduates over the years is that they are heavily involved in teaching. They are not focusing only on research, but are doing an enormous amount of teaching...at all different levels.

Watson Conference Oral History #4: Classical Rhetoric in the Present and Future of Composition Studies October 1996 Edward P. J. Corbett, Frank D'Angelo, Winifred Horner, James Kinneavy, and C. Jan Swearingen

Jack Ramey, interviewer
edited by Pamela Takayoshi

Jack Ramey: Who were your influences? What role did you hope your own work would play in the field?

Frank D'Angelo: I would say that Ed [Corbett] was an early influence in the shaping of my interests in rhetoric and comp. I was especially influenced by *Classical Rhetoric for the Modern Student* and later on his book on rhetorical criticism. I had used Ed's book and met him in the summer institute, and then I got some other things through Project English from him. I thought of classical rhetoric as an analogical base to which I could relate things. I could better understand the methods of development by relating them to the classical topoi, for example.

Edward Corbett: During those years during Project English, my first acquaintance was Francis Christiansen.

Winifred Horner: I think it's interesting that all of us started out as high school teachers and adjunct part-timers and MA's. All of us have that kind of background.

James Kinneavy: It is common to all of us. We were all drawn into a rhetorical situation, but we had to produce teachers of composition. We were produced by the exigencies of our different situations. This is true of Winterowd, it's true of people at Carnegie Mellon, it's true lots of places. We had to produce composition programs. We were a bankrupt discipline as far as rhetoric goes. We all just dove in in different ways. We grabbed at different places to try to put some kind of a fragment together to make a discipline that would work. It was very pragmatic. We had to be in class, and some of us ended up using the same things. Many of us ended up using some classical rhetoric eventually.

JR: Do you think that's the reason for this strong emphasis on classical rhetorical theory in the early days? Perhaps it's even a reason for the modes themselves.

JK: We inherited the modes. That was a part of the textbook. That was part of the situation.

FD: I wish that Connors had not used the term "modes" in his article, "The Rise and Fall of the Modes of Discourse," because only one 19th-century textbook writer that I know of used the term "modes." They used the term "forms of discourse," and they were conceived generically—description, narration, exposition, argument. So today, when people look at a textbook and they say, "Oh, you're using a modes approach?," what they really mean is a *generic* approach using description, narration, exposition, argumentation. That configuration of categories is quite different from Kinneavy's theories of modes, which are *strategies* of discourse.

WH: One of my reasons for going into the history of rhetoric was that in a literature department, that was considered legitimate. Being purely in composition was not, and it still isn't. If your work is in the history of rhetoric, you're okay. There's a break between people who call themselves compositionists and people who call themselves historians.

Jan Swearingen: Now the prejudice is going in reverse. I've seen this in searches, whether at the senior level or an entry level, if it's a true comp job—you know, true-blue, pure comp job—you're regarded as a mongrel or tainted by some affection for literary or historical studies, and I think that's a very insidious resurgence of that old split we need to work on. I hate to see that gap opening up again.

JK: I hope this won't be misunderstood, but in the beginning, we all had a common enemy. That was the enemy from without that I talked about. Secondly, we were so bankrupt that we could find a corner for anything that worked at all. If not a corner, maybe even a major table place. Sentence-combining was and still can be very useful. The Christiansen stuff can be and was very useful. We needed so to occupy this bankruptcy that almost everything was useful for a while and still, to some extent, is, and we became very eclectic. Then the common enemy was always there.

WH: That's so true. You could see it in the early Conference on College Composition and Communication meeting. It was like going home. "Here are my people. They understand me. I understand them." There *was* the common enemy. We were isolated in our departments, and it was wonderful to go someplace where everybody understood what we were all facing.

JK: Yes, there were some people who could not put up with composition, and we all had them in our departments and they're still around. But there were other people in literature, ones who had literary backgrounds. Some of us were willing to take on the exigency of the situation and say, "We've got to do something about composition, so let's use what we can from literature and everything else too."

WH: At TCU, more than half of the graduate students were in Rhetoric Comp. We had three, maybe four professors who could teach the graduate courses and direct those dissertations. What happened is all of us had no time to teach Freshman Comp. I remember being at a WPA meeting with a group of the people who were doing writing-program evaluation around the country. Lynn Bloom and I started talking and I said, "You know, I'm not teaching Freshman Comp anymore." She said she wasn't either, so we asked the 20 or so people there, "Okay. How many of you are teaching Freshman Comp?" Only two people raised their hands—and we were going all around the country reviewing writing programs. Most of us are so involved in graduate programs because of this great demand, and in a way we've lost our connection. To get back to the second question you've asked, Jack, I have always tried in my papers, my seminar teaching, to keep the connection between theory and what we do in the classroom. In the International Society for the History of Rhetoric, we have people whose scholarship only generally mentions connections to teaching rhetoric, but I have always tried to make that connection because I think it's important.

JS: You pioneered historical studies and rhetoric that are tied to classroom practice. I think you were one of the very first people to do bibliographical work and history of rhetoric in such a way that it could be applied to classroom practice. Because there are tons of bibliographers in straight English, but not in a way that you can say, "Oh, I see how this relates to teaching."

WH: Now, I'll tell you something. I think I have moved toward what I think is important. I have tried an indepth classical rhetoric book and tried to revive the last two offices of rhetoric, memory, and delivery, which are with us in television and computers. We don't know what to do with the new technology. We know that Quintilian wrote extensively about how to drape the toga. Well, look at our debaters. My gosh! They're telling them what colors to wear and how to wear their makeup. We're back to delivery. Those two offices are going to be extraordinarily important in the years to come as we move into visual media.

JK: The thing I'm most proud of is having run what I think of as a good freshman English program for 10 years. Another thing which I'm proud of is that I have a good graduate program going. In '79, it was approved and it's been a good graduate program ever since. I fought some royal battles both nationally and in Texas. Rhetoric has had to fight those battles, and I think that rhetoric has reaped some of the good that Ross [Winterowd] and I and the other wounded warriors carried away [*laughs*]. I also think that my work on theory and discourse and my textbooks are good. So those are some of the things that I think I would kind of highlight. Finally, I think that I'm kind of proud of the students that I have. I think that they're going to keep on speaking after I'm dead and gone.

JS: Someone asked me to ask you all: How would all of us, since we've all done work in classical rhetoric, how would we rewrite *Classical Rhetoric for the Modern Student* today? It has been done recently by Win and by Sharon [Crowley], as you've noticed, but one of the things I've tried to do in my book, which is not a textbook, was to talk about the connection for issues like ethics, multiculturalism. I think we've got a whole vast area stretching ahead of us where we're going to be dealing with multicultural student constituencies and multiple forms of discourse from different cultures. Classical rhetoric was formulated in just such a culture in Plato's, Aristotle's, and Cicero's time. It was a very cosmopolitan culture, and I think we can bring it back as a way of looking at the common topics. And decidedly artificial; they were created to form a common language in a very multicultural society, originally. Can you add women to the history of rhetoric without changing the definition of rhetoric? Should you add them to the history of rhetoric? Do we want to do this great figure, this model, or not?

JR: Ed, you said earlier that you took old ideas and reinterpreted them or revamped them for a new contact or a new worldview. How do you see, in 1996, students using classical rhetoric as heuristics or ways of getting into writing? There must have been a timeliness to your contribution, and it came about just exactly at the right time. Do you think that had anything to do with the success of your work and its influence?

EC: During those early years, there was conflict with young people. I think we've moved on from that, but I think it was a moment in rhetoric, and there were two kinds of things. There was rhetoric of rational things, and then there were the questions that were there so we could get what we wanted. I don't know if that was a major contribution, but I do think it was a change in the utility of rhetoric and a way of seeing that change. Then, too, I think we are getting back to the visual, and we're going to be using that even more.

JS: I think there's an interesting criticism of *Classical Rhetoric for Modern Students* and other classical rhetorical textbooks that's been leveled by people like [James] Berlin—that it's pandering to the abilities of all of these literature people who want something respectable. That criticism of it is very interesting along the lines of what Peter Elbow was just describing, because in its own way, the dogmatism behind the criticism is more reactionary than the textbook, which is very fluent, flexible, and adaptable. It's a very odd paradox.

WH: As though nothing that comes out of a sexist, racist society has anything to say for us. That's really sad.

JS: Well, misguided feminist theory says that rationality is male, so we should be irrational. Oh, please!

FD: There's an interesting irony in Pat Bizzell's work. In the last essay in her collection of essays, you see her moving into postmodernism. The latest thing is her interest in [Mary Louise] Pratt's contact zone stuff. The irony is that in her last essay, what she calls for is exactly what we're doing—the teaching of civic virtue. We're right back again to classical rhetoric. Jan, you've raised some questions about classical rhetoric and its relationship to feminist ideology. Would you and Win talk about that?

JS: Well, I'm getting pretty radical in my historiography because I've had to defend doing that kind of history to some pretty strong opponents who say you can't do history and you can't recuperate figures because all history is contaminated and unreliable. What I'm getting especially interested in is the huge amount of new evidence we have that women were teachers of rhetoric throughout classical antiquity, Aphasia for example. She may be a joke in Plato's dialogue, but she's not a total joke. There's a whole history there that needs to be uncovered. The jokes that are made about women who taught rhetoric are very interesting evidence of misogyny in antiquity, but they're also evidence of how familiar attitudes about rhetoric came about. This was by association with female teachers and female forms of discourse. I think that association is a real interesting theme.

EC: In the last 10 years, women have been most prominent in rhetoric. They're so dominant in numbers. That's the most promising thing I see in the future of rhetoric.

WH: I think you can see that all of us are very open to new ideas. We haven't started to really solidify our brains yet. I think that's true of all of us all along. We've been open to ideas. We're open to finding help, as you put it, and that's really good. We want to see what's going on now. These are our students, and we're always wondering.

JR: Now that you've got us going in that direction, why don't we just briefly sort of outline what your vision of the future of the discipline is all about. How do you see it going right now?

EC: Every morning, I correspond through e-mail. It's a different kind of thing. I don't worry about typos or misspellings, but the rhetoric of it is one of the most delightful ways of communicating with people. I think that e-mail is going to play a great part in the future of our writing.

WH: It's back to writing!

JR: Which gets right into rhetoric. Do you see that e-mail is positioned as a form of discourse particularly suited to classical rhetoric?

JK: Well, it's a new mode of classical rhetoric. It's a new adaptation of classical rhetoric, I think. That's true of not only email, it's true of the Web, too. If you look at websites, media dominates—websites are aural, visual, and written. That's going to complicate rhetoric. It's going to change the whole complexion of rhetoric, and we're going to have to teach people how to negotiate this new rhetoric.

WH: How to interpret it.

JK: That involves ethical and logical techniques too. I don't see how we can avoid that. In Texas right now, we are using the Web and e-mail to teach foreign languages. Students are talking to people in French, Spanish, German. The Internet is bringing us a very complicated medium. English departments right now are at the forefront of some of that. The Daedalus people have been spearheading that movement. That's good for us.

JS: One of the future possibilities that interests me with the Internet is that it's bringing back dialogue. In terms of reading something in a dialogical sense versus reading something in a passive recipient sense, television is a real passive medium. In some ways, reading a novel is also passive. It's sort of a one-way street, but on the Internet, I hope students will become more fluent in dialogical interaction.

Part IV

The Development of a Profession

chapter 12

Professionalizing Politics

Richard Ohmann
Wesleyan University

This chapter is about the troubled relations between professionalization and politics in general, and about some agenda setting that went on from the 1950s through the 1970s, as composition professionalized itself, in particular. I will point to what seems an anomaly in the brief professional history of writing instruction, and end with questions about that anomaly.

A group of workers turns itself into a profession by grounding its practice in a body of knowledge, developing and guarding that knowledge within a universally recognized institution such as a university; limiting access to its lore and skills by requiring aspirants to pass through graduate or professional programs; and controlling the certification of those aspirants for practice either by widespread agreement among employers (for example, to hire only those philosophers or biologists who have earned doctoral degrees) or with the backing and enforcement of the State (as in medicine, law, public school teaching, and so on). When a group fully achieves these goals, it turns its resources into artificially scarce commodities, creates a monopoly over their sale, and controls the conditions of its own work with little or no regulation by outside agencies (see Larson, 1977, for a thorough analysis). Of course, no group of workers could make such a safe and comfortable haven for itself in a market society without persuading consumers and authorities that the service it renders is a needed one, that only certified practitioners can meet the need, that they understand it better than their clients do, and that they will supply it in an objective and disinterested way—that is, in the interests of the client and by extension of the whole society, but to no special advantage of the practitioner, other than his or her fee. Professionalization is a social process, not an achieved and static condition, as witness to heavy losses suffered even by physicians—the supreme professionals at mid-century--since I wrote about these things in *English in America* (Ohmann, 1976).

The historical condition of possibility for modern professions was the triumph of industrial capitalism, with its increasingly specialized division of labor, its huge expansion of goods, services, and infrastructures, and its incorporation of all needs within markets. For instance, it built great cities; created intricate systems of energy, water, and waste; and spanned a continent with canals, railroads, and bridges. This project offered *engineers* an unprecedented chance to specialize and elaborate their practices, demonstrate the absolute need for their expertise, build a wall of "cognitive exclusiveness" (Larson, 1977, p. 25) around it, and turn that into monopoly—though never so successfully as did physicians, mainly because engineers' clients were powerful corporations rather than individuals. Again, capitalism needed to clarify and limit risk, redefine rights, and solidify control of property and labor power in the era of the corporation: this project offered *lawyers* their main chance to professionalize. *Doctors* were able to make their move for more complicated reasons, including the cacophony of practices and theories after mid-century, the virtual absence of regulation, the outrageous lies of proprietary healers and patent medicine makers, and the consequent public distrust of almost all practitioners other than the beloved family doctor. Then there were the manifest successes of medical research—anesthesiology, bacteriology, epidemiology—and the practical control of diseases such as typhus and cholera. Professionalizing "regular" doctors really did, for the first time in history, have more to offer the sick than a kindly or imposing manner. But the capitalist transformation of U. S. society was critical for medicine, too, as the massing of people in cities and factories brought new health crises, and new risks to the affluent from the illnesses of the poor. Doctors offered both public hygiene and private cures in response to the hazards of industrial capitalism.

THE RULE OF NEUTRALITY

The academic fields that professionalized around the same time intervened similarly in the new economic order, promising to help make it run efficiently, rationally, and without devastating social conflict. The point is especially clear for the emergent social sciences. At its founding in 1886, the American Economic Association (AEA) offered to speed "human progress" by rationalizing the economy, and help bring peace in the "conflict between capital and labor" (Coats, 1988, p. 358). Professionalizing political scientists offered expert and disinterested help a bit later in mediating political conflict and smoothing the political process, at a time when machine politics and corrupt government were scandals to the middle class, and fears of anarchy or revolution were widespread. These occupations professionalized through a period of conflict at least as distressing as, and certainly more systemically profound than, the conflicts of the 1960s and 1970s, during which composition made its move. In such times, the first modern professions claimed neutrality; they would take no sides in, for instance, the "conflict between capital and labor" that figured in early AEA discussions, but instead show a way toward peace in such conflicts through social planning, meliorative legislation, and expert management.

The AEA flirted with class-aligned views; one of its founders was Richard Ely, who identified "human progress" with Christian socialism. But he took much heat for such ideas both within the Association and from public figures in Wisconsin, where he taught at the University through the 1890s. By 1900, most economists seem to have agreed with Arthur T. Hadley of Yale, who in his presidential address held that the economist would have the most influence if he maintained a "dispassionate and critical attitude...that it is his mission to be the representative and the champion of the permanent interests of the whole community, in face of conflicting claims from representatives of temporary or partial ones" (Coats, 1988, p. 371). Never mind that Hadley was himself a partisan of *laissez-faire*; the point was to perform neutrality, convincing colleagues as well as the laity that the profession stood above class and faction, partisan only for modernity and the common good—and, of course, that *laissez-faire* was itself neutral, natural, and inevitable. Successful in this maneuver, the new professions and the new class of which they were the core made themselves indispensable, winning authority and comfort in the social order of this century.

In the years after they cleared pathways toward professional standing, familiarized all with its conventions, and established the legitimacy of its claims over a broad range of fields, many other groups of workers sought to gain the obvious advantages it afforded, often in connection with new technologies, products, and economic activities. Some groups have succeeded unequivocally (psychiatry, computer science), others partially or unsteadily (journalism, advertising). Composition seems a late arrival in that intermediate state. It has a moderately cohesive, though also variable and contested base of knowledge, or at least a disciplinary conversation with recognizable topoi. That conversation goes forward at conferences and in learned journals and professional publications of all sorts. Composition has a well established professional organization (now nearly 50 years old) and many specialized or regional groups. It has M.A. and Ph.D. programs whose graduates have privileged or exclusive access to some well-paying jobs, and substantial control over content, method, and working conditions in those jobs. I won't comment on the obvious shortfalls in professionalization, most notoriously the failure of composition to secure a lucrative monopoly in the provision of its primary service, writing instruction. The field *has* professionalized, if unevenly, and a comparison to other professionalizing groups is legitimate.

One could, for instance, focus on the historical conditions of possibility for its emergence. As at the time of the first wave of professionalization 100 years ago, there was when composition set its course a very rapid expansion of the economy (the postwar boom) and of demand for the kind of service composition offered: skill in the organization, development, and transmission of knowledge, for an "information society." There was virtually open warfare in the 1960s over the nature and control of that society, as there had been in the 1870s, 1880s, and 1890s. And there was, some think, a comparable realignment of capitalism—from competitive to corporate around 1900; and from a Fordist regime to the flexible, global capitalism we now know, through the time when composition professionalized (Harvey, 1989).

To be sure, many particular and even peculiar conditions made an opening for composition, including its prior embodiment in a college course that was required for almost all students; its subsumption within English during the first wave of professionalization; its 80-year subordination to literary studies; the failure of English to theorize composition; and its exclusion of *pedagogy* from a place among its professional secrets—as if medicine had left clinical practice to the whims of individual physicians! For all these local contingencies, the professionalization of composition seems to have gone forward in the sort of historical conjuncture most hospitable to such transformations.

And along the usual paths. Those who sought to make CCCC a semi-autonomous professional organization from 1950 on announced goals that resonate with those of other aspirant groups. They wanted better pay and lower teaching loads (to end the "drudgery" of writing instruction). They wanted respect for their work from English department colleagues. Departments should recognize the centrality of composition; every member should share in teaching it; and when the department hires, it should look for people with credentials in composition. That proposal of course entailed that there *be* such credentials: that Ph.D. programs in English offer composition studies and *prepare* graduate students to teach writing, rather than assuming that the practice was an art, an innate ability, or a craft learnable only from experience. The CCCC leaders wanted to behave like a profession, with systematic exchange of ideas, a "coordinated research program" (Gerber, 1950, p. 12), and normalization of procedures and standards across the nation. Like doctors earlier, they did not have to persuade the public that it needed their service, but did have to distinguish that service from the public's image of it—the much disdained "Miss Fidditch" approach, with terroristic enforcement of spelling rules, grammar, correct usage, and the mysteries of the five-paragraph theme. Like any professionals, they knew better than their "clients" what the latter needed.

What these people lacked was a way of theorizing their work, a coherent body of knowledge that would organize practice and validate composition in the eyes of university peers and administrators. On the written record in *College Composition and Communication*, the professionalizers were slow to take up that challenge. Only in the late 1950s did some begin to propose a revival of rhetoric. By the mid-1960s, a number of voices nominated rhetoric as, in effect, the theory of composition. In a 1965 article (interestingly, in the first issue of *CCC* edited by William Irmscher), Virginia Burke wrote of the "chaos" in composition, attributed it to the absence since 1900 of an "informing discipline," asserted the "power of a discipline [i.e., a body of theory] to identify and maintain a field," and invited her colleagues to "restore rhetoric as the informing discipline in the practice of composition at all levels" (1965, pp. 5–6). Over the next few years, many noted a revival of interest in rhetoric, hoped it was not a fad, and proposed one or another rhetorical tradition as theoretical foundation for their field, maybe even for all liberal education. These advocates included such influentials as James Murphy, Richard Braddock, Robert Gorrell, Richard Hughes, Edward Corbett, and Joseph Schwartz. Others began domesticating rhetoric, connecting it to the practice of composition; the work of Francis Christensen seemed especially promising for a while.

Alternative candidates for the role of theory came forward through the 1950s and 1960s: semantics, structural and then transformational linguistics, Bruner's psychology, tagmemics, and, of course, communication theory, whose affinities with composition had been hopefully anticipated in the naming of the organization. Unless I've missed something, composition never did agree upon a single "informing discipline" or theory, but has made do with a shifting assortment of issues and texts that frame the professional discourse and give it continuity. This has sufficed to mark composition off from other fields and build its scholarly respectability—and why not, given that a number of more established professions, including the parent field of English, are even less focused?

POLITICS IN COMPOSITION

What struck me in scanning *CCC* from 1960 to the mid-1970s was that the moment of professional articulation and purposeful disciplinarity did not dampen political engagement, as in economics and other professionalizing fields of the last century, but quite the reverse. That is, in the *pre*-professional phase of composition, up through the early 1960s, *CCC* admitted virtually no explicitly political discussion—for instance, on the Cold War, anti-Communism, and matters of free speech—and in fact published a few pleas for professional detachment (see, for example, Graves, 1963). However, by the end of the 1960s, the journal was addressing a range of issues taken from the noisy arena of national politics: disadvantaged students, two-year colleges and egalitarian education, racial oppression (indeed, the assassination of Martin Luther King—see Kelly, 1968), the question of dialect and power, campus uprisings, the rhetoric of confrontation, student power—almost everything except Vietnam itself and, until much later, feminism. Furthermore, these political energies invaded discussion of teaching practices, putting up for debate the decorums of classroom hierarchy, standards, grades, and even the question of whether composition can be systematically taught at all. In short, the conventions of authority and dignity a nascent profession would ordinarily call upon to set practitioner apart from client were all interrogated, and in the core venues of the discipline. Likewise, questions of political derivation were allowed to subvert academic conventions of writing *in* the journal: the passionate appeal, the free-form essay, the collage, gained admittance to *CCC*, as if to forgo the exclusions and reassurances implicit in a shared, specialized, and emotionally restrained style of address. Composition was airing unseemly questions about neutrality, detachment, and partisanship, and even about whether to act like a profession. I recall vividly, of course, the flow of politics into the pages of *College English* at the time, facilitated at first by my editorial tolerance and then by my more principled determination. But William Irmscher, who edited *CCC* through the same years, espoused politics very different from mine, and was more committed to sober professionalization; yet *CCC* put on display the same tensions and disruptions.

For a brief while, it might have seemed to readers of *CCC* that politics was allowed an occasional hearing, in segregation from the ongoing disciplinary project. The December 1968 issue dealt with education and inequality, the question of black language and identity, teaching Native Americans, the troubles at San Francisco State, and more. The next issue (February 1969) returned to a scholarly conversation about rhetoric and allied topics, with no effort to bridge between these and the politics of December, and no acknowledgment of a disjunction. Soon, however, the theoretical conversation began to notice the political. A pivotal moment, perhaps, was the publication of Edward P. J. Corbett's celebrated article, "The Rhetoric of the Open Hand and the Rhetoric of the Closed Fist" (1969), which accorded radicalism the dignity of rhetorical analysis even while preferring the disinterestedness of the open hand and mind. Increasingly, over the next few years, the professional and political conversations mingled. Can one say that the professional internalized the political? That compositiion took social conflict as part of its domain, rather than exiling it or offering to resolve it through the ministrations of experts, as with economics and political science earlier?

I'm not sure, but my strong impression is that although the disciplinary project went forward briskly, it did not leave behind the political themes of the movements of the 1960s. Questions of inequality (including now of gender as well as of race and class) remained on the professional agenda. Language retained its political dimension, as in the famous CCCC 1974 statement on "Students' Right to Their Own Language." The CCCC, along with the NCTE, engaged vigorously in battles over testing, basics, literacy, and so on, right through to the culture wars of the 1980s and early 1990s. And, as Bizzell (1996) has suggested at the Watson Conference, much of the most notable work in composition through that later period has dealt with "multiplicity and conflict," the social and the historical. Moreover, the profession seems to me to have taken *sides* in social conflict—taken sides, broadly speaking, with the less privileged and against centers of power.

Be that as it may, I hope to have sketched out a reasonable case for seeing conflict and politics as durable presences through the time of composition's professionalizing movement, and for seeing that presence as unusual, across the range of such movements in U.S. history. The obvious questions, then, would be: Why did it happen this way? and, with what consequences for current work and future prospects in composition?

REFERENCES

Bizzell, P. (1996, October). *Discourse and politics: New agendas for composition.* Paper presented at the Thomas R. Watson Conference on Rhetoric and Composition, University of Louisville, KY.

Burke, V. M. (1965). The composition-rhetoric pyramid. *College Composition and Communication, 16*, 3–7.

Coats, A. W. (1988). The educational revolution and the professionalization of American economics. In W. J. Barber (Ed.), *Breaking the academic mold:*

Economists and American higher learning in the nineteenth century (pp. 340–375). Middletown, CT: Wesleyan University Press.

Conference on College Composition and Communication. (1974). Students' right to their own language. *College Composition and Communication, 25*(3), 1–32.

Corbett, E. P. J. (1969). The rhetoric of the open hand and the rhetoric of the closed fist. *College Composition and Communication, 20*, 288–296.

Gerber, J. C. (1950). The Conference on College Composition and Communication. *College Composition and Communication, 1*, 12.

Graves, J. (1963). On the desirable reluctance of trumpets. *College Composition and Communication, 14*, 210–214.

Harvey, D. (1989). *The condition of postmodernity: An enquiry into the origins of cultural change*. Cambridge, MA: Blackwell.

Kelly, E. B. (1968). Murder of the American dream. *College Composition and Communication, 19*, 106–108.

Larson, M. S. (1977). *The rise of professionalism: A sociological analysis*. Berkeley, CA: University of California Press.

Ohmann, R. (1976). *English in America: A radical view of the profession*. New York: Oxford University Press.

chapter 13

Evocative Gestures in CCCC Chairs' Addresses

Ellen L. Barton
Wayne State University

INTRODUCTION

The tradition of the Chair's address at the opening session of the Conference on College Composition and Communication (CCCC) began in 1977, and the published versions of these talks provide a body of texts with a rich historical view of two decades of composition as a professionalized field.[1] CCCC Chairs' addresses, perhaps in response to the rhetorical situation of opening the annual meeting of an academic discipline, follow a tradition of what can be called "evocative gestures"—the articulation of broad concerns in the field. Perhaps in response to the nature of composition as a fairly new field in the academy, CCCC Chairs' addresses typically concern themselves with professionalism, specifically the traditional representation of an academic career or disciplinary field as comprised of research, teaching, and service. What is particularly interesting about the set of CCCC Chairs' addresses, however, is that the evocative gestures made toward teaching and service remain fairly constant over time and seem to reflect a shared consensus, but the gestures articulating the field's representation of itself as a research enterprise vary widely and seem to reflect much conflict. A history of the consistent articulation of teaching and service and the changing articulation of research in the CCCC Chairs' addresses thus offers a discourse-based account of the field's self-representation of its professionalism.

GESTURES ARTICULATING THE TEACHING AND SERVICE OF COMPOSITION

In 20 years of chairs' addresses, the evocative gestures articulating the importance of teaching and service have not changed substantially: CCCC Chairs have argued consistently that the teaching of writing is a complex and important activity, one that is of service not only to students in their pursuit of higher education, but also to citizens in their attempts to improve society at large.

Teaching

In the first CCCC Chair's address, delivered in 1977 and published one year later,[2] Richard Lloyd-Jones (1978) makes the argument that the teaching of writing is a complex activity, articulating a view that has been repeated in every Chair's address since. Lloyd-Jones critiques those in the academy or in society who would argue that the teaching of composition is a matter of simple basic skills, a matter of "one course or a pattern of courses [that] ought to do the job of teaching a person to write.... We thus encourage people to think that language is a child's toy rather than a person's lifelong other self" (p. 26). The next year, Vivian Davis (1979) agreed with Lloyd-Jones:

> Many students do not know how to write when they come to college, and freshman composition for most of them, given the curricula of the majority of our institutions, is their last chance. It is absurd that we allow them and our schools to believe that we can essentially help them to master the writing process in a year of freshman composition. All evidence indicates that good writing is the result of processes that develop slowly. If our society wants writers, we will have to make them understand that the job cannot be done overnight and that the cost is not cheap. (p. 29)

Jumping ahead 15 years, Lillian Bridwell-Bowles (1995) characterizes the complexity of teaching in much the same terms: "Although some teachers and textbooks do offer students cookbooks, most of us know that the characteristics of writing in different fields are cloudier and harder to pin down than the recipes acknowledge.... [F]inding our common pedagogical ground is far more complicated than simple either-or thinking" (p. 56). From Lloyd-Jones's address in 1977 to Nell Ann Pickett's in 1997, CCCC Chairs have made similar, if not identical, arguments for the complexity, challenge, and importance of teaching writing in the university.

Within the broad gesture forwarding this perspective on teaching, three particular addresses—one from the early 1980s, another from the late 1980s, and one more from the early 1990s—stand as landmark articulations of this shared sense of teaching: Lynn Troyka's "Perspectives on Legacies and Literacy in the 1980s" (1982), Miriam Chaplin's "Issues, Perspectives, and Possibilities" (1988), and Jane Peterson's "Valuing Teaching: Assumptions, Problems, and Possibilities" (1991). Troyka (1982) argues for the especial challenge and importance of teaching writing to nontraditional students, many of whom are basic writers. Using the word *legacy* in order to invoke the program initiated by Mina Shaughnessy, Troyka's address presents the state of the art of research on teaching, laying out what the field has learned from its work with these new students entering the academy. Inexperienced writers, especially basic writers, Troyka argues, learn through social interaction; these student writers prepare to write by talking and thinking holistically and concretely, a cognitive and operational style that remains in opposition to the inductive and analytic thinking and writing styles of many academics, including writing teachers. Troyka defines the legacy of these students in terms of the changed nature of teachers and teaching in student-centered composition programs: "College faculty, most especially teachers of writing, can welcome these students with warm encouraging classroom atmospheres and with informed, innovative teaching strategies that will help all students to meet the expectations they have set for themselves" (p. 261).

Like Troyka, Chaplin (1988) starts by describing the many nontraditional students who fill writing classrooms and argues that conventional teaching strategies are not effective with students who learn best through "meaningful learning experiences which allow them to relate instruction to their personal lives" (p. 55). Chaplin broadens Troyka's argument to conceptualize both students and teachers as learners in "classrooms which are democratized communities of learners" (p. 55). She suggests that the teaching of writing must "move away from the model of instruction based on skill proficiency or the lack of it toward a model based on students' experiential backgrounds" (p. 60), arguing that experience forms the essential background for articulating and understanding the importance of diversity within community.

Peterson (1991), in her Chair's address at the 1990 CCCC, also makes the standard gesture articulating the complexity and importance of teaching writing, pointing out, like Chaplin, Troyka, and every other Chair since Lloyd-Jones, that the CCCC grew up as an organization with a central commitment to this kind of teaching. However, Peterson takes on the profession's complacent gestures towards its commitment to teaching, noting that qualifications, credentials, prestigious career paths, and conventional academic honors are moving increasingly to reward research rather than teaching. Like her predecessors, Peterson offers a characterization of the teaching of writing as a complex activity: "We see writing now not as a matter of mechanically encoding a known message but as active and interactive processes of creating meaning.... And we see learning not as logical, linear, predictable process but as a dynamic, active and interactive, recursive process" (p. 29). Unlike her predecessors, Peterson warns that the field runs a risk of losing its focus on teaching by incorporating the traditional academic hierarchy that privileges research alone. Peterson asks for a recommitment to teaching by CCCC members, a commitment that validates teaching "as a mode of inquiry, a way of learning and knowing" (p. 28) and a commitment to teacher-research that will ultimately lead to "new knowledge": "The immense gains we have made from a deeper understanding of reading, writing, and learning will be fully matched, I believe by a deeper understanding of teaching and its transformation into a genuine way of learning and knowing" (p. 33).

Service

In the CCCC Chairs' addresses of the past 20 years, this commitment to the teaching of writing is vitally connected not only to students and to the university, but also to citizens and to society at large. In 1977, Lloyd-Jones referred to the literacy crisis, then reported extensively in the media, and argues that this public attention allows composition to remind society of the importance of its mission: "[S]till we hear that the culture needs the exactness of good writing.... [W]e are for the moment news, and that is our opportunity" (p. 28). He suggests that composition makes an important contribution to society, responding to "cries for help in fixing the cultural mosaic that makes up the nation" (p. 28). Davis, the Chair in 1978, takes up this gesture, arguing that the field of composition must take advantage of its position in "the public view" (p. 26). Davis declares that "the American people have a right to know what we do, what we do not do, and why.... We have chosen to play significant roles in carrying out [the] responsibility [to educate all American citizens]" (p. 27). She devotes much of her address to the argument that composition must communicate with the general public: "We are taking gradual steps toward open dialogue with the public.... Certainly it is an ambitious move to make, but if an informed public is our best weapon against the loss of freedom and human dignity, we cannot ignore the challenge" (p. 27). Jumping ahead, Bridwell-Bowles (1995) makes the same connection between the teaching of writing and its potential service to society: "[W]e must continue to make our classrooms vital places where students learn not only the various conventions of academic writing but also the power of communication to change things, to transform...[to] create community in a world that often seems torn apart by difference" (p. 47). From Lloyd-Jones's "View From the Center" (1978) to Pickett's description of "The Community College as Democracy in Action" (1997), CCCC Chairs make similar arguments that the teaching of writing makes a significant contribution to the development of informed citizens in a diverse but democratic society.

Within this broad gesture forwarding the social importance of composition, Lester Faigley's 1997 address stands as a landmark articulation of this shared sense of cultural service. In the CCCC Chairs' addresses, it is common for Chairs to discuss composition in terms of social issues in higher education. Troyka (1982) and Chaplin (1988), for example, discuss the changing demographics of college students: Troyka notes that the number of nontraditional students in colleges nationwide is expected to grow significantly, and Chaplin notes that these nontraditional students are extraordinarily diverse in their ethnic and socioeconomic backgrounds. Both Troyka and Chaplin, along with many other CCCC Chairs, argue that composition has a responsibility to serve these students and to provide higher education with a model of how to teach these students successfully. In his address, however, Faigley articulates the broadened version of this argument, referring to the work of James Berlin and claiming that composition provides a model of teaching all students successfully in part by concentrating upon the service mission of the profession. Looking backward to 1977, his first year in the profession, Faigley presents the cherished commonplace of composition, "That the good classroom could help produce the good society seemed self-evident when I began teaching college writing courses" (p. 31). Looking at the developments of the past 20 years, however, Faigley notes that the good society has been moved increasingly out of reach for many students, especially nontraditional ones. He retains his faith in composition, though, arguing that the field should rededicate itself to its central value of "encouraging our students to use literacy to participate in democratic community life, to engage civic issues, and to promote social justice" (p. 31).

Contexts of Teaching and Service

Within the context of a CCCC meeting, these gestures toward the complexity of teaching and the importance of cultural service are deeply meaningful, evoking a welcomed sense of the field's shared self-representation of its professionalism. It is ironic to note, however, that neither perspective has achieved such shared currency in the larger contexts that CCCC Chairs cite as the surrounding contexts of composition. Within the university and within American society, neither the view of writing and its teaching as a complex learning activity nor the view of writing as an important means of social understanding has been well disseminated or well received. Within universities, for instance, it remains common for teachers and teaching to be devalued, as Peterson (1991) argued, in an institutional "hierarchy that places teaching far below research and scholarship" (p. 26). As almost all CCCC Chairs have pointed out (most dramatically and humorously by Chaplin's [1988] reading of a letter written by a hypothetical part-time instructor suffering from institutional indignities), composition remains taught by the academy's lowest-paid, most-marginalized part-time instructors. And despite the field's attempts to open a dialogue with the public, as Lloyd-Jones (1978) and Davis (1979) suggest, and its attempts to contribute to the democracy of the public through the analysis of self, community, and diversity, as Bridwell-Bowles (1995), Faigley (1997), and others suggest, the perception of writing within society at large stubbornly remains the perspective of basic skills. A recent report on the state of writing instruction in my own state, for example, excoriated approaches to teaching based on analysis of society or self, calling for "real" instruction in writing:

> Most college graduates more than forty years old will recall taking freshman English composition. That's the course in which they learned the fundamentals of written exposition, including a review of grammar and syntax and some lessons in informal logic and the rules of evidence. A tedious but valuable course, freshman composition once sharpened universally applicable skills that helped students deal with future courses and careers. But at our state universities today, much of what passes for freshman composition is trivial and irrelevant, or worse.... Course syllabi and related materials from English departments and writing programs throughout Michigan's universities reveal a general lowering—and in some cases, an abandonment—of standards of correct writing. Self-expression and moral liberation...are emphasized over prose competency. Consider this professor's advice from a freshman composition course syllabus at [a state university]: "Don't worry about writing perfect papers. I do not have a set standard for what I consider 'good writing'." (Bertonneau, 1997, pp. vi–vii)

The last sentence points simultaneously to the two contexts that the field of composition occupies. A CCCC Chair might admire it as a statement reflecting growth and development in teaching, a movement away from reductive, skill-based approaches and standardized evaluation in favor of the complexity of sophisticated analysis and textual experimentation. But the statement is actually embedded in a public context that belittles the field's representation of its teaching and service missions. Within the venue of the CCCC, Chairs' gestures seem evocative of a professional commitment to teaching and service. Within the academic and public venues, which CCCC Chairs claim that we serve, however, these same gestures seem evocative of misplaced effort and declining standards.

GESTURES ARTICULATING COMPOSITION AS A RESEARCH FIELD

Evocative gestures articulating a shared sense of professional commitment to teaching and service reflect a high degree of consensus in the self-representation of composition, and another evocative gesture in CCCC Chairs' addresses over the past 20 years seems to articulate a shared sense of professional commitment to the importance of research in the field. The broadest gesture toward the place of research in the field is celebratory. As Lloyd-Jones argued in 1977, there is much "evidence that serious study of composition does exist.... At our conventions the sessions dealing with theoretical, scholarly, and research knowledge overflow. Keeping up with new work is getting harder all the time" (1978, p. 28). A number of CCCC Chairs repeated this cliché of a vibrant research life. In his 1988 address, for example, David Bartholomae noted, "We have even reached that pinnacle of disciplinary status, we now produce more words than any single person can possibly read. We cannot be kept up with" (1989, p. 48). Within this broad gesture of consensus with respect to the importance of research, however, CCCC Chairs' addresses actually reflect much conflict with respect to the nature, place, and value of research when research is considered more specifically. In fact, two decades of Chairs' addresses reveal a variety of conflicting gestures that attempt to articulate the place and nature of research within the field of composition. This section will focus on two such areas of conflict: first, the gradually submerged conflict between empirical versus humanistic paradigms as the explicit or implicit standard for the field; and second, the highly visible conflict between disciplinary autonomy and intradisciplinary fit with respect to English studies.

Humanism and Empiricism

Discussions of the place and value of research were well underway by the time Lloyd-Jones presented the first Chair's address in 1977.

Lloyd-Jones entitled his address "A View from the Center" (1978) and argued that composition should occupy a central position within the university by virtue of its scholarship. In this view, composition professionals are "the ones at the center who reach to all other disciplines and to all other people. We synthesize knowledge and unite people.... [O]ur central position in scholarship is to make a coherent whole of all this diversity [of scholarship]" (p. 27). Lloyd-Jones calls this interdisciplinary sense-making the "intellectual responsibility" of composition (p. 27).

Lloyd-Jones's (1978) argument for this central place of research, however, placed composition in the center of the humanities. In the introduction to his address, Lloyd-Jones characterizes composition's practitioners as "those who are fascinated, entranced, and enthralled by language," especially by the "subversive" metaphor (p. 24). He thereby aligns the field squarely within literature and the humanities, with their traditions of studying the literary language and aesthetic texts of high culture. Like many humanists, however, Lloyd-Jones was ambivalent about studies of language from the sciences, social sciences, and empirical traditions generally. In fact, he valorized composition scholarship as resistance to empiricism. What I would call Lloyd-Jones's gesture of suspicion occurs in the second paragraph of his address: "In an age of quantification, allegiance to the metaphor is subversive, because it upsets the deductive electronic gadgets we have elected to be our masters. Those machines need immutable categories, precisely defined. Each little quaver of doubt, each fuzzy borderline of meaning rouses the computer to be angry with the operator" (p. 24). Having ritually disposed of traditions of research based on quantification, categorization, and formalization, then, Lloyd-Jones goes on to assume the traditional paradigm of scholarship within the humanities.

The second Chair's address, however, asks "Where Do We Grow From Here?" (Davis, 1979) and serves as a counterpoint to the assumption that the humanities alone stand as the standard for composition studies. Davis identifies the same CCCC community as Lloyd-Jones: she notes that "we have dedicated ourselves to the study of language" (p. 26), but Davis answers her title question by arguing that one direction for the field of composition is empirical research. Forwarding a pointed critique of anecdotal research that has arisen mainly out of "the special interests of circumstances of the individual researcher" claiming success for particular approaches or materials in the teaching of writing (p. 28), Davis suggests more controversially that "our most significant theories about the teaching of composition should be submitted to tests of verifiability.... We need to...identify analytical methods especially adaptable to our own discipline" (p. 29). Davis warns that a lack of research sophistication leaves the field vulnerable, presumably to the narrow perspective of competing frameworks of educational research:

> [W]e cannot depend on others to have the required sensitivity to the complexities of the composition that we have. As long as others know more about what we do than we know, we will find ourselves at their mercy for funding, for professional prestige, and for answers to fundamental questions about our own discipline." (p. 29)

Davis's address argues that the field of composition must overcome its "suspicions of any analytical approach" and develop its own sophisticated empirical tradition that responds to "the needs of the profession" (p. 28).

For a while, the field seemed to follow both directions suggested by Lloyd-Jones (1978) and Davis (1979), incorporating and integrating both empirical and humanistic paradigms without devaluing either tradition. In addresses from the mid-1970s to the mid-1980s, Chairs seemed to make an active effort to explore the possible place of empirical studies in a traditionally humanistic field. Lloyd-Jones (1978) himself actually makes a brief gesture in this direction of interdisciplinarity, citing Carl Klaus's list of disciplines that composition can draw from, a list that includes several empirical fields: "rhetoric, linguistics, literary criticism, cultural history, sociology, psychology, neurology, speech therapy, politics, communication theory" (p. 27). Other Chairs consider this integration of empirical scholarship in more detail. William Irmscher (1979), for instance, talks about cognitive research on problem-solving and intellectual development, and he describes Janet Emig's work in detail. Frank D'Angelo (1980) mentions the importance of research on symbolic action in science and on narrative in social sciences, claiming, like Lloyd-Jones, that composition occupies a central place in the scholarship of the university since language "is the bridge between the literary arts and the sciences and social sciences" (p. 424). Similarly, Lee Odell, in his address subtitled "Toward a Maturing Discipline" (1986), devotes some attention to the need for integrating research from cognitive psychology and research from rhetoric, arguing that "as long as they are isolated from each other, both rhetoric and cognitive psychology are impoverished" (p. 399). But around the time of Odell's address, which itself was perhaps the last substantive appearance of empirical studies in CCCC Chairs' addresses, the relationship between empirical studies and composition research became one of overtly suspicious and/or empty rhetorical gestures alone.

In Maxine Hairston's famous CCCC address in 1984, for example, perfunctory rhetorical gestures toward empirical studies are quickly contradicted by overt gestures of suspicion. Hairston notes that new theories of writing instruction draw upon "the insights of cognitive psychology about how people learn" (p. 277). In a sweeping gesture of suspicion, however, she rejects empirical studies as one of the research paradigms for the field, stressing that "ours is a humanistic discipline, and we cannot yield to what Lewis Thomas calls 'physics envy,' the temptation to seek status by doing only empirical experiments that can be objectively normed and statistically validated" (p. 279). Using empirical approaches, Hairston cautions, "will narrow our field of inquiry to investigations that are so limited that what we find out will be worthless to us as writing teachers" (p. 279). Hairston employs here what could be subcategorized as a gesture of reduction: contrary to her depiction, however, the tradition of empirical research is far broader than a single method of experimental design with statistical analysis. In fact, an empirical framework is set up to deliver exactly the kind of research that she recommends for the field in her next paragraph: "We have to learn to formulate good questions, to examine data—especially data that come to us in language—sensitively and meticulously, to control for bias, and to be careful not to claim too much for our findings" (p. 279). Substituting the word *systematically* for *meticulously* here returns to the empirical paradigm that Hairston just eliminated.

This explicit claim for the humanities as the reigning standard for the field was cemented in place by Bartholomae's 1988 CCCC address, which implicitly assumed a humanities paradigm without question or argument. In this address, even rhetorical gestures toward an empirical paradigm were disappearing. Like Davis (1979), Hairston (1985), Lloyd-Jones (1978), and most other early CCCC Chairs, Bartholomae calls for research on language, with this project generally defined as the "common (and unconventional) things people do with language" (1989, p. 47). Bartholomae's definition of the field's object of study here extends but echoes Lloyd-Jones's (1978) similar identification of language and metaphor as the common interests of composition scholars: While Bartholomae appears to include empirical traditions of looking at what is common in language, he nonetheless uses what could be considered subversive parentheses in order to subtly privilege humanistic traditions of looking at what is unconventional about language. Nor does Bartholomae make any further gestures toward the empirical study of language.

More specifically, Bartholomae (1989) situates the research project of composition firmly within the contemporary humanities. Presenting a history of the CCCC as an organization that resisted "the commonplaces of the [old] humanistic tradition...[of] a unified culture, a refined moral sensibility and a perception of eternal truths" (p. 42–43),

Bartholomae locates the field of composition in today's English departments, currently "a site where English [is] open for negotiation (or renegotiation)" (p. 42) within the paradigm of the contemporary humanities. When Bartholomae positions composition here, he aligns it with other areas in English studies specifically and the contemporary humanities generally: "women's studies, black studies, film studies, gay studies, critical theory, culture study, studies of working-class language and literature, pedagogy" (p. 42). This is a much narrower list than Lloyd-Jones's (1978) mix of empirical and nonempirical approaches ranging from poetics to linguistics. Although Bartholomae speaks of interdisciplinarity, his list actually is much more intradisciplinary, looking at permeable boundaries between composition, English studies, and other closely related areas of the humanities as they combine to investigate the instability of language and as they are joined by their common opposition to unified theoretical explanations. This contemporary humanism represents the stance that most CCCC Chairs have assumed implicitly for the past 10 years.

Disciplinarity and Intradisciplinarity

The two most famous CCCC Chairs' addresses—Hairston's (1985) and Bartholomae's (1989)—are worth a closer look not only because they reflect the tension within the field in terms of the broad context of humanistic and empirical paradigms, but also because they reflect the tension between the field and its more local context of English studies.

Hairston's impassioned argument for disciplinary autonomy in "Breaking Our Bonds and Reaffirming Our Connections" (1985) still stands today as an excellent articulation of the problems that composition faces when it has to struggle toward academic professionalism within research-based English departments. In developing the position that "our worst problems originate close to home" (p. 273), Hairston's most convincing argument points to the one-way interdisciplinarity that still characterizes the relationship between composition and literary scholarship: "[Literary theorists] don't know writing theory and, as far as I know, are making no attempt to learn" (p. 274). To see whether Hairston's claim is borne out, I conducted a small citation study. In the CCCC Chairs' addresses of 1991 to 1996 (the last five published addresses), literary authors and scholars are well represented, with citations to Gloria Anzaldua, Maya Angelou, Nora Zeale Hurston, Toni Morrison, Homi Bhabha, Henry Louis Gates, Gerald Graff, Helene Cixous, bell hooks, Mary Louise Pratt, Gayatri Spivak, Cornel West, Patricia Williams, Frederick Jameson, plus the notables Michel Foucault and Jacques Derrida. In the comparable body of texts from the Modern

Language Association, the 1991 to 1996 presidential addresses (Baker, 1993; Gilman, 1996; Marks, 1994; Spacks, 1995; Stimpson, 1991; Valdes, 1992), many of the same literary figures and theorists are cited, but no composition scholar is referenced—not James Berlin, Linda Flower, Susan Miller, Andrea Lunsford, Lester Faigley, or any other figure whose research career is primarily in composition. The only crossover figure between these two forums was Paulo Freire, a scholar whose disciplinary identity in education cannot be claimed either by literature or by composition.

Bartholomae (1989), however, differs sharply with Hairston (1985), definitively rejecting disciplinary autonomy and explicitly specifying the local context of composition as English studies. In arguing that composition should "acknowledge our roots in English, not deny them" (p. 49), Bartholomae effectively silences Hairston's call for disciplinary autonomy; her gesture does not reappear in the CCCC Chairs' addresses. It is worth noting, however, that Hairston and Bartholomae argue more or less across each other, not taking up the other's most convincing points. Bartholomae argues that composition should retain its intradisciplinary focus within English studies, but he doesn't answer Hairston's charge that this relationship currently resembles a one-way street. Hairston argues that composition should attain the autonomous status of an independent discipline, but she doesn't articulate what interdisciplinary relationship composition should then negotiate with English and its foundational theoretical and methodological frameworks.

Nevertheless, in the body of Chairs' addresses, Bartholomae's (1989) implicit assumption of the paradigm of the humanities and his explicit positioning of composition within the discipline of English studies carried the day. In subsequent addresses, CCCC Chairs politely but definitively dismiss Hairston's gesture, while eagerly and explicitly taking up Bartholomae's. Andrea Lunsford (1990), for example, adopts Bartholomae's intradisciplinary perspective (although she, like Bartholomae, calls it interdisciplinary):

> Maxine Hairston presented one such perspective in her powerful "Breaking Our Bonds" address of 1985, and David Bartholomae last year placed *that* perspective into incongruity, suggesting that breaking bonds might not be as advantageous or as richly rewarding as interrogating and stretching those ties that bind us in various interdisciplinary ways. (1990, p. 72).

Similarly, Peterson (1991) notes that "David Bartholomae...urged us to remain open rather than to close the boundaries by defining ourselves too narrowly as a discipline" (p. 25). Echoing Bartholomae's list of participating disciplines, Bridwell-Bowles (1995) enumerates the areas that composition and English studies have in common:

> [W]e have centered our profession by aligning it with some of the most exciting, formerly 'marginal,' theoretical developments within the academy: feminist theory, multicultural and postcolonial theory, poststructuralism, and the new rhetorics with their connections to contemporary critical theory. (p. 52)

In setting forth what he calls the "stated and unstated projects" of composition situated within English studies, Bartholomae (1989) offers the theoretical project of English studies as a project for composition, too: "[O]ur central purpose has been to make room for these many voices, to imagine a multivocal, dialogical discipline that reflects in its actions its theoretical opposition to a unifying, dominant discourse" (p. 49). Most CCCC Chairs' addresses after Bartholomae's can be seen to be working out different aspects of this project aimed at self-reflexively theorizing a dialogic composition within English studies. For example, a number of Chairs work to incorporate a diversity of voices, personal and academic. In "Living In—and On—the Margins," for instance, Donald McQuade (1992) mixes creative and analytic genres, as does Bridwell-Bowles (1995) in "Freedom, Form, Function." In "Kitchen Tables and Rented Rooms: The Extracurriculum of Curriculum," Ann Ruggles Gere (1994) works simultaneously within the genres of history, personal narrative, and composition theory. Other Chairs take up self-reflexive theorizing. In "Composing Ourselves," Lunsford (1990) develops a post-modern reflection on composition, working "historically and subjectively" (p. 72) by discussing concepts such as authors, texts, differences, and the nature of being composed by others and composing ourselves in response. Similarly, in "Writing in the Spaces Left" and "When the First Voice You Hear is Not Your Own," William Cook (1993) and Jacqueline Jones Royster (1996) theorize diversity in composition, exploring concepts of voice, resistance, literacy, and liberation. These latter three addresses in particular take up Bartholomae's challenge to self-reflexive theorizing in opposition to grand narratives: Lunsford, Cook, and Royster all argue from positions of personal experience, of partiality, of post-modern difference and instability, of what all three call "the margins." These three addresses are especially interesting in their celebration of composition at the margins. In some ways, the focus of the CCCC Chairs' addresses made a radical move—from Lloyd-Jones's center in 1977 to the margins celebrated by Lunsford, Cook, Royster, and others 20 years later. But the shift may not be as radical as it appears. The field did not move from the center of the humanities, although it did move to the margins of English studies.

Contexts of Research

As Connors (1992) notes, any historical account "is provisional [and] partial" (p. 21), and this account of the changing articulation of research in CCCC Chairs' addresses is similarly interpretive, perhaps even biased to the point of constructing a nostalgic view of the good old days when empiricism and humanism lived happily together within composition. But foregrounding the tensions between humanism and empiricism and between disciplinary autonomy and intradisciplinary fit within English studies does reflect an intuitive sense of a division between earlier and later chairs' addresses, especially when read from the perspective of an empirical researcher.[3]

Earlier CCCC Chairs' addresses—for example, those by Chaplin (1988), D'Angelo (1980), Davis (1979), Hairston (1985), Irmscher (1979), Odell (1986), and Troyka (1982)—seem united in their sense of developing composition as a field within its own projects and interests, a field with its own object of study, to borrow terminology from empirical studies. The early CCCC Chairs' addresses can be read as contributions to the development of a theory specifically of composition, with this theory defined broadly by its attention to written language—its production and interpretation, its teaching and learning. To borrow Lloyd-Jones's (1978) terminology, these essays remind us that the field of composition was at this time centered upon itself. To recall Lloyd-Jones's list of participating empirical and humanistic disciplines, these essays also remind us that the interdisciplinary reach of composition was at this time extraordinarily broad and that the interdisciplinary question of integrating empirical and humanistic approaches was timely and significant.[4]

Later CCCC Chairs' addresses—for example, those by Bartholomae (1989), Bridwell-Bowles (1995), Cook (1993), Lunsford (1990), McQuade (1992), and Royster (1996)—take on the projects and interests of English studies, such as the inclusion of multiple voices and the development of self-reflexive theorizing. These later addresses, while increasingly sophisticated, can be read primarily as applications of the questions of contemporary theories to composition, and the list of participating critical approaches mentioned by Bartholomae (1989) and Bridwell-Bowles (1995) is much more intradisciplinary than interdisciplinary. To borrow Lloyd-Jones's (1978) terminology again, and to use it more in the sense that he did, these later essays show us how research in the field of composition has come to center itself within the humanities and English studies.

CONCLUSION

The major areas of consensus and conflict reflected in the body of CCCC Chairs' addresses ultimately revolve around professionalism—the relationship between research, teaching, and service in an academic field. As previously argued, the field's representation of the complexity of its teaching and the importance of its service is one of its consistent gestures over time, despite resistance to its missions of innovative teaching and social service. And despite conflict within considerations of research, another consistent gesture over time is the field's representation of itself as one that integrates research with teaching and service. Returning again to 1977, Lloyd-Jones (1978) described the integration of research and teaching in the figure of the scholar-practitioner who "synthesize[s] knowledge and unite[s] people" (p. 27), and, jumping again to 1994, Bridwell-Bowles (1995) also celebrates the integration of research, teaching, and service:

> For a long time we have looked for and found common ground, common theories, common pedagogies.... [W]e also have to come to grips with difference—among ourselves, among our students, among our institutions, among our nations as we see ourselves as global citizens. (p. 54)

This representation of professionalism in the CCCC Chairs' addresses is a nonconventional one for the modern academy. CCCC Chairs argue consistently that the field stands in contrast to traditional academic identity-formation solely in terms of research (think science, or, perhaps, literary theory). Bartholomae's (1989) address stands as a widely respected articulation of this position:

> [C]omposition seemed to me to provide the terms and context that allowed people to get to work and to work with energy and optimism, not cranking out just one more paper, not laddering their way up to the top, not searching for difficult texts and dull readers, not bowing and scraping before another famous book or another famous person, but doing work that one could believe in, where there was that rare combination of personal investment and social responsibility. (pp. 38–39)

In this critique of research-based careerism, work here involves research, but emphatically includes teaching and service as well.

But this integrative definition of the field coexists with traditional concepts of professionalism, particularly with regard to the primacy of research. In forwarding his argument for research in the field of composition, Lloyd-Jones (1978) warned against a field without research in traditional terms: Composition scholarship can occupy the center of research in the academy, but if it does not pursue this research role, "we deserve our present basic position, that is, our traditional place in the damp cellar of the house of the intellect" (p. 28). Similarly, in arguing for disciplinary autonomy, Hairston (1985) also pointed to the need for traditional disciplinary professionalization:

> [W]e must be productive researchers and scholars who contribute to the growth of our discipline.... [We] also have to publish: in the league we're in, that's a given.... [W]e also have to set high standards for our research, our conferences, our publications, and for our own writing, and we have to do first-class work in all our diverse activities. (p. 279)

Echoing Bartholomae, however, Peterson (1991) warns that traditional research-based criteria play an ever-increasing role in the field, arguing that there is considerable "evidence that a hierarchy exists within the profession, evidence that we consider teaching far less important than research or scholarship" (p. 27).

I suspect that CCCC Chairs will continue to take up both Bartholomae's gesture of integration as well as Peterson's gesture of critique, reflecting the continuing struggle to build a field that truly integrates research, teaching, and service into its definition of professionalism. It is a struggle worth continuing: If the field succeeds in building up rather than gesturing toward an integration of research, teaching, and service, it may well provide a model of professionalism for the university of the future.

NOTES

[1]Unfortunately, this body of texts is not complete. Three CCCC Chairs did not publish their addresses: James Hill, in 1982; Donald Stewart, in 1983; and Rosentene Purnell, in 1984.

[2]CCCC Chairs generally publish their addresses in the following year's journal. Thus, citation years (for example, Lloyd-Jones, 1978) usually post-date the year of the address (for example, 1977 for Lloyd-Jones). In this chapter, publication years appear as the official citations in parentheses. The year a particular address was delivered is occasionally given in the text.

[3]There are undoubtedly many other interpretations of the set of CCCC Chairs' addresses. For one interpretation that foregrounds issues that are quite different from the ones discussed in this chapter, see Ellen Halter's portion of our Watson Conference paper (Barton & Halter, 1996).

[4]This is not to say that the question of integrating empirical and humanistic paradigms is no longer timely or significant, although it is to say that this question disappeared from the representation of composition research by later

CCCC Chairs. A number of researchers in composition continue to explore this theoretical and methodological question (see, for example, Cheryl Geisler's 1994 work on academic literacy), but the major statement describing this approach—Linda Flower's "Cognition, Context and Theory Building" (1989)—has never been mentioned in a CCCC Chair's address.

REFERENCES

Baker, H. (1993). Presidential address 1992. Local pedagogy; or, how I redeemed my spring semester. *PMLA, 108*, 400–409.

Bartholomae, D. (1989). Freshman English, composition, and CCCC. *College Composition and Communication, 40*, 30–50.

Barton, E., & Halter, E. (1996, October). *Evocative gestures in professionalized composition: An interpretive discourse analysis of CCCC Chairs' addresses.* Paper presented at the Thomas R. Watson Conference on Rhetoric and Composition, University of Louisville, KY.

Bertonneau, T. (1997). *Declining standards at Michigan public universities* (2nd ed.). Midland, MI: Mackinac Center for Public Policy.

Bridwell-Bowles, L. (1995). Freedom, form, function: Varieties of academic discourse. *College Composition and Communication, 46*, 46–61.

Chaplin, M. (1988). Issues, perspectives and possibilities. *College Composition and Communication, 39*, 52–62.

Connors, R. (1992). Dreams and play: Historical method and methodology. In G. Kirsch & P. Sullivan (Eds.), *Methods and methodology in composition research* (pp. 15–36). Carbondale, IL: Southern Illinois University Press.

Cook, W. (1993). Writing in the spaces left. *College Composition and Communication, 44*, 9–25.

D'Angelo, F. (1980). Regaining our composure. *College Composition and Communication, 31*, 420–426.

Davis, V. (1979). Our excellence: Where do we grow from here? *College Composition and Communication, 30*, 26–31.

Faigley, L. (1997). Literacy after the revolution. *College Composition and Communication, 48*, 30–43.

Flower, L. (1989). Cognition, context and theory building. *College Composition and Communication, 40*, 282–311.

Geisler, C. (1994). *Academic literacy and the nature of expertise: Reading, writing, and knowing in academic philosophy.* Hillsdale, NJ: Lawrence Erlbaum.

Gere, A. R. (1994). Kitchen tables and rented rooms: The extracurriculum of composition. *College Composition and Communication, 45*, 75–92.

Gilman, S. (1996). Presidential address 1995. *Habent sua fata libelli*; or, books, jobs, and the MLA. *PMLA, 111*, 390–394.

Hairston, M. (1985). Breaking our bonds and reaffirming our connections. *College Composition and Communication, 36*, 272–282.

Irmscher, W. (1979). Writing as a way of learning and developing. *College Composition and Communication, 30*, 240–244.

Lloyd-Jones, R. (1978). A view from the center. *College Composition and Communication, 29*, 24–29.

Lunsford, A. (1990). Composing ourselves: Politics, commitment, and the teaching of writing. *College Composition and Communication, 41*, 71–82.

Marks, E. (1994). Presidential address 1993. Multiplicity and mortality. *PMLA, 109*, 366–374.

McQuade, D. (1992). Living in—and on—the margins. *College Composition and Communication, 43*, 11–22.

Odell, L. (1986). Diversity and change: Toward a maturing discipline. *College Composition and Communication, 37*, 395–401.

Peterson, J. (1991). Valuing teaching: Assumptions, problems, and possibilities. *College Composition and Communication, 42*, 25–35.

Pickett, N. A. (1997, March). *The community college as democracy in action*. Paper presented at the 48th Annual Convention of the Conference on College Composition and Communication, Phoenix, AZ.

Royster, J. (1996). When the first voice you hear is not your own. *College Composition and Communication, 47*, 29–40.

Spacks, P. (1995). Presidential address 1994. Reality—our subject and discipline. *PMLA, 110*, 350–358.

Stimpson, C. (1991). Presidential address 1990. On differences. *PMLA, 106*, 402–411.

Troyka, L. Q. (1982). Perspectives on legacies and literacy in the 1980s. *College Composition and Communication, 33*, 252–261.

Valdes, M. (1992). Presidential address 1991. One more time: Explanation and collective understanding. *PMLA, 107*, 426–433.

chapter 14

Whispers from the Margin: A Class-based Interpretation of the Conflict between High School and College Writing Teachers

Irvin Peckham
University of Nebraska at Omaha

In early 1996, I received a call for papers for the first Thomas R. Watson Conference in Louisville, Kentucky. The conference organizers advertised it as "History, Narration, and Reflection: The Professionalization of Composition, 1963–1983." The 22 featured speakers, starting with Bartholomae and ending with Young, represented the "Who's Who" in composition. I looked forward to the forum of multiple voices recapturing that period's extraordinary transformation in writing instruction—and in education. I also looked forward to revisiting my own transformation as a high school teacher during those years.

But when I measured my experience against who would be representing the period, I thought we would be gathering in Louisville to tell only part of the story—the college part, because the speakers were researchers, theorists, and teachers of college composition. With the possible exceptions of Charles Cooper and Janet Emig, few of the others would have been known to high school teachers. The absence of figures associated with pre-college teaching led me to think about the enduring conflict between high school and college writing teachers, which is the subject of this essay. The conflict between high school and college teachers is only one flash point. The larger conflict occurs between pre-college and college teachers. Within each group lie other conflicts—between, for example, high school and middle school teachers, or between two- and four-year college teachers. I am focusing on the conflict at the high school and college levels for two reasons: first, I am speaking through my two vastly different experiences at those levels; and second, the conflict is most visible between these groups as a consequence of the dramatic difference in working conditions, marked, for instance, by compulsory or noncompulsory student attendance and the presence or absence of time-clock requirements for teachers.

I begin this essay by locating myself as a high school teacher and naming the people who influenced me and my high school colleagues in the early 1970s. I then name the different sets of people who influenced me when I returned to graduate school in the mid-1980s. The difference is only one marker of the schism between the two groups of educators. It is more visible in the stories that high school and college teachers tell about each other. In these stories, high school teachers characterize college teachers as having their heads in the clouds, and college teachers think of high school teachers as having their eyes glued to the ground. North (1987) in *The Making of Knowledge in Composition* has provided the hierarchical oppositions (oral/text; narrative/expository; practice/praxis) governing these images. While North's focus is on the differences between practitioners and scholars, researchers, and theorists at all levels, the primary split occurs between high school and college teachers because, as both North and Kantor (1990) make clear, high school teachers simply do not have time for the research and scholarly inquiry that promote critical thinking; they are by necessity fundamental practitioners.

I interpret the images that high school and college teachers have of each other as class-based because they mirror the images working and professional/managerial classes have of each other. My central argument is that the conflict between high school and college teachers is a manifestation of class conflict played out within the academic hierarchy. The congruence between these conflicts explains both the function and tenacity of the conflict in the academic hierarchy. The congruence also accounts for the absence of high school teachers when we tell the story of our discipline.

INFLUENCES

I drifted like a hobo into teaching. The drift was part idealistic, part accident, and part panic. In the mid-1960s, young idealists like me were passing around books by Herndon (1968), Holt (1964), Kohl (1967),

Kozol (1967), and Postman and Weingarten (1969). The reading list wasn't so much a consequence of our interest in teaching; it was more an expression of the prevailing disestablishmentarianism: anything that challenged the dominant culture was worth reading, and these folks were challenging the primary socializing process—how kids were indoctrinated into (or kept out of) the dominant culture.

After a little trouble with the draft, I found myself in the middle of the Canadian free school movement, where Neil's *Summerhill* (1960) was the bible. I don't want to exaggerate my commitment, but I got hooked on teaching. It didn't take an Einstein to realize that the free school movement had the future of snow in April, so I went to the Ontario Institute for Studies in Education (OISE) at the University of Toronto to get a teaching credential. Academics like to trash educational programs, but I had excellent teachers at OISE. We learned about teaching by watching and doing. We also did some reading: the important books were Dixon's *Growth through English* (1967), Moffett's *Teaching the Universe of Discourse* (1968), and Dewey's *Experience and Education* (1938/1963). I think I first came across Wigginton's *The Foxfire Book* (1972) there.

In 1973, I returned to the United States, where I got a teaching job in a California high school by saying that I would also coach football, wrestling, and track. After a few years of disasters, I learned how to structure my curriculum around Moffett's (1973) ideas. Macrorie became another important influence after I stumbled across a class set of *Writing to be Read* (1969) in the English department bookroom. Both Macrorie and Moffett emphasized what Britton and colleagues (1975) later called "impelled" writing and interpreted grammar and conventions as a transcription activity. Macrorie and Moffett taught me how to step to the back of the classroom and let the student writing circulate. It wasn't hard to figure out that the best way to help students with their writing was to have them write on subjects that would make them want to read each other's writing. The perennial favorite was "My First Experience with the Opposite Sex"—students loved to read what the other students had written about that. I remember one story called "The Dreaded French Kiss," written by a young girl who knew how to make fun of herself. The story had everyone in stitches. It became the centerpiece for a magazine that my students put together to sell throughout the school. They called it *The Dreaded French Kiss and Other Stories*, and it sold like hotcakes. The success of the title was a lesson in rhetoric.

You could extrapolate the essence of my pedagogy from "The Dreaded French Kiss." I can imagine a few professorial fingers wagging, but even now, after 20 years of teaching and reading everyone from Anson to Zebroski, I can't think of a better way to teach writing. The rule is very simple: have students write about something that will sell.

Many other people influenced my teaching. I learned through teachers talking to teachers—in the staff room, at conferences, and in *English Journal*. North (1987) calls this "lore" (although he might admit that some articles in *English Journal* edge into scholarship). We called it "what works."

Let me finish this vignette by naming a few other people who were important to me. I have to mention with particular affection Stephen Judy, the editor of *English Journal*. I learned a lot from his writing, conference presentations, and the essays he included in *EJ*. Jim Gray deserves a front page in composition's history for his work with the Bay Area Writing Project (BAWP) and the National Writing Project. Miles Myers, who was co-directing BAWP with Jim, particularly influenced me. So did Keith Caldwell, Mary Kay Healy, Mary Lee Glass, Gerald Camp, Ruby Bernstein, Rebecca Caplin, Bill Robinson, Rich Murphy, Leo Ruth, and a host of other BAWP people whose names were never mentioned in the Watson Conference. I learned by example from Walter Loban, who helped me and about 15 other teachers on the Santa Clara County Committee on Writing forge countywide guidelines for teaching writing. And finally, I want to mention Cooper and Odell (1977). Their book, *Evaluating Writing*, helped our committee battle in the late 1970s the juggernaut demanding minimum competency testing by objective exams. I mark that book as my first hint that research could be useful. Charles became doubly important to me because as my mentor at the University of California, San Diego, where I completed my doctorate, he brought me into a new world. To Charles, I owe more than I can ever say.

My motivation for enrolling in the graduate program at UCSD was purely selfish: the press of teaching high school was wearing on me. I was teaching about 180 students a day. In some semesters, my classes ran as high as 40 per section. With a little math, you can figure out what happened when I had the students write three or four pages every other week or so—the accruing papers are only part of the planning, checking other work, record keeping, and coaching that went along with the job. I learned how to keep on top of this demand within a 40- to 45-hour week, but I didn't have a lot of time left for intellectual development. I wasn't reading essays by scholars who were obsessed with the semiotic constructions of subject positions. Only the elite have time to think about such things. This division of "labor" has a long history.

In graduate school, I switched from practice to theory. I struggled through theorists like Derrida, Culler, Bloom, de Man, Cixous, Kristeva, Irigaray, Foucault, Barth, Said, Jameson, Fish, and so on. A little later in the program, we segued into composition. Reading here got a bit more practical as I read work by Larson, Elbow, Bizzell, Lunsford, Rose, Shor, Berlin, Bartholomae, Flower and Hayes, Lauer, Kinneavy, D'Angelo, and Connors.

Let me return to my point: Many of the people on the composition page of my graduate school reading list were featured speakers at the Watson Conference, which billed itself as a place where the history of composition in 1963 to 1983 would be told. As a high school teacher during this period, I had heard of only Cooper, Odell, and Emig. If high school teachers had organized the conference, they would have invited a far different set of speakers. High school and college teachers read (and are written by) different people.

This miswriting (or overwriting) of the history of composition is not surprising: histories are generally the histories of the upper classes—for good reason. Only the upper classes are textualized: they are the ones who, like college teachers, have time to write, and they are the ones who are written about. So they are the ones whom histories trace. Working-class people (and high school teachers) are left on the margins or off the page.

THE CONFLICT

This difference in whom we read and by whom we are (or are not) written marks the gap between the two groups. The gap is not empty: it is the site of conflict. Let me introduce this conflict through one of my current students, named Mike. He is in his early 40s, just shy of 6 feet in height, and is heavy set. He has a rough complexion, a scraggly beard, and a voice like gravel. His hair is thin, dramatically receding. His eyes seem small, set deep within the folds of his skin.

Mike has worked all of his adult life for Union Pacific. He looks like an angry railroad man. He told me yesterday that he wanted to study sociology because he is interested in class politics, but he realized there is little future in social work. He decided instead to become an engineer—although he hates the way they look down on blue-collar workers like himself. The engineers, Mike said, don't listen to anything the line workers tell them because they think the line workers are as stupid as shit. Mike sputtered as he talked. Bourdieu (1991) would say his ineloquence was a consequence of his working-class habit of getting entangled in his own words. Mike will have a hard time taking off his blue collar; it is sewn into his language and skin.

Mike's anger is born from the conflict. As a former member of the working class, I grew up with this anger and understand it. Working-class people like Mike are angry because they think people from the upper classes consider them stupid. The working-class anger and the upper-class dismissal are the more obvious manifestations of the class conflict played out in the railroad yards and in the educational hierarchy that situates professors above high school teachers.

High school teachers will understand how I have framed this conflict. They know that college teachers dismiss high school teacher knowledge. Some of us may pretend we do not share this dismissal, but it is sewn into our skins as deeply as Mike's blue collar is into his. I heard it, for example, in Emig's talk at the Watson Conference when she spoke of what she had seen in her granddaughter's high school English classroom. On the wall, Emig said, were posters describing the linear "writing process"—prewrite, write, revise, edit. This picture drew a good laugh from the knowing compositionists in the crowd. Emig went on to describe the teacher's wild misinformation on the dates of the Romantic artists. There was more knowing laughter.

I do not tell this story to derogate Emig or those who laughed at the mythologized ignorance of high school teachers. The dismissal of high school teachers' knowledge is in the air we breathe. Although I come from a blue-collar and high school teaching background, when I work with area high school teachers, I can feel within me the superiority that comes from being called Dr. Peckham. Because I have read (and somewhat understood) Burke and Bakhtin, I think I know more than these teachers. What's worse, they think I do, too.

Although high school teachers resent this superiority, they adulate college teachers in a kind of double-voicing that occurs whenever dominant and dominated cultures live within the same sphere (Freire, 1968/1970).[1] According to Freire, the dominant culture creates the myth of ignorance in the dominated culture to establish their own authority as "knowers." To be a knower, one must have nonknowers. To construct nonknowers, the dominant culture invades the psyches of the dominated to implant in them the image of the dominators. Freire calls this "cultural invasion" (p. 151). The dominated then see themselves through the eyes of the dominators: they see themselves as ignorant and the dominators as wise. At the same time, a voice within the dominated asserts their essential humanity, which is to be thinking, acting beings who can transform rather than merely accept reality. These two voices—the authentic and ventriloquated voices—are in conflict, as if the outer conflict is housed within the inner self.

The picture is complicated for people who cross from the dominated to the dominant culture. We double our double-voicing. When I was a high school teacher, I didn't like college teachers because they dismissed us. I also admired them because they had Ph.D.'s, which is why I got mine. Now I hear in my mind the muted voices of high school teachers insisting on their subjectivity. Still, I was in the Watson audience and, like most others, I laughed at the lore-ridden high school teachers who think of writing as linear or who may not have researched carefully the precise dates of Delacroix. This is not a mea culpa: it is being out front. In me is written the conflict between college and pre-college teachers and, on a different field, the conflict between the upper and lower classes.

MYTHS OF THE CONFLICT

The myths that support the class-based conflict between college and high school teachers are as old as Plato's parable of the cave. They have been recodified to distinguish dominant from dominated cultures—masters from slaves, nobility from peasants, men from women, Anglo from Native or African American, professional/managerial from working class, teachers from students, and college from high school teachers. The governing hierarchical oppositions are oral/text and narrative/expository. The consequences of these oppositions are practice/praxis. Practice is unthinking action; praxis is reflective action. Slaves practice; masters praxis.

The naming game, by which we imagine classes with attributes, is always saturated by the social spaces of those who name (Bakhtin, 1981; Bourdieu, 1991). The dominant culture has cornered the market on legitimate metaphors and names (Bourdieu, 1991)—thus, we think of the dominated groups as the "lower" classes, a metaphor that allows language users to knit them to lower ability thinkers. In his parable, Plato—a member of the dominant culture—describes the lower class thinkers as chained in the cave with their eyes fooled by the shadows on the wall. Like children (or like slaves and women in Plato's social hierarchy), they are captivated by the stories enacted by those shadows. Retranslated into the upper/lower class myth, they pass on knowledge via oral narratives. They are illiterate hillbillies telling big ones while swigging from a jug of hooch; they are housewives gossiping over backyard fences; they are high school teachers swapping stories in faculty lounges.

By contrast, upper-class thinkers have broken their narrative-linked chains and escaped the cognitive cave to the outside, where they can look in the Heavens and see the Forms. Because they are free of the necessities (provided for them by the lower classes), upper class thinkers can abstract from the particulars to theorize on the relationships between categories. They gain and pass on their knowledge through exposition and logical argumentation. They are us. We do not have to worry about shelter and food; most of us do not have to worry about jobs.

North's (1987) distinctions between practitioners and scholars, researchers, and theorists parallels Plato's parable. The categories here are being named and described by a member of the dominant class, a research university professor; the practitioners predictably get short shrift—they are linked with the slavish nonthinkers chained in the cave. Because of their reliance on oral narratives, they are submerged in their own experience and consequently are incapable of thinking critically about their practices. North offers the excuse that because they are overwhelmed by classroom demands, practitioners are never free to read, research, theorize, and write—the activities necessary for the critical, disinterested gaze of college professors.

North's (1987) categories of scholars, researchers, and theorists are linked with Plato's upper-class thinkers. Although they may not have achieved the highest level of thinking necessary to perceive the Forms (blinded as they are by postmodern irruptions), they have at least broken the chains of their experience. They have turned their heads to see that the narrative shadows are cast by the figures high on the wall behind them. These figures are in turn manipulated by the master narrators. Disenchanted by the play of shadows, most scholars, researchers, and theorists have escaped the cave to the world outside their own experience (frequently diminished to one or two classes a semester). The modernists among them have learned how to see the real things. The structuralists have looked to the Heavens to find the patterns for these things. God knows where the postpeople are looking, but one thing is sure: they aren't seeing narratives. At times, one could wish for a good story.

North (1987) takes pains to divorce his description from privileging according to function and position in the academic hierarchy, but readers aren't fooled—at least one group of my composition theory students weren't. Because most of them were going to be high school English teachers (that is, practitioners), they were irritated by what they perceived as North's privileging and condescension. I was initially surprised by their irritation; situated as a college teacher, I had thought North was being fair-minded. Now I think he was merely grafting the academic hierarchy onto Plato's parable, giving us a framework within which to understand why college teachers are higher and high school teachers lower in the game.[2]

The governing hierarchical oppositions within North's framework are oral/text, narrative/expository, and practice/praxis. My theory and practice students clearly understood that the attributes of practitioners (oral/narrative/practice) were the weak members of the oppositions and that the attributes of scholars, researchers, and theorists (text/exposition/praxis) were the privileged. More bluntly, practitioners (like high school teachers) are sort of dumb; scholars, researchers, and theorists (like college teachers) are sort of smart. That's why they are what they are.

One hears variations of these descriptions in our halls or department meetings when the subject turns to how poorly prepared incoming first-year students are; one hears them in our conferences, and one hears them on listservs—although as soon as they are uttered, a group reflexivity takes over, causing several people to come to the high school teachers' defense. Perhaps one of the more notable self-reflexive instances of this sort occurred in Kantor's 1990 article, "Learning from Teachers." Kantor begins with his reflections on an article he had published nine years previously in *English Journal*. The article had, as he noted, the "somewhat condescending title, 'Research in Composition: What It Means for Teachers'"(p. 61). Kantor was taking it upon himself to summarize current theory and research for high school teachers and explain its implications for practice. The subtext was that high school teachers were like the peasants in Brueghel's "Blind Leading the Blind." Kantor was assuming the role of a priest suggesting they might walk better if they removed the blindfolds from their eyes.

Kantor (1990) describes the different reactions to his article. One high school teacher, in particular, assailed Kantor for his jargon-ridden prose and for not understanding the real needs of practicing teachers. Kantor recounts his initial defensive response, which was essentially to dismiss the teacher's critique because the critic had revealed in his "diatribe" (p. 62) his total innocence of Britton's theory of cognitive development. Kantor then tracks his own ideological development as it was revealed in his subsequent articles, critiques of those articles, and his reactions to those critiques. The point was that he recognized in reflection the condescension that he had displayed toward high school teachers during the early part of his career. The confession genre requires that one speak from subsequent enlightenment. Kantor's particular enlightenment was that he recognized the need to valorize high school teachers' knowledge and research, that university professors and pre-college teachers need to work not from their relative positions on a hierarchy in which the theoretical and research-oriented knowledge of the university professors is privileged, but on an egalitarian footing to contribute collaboratively to the larger educational project.

There are layers to my point. I made the same mistake with Kantor that I had previously made with North. I thought Kantor's would be a good article to have my theory and practice students read because it highlighted the schism between theory and research and practice through the eyes of a sensitive college teacher who had learned to see the issue from the high school teachers' point of view.

Several students, however, strenuously objected to Kantor's jargon-ridden, condescending article (the one that was supposedly representing an enlightened vision). I acted defensively: after all, I had made them read it. But upon rereading it, I saw that it was threaded with condescending jargon. Worse, I was condescending in my reaction to their reaction: I tried to explain Kantor's point to them. To do my students justice, they tolerated me—as they have learned to tolerate most professors.

Kantor's (1990) article lays bare the rift between high school and college teachers. College teachers think they know more than high school teachers about teaching writing. Even when college teachers come to the issue with Kantor's sensitivity, they have absorbed a kind of class structure they can't escape. It takes a Freire to be able to peel off the layers of ideologically saturated patterns of thinking, to understand what egalitarian means. Although I have thought about this for years, I am not close to understanding. That's why I laughed when Emig told the old joke about the rote-minded high school teacher.

ORIGINS OF THE MYTH

As with most myths, there are grains of truth in the contrasting visions high school and college teachers have of each other. High school teachers are submerged in their everyday realities. Because they are inundated with students and papers, it is difficult to gain a critical perspective. Worse, the high school teachers' myth of college teachers inspires a certain disdain of research. When I was a high school teacher, I read *English Journal* regularly—it was characterized by practical assignments, narratives, and testimonials. I had looked at the journals *College English* and *Research in the Teaching of English*. To my mind, *CE* was full of hopeless philosophizing and *RTE* was full of nit-picking research that discovered what any good teacher would already know. My submersion, characterized by my defensive reaction toward *CE* and *RTE*, blocked my vision.

The other grain of truth is that many college teachers do have their heads in the clouds, rattling on about positionality, interpellation, irruption, and erasure. Like really. And many of us do not know how to teach. As Bob Connors lamented in the opening keynote address at the Watson Conference, many of us, after all, don't do very much of it. In addition, most of our writing classes are small, with students who have paid for the privilege of being in them—a far different "teaching" situation than one finds in high schools. We also know that when push comes to shove, teaching isn't what counts in our game. Teaching is what we do on the side so that we can have space within which to make ourselves textually visible.

There are consequently different orientations at the high school and college levels. At the high school level, teachers are oriented toward teaching; at the college level, professors are oriented toward research, theory, and publication. These different orientations mirror the different orientations among classes.

Class Orientations

Using data obtained from 1,217 detailed questionnaires, Bourdieu (1984) analyzed and reported in *Distinction: A Social Critique of the Judgement of Taste* the different orientations of class fractions. Although I am doing a bit of violence to Bourdieu's concept of social spaces, I imagine these class fractions on a continuum from lower to upper with privileges and autonomy distributed accordingly. This distribution accounts for the metaphors of lower and upper, reflecting the dominant class' self-justification of privilege.

According to Bourdieu's (1984) analysis, the lower classes are oriented toward function; the upper classes toward form. The lower classes are immersed in concrete experience—what counts is what a thing does, how it contributes to one's work or living conditions. Because the upper classes do not need to concern themselves with the functions of things, what counts for them is form. Being able to focus on form, or significant features *abstracted* from the particularity, is one of the markers of upper-class existence. Bourdieu associates it with the Kantian "pure" gaze—the ability to look at experience from a distance. This difference in immersion/function and distance/form is manifested in such things as the food the different class fractions eat, the clothes they wear, the books they read, the art they buy, the music they listen to, the language they use, and the sports they watch or play. Bourdieu describes these manifestations of social space as a person's *habitus*. One carries one's habitus within; it is embodied.

Bernstein's (1971–75) related research among school-age children in England adds to these distinctions the notion of restrictive and nonrestrictive language and cognition. The foundation for Bernstein's research can be put like this: Working-class men live in restrictive work environments.[3] They are not given much room within which to make decisions. They are told what to do. They consequently become rule-oriented. These men bring these restrictive worlds home with them in their language and worldviews. At home, they try to objectify themselves in their wives and children, reproducing the employer/employee relationship that they experience in their work.[4] Freire describes this situational reproduction as ventriloquism, with the working-class men playing the role of boss in order to salvage their self-image, but it also seems as if they are trying to prepare their children for what the working-class men imagine is the "Real World."

By contrast, the situation of professional/managerial class workers is relatively nonrestrictive—that is to say the kind of environment in which I now find myself. At the moment, I am sitting in my study on a Tuesday morning, writing merrily on my laptop about an issue that strikes my fancy. I have no serious deadline on this chapter. Only my wife and a few friends know I am writing it. I teach three classes a semester—all of them my own choosing. Within some wildly loose restrictions, what I teach and how I teach is up to me. Basically, I am free to construct most of my working reality—as long as I keep producing with some demonstration of research, scholarship, and intelligence articles at the rate of one every year or so. I have learned how to operate within ambiguity and have embraced the relativism of postmodernity with enthusiasm. I have learned how to live within many different kinds of discourses and behaviors. What marks success in my world is an ability to negotiate different positions, to abstract from particulars, and to imagine interesting relationships among categories—in this chapter, for instance, between the categories of teachers and social classes. This is the world I bring home to my children, and I try to construct an environment that I think will teach them how to succeed in the kind of world I imagine. For me, this world is not one of hard rules and fast obedience. It is one of questioning—and of knowing when it is time to set aside questioning for performance.

My point is this: The working class and high school teachers share the same habitus; likewise with the professional/managerial class and professors.

Distribution by Class Origin in the Educational Hierarchy

The shared habitus is a consequence of the correlation between class origin and position in the educational hierarchy—that is, the higher one's position in the educational hierarchy, the higher one's class origin (Bourdieu, 1991; Bowen & Schuster, 1986). There are obviously exceptions to this correlation—women with working-class origins teaching, for example, at Stanford—but a place for these *parvenues* is woven into the fabric of social reproduction, clearing a space for the myth of class mobility (Bourdieu, 1984). This myth helps to maintain the illusion that privilege is assigned by virtue of industry and intelligence, allowing those who benefit most from the system to believe in their own worthiness, and preventing those who benefit least from grasping how privilege is really assigned (Bourdieu, 1991).

The distribution is further complicated by such things as gender (working class women are disproportionately represented at the elementary school level [Kline, 1995]), ethnicity, fractions within each level, discipline, and concentrations within disciplines. Working-class students gravitate toward education (which explains their disproportionate distribution among elementary and high school teachers), sociology, and business (the smart way to crawl up); professional/managerial class students gravitate toward high status fields like physics, law, and medicine (Bourdieu, 1984; Bowen & Schuster, 1986; Ryan & Sackrey, 1984). Although I have found no research on this question, I suspect that a survey among English departments would reveal more working-class academics (and women) in composition than in literature, and within composition, more with a focus on technical writing than with a focus on cultural studies. The pattern is predictable: in the more marginalized fields you will find members of the marginalized classes.

Cause of the Distribution by Class Origin

This distribution by class origins bears out Durkheim's (1915) thesis that social groups generate structures to reproduce themselves as if the group were an organism; for this kind of structural reproduction, people have to stay more or less in place. Bourdieu's (1991) gravitational theory of symbolic capital explains what keeps them there: symbolic capital, he claims, attracts symbolic capital. Symbolic capital is broadly defined as practices (for example, table manners) and material realities (for example, houses) that have social value. People with similar kinds and amounts of symbolic capital occupy a common social space within which they recognize and valorize each other. In school, teachers with working-class origins who teach at the lower levels in the educational hierarchy may reward students with working-class origins, but as working class students progress, they move into levels populated by teachers with progressively more professional/managerial-level origins—or pretensions. Working-class children may consequently experience success in their early years, but as they advance through high school and into college (the place where they have to entirely make themselves over so as not to reveal their class origins), academic success comes more dearly.

This filtering effect, according to linguistic, cognitive, and social habits of the different classes, has been extensively theorized and documented (Bernstein, 1971-75; Clark, 1960; Heath, 1983; Ohmann, 1987; Rose, 1989; Shor, 1980, 1986). Bourdieu (1991) ties the filtering to the curriculum shift from intrinsic to extrinsic materials. In the early years,

Bourdieu explains, students are rewarded for mastering intrinsic knowledge, that is, what is taught in the school; as students move up, they are increasingly rewarded for extrinsic knowledge, the kind of knowledge that is the very air upper-class students breathe. Professors are impressed by students who are familiar with Djuna Barnes or Franz Liszt (or who correctly date Delacroix); they are not so impressed by students who read Steven King and listen to Pearl Jam. We move, in other words, from rewarding according to one's scholastic to one's cultural capital.

THE ABSENCE

The filtering effect explains both the reproduction of culture and the distribution of status and privilege in the educational hierarchy along class lines. When working class students like me misread our mediocre performances at the undergraduate level, we start looking for soft landings in fields like education and sociology where, rumor has it, good grades are easier to get. When I began this essay, I said I had drifted into teaching, but I could more accurately say I had nowhere else to go. I thought I was stupid, but I was just working class. I realize that this interpretation of my academic performance might be self-serving, but in my own mind, I know that I have gone beyond the need to excuse myself. Rather, I have realized how I was herded into my position; I also know that I escaped into the professional class as a consequence of having married into a family in which the males had Ph.D.'s. My struggle to get one was my attempt to erase within my adopted family my lower-class status.

Although there was a time when I tried to, I have not forgotten my working class, high school teacher origin. I know the stories and underlying myths from both sides of the great divide: I know how the myths miswrite the Other as well as the grains of truth that give rise to these myths. High school teachers know much more than college teachers give them credit for, but many of them are submerged in their practice; professors are prone to theorize water out of rocks, but many of them are also very good teachers. In a nutshell, intelligence and pedagogical competence are probably about equal in both camps. Nevertheless, we tell these stories about each other because we have been trained to do so by a social system that perpetuates a hierarchical structure by mythologizing the ignorance of those below us.

The alignment of class origin and position in the educational hierarchy explains not only the stories we tell about each other, but also the enduring character of the conflict. We may think like Kantor that we are engaged in a common project, but a submerged social agenda undermines cooperation. We are facing off against each other and in this action reenacting class conflict. This in part explains why when we gathered in Louisville to tell the story of the professionalization of composition, we left out the chapters about elementary, middle school, and high school teachers. This omission is an important part of the story.

NOTES

[1]Freire (1970) labels two groups "oppressed" and "opressors." These labels seem too strong to describe the relative positions of high school and college teachers.

[2]I need to reiterate that the hierarchy occurs on a continuum—for example, two-year college teachers slide between high school and four-year college teachers; and state college teachers in Nebraska are quite a bit lower in the hierarchy than professors at UC Berkely.

[3]At the time of Bernstein's (1971–75) research, most working-class women were not in the workforce.

[4]I am in sympathy with Ohmann's (1987) critique of Bernstein's work, particularly of the pedagogical implication that working-class students will succeed only in restrictive educational environments. From my own experience (see Peckham, 1995), many of Bernstein's descriptions of the class differences in language and cognition ring true. They also match many of Bourdieu's (1984) descriptions of the differences between class fractions.

REFERENCES

Bakhtin, M. M. (1981). *The dialogic imagination* (M. Holquist, Ed.; C. Emerson & M. Holquist, Trans.). Austin, TX: University of Texas Press.

Bernstein, B. (1971–75). *Class, codes, and control.* London: Routledge & Kegan Paul.

Bourdieu, P. (1984). *Distinction: A social critique of the judgement of taste* (R. Nice, Trans.). Cambridge, MA: Harvard University Press.

Bourdieu, P. (1991). *Language and symbolic power* (G. Raymond & M. Adamson, Trans.). Cambridge, MA: Harvard University Press.

Bowen, H. R., & Schuster, J. (1986). *American professors: A national resource imperiled.* New York: Oxford University Press.

Britton, J., Burgess, T., Martin, N., McLeod, A., & Rosen, H. (1975). *The development of writing abilities.* London: Macmillan.

Clark, B. R. (1960). The cooling out function in higher education. *American Journal of Sociology, 65,* 569–576.

Cooper, C., & Odell, L. (Eds.). (1977). *Evaluating writing: Describing, measuring, judging.* Urbana, IL: National Council of Teachers of English.

Dewey, J. (1963). *Experience and education.* New York: Collier. (Original work published 1938)

Dixon, J. (1967). *Growth through English.* Reading, England: National Association for the Teaching of English.

Durkheim, E. (1915). *Elementary forms of religious life.* London: Allen & Unwin.

Freire, P. (1970). *Pedagogy of the oppressed* (M. B. Ramos, Trans.). New York: Herder & Herder. (Original work published 1968)

Heath, S. B. (1983). *Ways with words.* Cambridge, MA: Cambridge University Press.

Herndon, J. (1968). *The way it spozed to be.* New York: Simon and Schuster.

Holt, J. (1964). *How children fail.* New York: Pitman.

Kantor, K. (1990). Learning from teachers. In D. A. Daiker & M. Morenberg (Eds.), *The writing teacher as researcher.* Portsmouth, NH: Boynton/Cook.

Kline, C. (1995). Rock shelf further forming: Women, writing, and teaching the young. In L. W. Phelps & J. Emig (Eds.), *Feminine principles and women's experience in American composition and rhetoric.* Pittsburgh, PA: Pittsburgh University Press.

Kohl, H. (1967). *36 children.* New York: New American Library.

Kozol, J. (1967). *Death at an early age: The destruction of the hearts and minds of Negro children in the Boston public schools.* Boston: Houghton Mifflin.

Macrorie, K. (1969). *Writing to be read.* Rochelle Park, NJ: Hayden.

Moffett, J. (1968). *Teaching the universe of discourse.* Boston: Houghton Mifflin.

Moffett, J. (1973) *A student-centered language arts curriculum: Grades K-13.* Boston: Houghton Mifflin.

Neil, A. S. (1960). *Summerhill: A radical approach to education.* New York: Hart.

North, S. (1987). *The making of knowledge in composition: Portrait of an emerging field.* Portsmouth, NH: Boynton/Cook.

Ohmann, R. (1987). *Politics of letters.* Middletown, CT: Wesleyan University Press.

Peckham, I. (1995). Complicity in class codes: The exclusionary function of education. In C. L. B. Dews & C. L. Law (Eds.), *This fine place so far from home: Voices of academics from the working class* (pp. 263–276). Philadelphia: Temple University Press.

Postman, N., & Weingarten, C. (1969). *Teaching as a subversive activity.* New York: Delacorte Press.

Rose, M. (1989). *Lives on the boundary.* New York: Penguin Books.

Ryan, J., & Sackrey, C. (1984). *Strangers in paradise: Academics from the working class.* Boston: South End Press.

Shor, I. (1980). *Critical teaching and everyday life.* Chicago: University of Chicago Press.

Shor, I. (1986). *Culture wars: School and society in the conservative restoration, 1969–1971* . Boston: Routledge & Kegan Paul.

Wigginton, E. (Ed.). (1972). *The Foxfire Book.* New York: Anchor Books.

chapter 15

Professing Rhetoric and Composition: A Personal Odyssey

Frank J. D'Angelo
Arizona State University

When we think of the shaping of rhetoric and composition as a discipline, we tend to think of the contributions of professional organizations such as the Conference on College Composition and Communication (CCCC), with its annual meetings and its journal, which established a forum for the dissemination of ideas about the content and administration of writing courses. And although the CCCC deserves much credit for developing knowledge, methods, and standards for the emerging discipline, I would like to discuss the role that individuals, interacting in small groups, played in bringing people together, identifying teaching needs, and expanding knowledge. I want to focus on the period between 1970 and 1980. I have divided my narrative into three phases for the sake of convenience.

THE INITIATION STAGE

In the first phase, the "initiation" stage, I took a teaching position at Arizona State University in 1970. In 1971, I became Director of Composition, and both Jerry Archer, the department chair, and Bill Ferrell, the assistant chair, encouraged me to get on the CCCC's program the following year.

Their main purpose was to initiate me into the emerging discipline. For the 1972 conference in Boston, I accepted a role as recorder, mostly to find out what was going on and to learn how to conduct myself as a professional. The next year, 1973, I gave my first paper at the CCCC meeting in New Orleans.

I must have met Ross Winterowd that year because the following year, 1974, at the Anaheim meeting, he invited me to a meeting of the emerging Rhetoric Society of America. The meeting was held in Winterowd's living room in Huntington Beach and chaired by Ed Corbett. Others who attended were Janice Lauer, Jim Kinneavy, Richard Lloyd-Jones, Dick Larson, Walter Fisher from the Speech Communication Association, and a number of Winterowd's graduate students from USC. This was an important early meeting of a small group of teachers and scholars who were to form the nucleus of the Rhetoric Society, which gave impetus to scholarly interest in classical rhetoric and in the history of rhetoric. George Yost, a founder of the Rhetoric Society, could not make that particular meeting, but he influenced the direction of the society by his editorship of the newsletter.

In that same year, Tommy Boley invited me to address a special interest group of composition teachers at the Rocky Mountain Modern Language Association (RMMLA) meeting in El Paso, Texas. Boley was part of an active group of writing teachers at the University of Texas at El Paso, which included Maureen Potts, Bob Esch, Larry Johnson, and Nancy Wood. Boley had been a student of Jim Kinneavy's at the University of Texas at Austin, and, filled with enthusiasm for the teaching of writing, he and his colleagues developed one of the first M.A. programs in professional writing and rhetoric in 1976. In addition to setting up special interest groups in rhetoric and composition, they sponsored lectures and workshops in the 1970s, and they invited prominent teachers and scholars to share their knowledge about recent developments in rhetorical theory and practice.

Maureen Potts, a member of that Texas-El Paso group, had gotten her Ph.D. at Texas Woman's University. In the early 1970s, Texas Woman's University nurtured an active group of writing teachers, including Bill Tanner, Dean Bishop, and Turner Kobler, who put together one of the first Ph.D. programs in rhetoric and composition, under the direction of Autrey Wiley, a remarkable woman who was a distinguished 18th-century Restoration drama scholar. Bill Tanner tells me that when she was 70 years old, as department chair, she called faculty members into her office and "persuaded" them to develop courses in the history of rhetoric. "You teach courses in medieval literature," she said to one faculty member. "You will develop a course in medieval rhetoric." To another who taught courses in Renaissance literature, she said, "You will develop a course in Renaissance rhetoric." And so on.

I got to know members of that group when I was invited by Tanner to give a talk at a symposium in rhetoric in 1975. Ross Winterowd, Dick Larson, Richard Coe, and Tom Sloane, chair of the rhetoric program at Berkeley, were on the same program. The previous year, the group had invited Ed Corbett, Gary Tate, and Winston Weathers. The symposium was sponsored by the English Department of Texas Woman's University, in cooperation with the Federation of North Texas Area Universities. In a period of six years, from 1974 to 1980, the Federation invited leading scholars such as Kenneth Burke, Wilbur Samuel Howell, Jacques Barzun, and Gerald Prince to deliver papers. I believe that it was groups such as these that constituted a genuine turning point in the professionalization of composition studies. They gave composition teachers, who had neither identity nor status in their own departments, a place to gather, to talk, to deliver papers, to exchange ideas, and to develop professionally.

During the early 1970s, Ed Corbett chaired a special-interest session in rhetoric and composition at the Midwest Modern Language Association in Chicago, Ed Corbett and Richard Young addressed a special-interest group at the MLA, Tommy Boley chaired a session at the RMMLA, and J. Dean Bishop chaired a meeting at the South Central Modern Language Association. In 1975, Janice Lauer began a series of seminars in the teaching of writing at the University of Detroit, and Forrest Burt and his colleagues at Texas A & M organized a series of seminars on writing as process to instruct teachers of writing about recent developments in composition theory and practice. There was a powerful urge to professionalize in the early 1970s, to claim a field for rhetoric and composition. Part of the impetus came from university professors who were required to teach writing courses and to direct composition programs, but were given no systematic guidance in graduate school to teach composition or to direct programs.

THE QUEST STAGE

In the second phase of the professionalization of the discipline of rhetoric and composition, which I shall label the "quest" stage, we ventured forth to claim an identity. We read everything that was available and that might make us better teachers of writing. We were enthusiastic about Christensen's generative rhetoric and the possibilities of new rhetorics. We were excited about Kinneavy's theory of discourse, Corbett's classical rhetoric, tagmemic rhetoric, linguistic stylistics, transformational sentence combining, literary structuralism, and more. We did not separate the professional from the personal. We identified with other teachers in the field on a personal level; interdependent, we shared many interests. Ross Winterowd said that we were "Pentecostal" in those days, rolling around the floor in ecstasy. Now, he says, we are "High Church."

The 1970s was a period that gave direction and method to our teaching and scholarship. These small groups gave us a place to gather, to talk, and to share ideas. And we talked everywhere—at conferences, symposia, summer institutes, publishers' parties, in lobbies, restaurants, and bars. Out of these gatherings came newsletters, bibliographies, new courses, graduate programs, articles in books and journals, and support for our colleagues for tenure and promotion.

The goals of the quest varied from person to person. For some, it was to identify a common subject matter and a methodology. For others, it was the development of an academic field that would bring prestige and status. For still others, it was to obtain publication sites and research grants. And for a few, it was some mysterious source of meaning in the service of an ideal—in the words of Tennyson, "To follow knowledge like a sinking star/Beyond the utmost bound of human thought."

For some members of these groups, rhetoric and composition defined itself by its opposition to literary studies. However, there was no historical reason for doing so. Historically, rhetoric aligns itself with dialectic and poetic. In addition, almost all of us had Ph.D.'s in literary studies. Nevertheless, many had to do battle with the ogres of what Ross Winterowd calls the "literarist empire." In my own department, I felt no animosity by literary scholars toward composition studies until the mid-1970s, when John Gage and I presented a proposal to the PhD graduate committee at Arizona State University for a new concentration in rhetoric and composition. It was only then that the dragons guarding the literary canon came out of their caves breathing fire, but they were defeated by the forces of rhetoric.

The years 1976 and 1977 were important in the shaping of the discipline. In the summer of 1976, John Warnock and Ross Winterowd, sensing that things were beginning to happen in rhetoric and composition, put together a summer institute in rhetoric at the University of Wyoming. To that meeting, they invited George Yost, the founder of the Rhetoric Society; Janice Lauer; Richard Young; Patty Sullivan, a composition instructor at Wyoming; Dorothy Guinn, one of Ross's graduate students; E. D. Hirsch; and me. There was no money involved; we had to pay our own way. We met in a small cabin in the mountains to talk about what we were doing and what we were reading, as chipmunks jumped in and out of the windows.

Later, when I asked John Warnock and Richard Young what the main purpose of the meeting was, they said it was to educate Hirsch about rhetoric and composition, and they added, "But we failed." At that time, Hirsch's *The Philosophy of Composition* (1976) was about to appear, and he seemed genuinely interested in the teaching of writing. I'm not sure if any great issues were resolved at that meeting, but it was groups such as these that preserved the spirit of social interaction. I am convinced that it was in these small groups that professionalism was emerging as a way of holding ourselves together. Warnock, of course, was to take over the leadership of the Wyoming conference from Art Simpson in the years that followed, when important issues about teaching were emerging.

Between 1976 and 1977, I attended at least 11 professional meetings. Writing conferences and special-interest groups in rhetoric and composition were springing up everywhere—at the MLA, the National Council of Teachers of English, the Speech Communication Association, the Texas A & M Summer Institute organized by Forrest Burt, the University of Texas at Arlington's Issues in Writing Symposium, the Association of Departments of English meeting of the MLA, and at Livingston College in Alabama. I cite these figures to illustrate the contribution of small groups to the growth of interest in rhetoric and composition as a discipline.

One of the most important of these early meetings was the Conference on Language and Style, put together by Don McQuade and his colleagues in 1977 at the Graduate Center of the City University of New York (CUNY). That meeting put me in touch with the CUNY writing teachers, a very important group of writing teachers at that time. The conference prominently featured Ken Bruffee, Dick Larson, Sondra Perl, Sandra Schor, John Clifford, Robert Di Yanni, Judith Fishman, Robert Lyons, and others. This group, most of whom were writing-program directors, met once a week at the CUNY graduate center with Mina Shaughnessy and Janet Emig to talk about important issues in the teaching of writing. They called themselves CAWS, the CUNY Association of Writing Supervisors. Out of these early meetings came collaborative learning, the Writing Program Administration (WPA), and the *Journal of Basic Writing*. Many of the CUNY writing teachers were to play a prominent part in the CCCC program I chaired in 1979.

Much of the conference was devoted to linguistic stylistics, but, in addition to the linguists, McQuade and his colleagues invited writing teachers "to chart the interconnections of linguistics, stylistics, and the teaching of composition." That was a raucous meeting. Stanley Fish was asked to sum up the proceedings, and, after taking issue with Samuel Keyser's reading of a Wallace Stevens poem, he pronounced the conference a failure. Linguistics, he said, is useless in the interpretation of literary texts because its methods are circular and arbitrary, and its categories refer to nothing except the categories of the system that produced them. I wonder what he might have said about *our* sessions had he attended them, but out of that conference came *Linguistics, Stylistics, and the Teaching of Composition* (1979) and the revised and expanded *Territory of Language* (1986), edited by Don McQuade.

McQuade himself was a member of an earlier small group that was loosely connected at Rutgers University. Pat Bizzell, a member of that group of writing teachers, told me recently that Don McQuade and Robert Atwan preceded her at Rutgers. Pat was part of a group that included Bruce Herzberg, David Bartholomae, and Linda Flowers; and Janet Emig was a faculty member at that time.

Bizzell says that they fancied themselves as budding literary critics. She did her dissertation on F. Scott Fitzgerald. Bartholomae did his on Thomas Hardy. While he was a graduate student at Rutgers, Bartholomae put together the basic writing program. When he left to take a position at Pittsburgh, Bizzell took over his responsibilities. She also helped to direct the writing program, and that experience helped her get a job at the College of Holy Cross after she got her Ph.D. Both Bizzell and Bartholomae told me that they got no help from their graduate studies in learning how to do their jobs teaching writing. But they were avid readers of books and journals, and they and a few colleagues would occasionally meet over drinks to talk about what they were doing.

I met Bizzell at an NCTE meeting in the mid-1970s. At that meeting, we shared our enthusiasm for new developments in rhetoric and composition. In subsequent years, I saw Bizzell and Herzberg both at professional meetings and publishers' parties, and we renewed our acquaintance. Publishers' parties in the 1970s were modest affairs. Publishers would rent a suite of rooms, put some beer on ice in the bathtub, and provide snacks for our hungry appetites. I would be remiss if I did not mention the important role that editors and publishers such as Paul O'Connell, Chuck Christensen, Bill Oliver, Eben Ludlow, Nancy Perry, Phil Miller, and Carolyn Potts played in the development of interest in rhetoric and composition. They not only provided places where we could meet and talk, but they also encouraged us to disseminate our ideas in a wide range of books and publications.

I was involved with a group of writing teachers in the mid-1970s, consisting of Erika Lindemann, Bill Coles, Gary and Priscilla Tate, Bob Bain, Rick Coe, and Joe Comprone. We met regularly at NCTE meetings to drink and talk. Perhaps our most important contribution as a small group was to get writing sessions on the NCTE program. We also formed lasting friendships, and we influenced each other in significant ways. In addition, members of this group connected with other groups as we continued to seek internal legitimation.

Lindemann did her graduate work in literary studies at Chapel Hill. After she got her Ph.D. in 1972, she took a position at the University of South Carolina directing the writing program. Because she didn't know anything about the field, she attended her first CCCC meeting in 1973. Lindemann told me that she was so naive that when she registered for the conference she thought she was also registering for the hotel. When she got to the hotel, she discovered she didn't have a room. Erika met Ed Corbett, Joe Comprone, and others, just hanging around the meeting rooms. Joe asked her if she had read Kinneavy's book, and she replied that she hadn't read anything. She was just getting started in the field.

Erika Lindemann, Joe Comprone, David Bartholomae, Susan Miller, Rick Coe, and Jim Raymond formed an important small group in the 1970s. With the help of the others in the group, Lindemann got an NEH grant in 1977 to bring secondary and college teachers to the campus for a summer conference to help them integrate writing into their teaching. Tom Waldrep gave them a place to stay. This group stayed in touch after that conference. They put together sessions at the CCCC. They helped each other get published. They read one another's papers. They competed with one another. Comprone told me recently that "We were just people trying to help out other people. We were young turks with a heart. We had an idealistic streak." All of the members of that group went on to make significant contributions to the discipline.

I got to know Gary and Priscilla Tate in 1974. Gary got his Ph.D. in Renaissance literature at the University of New Mexico. He taught at Wyoming in 1957 and 1958 and Ohio Wesleyan in 1959. In 1960, he took a position at the University of Tulsa, where he directed the composition program from 1965 to 1970. Gary was part of a small group of teachers interested in composition, including Winston Weathers and Otis Winchester. Bill Tanner, who was to play an important role at Texas Woman's University, was a graduate student at Tulsa. Gary tells me that Weathers was a legendary writing teacher in those days. In 1965, Gary directed a National Defense Education Act (NDEA) Institute, featuring Ed Corbett and Dick Larson as guest speakers. Out of that collaboration, Tate and Corbett went on to edit an important series of books, including *The Writing Teacher's Sourcebook* (1981).

In 1971, Gary accepted a position at Texas Christian University to direct the writing program. In 1972, both Gary and Priscilla Tate put together, in mimeographed form, the first issue of *Freshman English News*. Their aim was to encourage teachers to send in reports about teaching writing; but teachers kept sending essays on theory. In 1976,

Gary and Priscilla devoted the entire winter issue of *Freshman English News* to Winston Weathers' provocative essay "The Grammars of Style: New Options in Composition." In 1977, I had supper with Gary and Priscilla at a CCCC meeting in the restaurant at the Radisson-Muehlebach Hotel in Kansas City, Missouri. The place was packed with participants from the conference. Almost anybody who was anybody was there. Looking around at the writing teachers gathered there, Gary said half-seriously: "If somebody were to bomb this place, rhetoric and composition would disappear from the face of the earth." It might have been at that same conference that Ross Winterowd, looking around at the teachers in attendance, announced that "we were the cream of the scum."

Bill Coles got his Ph.D. at Minnesota in 1958. He did his dissertation on Thomas Love Peacock. Coles told me recently that he never took a course in composition and that he thought teaching composition was a racket until he went to Amherst College in 1960. There, he said, he met people who were actually interested in teaching writing. At Amherst, everyone taught freshman composition, and Coles took as his models the teachers he found there. They included Alfred Kazin, a prominent American literary critic; Leo Marx, a cultural historian; and Theodore Baird, who developed the writing program at Amherst.

In 1974, Coles took a position as composition director at the University of Pittsburgh "to lead them out of the swamp." In 1975, David Bartholomae joined Coles to assist him in directing the program and to develop the basic writing program. Bartholomae said that he learned a lot about writing from Coles. Coles authored an important series of books in the 1970s, including *Composing* (1974) and *The Plural I* (1978). When I chaired the CCCC meeting in 1979, Coles put together a number of sessions on literacy and writing across the curriculum.

In 1977, Forrest Burt invited me to participate in the Texas A & M Summer Institute in Dallas, one of several seminars that Forrest, Elizabeth Cowan, and Greg Cowan put together in the 1970s. This was an interesting group of writing teachers. Besides their interest in the traditional areas of rhetoric and composition, they were making connections between creativity, Gestalt psychology, humanistic psychology, and the teaching of writing. Elizabeth and Greg Cowan, Barrett Mandell, and Joanne Cocklereas put together an interesting session on humanistic psychology and the teaching of writing at the CCCC meeting I chaired in 1979.

THE TRIUMPH OF THE IDEAL

In the third phase of the professionalization of the discipline, which I shall call the "triumph of the ideal," the academic discipline of rhetoric and composition had finally emerged. However, it is less clear if it achieved the prestige and status for which its practitioners had fought. I will arbitrarily give the years 1978 to 1980 as important dates, although I believe that this phase continued well into the 1980s. In this phase, the number of opportunities for scholars and teachers of composition to give papers, to conduct workshops, and to publish increased geometrically.

Between 1978 and 1980, I participated in 22 conferences and symposiums, four workshops, and four colloquiums, at such diverse institutions as Lubbock Christian College, the University of Utah, Utah State University, the University of Alabama at Birmingham, St. Edwards University, Texas Woman's University, the University of Illinois, the University of Louisville, Brigham Young University, and the University of Alabama. You could probably multiply the number of speaking engagements, colloquiums, seminars, and workshops by a hundred if you were to ask other scholars what they were doing at this time. The sheer magnitude of opportunities was amazing. Again, I give these figures to illustrate the growth of interest in rhetoric and composition and in the professionalization of the discipline. Willis Pitkin invited me to a colloquium at Utah State University on May 26, 1978. Pitkin got his Ph.D. at USC in 1973. Francis Christensen directed his dissertation. Bill Smith directed the composition program at Utah State in 1973, where he and Pitkin and others formed an interesting small group. Pitkin told me that Mina Shaughnessy was a big influence on him at this time. He met Mina at an MLA meeting in Chicago. Because Pitkin expressed admiration for her work, they spent the afternoon walking around Chicago. That's how it was in the 1970s—you could walk up to anybody in the profession and go out for coffee or lunch or for a drink to talk about writing. We had little regard for rank and authority.

Before he took a position at Utah State, Pitkin worked for a computer company, looking to develop a computer dictionary. Richard Ohmann published two of his essays in the same issue of *College English*—"Hierarchies and the Discourse Hierarchy" (1977a) and "X/Y: Some Basic Strategies of Discourse" (1977b). Many teachers found Pitkin's work difficult to understand, yet he used his ideas about discourse structure in Utah State's Writing Center, and he successfully taught those same materials to huge classes of up to 100 students. Pitkin's textbook, *Generating Prose*, was published by Macmillan in 1987. Pitkin quit going to conferences for awhile. But in 1988, he presented a paper entitled "The Reader as Organizer" at a session I put together with Victor Vitanza, "Organizing

Texts," at the CCCC meeting in St. Louis. Discouraged by the lack of response to his paper, Pitkin told the audience this would be his last CCCC meeting. Pitkin is currently working on a book on the limits of language, called *Feeding the Dinosaurs*.

In 1979, Jim Raymond invited me to a symposium on literacy at the University of Alabama. Raymond did his dissertation on medieval literature at Texas-Austin. He got his job directing the composition program at Alabama because of his experience assisting Maxine Hairston at Texas-Austin. He counts as his influences Mina Shaughnessy and James Sledd. Raymond, Ralph Voss, and Bill Smith formed a group (of sorts) at Alabama, and he was loosely connected to Lindemann's group. I think he invited me to speak because he liked my New Orleans accent.

Most of the symposiums given by the university dealt with English and American literature, but Raymond persuaded his colleagues to do a conference on literacy, to which he invited John Simon, James Sledd, E. D. Hirsch, Walter Ong, Richard Lloyd-Jones, Vivian Davis, Ed Corbett, and me. Sledd gave his usual polemical talk, and when Hirsch got up to speak, Sledd's graduate students rose from their seats and turned to the audience. On their sweaters was emblazoned a message—something like "Hirsch Sucks." This symposium is another example of the drive to professionalize in the 1970s. Jim Raymond and other members of small groups of writing teachers made places for us at important meetings. The papers we delivered subsequently got published in books and journals, lending a scholarly air of authority to what we were doing. Jim edited the proceedings of that conference in a book titled *Literacy as a Human Problem* (1982). There were many other small groups that helped to shape the discipline in the 1970s, but due to the limitations of space, I am including only those with which I had some personal contact.

The culmination of this third stage came for me at the CCCC meeting I put together in 1979. The title of the conference was "Writing: A Cross-Disciplinary Enterprise." Whatever measure of success that conference had I attribute to the members of the small groups who wrote to me proposing sessions. My favorite story concerns the role that Elaine Maimon, Art Young, and Toby Fulwiler played in shaping the conference. At the 1978 CCCC conference, knowing that I was to chair the program the next year, they took every opportunity to convince me to feature writing across the curriculum. What happened was surreal! It seems that every time I waited for the elevator in the conference hotel, three heads would mysteriously pop out of the elevator door, shouting in unison, "Writing across the curriculum!". This went on for three days. Finally, Maimon, Young, and Fulwiler cornered me and convinced me that the CCCC should validate what they and others were doing. "We had just come from the bar," Maimon said. Now I don't want you to think that I think that alcohol has anything to do with creativity, but I am surprised at the number of occasions when moderate drinking led to conviviality and to getting important work done. They and others helped me to put together 11 sessions on writing across the curriculum, which featured faculty members from English, philosophy, music, history, government, engineering, and biology.

That was the first conference to feature new research on invention, cognition, and the composing process. Ann Berthoff chaired a session entitled "New Research in Composing and on Cognitive Processes," which featured Sondra Perl, Linda Flower, and Nancy Sommers. Janice Lauer and Janet Emig did a seminar on the composing process. Richard Young chaired a session on invention that featured Lisa Ede, Charles Kneupper, and Victor Vitanza.

The rhetorical tradition, classical rhetoric, and the history of rhetoric were well represented, with 10 sessions. Michael Leff and Mike Halloran gave presentations on the essentials of Aristotle's rhetoric. John Gage, Larry Green, and their colleagues from Berkeley gave papers on the enthymeme. George Yoos and David Harrington discussed the "Ethical Dimensions of Rhetoric"; Bob Gorrell, Lee Odell, John Poulakos, and Craig Gannon put together a session on rhetorical theory; and Don Stewart, Andrea Lunsford, James Berlin, and Wally Douglas discussed 19th-century historical figures in rhetoric and composition.

At that same conference, Pat Bizzell, David Bartholomae, Judith Fishman, Sara Garnes, and Marilyn Sternglass put together a series of sessions on basic writing. Ken Bruffee, Lil Brannon, Muriel Harris, and Janice Neuleib did the same for writing labs. Similarly, the technical communication teachers and scholars put together eight sessions across the program from theory to practice. Richard Lloyd-Jones, Ed White, Rick Coe, and Bill Lutz handled the sessions on testing. Dixie Goswami, Ellen Nold, Ann Matsushashi, and Richard Beach participated in the sessions on revising and evaluating student writing.

That conference, I am convinced, made many careers, but Ann Berthoff was none too pleased with the prominent role that cognitive science played there and with my attempt to get as many people on the program as possible. I tell these stories because the collective memory of a discipline might have a significant effect on its future. There arose in the 1970s a peculiar situation in which writing teachers learned more about what they were doing by meeting in small groups outside the academy than they did in pursuing their doctorates. They taught even the most elementary writing courses with a sophistication not always shared or understood by their literary colleagues. They recognized that the students they were teaching were eager and responsive and a joy to teach.

Here, then, is a rough chronicle of the individuals and small groups I have been acquainted with that helped to shape the discipline of rhetoric and composition in the 1970s. In my narrative, I have persistently emphasized the role that small groups, meeting informally, played in the development of our discipline. These small groups gave us a place to gather, to talk, to share ideas, and to develop professionally. They preserved a spirit of social interaction. They helped members of the group to get published. They fostered a greater interest in research. They began to establish journals to record and disseminate the results of their research. They argued that departments of English needed to take composition more seriously. And most importantly, their collaboration gave direction and method to the teaching of writing.

Whenever a small group of people comes together for whatever reason, there is a potential for action. In such groups, decisions can be made more easily, and friendships can develop. Small groups can dramatize the quest for knowledge, making it real and alive, not merely an abstract, academic pursuit. As members of these small groups in the 1970s, we did not seek to occupy a position of advocacy. Rather, our goal was to participate with others to achieve a common goal. And that goal was to make us better teachers of writing and to see the activity of composition from the student's point of view. Since advocacy was not our goal, we did not attack the ideas of others, but allowed each person the right of self-expression without feeling hidden threats. We knew there were often differences of opinion, but we asked ourselves: What are the things that we can agree on? We considered each person in the group to have potential value.

However, since those early years, there have been schisms between practitioners and researchers and between compositionists and rhetoricians, not to mention all kinds of ideological confrontations. Perhaps we were naive in the 1970s about the enemy within, but we could disagree, without being disagreeable, and contend, without being contentious. The historians among us have tried to explain the problems that face us in terms of the postmodern unsettling of traditional boundaries and the loss of a grand narrative that could unify competing discourses. But perhaps we need no grand narrative to tell us what we have known all along—that people can disagree and still cooperate and be intelligent and decent people. In the 1970s, we integrated our personalities into the groups without losing our identities. This integration provided a proper synthesis of intelligence, creativity, and values. That is the lesson I learned from individuals in small groups in my personal odyssey in the 1970s.

REFERENCES

Coles, W. E. (1974). *Composing: Writing as a self-creating process.* Rochelle Park, NJ: Hayden.

Coles, W. E. (1978). *The plural I.* New York: Holt.

Hirsch, E. D., Jr. (1976). *The philosophy of composition.* Chicago: University of Chicago Press.

McQuade, D. A. (1979). *Linguistics, stylistics, and the teaching of composition.* Akron, OH: University of Akron, Department of English.

McQuade, D. A. (1986). *The territory of language.* Carbondale, IL: Southern Illinois University Press.

Pitkin, W. L., Jr. (1977a). Hierarchies and the discourse hierarchy. *College English, 38*(7),648–659.

Pitkin, W. L., Jr. (1977b). X/Y: Some basic strategies of discourse. *College English, 38*(7),660–672.

Pitkin, W. L., Jr. (1987). *Generating prose.* New York: Macmillan.

Pitkin, W. L., Jr. (1988). *The reader as organizer.* Paper presented at the meeting of the Conference on College Composition and Communication, St. Louis, MO.

Raymond, J. C. (Ed.). (1982). *Literacy as a human problem.* University, AL: The University of Alabama Press.

Tate, G., & Corbett, E. P. J. (Eds.). (1981). *The writing teacher's sourcebook.* New York: Oxford University Press.

Weathers, W. (1976). Grammars of style: New options in composition. *Freshman English News, 4*(3),1–18.

Watson Conference Oral History #5: Discourse and Politics in Composition Studies October 1996 David Bartholomae, Pat Bizzell, Patty Harkin, and Richard Ohmann

Camille Newton, interviewer
edited by Pamela Takayoshi

Camille Newton: Yesterday, James Zebroski said that Pat Bizzell and David Bartholomae, through their publications and research focuses, kept cognition from becoming the main direction of rhetoric and composition in the early '80s. And it was suggested today that Richard Ohmann, as editor of *College English,* and Patty Harkin, as co-editor of *Contending with Words*, selected what would be included in influential texts in the discipline. Could you discuss the individual choices you have made as administrators, teachers, writers, and researchers that you think have been significant for the formation of the discipline?

Pat Bizzell: Zebroski must have said that about me because of "Cognition, Convention, and Certainty," a 1982 essay that I talked about this morning. That has been a much cited essay and people have told me that it helped them see a way of doing composition studies that didn't involve empirical research.

Patty Harkin: There is something very generational about the way in which this profession has developed itself, in that the people of our age who are now in their late 40s and early 50s are people who were largely educated in departments of literary studies where it was not possible to take a degree in rhetoric. Yet, we were really carefully trained theorists. Our impulse was to try to find a way of theorizing this work that we were doing in such a way as to give it an overarching reason. That led us, I think, all at once to discuss the fact that we have a post-disciplinary profession. We don't have a discipline in the sense of a regulated way of raising and answering questions that is agreed-upon by everybody. But we have a professionalization—you can get tenure in what we do, you can have series of books about it, you can have Ph.D. programs in it. Engineers are a great deal more agreed about how to get a bridge go all the way across a river than we are about how to get a message to somebody.

Richard Ohmann: The farther over you go toward the natural sciences, the more that is going to be true. Obviously, economics has a body of theory that everybody in the field must know, but I'm sure it is possible to get a Ph.D. in rhetoric without knowing X, Y, or Z; what are the important texts? Certainly in literature it is possible to get a Ph.D. without having read Foucault, probably without having read Shakespeare. However, people of the current generation are all in on a conversation that everybody afterward will be able to join if they are in a graduate program in rhetoric and composition—there's a kind of informal canon and collection of problematics.

David Bartholomae: The work graduate students produce is constrained by the training programs they are in or the work they have read in the ways that seem to me to be different from the positions that we faced when we were getting started, when it seemed more like open territory.

RO: To go back to Camille's original question: When I went to graduate school, I had no thought of going into composition studies or even composition teaching. That is, I was somebody who liked to read books, somebody who wanted to study and teach literature like everybody in my generation. But when I applied for teaching fellowships after my first couple of years of graduate school at Harvard, I got one in the writing course. "General Education A," it was called. I invested quite a lot of energy, time, and interest in that course and ended up joining with its director, Harold Martin, in producing a textbook, an anthology, called *Inquiry and Expression*, and I then later joined with him in the second and third editions of *The Logic and Rhetoric of Exposition*. So I had actually done work connected with a writing course by the end of the '50s, and that interested me in the field. Now, again, I never thought of that as my specialty. A career in writing instruction was not what anybody did then. But I took the work seriously so that when I began editing *College English* in 1966, I thought that interesting things could be written and said about writing instruction, and I was open to them as submissions to the magazine.

PB: That was no small thing.

DB: No, that was actually a terrific thing. Because I think *College English* at the time was different from *CCC* both in its standing and also the number of surprises it was willing to offer. That was your contribution.

CN: That is particularly interesting, given your call today for more exploration of experimental stylistics in prose and forms. How do you see that happening?

DB: I thought Pat gave one very powerful answer which is that it *is* happening. What the culture has been producing and valuing has been people whose prose does this—Patricia Williams, Gloria Anzaldua, everybody has their own favorite list. Teachers can bring that work into play both as material to read in the curriculum, but also by having students read it to think about what is at stake if you write that way, think that way.

PB: Yeah, I think that is exactly right. Students are very hip to that, by and large. I think if we only look at the professoriate, we don't have a complete picture of the forces in play in this area. If you just look at comp people versus literature people in the typical English department, you would say "That is obviously ridiculous, Pat. It is never going to happen." But I think the students themselves are a powerful force, the most powerful force. Students have forced dramatic changes in the academy since I began teaching in 1972 and will continue to do so. I think, in general, they are forcing changes in the direction I want to go and that I want comp studies to go. I think we have a better product than traditional literary studies. We are going to have some clout in that sense in shaping the curriculum of English departments. I think the students are going to vote with their feet and say "We want this kind of literary study. We want this kind of address to reading and writing more than this other kind." I am hoping this will give us some kind of leverage in trying to set the agenda first of the discipline of English studies and then maybe a larger agenda of undergraduate education at least in the humanities if not across the curriculum. That is the optimistic scenario. It is kind of a necessity-driven scenario.

I think more diverse students are in the academy now because the academy needs them, not the other way around. Oftentimes, in comp studies, when we talk about basic writing, we still talk about basic writing students like charity cases. "Out of the goodness of our hearts, we brought them into the academy, now we have to figure out how to take care of them." Whereas, in fact, those populations are coming into the academy because the academy needs them. The academy needs the bodies. The academy needs the money. It needs the credibility with the culture at large that comes with educating broadly for the democracy. As those populations increase in the academy, I think the power shifts, I am hoping the power shifts, in the direction that I would like to see us going.

PH: It is important, too, to encourage students to understand and analyze the commodity that they have come to school to purchase. Any traditional knee-jerk Marxian analysis would say by now we are commodified. Our work is commodified. Well, sure, but students come to you and say, "I want to get a job" and corporations say, "Send me a man who can write a memo." We ought to be able to ask our students to look critically at that request. It seems more appropriate to do that than to refuse to teach them how to write a memo. To say, instead, why is it that the culture prefers these genres of writing to those genres of writing?

RO: Going back to your point, Pat, about what students will want, you mentioned in your talk the risk of going in the direction you were proposing. That risk is not only from other people in the English department or the academy but also from pressures on the university from the outside. It seems whenever the public, if I can use that mystification, takes notice of our work, it does so with quite a bit of suspicion, hostility, misunderstanding, and resentment—as in the back-to- basics movement, the culture wars, and the various literacy crises. So, to the extent that what you are proposing is perceived as multiculturalism, there is going to be some choppy water for it outside the academy. I am sure you'd agree.

PB: Oh, of course I'd agree. I would prefer to talk about it in language that was offered to us this morning: increasing opportunities for democracy, literacy for democracy. It can be presented that way because we are willing to say we want to help students do things in the world that they want to do. That's another area, again, where I think we are better prepared than some literary scholars. It is chancy; it could go either way. I think we at least have a chance to make the case. It is true that we also have to make the case more than we have done.

DB: Why do you describe this in terms of us and literary scholars? It's hard to imagine a definition of literary scholar that wouldn't include you. In fact, your new textbook, which is a remarkable book, in many ways could be thought of as a literature textbook and not a composition textbook.

PB: I couldn't agree more. I have a number of responses to that. I describe it this way partly because it is traditional discourse in comp studies that somehow literature is the enemy. I think I am able to make this critique precisely because I don't see any difference. I teach literature courses and composition courses all the time. I teach them exactly the same way. I was hired to be both in some sense in my department. And I think my department is remarkably integrated. One of the things I like about my department is that everyone teaches composition, everyone teaches literature, and many people also teach what is called creative writing elsewhere. I live in a departmental culture where these things are interanimated to a much greater degree than they are in many other universities. That is a perspective that I value and would like to see dispersed. But I understand that most people don't live in climates like that, so when I make public pronouncements, I use this language that is part of the conventional way of talking about things.

You yourself spoke this morning about competing models of how to address texts and how to interact with texts. I think in general there is a kind of cluster on the comp side and a cluster on the literary side and I tend to gravitate toward those on the comp side and want to promote those. I am agreeing with you, I think, that one doesn't want to dichotomize those. It was kind of a rhetorical device. How about answering your own question, David? It seems to me that you are in the same position.

DB: Yeah, that's right. I actually made it a rule not to use the dichotomization that you were relying on for a variety of reasons. One is that I am not convinced that everyone else lives in a world where those divisions are fundamental. The real divisions, and I think they are deep and fundamental, are often ideological divisions having to do with what it means to do work in the field as a professional teaching. What work am I responsible for? Am I responsible for working closely with students? I think that cuts across creative writing, literature, and composition divisions. These are theoretical and epistemological divisions. It is destructive to English departments to fight along those lines and I think it hurts us. It is clearly the case in most schools that the administration would be happy to get rid of the English department, but it needs to support the composition program. That we allow the world and the administration to think in those terms is more troubling to me than it is positive. Because we have to convince even our own colleagues to imagine that the real commercial value of English is not the one semester required course but some larger project.

PB: I totally agree with that.

CN: Do you see the professionalization of rhetoric and composition as reinforcing that split?

RO: I don't know. My former department will never hire anyone from your program, Patty, or a writing program, Dave, because there is no composition studies position, nor is there a basic writing course. There's lots of writing going on in lots of courses. I would think, even though I understand that my experience of this one little place is peculiar, that the whole field of English is still very much divided in many people's minds and that affects things such as hiring decisions. So yes, the professionalization of composition studies has required this antagonism or opposition, and maybe, given an optimistic reading like Dave's, it won't need to do so in the future. I am not sure.

PH: Your question is in part a question about class. Class, not only in its classical, traditional definition of how close you are to the mode of production, but also as a question of common interests. Years ago, Richard Lanham predicted that the most exciting work in composition studies would take place in "state universities of the second rank." Having spent the first 20 years of my professional life in such institutions, I think he was quite right. In places like the University of Akron and the University of Toledo, where the vast majority of the students were open admissions students, the very first kids in their families that had ever gone to college, writing and the teaching of writing were not particularly denigrated by the rest of the staff, except for a very few elitists who taught seminars on Henry James to two people. Then, when the budget got cut, so did Henry James. But we went ahead, plugging right along. And there is distinctly a class difference in terms of graduates getting hired. People in rhetoric get jobs. People in literary studies do not get jobs. At Purdue, the rhetoric program has a 98 percent placement rate and in literary studies, it's about 15 percent. I think it is important that departments of English analyze the ways in which discourse constructs subjects, values, and knowledge.

DB: I think there is a big difference between our program and Purdue's program because we don't have a separate tract in composition and rhetoric. That was an argument that I made some time ago, and I've often been accused of betraying my subdiscipline by not guaranteeing its identity inside of a graduate program that works on open market principles. The thing that concerns me most is not so much how the graduate program organizes its work, but how the profession is organized. What does it mean to be in composition right now? One thing that concerns me is the degree to which composition as a field now, by producing specialists, has furthered this particular problem. The great irony of the time for me is the production of the composition specialist, who is identified with a line in a departmental budget who then comes and never teaches composition but teaches theory or manages people. So little of our energies are spent right now getting faculty, however they are conceived, to imagine their commitment to lower-level undergraduate curriculum, to general education, and to composition. There is a large movement that is turning all of that over to part-time faculty and to graduate students. I think it is going to happen more rather than less. The pressures are there to create more research faculty than teaching faculty. That is the bleakest future that I can imagine, I mean barring the complete collapse of the university system. I could imagine working happily on something called a program of undergraduate studies. I'd be happy there. But I wouldn't be happy in an English department whose tenured faculty taught only majors and graduate students and where all the general education courses were being taught otherwise. And that's a more pressing issue, it seems to me, than trying to control the definition of graduate study in composition right now. I worry that the time 4Cs spends trying to control and, in a sense, legitimate graduate programs is only going to feed into a destructive scenario rather than prevent it. That is, it is just part of the whole production of the specialist and the leaving of everything else to somebody who is poorly paid and who doesn't have an office.

PB: On the other hand, I am not inclined to see the professionalization of comp studies, however that is defined, as a bad thing. My ground for optimism with the scenario you just sketched is that I think it is still the case not only that comp studies has to some degree taken sides as you suggested, but that I can't think of an example of an important work in composition studies that didn't begin from a classroom problem, from somebody saying "There is something I want to do with my students and it is not working, or I want to do it differently, or they want to do it differently." I can't think of an example of any kind of important work in comp studies that didn't come from that and is still coming from that. So that connection with the earth that Robert [Connors] was nostalgically invoking Wednesday night seems to me has never been broken, has never been dissipated, except for people in advanced graduate programs like his. Most of us are very nicely in touch with the earth, thank you.

Part V

Future Prospects and Challenges

chapter 16

Rethinking Research on Composing: Arguments for a New Research Agenda

Lee Odell
Christina Lynn Prell
Rensselaer Polytechnic Institute

In the 1978 volume *Research on Composing*, Cooper and Odell claimed that "What we have needed for decades and what we must have soon is a period of vigorous research on written discourse and the composing process" (p. xi). At the time, it seemed that this claim might be true, but it also seemed, at least to Odell, that he and Cooper were engaging in wishful thinking. Certainly, neither of them could have predicted the flood of research that has been done in the past two decades.

All this effort notwithstanding, the authors of this chapter want to make another wishful but confident-sounding claim: What we have needed for at least a decade and what we must have soon is a period of vigorous research on composing. Not just writing—composing. To modify a phrase from Richards's *Philosophy of Rhetoric* (1965), we need studies not solely of "the interanimation of words," but the interanimation of words, visual images, and page (or screen) design. What is the nature of this interanimation? That is, for example, how do visual images amplify (or subvert) the explicit and implicit messages conveyed through words or page layout? How does this interanimation affect the composing process?

How is it reflected in a completed product? How does it affect an audience's understanding of, response to, or assessment of that product?

Such questions will surely lead composition teachers and researchers into areas where we may have neither the experience, the training, nor perhaps even the inclination to venture. In many departments of English, there was a time when even so timid a gesture as underlining a word for emphasis was frowned upon. Emphasis was to be achieved through logic, diction, and effective syntax. Resorting to underlining was admitting failure: as a stylist, as a thinker, and, by implication, as a person, since underlining suggested that one was too lazy to do the hard work demanded by good writing. That's *writing*, not *composing*. Although an essay might be referred to as a composition, that terminology confused no one. Musicians composed; what we were doing was writing.

This point of view persisted well after our profession began to talk about research on composing or the composing process. Early on, our studies were of written texts: Did professionally written texts typically have topic sentences? How did syntax change as students matured? When we began to look beyond completed written texts—at the composing process, for example, or the social contexts in which texts were composed or read—we were still primarily interested in writing: How can we help students engage more fully, more thoughtfully in the composing process so that they can increase their chances of creating effective written texts? How do social or interpersonal factors influence the choices writers make?

This equation of *composing* and *writing* also appears in current textbooks on composition ("technical writing" texts are a different matter altogether). Many of these composition textbooks are truly wonderful, especially when compared to what we had available 20 or 30 years ago. The best of them help students work through the writing process; they emphasize audience and purpose; they introduce students to different genres. But at no point do they suggest that students might need to worry about the way a page of text looks—about whether the explicit message they convey in their written text is enhanced by page layout and visual images. Nor do they deal in any systematic way with what students need to do if they are composing online—in hypertext, for example—or if they are creating a multimedia presentation that integrates words and static images with footage from a videotape.

Consequently, most of us have no personal or professional tradition that lets us integrate visual and verbal information in a comprehensive view of composing; yet we need to develop such a tradition—and soon. Outside the "composition" classroom, people's understanding of composing has changed dramatically. This is obviously true in television—not just in sitcoms and advertising, but also in serious, thoughtful news programs and documentaries, where messages are composed through an integration of spoken language, visual image, and sound. Even when messages are composed on a printed page, those messages depend as much on visual information—pictures, color, typography, page layout—as on the written text. And, of course, hypertext allows even young children to create compositions that integrate written text, with video, static images, spoken language, and sound. Current work in all these media—video, print, and hypertext—requires that we rethink what we mean by composing and that we develop research agendas that will carry us well beyond examining written texts and writing processes.

COMPOSING WITH VIDEO

For most of us, composing with video may seem completely beyond the pale, the province of television journalists or educational media specialists. Yet the resources needed to do this sort of composing are increasingly within our grasp. High quality, portable video cameras are now readily available and video-editing machines are increasingly accessible to people with little technical training. More important, the work of Sipple and his colleagues at Robert Morris College suggests that video can be an important medium of communication within our own profession.

When Sipple and his colleagues decided to contribute to the ongoing discussion of writing across the curriculum (WAC), they chose not to publish conventional books and articles, but, instead, to work with the Public Broadcasting Service to produce a series of nationally broadcast video conferences on WAC. These video conferences included comments by panelists and also the showing of relatively short videotapes, which represented a unique but powerful form of composing—an editor's distillation of two or three hours of videotape from each of the WAC programs represented in the video conference. These videotape compositions give us a new way to think about the time-honored writing teacher's injunction: "Show. Don't tell."

The PBS video conferences did a good bit of "telling," not only in the form of panelists' remarks, but also of voiceover commentaries that accompanied videotape shots of students and teachers who were participating in the WAC programs. This telling was also accompanied by a lot of "showing" in the form of footage of students and teachers going about their daily business in carrying out the program under discussion. These videotapes do not argue that showing is more important than telling. But they do suggest we need to reconsider the relation between showing and telling in this form of composing. Specifically, when people compose in video, they have to think about:

- the multiple claims that are implicit in their "showing," that is, in their selection of visual images;
- the "interanimation" of showing and telling, that is, the ways visual images reinforce, amplify, and/or subvert explicit spoken claims of "telling" statements; and
- the ways these interanimations help anticipate and respond to objections a viewer/reader might raise to the implicit and explicit claims made in the video.

The importance of these points becomes clear in the 1994 WAC video conference, which focused on ways schools, colleges, and the larger community could work together to promote meaningful learning for students in all subjects at all grade levels. One of the principal claims running throughout this conference was that people of all ages and abilities can do far more interesting and sophisticated work than teachers often assume. As partial illustration of this claim, the video conference showed an edited videotape from the Fort Worth (Texas) Applied Learning program.

This videotape was composed by Barbara A. Levine (1994), who had access to extensive footage of children working in a number of Applied Learning classrooms as well as tapes of parents and teachers discussing the Applied Learning Program. For one segment of the video, Levine extracted the audio from one of the parent–teacher discussions and used it as a voiceover for scenes taken from one of the classrooms.

In the audio, Applied Learning teacher Deborah Gist-Evans asserted that her third grade students were able to undertake an extraordinary project—conducting a "Young Authors Conference" that ultimately involved some 2,000 parents and elementary school children from the Fort Worth Independent School District. This meant, Gist-Evans reported, that third graders (8-year-olds)

- identified, invited, and negotiated with popular children's authors who would serve as principal speakers at the conference;
- scheduled all the conference sessions, many of which had other children reading and discussing their own work;
- made all the arrangements for using a local high school as the site for the conference; and
- did all the work of advertising the conference, making sure the conference had an official place on the school district's calendar, and inviting local businesses to sponsor the conference.

This would be a formidable project, even for a group of adults. So Gist-Evans's claims about her children's work might normally invite questions, if not outright skepticism: Won't third graders be overwhelmed by such an enormous undertaking? Won't the teacher have to hold their hands at every step of the way, and perhaps even do all the

"I call this meeting to order."

"Who needs to share?"

real work for them? Won't they lose interest well before the project is complete? Do they have the organizational skills they will need? Won't they be intimidated by having to deal with adults, especially principals and other school administrators?

The videotape forestalled such reactions by presenting images of Gist-Evans's students at work. Before letting us hear any of Gist-Evans's claims about what the children had accomplished, Levine lets us see and hear images from one of the regular class meetings in which students reported on and assessed their ongoing presentations for the conference, depicted in the video frames on page 299.

Only after giving us this brief glimpse of the third graders in action does Levine let us hear Gist-Evans's description of all the work the children are undertaking. These descriptions appear in a voiceover that accompanies scenes from the class meeting. Taken together, the voiceover (the "telling") and the scenes from the class (the "showing") convey a powerful message about the children's competence. Is Gist-Evans telling the truth about what her students did? Is it possible for third graders to do this sort of work? Everything in Levine's video composition argues that the answer to both questions is an emphatic *yes.* She carefully selects visual images from the class meeting and juxtaposes these images with comments from the teacher. The net effect of her work suggests the following:

The children are not overwhelmed by the project. The two girls in the top picture on page 301, who "share" their report, do not look nervously at the video camera or at the teacher. They concentrate on the task at hand, providing information to their classmates and answering their questions. Furthermore, the classroom itself suggests an air of competence: Behind the children are neatly-hung papers and carefully stacked clipboards—things one might see in a well-run office. The teacher is present in the classroom, but she is not the focus of the camera's or the students' attention.

The children appear to be engaged. The two children in the bottom picture on page 301 do not appear passive or bored, as they might appear if they had been posed as props.

These children's faces seem focused and engaged. Both pairs of eyes are directed at the speakers and the expressions on their faces imply genuine interest. The girl on the right—mouth open, eyebrows raised—seems ready to speak; the boy on the left—sitting straight up, his mouth slightly open—reflects this same engagement.

They look like they have an organized approach to their work. The student in the picture on page 302 is recording information on a large chart that shows what has been done and what still needs to be done.

Perhaps what is most significant about this image is what is *not* shown; most notably, there is no teacher hovering anxiously over the girl.

Near the end of this segment of the edited videotape, Gist-Evans notes that this sort of work requires students to do "all kinds of things where they have to write and to call people outside the school. And they get all different kinds of responses. People react differently when 8-year-olds call or write to them." Gist-Evans goes on to comment about the confidence her children have developed. But before she does so, we see and hear a student (see video frame on page 303) reading from a memo she has written to the central administration:

"To: Fort Worth ISD Schools
From: Mrs. Gist-Evan's Third Grade Class
Re: Young Authors Conference"

This image presents us with a number of messages. This is clearly a child in a classroom; past her right shoulder we can see a chalkboard and a paper sheep.

Yet we simultaneously receive messages about her competence: We hear her reading the memo in a very clear, confident voice; she holds a clipboard in both hands, and the camera angle tilts up toward her face, giving her a highly authoritative air. Gist-Evans comments:

> One of my students wrote to Dr. Roberts [the district superintendent] to invite him to the Young Authors Conference and have him put it on the district calendar. And she got a letter back from the office that said they

needed to know the date or something. And she just...she knew she had put the date on it. So she goes and gets her folder. I put the date. So she writes him this letter back and—I think somebody else reading it might not have noticed, but underlying [her comments] there was this irritated tone coming out of this letter. And I thought "we must feel pretty good about ourselves to write a letter like that...."

Indeed, one of the principal claims made throughout this videotape is that students in the Applied Learning classes do "feel pretty good" about themselves. This is Gist-Evans's claim about her students, but it is also Levine's claim about other students in the program. She consistently selects images of students who are focused on their work, confident in their actions, and convinced that what they are doing is important. And she artfully juxtaposes those images against parent–teacher commentary in ways that give resonance to both.

This selection and juxtaposition suggest that the videotape is, at least in part, Levine's composition. Granted, she did not do some of the things we writing teachers associate with composing. She did not, for example, write out a script that would tell students and parents what to say and when to say it. Arguably, she was merely cutting and pasting, arranging snippets of other people's words into a pattern she found meaningful. But she, in effect, composed a report of information about the Fort Worth Applied Learning program, one that program participants felt nicely captured the essence of that program.

WORKING WITH PRINT

References to composing with video may make us nostalgic for a time when all we had to work with was plain old words on paper, a time when we and our students could focus all our attention on the verbal messages a writer was conveying. Unlike most nostalgic impulses, this one has a certain basis in historical fact. Until perhaps 10 or 15 years ago, we and our students had few choices as to how our writing would look. About all we could do was adjust the margins on our typewriters or try to use our best handwriting. The visual appearance of our work was determined by the typewriter we used, the condition of the typewriter ribbon, or, if we were writing longhand, the degree of small-motor control we possessed.

Of course, modern word-processing programs have changed all this. Even a woefully outdated computer (that is, one that's 3 or more years old) probably offers a choice of 20 or so typefaces, 15–20 type sizes, and one-, two-, or three-column page layouts, not to mention the capacity for integrating still pictures and video into written text. Whether we like it or not, the visual appearance of our written work now represents a set of choices—in typography, page design, and visual images. These choices are becoming almost as important for "writers" as are choices of diction, syntax, organization, and so on.

From one perspective, these visual elements may seem nothing more than ornamentation. However, as Keyes (1993) points out, visual elements can be central to readers' understanding of a text. The "visual information structure" (p. 639) of a text can reveal its underlying structure: "chunking," or creating distinctive blocks of text, both consolidates related pieces of information and separates one body of related information from other bodies; "filtering," or using different type sizes and styles, indicates the relative importance of different passages and discriminates one type of information from another; and the use of color "focuses attention, speeds search, [and] reveals organization and pattern." And, as Meggs (1992) argues, visual elements may be an important part of the message(s) a written text conveys.

Consider, for example, messages conveyed by the following three-page advertisement for Pravachol (pages 305–307), a cholesterol-lowering drug. In addition to conveying specific information about the drug,

You'd Give Your Life for Them.
But That's Not What They Want.
You're Everything to Me
Happy Birthday
DAD
HAPPY
BIRTHD
happy
Birthday
I Love You!

THEY JUST WANT YOU TO STAY HEALTHY. SO IT'S IMPORTANT THAT YOU KNOW ABOUT PRAVACHOL FROM BRISTOL-MYERS SQUIBB.

PRAVACHOL. THE ONLY CHOLESTEROL-LOWERING DRUG OF ITS KIND PROVEN TO HELP PREVENT A FIRST HEART ATTACK.

If you have high cholesterol, there's something you should know. You may be at risk of having a first heart attack, even if you have no signs of any heart problems. And the grim fact of the matter is, up to 33% of people do not survive their first heart attack.

If improving your diet and exercise is not enough, you should ask your doctor about PRAVACHOL. The first and only cholesterol-lowering drug of its kind proven to help prevent first heart attacks. It may be able to help you live a longer, healthier life.

A new landmark five-year study including over 6,500 males with high cholesterol showed a dramatic reduction (approximately one-third) in the number of first heart attacks and deaths due to heart disease among those taking PRAVACHOL.

PRAVACHOL, when used with diet, has been proven to reduce the risk of a first heart attack, reduce the risk of death from heart disease, and reduce the risk of heart surgery in people with high cholesterol but no symptoms or history of heart disease.

PRAVACHOL® is a prescription drug, so you should ask your doctor or healthcare professional if PRAVACHOL is right for you. Some side effects, such as slight rash or mild stomach upset, occur in about 2–4% of patients. PRAVACHOL should not be taken by women who are pregnant or nursing, people who are allergic to any of its ingredients or by anyone with liver disease. Your doctor may perform tests to check your liver before and during treatment. Be sure to tell your doctor right away if you experience any muscle pain or weakness, as it may be a sign of a serious side effect. Be sure to mention any medications you are taking so any possible serious drug interactions can be avoided. Please see important information on the next page.

Please keep this reminder.

***Ask your doctor** if Pravachol is right for you or **call 1-800-PREVENT** for more information on the first and only cholesterol-lowering drug of its kind proven to help prevent first heart attacks.*

PRAVACHOL
pravastatin sodium

PRAVACHOL HELPS PREVENT FIRST HEART ATTACKS.

Bristol-Myers Squibb Company

PRAVACHOL®

Pravastatin Sodium Tablets

CONTRAINDICATIONS: Hypersensitivity to any component of this medication. Active liver disease or unexplained, persistent elevations in liver function tests (see **WARNINGS**). *Pregnancy and lactation.* Atherosclerosis is a chronic process and discontinuation of lipid-lowering drugs during pregnancy should have little impact on the outcome of long-term therapy of primary hypercholesterolemia. Cholesterol and other products of cholesterol biosynthesis are essential components for fetal development (including synthesis of steroids and cell membranes). Since HMG-CoA reductase inhibitors decrease cholesterol synthesis and possibly the synthesis of other biologically active substances derived from cholesterol, they may cause fetal harm when administered to pregnant women. Therefore, HMG-CoA reductase inhibitors are contraindicated during pregnancy and in nursing mothers. **Pravastatin should be administered to women of childbearing age only when such patients are highly unlikely to conceive and have been informed of the potential hazards.** If the patient becomes pregnant while taking this class of drug, therapy should be discontinued and the patient apprised of the potential hazard to the fetus. **WARNINGS: Liver Enzymes** — HMG-CoA reductase inhibitors, like some other lipid-lowering therapies, have been associated with biochemical abnormalities of liver function. Increases of serum transaminase (ALT, AST) values to more than 3 times the upper limit of normal occurring on 2 or more (not necessarily sequential) occasions have been reported in 1.3% of patients treated with pravastatin in the US over an average period of 18 months. These abnormalities were not associated with cholestasis and did not appear to be related to treatment duration. In those patients in whom these abnormalities were believed to be related to pravastatin and who were discontinued from therapy, the transaminase levels usually fell slowly to pretreatment levels. These biochemical findings are usually asymptomatic although worldwide experience indicates that anorexia, weakness, and/or abdominal pain may also be present in rare patients. **It is recommended that liver function tests be performed before the initiation of treatment, at 6 and 12 weeks after initiation of therapy or elevation in dose, and periodically thereafter (e.g., semiannually).** Patients who develop increased transaminase levels should be monitored with a second liver function evaluation to confirm the finding and be followed thereafter with frequent liver function tests until the abnormality(ies) return to normal. Should an increase in AST or ALT of three times the upper limit of normal or greater persist, withdrawal of pravastatin therapy is recommended. Active liver disease or unexplained transaminase elevations are contraindications to the use of pravastatin (see **CONTRAINDICATIONS**). Caution should be exercised when pravastatin is administered to patients with a history of liver disease or heavy alcohol ingestion (see **CLINICAL PHARMACOLOGY: Pharmacokinetics/Metabolism**). Such patients should be closely monitored, started at the lower end of the recommended dosing range, and titrated to the desired therapeutic effect. **Skeletal Muscle — Rare cases of rhabdomyolysis with acute renal failure secondary to myoglobinuria have been reported with pravastatin and other drugs in this class.** Uncomplicated myalgia has also been reported in pravastatin-treated patients (see **ADVERSE REACTIONS**). Myopathy, defined as muscle aching or muscle weakness in conjunction with increases in creatine phosphokinase (CPK) values to greater than 10 times the upper normal limit, was rare (< 0.1%) in pravastatin clinical trials. Myopathy should be considered in any patient with diffuse myalgias, muscle tenderness or weakness, and/or marked elevation of CPK. Patients should be advised to report promptly unexplained muscle pain, tenderness or weakness, particularly if accompanied by malaise or fever. **Pravastatin therapy should be discontinued if markedly elevated CPK levels occur or myopathy is diagnosed or suspected. Pravastatin therapy should also be temporarily withheld in any patient experiencing an acute or serious condition predisposing to the development of renal failure secondary to rhabdomyolysis, e.g., sepsis; hypotension; major surgery; trauma; severe metabolic, endocrine, or electrolyte disorders; or uncontrolled epilepsy.** The risk of myopathy during treatment with another HMG-CoA reductase inhibitor is increased with concurrent therapy with either erythromycin, cyclosporine, niacin, or fibrates. However, neither myopathy nor significant increases in CPK levels have been observed in three reports involving a total of 100 post-transplant patients (24 renal and 76 cardiac) treated for up to two years concurrently with pravastatin 10-40 mg and cyclosporine. Some of these patients also received other concomitant immunosuppressive therapies. In one single-dose study, pravastatin levels were found to be increased in cardiac transplant patients receiving cyclosporine. Further, in clinical trials involving small numbers of patients who were treated concurrently with pravastatin and niacin, there were no reports of myopathy. Also, myopathy was not reported in a trial of combination pravastatin (40 mg/day) and gemfibrozil (1200 mg/day), although 4 of 75 patients on the combination showed marked CPK elevations versus one of 73 patients receiving placebo. There was a trend toward more frequent CPK elevations and patient withdrawals due to musculoskeletal symptoms in the group receiving combined treatment as compared with the groups receiving placebo, gemfibrozil, or pravastatin monotherapy (see **PRECAUTIONS: Drug Interactions**). **The use of fibrates alone may occasionally be associated with myopathy. The combined use of pravastatin and fibrates should be avoided unless the benefit of further alterations in lipid levels is likely to outweigh the increased risk of this drug combination. PRECAUTIONS: General** — Pravastatin may elevate creatine phosphokinase and transaminase levels (see **ADVERSE REACTIONS**). This should be considered in the differential diagnosis of chest pain in a patient on therapy with pravastatin. *Homozygous Familial Hypercholesterolemia.* Pravastatin has not been evaluated in patients with rare homozygous familial hypercholesterolemia. In this group of patients, it has been reported that HMG-CoA reductase inhibitors are less effective because the patients lack functional LDL receptors. *Renal Insufficiency.* A single 20 mg oral dose of pravastatin was administered to 24 patients with varying degrees of renal impairment (as determined by creatinine clearance). No effect was observed on the pharmacokinetics of pravastatin or its 3α-hydroxy isomeric metabolite (SQ 31,906). A small increase was seen in mean AUC values and half-life ($t^{1/2}$) for the inactive enzymatic ring hydroxylation metabolite (SQ 31,945). Given this small sample size, the dosage administered, and the degree of individual variability, patients with renal impairment who are receiving pravastatin should be closely monitored. **Information for Patients** — Patients should be advised to report promptly unexplained muscle pain, tenderness or weakness, particularly if accompanied by malaise or fever. **Drug Interactions** — *Immunosuppressive Drugs, Gemfibrozil, Niacin (Nicotinic Acid), Erythromycin:* See **WARNINGS: Skeletal Muscle.** *Antipyrine:* Since concomitant administration of pravastatin had no effect on the clearance of antipyrine, interactions with other drugs metabolized via the same hepatic cytochrome isozymes are not expected. *Cholestyramine/Colestipol:* Concomitant administration resulted in an approximately 40 to 50% decrease in the mean AUC of pravastatin. However, when pravastatin was administered 1 hour before or 4 hours after cholestyramine or 1 hour before colestipol and a standard meal, there was no clinically significant decrease in bioavailability or therapeutic effect. (See **DOSAGE AND ADMINISTRATION: Concomitant Therapy.**) *Warfarin:* In a study involving 10 healthy male subjects given pravastatin and warfarin concomitantly for 6 days, bioavailability parameters at steady state for pravastatin (parent compound) were not altered. Pravastatin did not alter the plasma protein-binding of warfarin. Concomitant dosing did increase the AUC and Cmax of warfarin but did not produce any changes in its anticoagulant action (i.e., no increase was seen in mean prothrombin time after 6 days of concomitant therapy). However, bleeding and extreme prolongation of prothrombin time has been reported with another drug in this class. Patients receiving warfarin-type anticoagulants should have their prothrombin times closely monitored when pravastatin is initiated or the dosage of pravastatin is changed. *Cimetidine:* The $AUC_{0-12 hr}$ for pravastatin when given with cimetidine was not significantly different from the AUC for pravastatin when given alone. A significant difference was observed between the AUC's for pravastatin when given with cimetidine compared to when administered with antacid. *Digoxin:* In a crossover trial involving 18 healthy male subjects given pravastatin and digoxin concurrently for 9 days, the bioavailability parameters of digoxin were not affected. The AUC of pravastatin tended to increase, but the overall bioavailability of pravastatin plus its metabolites SQ 31,906 and SQ 31,945 was not altered. *Cyclosporine:* Some investigators have measured cyclosporine levels in patients on pravastatin, and to date, these results indicate no clinically meaningful elevations in cyclosporine levels. In one single-dose study, pravastatin levels were found to be increased in cardiac transplant patients receiving cyclosporine. *Gemfibrozil:* In a crossover study in 20 healthy male volunteers given concomitant single doses of pravastatin and gemfibrozil, there was a significant decrease in urinary excretion and protein binding of pravastatin. In addition, there was a significant increase in AUC, Cmax, and Tmax for the pravastatin metabolite SQ 31,906. Combination therapy with pravastatin and gemfibrozil is generally not recommended. In interaction studies with *aspirin, antacids* (1 hour prior to PRAVACHOL), *cimetidine, nicotinic acid,* or *probucol,* no statistically significant differences in bioavailability were seen when PRAVACHOL (pravastatin sodium) was administered. *Other Drugs:* During clinical trials, no noticeable drug interactions were reported when PRAVACHOL was added to: diuretics, antihypertensives, digitalis, ACE inhibitors, calcium channel blockers, beta-blockers, or nitroglycerin. **Endocrine Function** — HMG-CoA reductase inhibitors interfere with cholesterol synthesis and lower circulating cholesterol levels and, as such, might theoretically blunt adrenal or gonadal steroid hormone production. Results of clinical trials with pravastatin in males and post-menopausal females were inconsistent with regard to possible effects of the drug on basal steroid hormone levels. In a study of 21 males, the mean testosterone response to human chorionic gonadotropin was significantly reduced ($p < 0.004$) after 16 weeks of treatment with 40 mg of pravastatin. However, the percentage of patients showing a ≥ 50% rise in plasma testosterone after human chorionic gonadotropin stimulation did not change significantly after therapy in these patients. The effects of HMG-CoA reductase inhibitors on spermatogenesis and fertility have not been studied in adequate numbers of patients. The effects, if any, of pravastatin on the pituitary-gonadal axis in pre-menopausal females are unknown. Patients treated with pravastatin who display clinical evidence of endocrine dysfunction should be evaluated appropriately. Caution should also be exercised if an HMG-CoA reductase inhibitor or other agent used to lower cholesterol levels is administered to patients also receiving other drugs (e.g., ketoconazole, spironolactone, cimetidine) that may diminish the levels or activity of steroid hormones. **CNS Toxicity** — CNS vascular lesions, characterized by perivascular hemorrhage and edema and mononuclear cell infiltration of perivascular spaces, were seen in dogs treated with pravastatin at a dose of 25 mg/kg/day, a dose that produced a plasma drug level about 50 times higher than the mean drug level in humans taking 40 mg/day. Similar CNS vascular lesions have been observed with several other drugs in this class. A chemically similar drug in this class produced optic nerve degeneration (Wallerian degeneration of retinogeniculate fibers) in clinically normal dogs in a dose-dependent fashion starting at 60 mg/kg/day, a dose that produced mean plasma drug levels about 30 times higher than the mean drug level in humans taking the highest recommended dose (as measured by total enzyme inhibitory activity). This same drug also produced vestibulocochlear Wallerian-like degeneration and retinal ganglion cell chromatolysis in dogs treated for 14 weeks at 180 mg/kg/day, a dose which resulted in a mean plasma drug level similar to that seen with the 60 mg/kg/day dose. **Carcinogenesis, Mutagenesis, Impairment of Fertility** — In a 2-year study in rats fed pravastatin at doses of 10, 30, or 100 mg/kg body weight, there was an increased incidence of hepatocellular carcinomas in males at the highest dose ($p < 0.01$). Although rats were given up to 125 times the human dose (HD) on a mg/kg body weight basis, serum drug levels were only 6 to 10 times higher than those measured in humans given 40 mg pravastatin as measured by AUC. The oral administration of 10, 30, or 100 mg/kg (producing plasma drug levels approximately 0.5 to 5.0 times the human drug levels at 40 mg) of pravastatin to mice for 22 months resulted in a statistically significant increase in the incidence of malignant lymphomas in treated females when all treatment groups were pooled and compared to controls ($p < 0.05$). The incidence was not dose-related and male mice were not affected. A chemically similar drug in this class was administered to mice for 72 weeks at 25, 100, and 400 mg/kg body weight, which resulted in mean serum drug levels approximately 3, 15, and 33 times higher than the mean human serum drug concentration (as total inhibitory activity) after a 40 mg oral dose. Liver carcinomas were significantly increased in high-dose females and mid- and high-dose males, with a maximum incidence of 90 percent in males. The incidence of adenomas of the liver was significantly increased in mid- and high-dose females. Drug treatment also significantly increased the incidence of lung adenomas in mid- and high-dose males and females. Adenomas of the eye Harderian gland (a gland of the eye of rodents) were significantly higher in high-dose mice than in controls. No evidence of mutagenicity was observed *in vitro*, with or without rat-liver metabolic activation, in the following studies: microbial mutagen tests, using mutant strains of *Salmonella typhimurium* or *Escherichia coli*; a forward mutation assay in L5178Y TK +/- mouse lymphoma cells; a chromosomal aberration test in hamster cells; and a gene conversion assay using *Saccharomyces cerevisiae*. In addition, there was no evidence of mutagenicity in either a dominant lethal test in mice or a micronucleus test in mice. In a study in rats, with daily doses up to 500 mg/kg, pravastatin did not produce any adverse effects on fertility or general reproductive performance. However, in a study with another HMG-CoA reductase inhibitor, there was decreased fertility in male rats treated for 34 weeks at 25 mg/kg body weight, although this effect was not observed in a subsequent fertility study when this same dose was administered for 11 weeks (the entire cycle of spermatogenesis, including epididymal maturation). In rats treated with this same reductase inhibitor at 180 mg/kg/day, seminiferous tubule degeneration (necrosis and loss of spermatogenic epithelium) was observed. Although not seen with pravastatin, two similar drugs in this class caused drug-related testicular atrophy, decreased spermatogenesis, spermatocytic degeneration, and giant cell formation in dogs. The clinical significance of these findings is unclear. **Pregnancy: Pregnancy Category X.** — See **CONTRAINDICATIONS.** Safety in pregnant women has not been established. Pravastatin was not teratogenic in rats at doses up to 1000 mg/kg daily or in rabbits at doses of up to 50 mg/kg daily. These doses resulted in 20x (rabbit) or 240x (rat) the human exposure based on surface area (mg/meter²). However, in studies with another HMG-CoA reductase inhibitor, skeletal malformations were observed in rats and mice. There has been one report of severe congenital bony deformity, tracheo-esophageal fistula, and anal atresia (Vater association) in a baby born to a woman who took another HMG-CoA reductase inhibitor with dextroamphetamine sulfate during the first trimester of pregnancy. PRAVACHOL (pravastatin sodium) should be administered to women of child-bearing potential only when such patients are highly unlikely to conceive and have been informed of the potential hazards. If the woman becomes pregnant while taking PRAVACHOL (pravastatin sodium), it should be discontinued and the patient advised again as to the potential hazards to the fetus. **Nursing Mothers** — A small amount of pravastatin is excreted in human breast milk. Because of the potential for serious adverse reactions in nursing infants, women taking PRAVACHOL should not nurse (see **CONTRAINDICATIONS**). **Pediatric Use** — Safety and effectiveness in individuals less than 18 years old have not been established. Hence, treatment in patients less than 18 years old is not recommended at this time. **ADVERSE REACTIONS:** Pravastatin is generally well tolerated; adverse reactions have usually been mild and transient. In 4-month long placebo-controlled trials, 1.7% of pravastatin-treated patients and 1.2% of placebo-treated patients were discontinued from treatment because of adverse experiences attributed to study drug therapy; this difference was not statistically significant. In long-term studies, the most common reasons for discontinuation were asymptomatic serum transaminase increases and mild, non-specific gastrointestinal complaints. During clinical trials the overall incidence of adverse events in the elderly was not different from the incidence observed in younger patients. **Adverse Clinical Events** — All adverse clinical events (regardless of attribution) reported in more than 2% of pravastatin-treated patients in the placebo-controlled trials are identified in the table below; also shown are the percentages of patients in whom these medical events were believed to be related or possibly related to the drug:

	All Events		Events Attributed to Study Drug	
Body System/Event	**Pravastatin (N = 900) %**	**Placebo (N = 411) %**	**Pravastatin (N = 900) %**	**Placebo (N = 411) %**
Cardiovascular				
Cardiac Chest Pain	4.0	3.4	0.1	0.0
Dermatologic Rash	4.0*	1.1	1.3	0.9
Gastrointestinal				
Nausea/Vomiting	7.3	7.1	2.9	3.4
Diarrhea	6.2	5.6	2.0	1.9
Abdominal Pain	5.4	6.9	2.0	3.9
Constipation	4.0	7.1	2.4	5.1
Flatulence	3.3	3.6	2.7	3.4
Heartburn	2.9	1.9	2.0	0.7
General				
Fatigue	3.8	3.4	1.9	1.0
Chest Pain	3.7	1.9	0.3	0.2
Influenza	2.4*	0.7	0.0	0.0
Musculoskeletal				
Localized Pain	10.0	9.0	1.4	1.5
Myalgia	2.7	1.0	0.6	0.0
Nervous System				
Headache	6.2	3.9	1.7*	0.2
Dizziness	3.3	3.2	1.0	0.5
Renal/Genitourinary				
Urinary Abnormality	2.4	2.9	0.7	1.2
Respiratory				
Common Cold	7.0	6.3	0.0	0.0
Rhinitis	4.0	4.1	0.1	0.0
Cough	2.6	1.7	0.1	0.0

*Statistically significantly different from placebo.

In the *Pravastatin Primary Prevention Study (West of Scotland Coronary Prevention Study)* (see **CLINICAL PHARMACOLOGY: Clinical Studies**) involving 6595 patients treated with PRAVACHOL (pravastatin sodium) (N = 3302) or placebo (n = 3293) the adverse event profile in the pravastatin group was comparable to that of the placebo group over the median 4.8 years of the study. The following effects have been reported with drugs in this class; not all the effects listed below have *necessarily* been associated with pravastatin therapy: *Skeletal:* myopathy, rhabdomyolysis, arthralgia. *Neurological:* dysfunction of certain cranial nerves (including alteration of taste, impairment of extra-ocular movement, facial paresis), tremor, vertigo, memory loss, paresthesia, peripheral neuropathy, peripheral nerve palsy, anxiety, insomnia, depression. *Hypersensitivity Reactions:* An apparent hypersensitivity syndrome has been reported rarely which has included one or more of the following features: anaphylaxis, angioedema, lupus erythematous-like syndrome, polymyalgia rheumatica, dermatomyositis, vasculitis, purpura, thrombocytopenia, leukopenia, hemolytic anemia, positive ANA, ESR increase, eosinophilia, arthritis, arthralgia, urticaria, asthenia, photosensitivity, fever, chills, flushing, malaise, dyspnea, toxic epidermal necrolysis, erythema multiforme, including Stevens-Johnson syndrome. *Gastrointestinal:* pancreatitis, hepatitis, including chronic active hepatitis, cholestatic jaundice, fatty change in liver, and, rarely, cirrhosis, fulminant hepatic necrosis, and hepatoma; anorexia, vomiting. *Skin:* alopecia, pruritus. A variety of skin changes (e.g., nodules, discoloration, dryness of skin/mucous membranes, changes to hair/nails) have been reported. *Reproductive:* gynecomastia, loss of libido, erectile dysfunction. *Eye:* progression of cataracts (lens opacities), ophthalmoplegia. *Laboratory Abnormalities:* elevated transaminases, alkaline phosphatase, and bilirubin; thyroid function abnormalities. **Laboratory Test Abnormalities** — Increases in serum transaminase (ALT, AST) values and CPK have been observed (see **WARNINGS**). Transient, asymptomatic eosinophilia has been reported. Eosinophil counts usually returned to normal despite continued therapy. Anemia, thrombocytopenia, and leukopenia have been reported with HMG-CoA reductase inhibitors. **Concomitant Therapy** — Pravastatin has been administered concurrently with cholestyramine, colestipol, nicotinic acid, probucol and gemfibrozil. Preliminary data suggest that the addition of either probucol or gemfibrozil to therapy with lovastatin or pravastatin is not associated with greater reduction in LDL-cholesterol than that achieved with lovastatin or pravastatin alone. No adverse reactions unique to the combination or in addition to those previously reported for each drug alone have been reported. Myopathy and rhabdomyolysis (with or without acute renal failure) have been reported when another HMG-CoA reductase inhibitor was used in combination with immunosuppressive drugs, gemfibrozil, erythromycin, or lipid-lowering doses of nicotinic acid. Concomitant therapy with HMG-CoA reductase inhibitors and these agents is generally not recommended. (See **WARNINGS: Skeletal Muscle** and **PRECAUTIONS: Drug Interactions.**) **OVERDOSAGE:** To date, there are two reported cases of overdosage with pravastatin, both of which were asymptomatic and not associated with clinical laboratory abnormalities. If an overdose occurs, it should be treated symptomatically and supportive measures should be instituted as required.

CAUTION: Federal (USA) law prohibits dispensing without prescription.

Consult package insert before prescribing PRAVACHOL® (pravastatin sodium).

Revised July 1996
D3-B001-7-96

J4-536D

the ad uses visual information to convey several messages about Bristol-Myers, the company that makes the drug. The overall message is that the company that makes Pravachol (Bristol-Myers) is an organization that represents the best of two different worlds: the compassion and caring associated with close family relationships, and the hard-nosed, objective reliability of science.

The visual emphasis on family appears strongly in the first page of the ad (page 305). The use of three birthday cards evokes a stereotypical view of the modern American family—mother, father, and two children all living (presumably happily) in the same household. The three different cards suggest three different but highly recognizable voices:

- that of a child whose youth and enthusiasm are apparent not only in his/her forthright declaration of love, but also in his/her childlike conception of a rainbow; his/her childlike conception of the horizon as a straight line with no gradation of color in the sky above it; and his/her childlike writing (using bright crayons);
- that of an early adolescent who makes no explicit reference to love but whose affection is suggested in the degree of care put into the making of the card (the filigreed red border of the card, the carefully pasted balloons, the stylized print); and
- that of a loving spouse whose mature understanding of love is captured in the beautiful photograph of a lily, the careful script, the relatively subdued colors of the card and its picture, and the loving message of "You're everything to me."

These cards, and the family relationships they imply, are given prominence by the ad's use of "visual tension," the juxtaposition of contrasting elements (for example, shapes, lines, and colors) that causes some discomfort for the viewer. (For a fuller discussion of visual tension, see Meggs, 1992, p. 94.) In this ad, the irregular appearance of the cards (they are different sizes; the typeface styles and pictures clash with each other) conflicts with the orderliness of the background in which they appear. This background consists of wallpaper with parallel vertical lines that lead the eye down the page. This downward eye movement is reinforced by a continuum of light, moving from bright (but not garish) in the upper left corner to relative darkness in the lower right corner. The lines in the wallpaper and the continuum of light serve to lead the viewer's eye toward the birthday cards, which (with their irregular contours, their relatively bold colors, and their clashing typefaces) disrupt the smoothness of movement established in the background. This disruption further emphasizes the cards and the family relationships they represent.

On the second page of the ad (page 306), the warmth and excitement generated by the birthday cards are completely absent, replaced by standard typography and a serious discussion, concerned for the well-being of the reader. The page's layout is very conservative and does several things to reinforce a notion of balance and seriousness. First, simple rectangles dominate the page: a large rectangular frame borders the entire page, a solid red rectangle is located in the top-center of the page, and a rectangle framed by a dotted line sits in the lower right corner. This lower rectangle holds a still smaller rectangle inside it, which is red and resembles the larger red rectangle at the top. All of these rectangles create a strong sense of stability and order. The evenly spaced and neatly arranged columns of text beneath the top rectangle further support this sense of order, encouraging the viewer to read the ad.

Whereas the first page strives to appeal to the viewer's emotion, and the second page conveys a profound concern for readers' health, the last page of the ad (page 307) focuses on delivering the facts and promotes the message that the maker of Pravachol is a serious scientific enterprise. Variations in typeface serve only to announce topics of concern to a doctor or to emphasize warnings that have to do with possible medical complications. The table in the second column is neat and unobtrusive, allowing just the facts to come through. The font size is small and information is densely packed, suggesting a greater concern for comprehensive, "objective" treatment of a complex subject than with the personal relationships that figure so importantly in the first page of the ad.

Advertising, of course, usually lies well outside the focus of composition courses, except perhaps when ads serve as the object of students' critical analysis. But the basic argument here—that visual appearance is important in conveying substantive messages—is supported from other sources, one perhaps less surprising than the other. For most of us, and certainly for anyone who has ever taught journalism, it's almost an article of faith that the design of the front page of a newspaper conveys messages about the nature and the relative importance of news stories. The most important "hard news" stories conventionally appear in the upper righthand corner of the page, accompanied by relatively large, bold type and perhaps a picture. Less important stories are likely to appear "below the fold," accompanied by smaller headlines and smaller pictures.

Familiar as these conventions are, they are a relatively recent development, dating back to the 1920s. Nerone and Barnhurst (1995) have shown that prior to the 1920s some newspapers gave few cues as to the relative importance of the stories they published. A front page, for example, was likely to contain a number of stories, many of roughly the same length, all with headlines of the same size and typeface. During the 1920s and 1930s, however, the papers studied began to give clues as to the relative importance of stories, using visual strategies such as those mentioned in the preceding paragraph. This new page design, Nerone and Barnhurst argue, represented papers' attempts to give order and meaning to the "turbulent change" of that era. According to Nerone and Barnhurst, the papers' message to readers was: "You feel the world is out of control, but don't worry, we'll explain everything" (p. 13). The look of these papers was a key part of their message to readers.

Much the same point comes from what might seem a less likely source, Strunk and White's *Elements of Style* (1979). Granted, the explicit focus of the text is primarily on features of written language—syntax, diction, usage, and so on. But the authors do make one brief nod in the direction of visual information:

> In general, remember that paragraphing calls for a good eye, as well as a logical mind. Enormous blocks of print look formidable to a reader. He [sic] has a certain reluctance to tackle them; he can lose his way in them.

15. *Put statements in positive form.*

Make definite assertions. Avoid tame, colorless, hesitating, noncommittal language. Use the word *not* as a means of denial or in antithesis, never as a means of evasion.

He was not very often on time.	He usually came late.
He did not think that studying Latin was a sensible way to use one's time.	He thought the study of Latin a waste of time.
The Taming of the Shrew is rather weak in spots. Shakespeare does not portray Katharine as a very admirable character, nor does Bianca remain long in memory as an important character in Shakespeare's works.	The women in *The Taming of the Shrew* are unattractive. Katharine is disagreeable, Bianca insignificant.

The last example, before correction, is indefinite as well as negative. The corrected version, consequently, is simply a guess at the writer's intention.

> Therefore, breaking long paragraphs in two, even if it is not necessary to do so for sense, meaning, or logical development, is often a visual help. But remember, too, that too many short paragraphs in quick succession can be distracting. (p. 17)

Although this explicit reference to visual elements is relatively brief, the implicit messages about the importance of these elements permeates the entire book. Consider, for example, "rule" number 15, on the preceding page.

As in all the other rules, the rule itself is numbered, printed in boldface italics, and set on the left margin. Explanatory information is presented in paragraphs set in regular type that is slightly smaller than that of the rule. Examples are presented in still smaller type and are often listed in columns, the incorrect example always appearing in the left column, and the correct example in the right. This use of typography and page design helps make Strunk and White's (1979) ideas more readily accessible to readers; one always knows where to look for a given kind of information, whether a rule, explanatory material, or examples of good or bad style. And in that ready accessibility, the visual elements further emphasize Strunk and White's explicit comments about clarity, conciseness, and decisiveness in written language. Thus, even so conservative a source as *Elements of Style* reminds us that the look of a page is, or should be, a matter of deliberate choice, one that is integral to the message(s) a written text seeks to convey. At one time, many of these choices were available only to graphic artists or publishing companies. Now, computer technology has made these choices available to all of us. For us and for our students, there is no longer any such thing as plain old words on paper.

COMPOSING IN HYPERTEXT

As Grice, Ridgway, and See (1991) point out, for many people the concept of hypertext implies complete lack of structure: "Say the word 'hypertext' and people will conjure up images of readers wildly flipping from one piece of electronic information to another with unlimited and unrestricted freedom to see any piece of information that catches their attention" (p. 48).

This point of view may be especially attractive to students, whose hypertexts may have only the structure that Pfaffenberger (1997) refers to as "random cool goodies"—a listing of "a few interesting items, in no particular order that you're sure your audience will like" (p. 49). However, Pfaffenberger points out, hypertext documents may have several different kinds of structures, ranging from "alphabetic," as in the index of a book, to division and classification, general to specific, persuasive, or chronological, and so on. All these terms, of course, should seem familiar to any composition specialist, if only because all appear in almost any "writing" textbook. The brave new world of hypertext may look a lot like territory we routinely cover.

This is especially true of those types of structures (for example, division and classification) that lend themselves to hierarchical view of a topic. Consider, for example, the following three screens from a hypertext document created by the second author. The screens were created to accompany a video presentation illustrating the harmful effects of industrial pollution in "Cancer Alley," a highly industrialized region located along the Mississippi River. It was not possible to reproduce "captures" of these screens with a high enough resolution to allow reprinting here, so we are including typed versions of those screens.

On the face of it, these screens may have little in common with the written texts we conventionally teach in composition classes. Yet these screens have a clear hierarchical structure, as the figure on page 314 shows.

Cancer Alley, Louisiana

Between Baton Rouge and New Orleans, there currently stands 93 chemical processing plants. This high concentration of plants coincides with the area's high number of cancer victims, the last of which having hallmarked the area with the nickname of "Cancer Alley." Many locals, and a growing number of researchers; feel the cause of these cancer cases lies directly in the present of so many chemical processing plants.

To learn more about Cancer Alley, please click on one of the links to the right.

History
gives backgrond information on Cancer Alley and a historical context.

The Where's Who's and What's
gives specific facts regarding the people and places involved.

Science
outlines scientific, environmental, and healtrh-related issues.

Economy
summaries key economical issues affecting the area's people and towns.

Cancer Alley: Science <—>

The chemical plants in Cancer Alley have dumped thousands of pounds of toxic pollutants into Louisiana's river, land, and air. These toxins, aside from the general pollution they cause, have harmfully affected the people in the area.

To learn more about the effects of hazardous chemicals, please click on one of the links on the right.

Environmental Harm
gives information gathered from a number of studies.

Harm to Personal Health
gives information gathered from a number of studies.

How Toxic Waste Reaches the People
outlines scientific, environmental, and health-related issues.

Tables
shows the different pollutants of Cancer Alley and their effects to health.

History | **The Where's Who's and What's** | **Science** | **Economy**

Cancer Alley: Science <—>

Harm to Personal Health

There isn't a lot of research on the effects to health of the toxic wastes found in Cancer Alley. Several of the toxins are known to be carcinogenic, yet proving direct links between the toxins and the area's high cancer rates is difficult

Listed to the left, and on the next few screens, are some facts gathered from what research exists.

* The EPA lists 13 chemical

plants in Louisiana where cancer risk from breathin the chemicals is 100 times above the acceptable level. These chemical plants are DuPont, Exxon, Shell, Dow, Copolymer, Union Carbide, Formosa, Freestone, BASF, Vulcan, Occidental, and Crown Zellerbach.

These companies refused requests to count the number of cancer cases existing in their plants; therefore, a direct comparison of the threat of cancer and the actual number of cases cannot be made.

Click here for more facts.

History | **The Where's Who's and What's** | **Science** | **Economy**

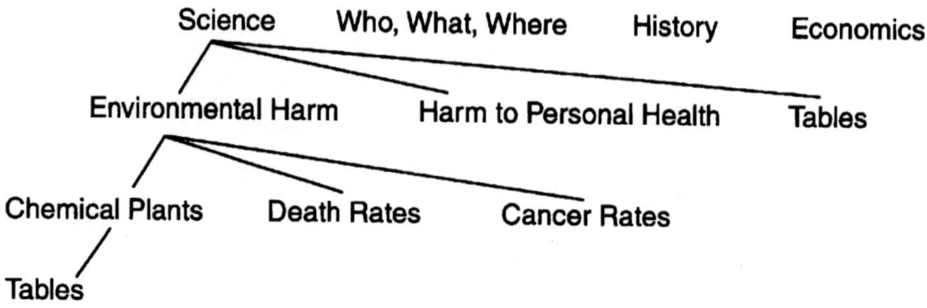

When viewing the tree diagram, we realize that the underlying structure of this hypertext begins to look very much like a conventional outline:

Cancer Alley
I. History
    A. Overview
II. Where? Who? What?
III. Science
    A. Environment harm
    B. Harm to personal health
        1. Chemical plants
        2. Cancer rates
        3. Death rates
    C. Tables
IV. Economy

We are not so rash as to argue that all hypertext has—or should have—this sort of hierarchical structure. It does seem, however, that some of the structural patterns familiar to teachers of composition may be useful even in what might otherwise seem a foreign medium.

POSSIBILITIES FOR RESEARCH

When Cooper and Odell published *Research on Composing* (1978), they realized that they could only offer "points of departure" rather than frame definitive research agendas. Nonetheless, all the contributors to that volume could go into some detail about research possibilities. If research on written composition was still a relatively new scholarly area, the medium—written text—was thoroughly familiar, and that familiarity allowed contributors to pose a number of new research questions. In the present case, however, the situation is reversed. We now know a good bit about research methodology, but the media under investigation, for most teachers of writing, are not well understood. Consequently, we suggest that scholars in rhetoric and composition might begin with some of the questions that have been so productive in understanding the composing of written texts. Specifically, scholars might begin investigating such topics as the following.

The Nature of the Composing Process

Over the past several decades, scholars in rhetoric and composition have claimed that the composing process: 1) often involves a process of discovery in which one constructed meaning rather than merely writing down ideas that were already fully formed in one's head; 2) is guided at least in part by the generative power of the medium (in this case written or spoken language) in which people composed.

Do these two claims also hold true for the kinds of composing described in this chapter? For example, in creating the PBS video on Applied Learning, Levine (1994) was working with videotapes that someone else had given her; at no point did she add a single word of her own to the "composition" she was creating. From one point of view, she merely assembled materials that someone else had gathered. So is it fair to say she constructed any meaning of her own? If she did, was this construction influenced by the visual content of the medium in which she was working—by, for example, the scenes of public school students at work in their classrooms? Was Levine's meaning-making process influenced by the constraints (or the possibilities) of the medium in which she was working?

Choices and the Bases for Choosing

One way to describe our work as writing teachers is to say we help students become aware of the options available to them and then help them choose wisely from among those options. When we are dealing with written texts, we have a pretty good idea of how to proceed. We can help students see the choices they can make with regard to the relative formality or informality of diction, complexity and structure of sentences, patterns of organization, and kinds of elaboration and reasoning present in (or absent from) a particular text. And we have some sense of how those choices might be guided by audience, purpose, or genre.

But the kinds of composing represented in this chapter may seem to take us well out of our depth, for talk of the linguistic choices we understand so well may sometimes be inappropriate or inadequate. Levine (1994), for example, had no power to shape the diction or syntax of the people who spoke in her videotape; nor was she able to include any of her own language in that videotape. Arguably, then, if Levine were a student in one of our writing classes, much of what we know about linguistic choices doesn't seem especially relevant. By contrast, the people who composed the Pravachol ad and the "Cancer Alley" hypertext could make choices of language and syntax. But those linguistic choices represent just one part of an array of choices available in these instances. Creators of both the ad and the hypertext had to make a number of choices about page (or screen) design: How much "white" space would there be? How large and what shape would the blocks of text be? How would they construct an "eyepath" for the reader? How would blocks of text be positioned on the page? And the creator(s) of the ad had to make still further choices—about color, light, typography, pictures, and so on.

It's the "and so on" in the previous sentence that may be of most concern to composition teachers and researchers. Are there other kinds of decisions that we don't have the training or knowledge to recognize? Suppose we asked, say, an experienced composer of hypertext to do a compose-aloud protocol or to review a draft of a hypertext document. Where would we find that person hesitating, weighing options? What would those options be? How might the experienced hypertext creator differ from the novice? Would we find that one of them focused on options that never figured in the deliberations of the other?

The Meaning-Making Processes of "Readers"

We know a good bit about what readers do when they encounter certain kinds of written texts. We know, for example, that they don't always read every word; rather, they tend to focus on those portions of a text that particularly concern them (see Redish, 1993). But our knowledge of readers is based on studies of what people do when they try to construct meaning from the printed page. What happens when "readers" encounter hypertext or presentations that include oral language, written language, and visual images? If readers pay selective attention to information presented through one medium, surely they must have to be even more selective when confronted with the barrage of information possible in a multimedia presentation. But what do they pay attention to? Do they rely on one sort of information (the content of visual images, for example) more than the spoken or written text that accompanies those images? And what can the field of technical communication tell us about what readers do when they try to "navigate" an online hypertextual document?

In addition to these familiar questions, we also need to consider issues that arise when people compose in new media or in combined media. By what criteria shall we judge communications that involve more than one medium? How relevant is our existing knowledge of composition and rhetoric?

Criteria or Standards

All three media previously discussed contain compelling visual images that convey a number of messages virtually simultaneously. Yet as Doheny-Farina (1995) has argued, the richness and speed of this sort of communication is not necessarily conducive to careful reflection. Consider, for example, the PBS video. Implicitly, the tape claims that the practices shown are typical of Applied Learning classrooms. But are they? Would one find comparable work going on in other such classrooms? Can this sort of work be done by any teacher of reasonable competence or does one have to be, as Gist-Evans is, a truly gifted teacher? How shall we decide whether a video presentation contains claims that are reliable and valid?

Furthermore, how shall we writing teachers assess our students' efforts to create videos, websites, or other multimedia presentations? Are there any criteria that will apply to both linguistic and visual features of a text? What sort of models shall we hold up to students? And how shall we articulate the reasons we find those models exemplary?

The Relevance of Our Existing Knowledge

Running through this chapter has been the assumption that we need to expand our notion of composing, opening it up to include such dimensions as oral language, page (or screen) design, static visual images, and video. Clearly, each new dimension requires us to move into a foreign territory, each with its own language and customs. So just how foreign is each of these new territories? How do the language, methodology, and guiding principles of each territory relate to what we already know?

For example, when visual artists talk about the "resonance" of typography and page design, they seem to mean something comparable to what writing teachers define as *voice*—the implicit or explicit stance a text takes toward its audience and subject. Do resonance and voice have roughly the same meaning? Would a graphic artist find nuances in resonance that a composition teacher would not find in voice? Similarly, in designing websites and other types of online information, technical communicators concern themselves with navigability or accessibility. How do these concepts overlap with what composition specialists mean when they talk about organization?

Even if we do find some areas of significant overlap, it's almost certain that we'll occasionally find ourselves wondering whether the critical apparatus we use in analyzing conventional text had any value in analyzing the media represented in an expanded view of composing. Consider hypertext, for example. This medium is founded on the assumption that readers will not move through the text in a linear fashion, but may, instead, enter the text at any number of points, thereby, in effect, creating their own structure for the text. What does this do to the notion of hierarchical structure that seems so important for many conventional texts? In the case of the "Cancer Alley" materials cited earlier, we saw that at least one hypertext reflected a fairly conventional-looking hierarchical structure. But will we find this structure in other hypertext materials? Is there any other conceptual (or pedagogical) baggage we will be able to take with us as we move into the unexplored territory represented by video, hypertext, or static visual images? What will we need to leave behind?

* * *

These questions, of course, only scratch the surface of the work that is to be done if we expand our definition of composing. But perhaps they will serve as points of departure that will justify the time-honored conclusion for research reports: Further research is clearly indicated.

REFERENCES

Cooper, C. R., & Odell, L. (1978). *Research on composing*. Urbana, IL: National Council of Teachers of English.

Dohney-Farina, S. (1995). *Rhetoric, innovation, and technology.* Cambridge, MA: MIT Press.

Grice, R. A., Ridgeway, L. S., & See, E. J. (1991). Hypertext: Controlling the leaps and bounds. *Technical Communication, 38,* 48–56.

Keyes, E. (1993). Typography, color, and information structure. *Technical Communication, 40,* 638–646.

Levine, B. A. (1994). *Applied Learning Program* [Videotape]. (Available from the Public Broadcasting Service, Pittsburgh, PA)

Meggs, P. B. (1992). *Type and image: The langauge of graphic design.* New York: Van Nostrand Reinhold.

Nerone, J. C., & Barnhurst, K. G. (1995). Visual mapping and cultural authority: Design changes in U.S. newspapers, 1920–1940. *Journal of Communication, 45*, 9–43.

Pfaffenberger, B. (1997). *The elements of hypertext style.* Boston: AP Professional.

Redish, J. C. (1993). Understanding readers. In C. M. Barnum & S. Carliner (Eds.), *Techniques for technical communicators* (pp. 14–41). New York: Macmillan.

Richards, I. A. (1965). *The philosophy of rhetoric.* New York: Oxford University Press.

Strunk, W., & White, E. B. (1979). *The elements of style* (3rd ed.). New York: Macmillan.

chapter 17

Intellectual Bureaucrats: The Future of Employment in the Twilight of the Profession*

Richard E. Miller
Rutgers University

For those who study the job market in higher education, it is clear that the nature of work in the academy is undergoing a radical reformation. The declining tax base, the rise of animosity for education as a kind of "social engineering," the steady replacement of tenured lines with temporary professionals, the encroachment of total quality management and outcomes assessment, and the public cries for tangible evidence of the "products" of education—all of these events have served to change what it means to be a teacher in the academy and what it means to be a graduate student training for entry into this profession. There are those who, in the wake of these changes, openly deplore the disappearance of students who embark on the adventure of advanced study purely out of a love for and devotion to learning. And there are others who lament the public's intrusions into our discussions about what should be taught and why. I, however, can find no compelling reason to mourn either the passing of these older ways of imagining the business of higher education as a pure pursuit nor do I regret the erosion of this

* Adapted from Richard E. Miller, *A Politics of Impuirity*. Copyright © 1998 by Cornell University Press. Used by permission of the publisher.

rhetoric's power to capture and mesmerize higher education's clientele. Rather, I think that we might see this change in the status of higher education as an opportunity to retool for a market much less inclined to support the ceaseless production of cultural critique. And, in this respect, at least, I think there are reasons to be cautiously optimistic that those who work in composition are well positioned to respond to the increasing demands that higher education reorient itself to meet the needs of beginning students. So, at the risk of breaking with the consensus that this shift in the job market and the ongoing redefinition of what constitutes work in the profession is to be *wholly* regretted, I would like to suggest that these changes are better understood as an emergent opportunity for those truly interested in becoming public intellectuals, those committed to improving the educational chances of the disenfranchised, those involved in the work of theorizing and disentangling encounters with difference. The twilight of the profession is best seen, in other words, as the slow dawning of a new profession, one that may well be more openly committed to meeting the needs of students on the margins of the academy, more responsive to the concerns of the local community, more likely to set into motion a range of pedagogical and bureaucratic practices designed to provide instruction in the arts of working within and against dominant systems of constraint.

That I find these possibilities exciting and even desirable does not allow me to forget for a moment that this new incarnation of the profession, where the boundary between the intellectual and the bureaucrat is blurred, is not what lures most people to graduate school. Nor have I lost sight of the fact that this shift in the job market has already occasioned a great deal of agony, disappointment, anger, and despair. But, in the interests of defamiliarizing a problem that has, as yet, appeared insoluble, I propose that we think through what exactly it is about the reformation of higher education's job market that is causing so much resentment. A good place to begin such an examination is with a consideration of how "composition" and the teaching of entry-level students have been figured in and by the profession's call to arms. If we turn, for example, to the work of Bérubé and Nelson, who have distinguished themselves in the general discussion of the academic job crisis by proposing specific and substantial changes in the way academics approach the business of education, we can see how the eminent possibility of labor in composition functions as a sign of the academy's collapse. A 1995 issue of *Academe*, which includes articles by both Nelson and Bérubé, has a cover that aptly captures their sense of what graduate school has become—it is a place where professionally attired graduate students ascend and descend a series of stairs leading nowhere, a factory for producing proto-professionals, all dressed up with no place to go.

THE EMBODIED ACCUSATION: GRADUATE STUDENTS AND THE JOB CRISIS

In the introduction to their jointly edited collection, *Higher Education Under Fire* (1995), Bérubé and Nelson insist that academics must now "admit that the long-term collapse of the job market is making the logic of graduate apprenticeship morally corrupt" (p. 20). "What does it mean," they ask, "to face an academic future in which many graduate students will have none? What are the ethics of training students for jobs that few of them will ever have?" (pp. 20–21). With these pointed questions, Bérubé and Nelson draw on the ever-serviceable figure of the anonymous student to animate their charges concerning the moral and ethical failings of the academy. In so doing, they offer a vision of the "graduate student" as a persevering entity struggling bravely to fulfill the requirements for joining the profession, while balancing the heavy demands of teaching entry-level courses that tenured faculty presumably no longer wish to staff. Within this rhetorical gambit, in other words, the "graduate student" functions as the embodiment of an accusation, a figure who haunts the academy like a guilty conscience, a constant reminder of the academic's inability to read, let alone control, the market forces that determine whether or not a job stands on the other side of all the courses, examinations, time, and debt that together make up the material costs of the creditialization process.

In better times, it was easier for everyone involved in the business of higher education to think of the "graduate student" as an apprentice training to enter a vaunted profession—a "secular vocation," as Robbins (1993) calls it. With the collapse of the job market, however, it now requires a great deal more work to conceal or explain the fact that academics are complicitous in the "morally corrupt" business of trading in human capital: some insist that higher education has nothing to do with generating employable end-products; others long for the days when students worried more about learning and less about the future; and nearly everyone blames an ignorant public and craven administrators for misconstruing the virtuous work of graduate education as exploitation. Unsatisfied with this ongoing exchange of critique and analysis of the collapse of the market, Bérubé and Nelson (1995) have argued for a packet of institutional reforms and administrative procedures that seek not only to shift the terms of the debate, but to actually alter the material practices of higher education. Thus, for example, they have called for reducing both the number and size of graduate programs across the country and strengthening the "gatekeeping function" of the master's degree (p. 21). Complementing these reforms, which would reduce the number of applicants competing for employment, Bérubé and Nelson want to further improve the employment picture by increasing the number of available jobs—an utterly unobjectionable goal that can be accomplished, they believe, by enjoining universities and colleges to put together attractive early-retirement packages and strenuous post-tenure reviews so that nonperforming faculty members can be eased out of the profession. Finally, in the interest of improving the treatment of graduate students prior to their entry into the job market, Bérubé and Nelson call for higher wages and better benefits for teaching assistants, better career counseling, improved training for teaching jobs at nonresearch colleges and universities, and more faithful fulfillment by faculty of their obligations to students entering the job market (pp. 22–23). In short, Bérubé and Nelson wish to respond to the current job crisis by implementing a set of procedures that would create jobs where none now exist; in this way, *their* students will get "good" jobs, their consciences will be cleansed, and the problem will be solved.

Putting aside the question of whether such a massive reform of academic culture could ever be enacted, it is worth noting how heavily these proposals rely on exclusively bureaucratic procedures for accomplishing the essentially social mission of insuring future employment for current graduate students: Indeed, Bérubé and Nelson (1995) have a remarkable faith in the power of such procedures to do a good job of discriminating between programs that should be allowed to continue and those that shouldn't; between students who are best qualified to pursue graduate work and those who aren't; and between advanced professors who are fulfilling their pedagogical, scholarly, and professional responsibilities and those who would best be encouraged to study the packet on early retirement. Nelson (1995) believes so firmly in administered change, in fact, that he has since gone so far as to codify his proposals into a "12-step program for academia," thereby transforming the massive bureaucratic system of higher education into a dysfunctional entity that needs only to move through the prescribed rigorous therapeutic regime to regain its psychic health and moral integrity. There should be a bill of rights for graduate students and teaching assistants, a union (which could exercise its power, in Nelson's now-famous example, by "organizing group shopping trips to other states for all purchases"), "a year's work for a year's wage" (or, more helpfully, a year's wage for a year's work). Also, community colleges should be encouraged to hire Ph.D.'s; research universities should exchange postdoctoral teachers; and the positive accomplishments of the academy should be publicized (pp. 22–25).

As laudable as it is that Bérubé and Nelson (1995) have drawn attention to the fundamentally bureaucratic nature of the educational enterprise, it is unfortunate that their insights into the business of education have not led them to rethink how reform comes about in this type of institutional setting. Instead, Bérubé and Nelson fall into what I call "the teacher's fallacy," constructing the academy as an unruly student, bereft of a personal history or a set of internal motivations, ready to do as told if only told forcefully enough. Furthermore, in occupying the role of reformer, Nelson and Bérubé can't shake the peremptory mode of address that comes to them by virtue of their long training as intellectuals, for, as Hunter (1994) has argued, it is "as the bearer of a prestigious spiritual demeanor and moral authority...that [the figure of the critical intellectual] finds its niche in the school system, alongside the figures of the citizen and the bureaucrat" (p. xxiii). Suffused with this moral authority, Bérubé and Nelson have now brought their message of reform to their colleagues, only to be met with a chilly reception. Nelson (1995), for instance, reports being surprised by his colleagues' anger at his efforts to have the administration use some "vacated faculty salaries to increase the size and number of graduate student fellowships" (p. 23). And Bérubé (1995), while conceding that "we can't do much about the larger economic issue at stake here, the wholesale conversion of full-time, tenure-track jobs to part-time adjunct positions," nevertheless insists that we use "our waning sanity and ever-precarious good sense" to decry the inflated requirements for entry-level positions, which have "heightened tensions and worsened working conditions in the profession" (pp. 28–29). In the face of such hearty hortatory admonitions, the faculty resists, the administration resists, and, following these good examples and the traits that got them into the higher echelons in the first place, the students themselves resist banding together and working for the improvement of all.

OF CRITIQUE AND OTHER DEMORALIZING PRACTICES

I would like now to draw attention to that part of academic culture that Nelson (1995) feels is not subject to change. As he puts it:

> [A]lthough I have taught composition and enjoyed it, I would now find it demoralizing and intolerable to have to grade hundreds of composition papers each semester. There is no way I could do it as carefully and thoroughly as my graduate students do. So what is to be done? (p. 21)

With this backhanded compliment, praising *his* graduate students for their ability to perform work he himself finds "demoralizing and intolerable," Nelson inaugurates his 12-step program for reforming the profession. And it is precisely because Nelson finds work in composition so repulsive that he must figure out what changes can be enacted that will improve the employment possibilities for his graduate students without imperiling his own position of privilege. Read in this light, his proposals to shut down marginal graduate programs, to better police the boundaries separating the master's degree and the Ph.D., to convince community colleges to hire instructors with doctorates, and so forth. all seem as concerned with preserving the primacy of research institutions as they are with addressing the putative needs of the oft-invoked suffering but dedicated graduate student. Presumably, Nelson and Bérubé are banking on the persuasive powers of this sympathetic figure to cover their proposals with the kind of moral authority necessary to shame their colleagues into action. In this state of shame, no one will bother questioning the desirability of preserving a system that promotes such a debased view of what it means to work with entry-level students.

To take note of this rhetorical deployment of the "graduate student" is not to deny the exigencies of the current job crisis nor is it to suggest that graduate programs are doing an adequate job of preparing their students to confront these exigencies. Deflating the rhetorical force of this figure does, however, make room for a consideration of the paradox that resides at the heart of these proposals: Just how is it that graduate students are able to do such a good job doing work Nelson and his colleagues find "demoralizing and intolerable"? Is it youthful enthusiasm? Naivete? A natural talent for dirty work? And what does Nelson do to insure that his students don't end up suffused with his distaste for such work so that, when the time comes for them to move into those newly minted positions at the local community college he and Bérubé have dreamed up, they don't somehow feel that they've been betrayed by a system that brought them to the heights of critical theory, only to drop them in what they have been so thoroughly trained to see as the deepest valley of the academy? Exactly what kind of "career counseling" is going to prepare future members of the profession for the shocking and vertiginous disjunction that exists between the demands of graduate work and the bureaucratic realities of academic employment, whether permanent or temporary?

In his ongoing battle with Sander Gilman, past president of the MLA, Nelson has recently called the Modern Language Association to task for its failure to communicate a more accurate representation of what it now means to enter the profession of English studies. Here is the advertisement Nelson satirically suggests might better reflect what graduate programs have in store for their teaching assistants: "Come and teach marginally literate business majors how to write! Help students increase their earning power! Loans available to help cover your expenses! Good job performance ratings will have no effect on plans to terminate your employment!" (1995, p. 21). Once again, even as Nelson offers a much needed critique of the MLA's refusal to come to terms with the realities of the marketplace, he can't help but be repulsed by the very kind of work that composition instructors—and graduate students throughout the profession—are regularly required to do. This is Nelson's Kurtzian moment, for the horror he imagines is a world where an English teacher might be forever compelled to move among the "marginally literate," forever lost to the work of teaching others to write, forever vulnerable to an indifferent employer who hires and fires at will, extracting labor without regard to the human consequences. However much one might agree with Nelson's analysis of the inequities in the academy's labor practices, it is hard to share in his panic at the thought that teaching in the profession might largely entail working with non-English majors or that the goal of such labor might be nothing more than assisting students in improving their social position. After all, these working conditions are the ones that composition teachers live with everyday: Students are required to take expository writing courses and that they are so required is understood by everyone involved to be an expression of the institutional belief that all students must be proficient writers if they are going to advance through the system. From the institutional standpoint, then, there's nothing personal about this pedagogical relationship: students must attend; teachers must be present; papers must be solicited, assessed, and returned. And, regardless of what actually happens during this process, instruction must be said to have occurred.

OF BUREAUCRACIES AND SOCIAL AGENCY

This denuded description of what teaching entails doesn't make for good ad copy, of course, but it does capture what it means to get into the business "on the ground floor" at present. And, for those who believe that being a teacher is supposed to lead to absolutely autonomous working conditions, the experience of actually working at this location in the academy is bound to be experienced as a betrayal of some sacred trust. There is no question that this felt sense of betrayal is both profoundly painful and all but completely disempowering: evidence of this is always on tap, as may be seen in the fact that the academic presses never tire of churning out their bookshelf-bending load of diatribes about the collapse of the university, the struggle for the soul of higher education, the imperiled academy, and so on. Perhaps the time is ripe, however, to leave off critiquing the academy for having failed to make good on its promise of delivering a meaningful, morally sacrosanct life and to begin, instead, to work within the fiscal and bureaucratic constraints that both enable the academic enterprise and limit its scope. With regard to teaching, this means recognizing that one is inescapably implicated in a bureaucratic system and that, therefore, the best that one can do is to commit oneself to the seemingly impossible project of becoming a "good bureaucrat." As noxious as such an idea is sure to sound to all, given the exclusively negative connotations linked to bureaucrats, this idea is likely to be seen as positively repulsive both to those who espouse a commitment to radical reform and to those wholly uninterested in how the business of higher education is carried out as long as their monthly paycheck arrives on time.

Under the barrage of this entirely predictable range of responses, the promise held out to those who would reconsider the relationship between intellectual and bureaucratic work is modest indeed: by letting go of the ideology of the intellectual's exclusively critical function, the opportunity arises for experiencing a real sense of agency in the world of local academic affairs. By "a real sense of agency," I do not mean that faithfully carrying out one's teaching duties, assigning grades fairly, promoting the academic success of all students regardless of race, class, sexual preference, gender, or political leanings, and actively serving on departmental and university-wide committees will change the nature of academic work. It will not. To think of agency only as the ability to alter massive cultural structures, to shift the thinking of large numbers of people, or to perform any number of similarly grand feats of conversion is to effectively remove agency from the realm of human action: no single individual, working alone, has ever realized any of these paradigm-shattering goals. If, however, agency is understood as the act of working within extant constraints, simultaneously preserving and creating the sense of self-worth that comes from participating in the social world, it is not unreasonable to reconceive the goal of higher education as promoting conditions in which everyone has the opportunity to learn how to be an agent for sustainable change.

The first step toward achieving this sense of agency is to develop a sufficiently nuanced understanding of power relations to see that constraining conditions are not paralyzing conditions. This understanding is always well within reach; indeed, as soon as one enters the school system and begins to learn about its ritualized practices, shortcomings, prejudices, and strengths, one inevitably discovers that "relatively autonomous working spaces" are there to be found somewhere—not all teachers have the same standards, require the same amount or kind of work, respond in the same way, demand the same level of respect and punctuality, act according to the same protocols of behavior, or ascribe to the same ethical or political belief systems. Unfortunately, this very fact tends to promote a surprisingly unsophisticated analysis of the dynamics of power in a bureaucracy. There are those places where one is free—for the student, this tends to mean those rare classes where the teacher values one's work; for the teacher, the sense of freedom is likely to arise in response to being allowed to decide the content of instruction. And there are all the other places where one is paralyzed, where one's work is nothing more than an empty response to mandatory requirements—for teacher and student alike, this could well describe the entire experience of schooling. When this is how life in a bureaucracy is experienced, it is not surprising that what results are fantasies of escape and thundering jeremiads about the system's gross inequities.

But, as I've meant to suggest here, even for those most interested in reforming the academy, escaping the bureaucratic machinery of assessing and evaluating the work of others is simply impossible; and, as we have seen as well, all the fulminating moral posturing in the world does nothing to change this essential aspect of modern life. So, what remains for those who want to change what can be changed, is tinkering on the margins of the academy, altering admissions standards, participating in the slow, sustained, all-but-anonymous work of designing curricula that are more responsive to a range of learning practices and cultural backgrounds, training teachers to think differently about the assumptions underlying the idea of native intelligence, participating actively in hiring decisions, providing instruction at all levels in the arts of discovering the possibilities that emerge when one sets out to enumerate and then work on and within extant constraints. The university won't be overthrown by such modest adjustments, capitalism won't be brought to its knees, and the manifest social injustices of an institution that trades in the business of naturalizing and then hierarchizing the citizenry's culturally produced differences won't be erased. Under the best circumstances, the most one can hope for is that fostering the development of this hybridic persona—the intellectual bureaucrat—will produce an academic environment that rewards versatility, as well as specialization, teaching as well as research, public service as well as investment in the self. But, by providing students with the opportunity to rethink the assumed opposition between the academy and the business world, the intellectual and the bureaucrat, it may just be possible to promote the development of sensibility that can bear thinking creatively about administrative matters, a state of mind that seeks to insure that institutional working and learning conditions approach the humane ideal that resides at the core of all efforts to democratize access to higher education.

The academy is actually already well positioned to make this modest shift. To begin with, recent work in cultural studies and postmodern theory, as well as ongoing efforts to understand subject formation in relation to the race, class, gender complex, has provided much of the critical material that is necessary for the production of what I have called the "good bureaucrat." That is, taking on the hybridic persona of the intellectual bureaucrat would appear to require a remarkable tolerance for ambiguity, an appreciation for structured contradictions, a perspicacity that draws into its purview the multiple forces determining individual events and actions, an understanding of the essentially performative character of public life, a recognition of the inherently political character of all matters emerging from the power/knowledge nexus—all attributes highly valued on the contemporary critical scene. And, regardless of one's disciplinary training or theoretical commitments, everyone who has risen through the ranks of the academy possesses a storehouse of knowledge about successful strategies for navigating a bureaucratic system and ideas about what would make the system function more efficiently, if not more humanely.

While this wealth of critical and experiential knowledge would seem to provide a promising foundation upon which one might construct a culture that valued the anonymous labor of the intellectual bureaucrat, it would be foolish to imagine that the current revulsion at the notion of bureaucratic work is going to be overcome either by reasoned argument or by gesturing to the collapse of a market for purely intellectual labor. One need only try to find a positive representation of the bureaucrat to realize how deep the contempt for this social entity runs: after all, how can one produce a positive representation of a petty-fogging, paper-pushing, rule-bound, ring-kissing, social automaton? Indeed, to commence such a search is to see how centrally bureaucracies figure across the entire narrative spectrum as the social space that true individuals avoid at all costs. For, regardless of whether the bureaucracy being represented involves personnel from the military, government services, law enforcement, education, or the political sphere, generic conventions require that all dignity, honor, and glory go to those who distinguish themselves from this faceless mass and from all who would be governed by dominant codes of behavior.

This is a fitting observation to close on, as it captures the conflictual relationship that exists between the intellectual and bureaucrat, despite the fact that both figures depend upon each other to make the work that they do possible and meaningful. It is certainly the case that the academy can continue to operate, as it has from the outset, by seeing work in these two spheres as fundamentally opposed. And there are undoubtedly compelling reasons for steadfastly refusing to see how these two spheres might be made to function in concert, and equally convincing arguments for insisting that we resist contaminating the educational process by trying to bring these spheres together. However, for those of us weary of feeling utterly powerless—those of us interested in translating into a workable plan of action the dissatisfaction with institutional life that makes itself known everywhere—overcoming the deep revulsion we all feel for the bureaucratic conditions that simultaneously constrain and enable our work in the academy may well be the best chance we have for shaping how the business of intellectual inquiry gets carried out in the future. That is, if the shift in the job market and hiring trends does indeed signal that the academy is undergoing a radical reformation at the hands of economic powers over which no single individual or corporate entity exercises control, the best strategy available to anyone seeking to enter or remain in the profession could well lie in the seemingly unimaginable, but immanently realizable project of fabricating for oneself and for the academic community at large the viable persona of the intellectual bureaucrat.

REFERENCES

Bérubé, M. (1995, November/December). Standard deviation: Skyrocketing job requirements inflame political tensions. *Academe,* 26–29.

Bérubé, M., & Nelson, C. (Eds.). (1995). *Higher education under fire.* New York: Routledge.

Hunter, I. (1994). *Rethinking the school: Subjectivity, bureaucracy, criticism.* New York: St. Martin's Press.

Miller, R. E. (1998). *As if learning mattered: Reforming higher education.* Ithaca, NY: Cornell University Press.

Nelson, C. (1995, November/December). Lessons from the job wars: What is to be done? *Academe,* 22–25.

Robbins, B. (1993). *Secular vocations.* London: Verso.

Watson Conference Oral History #6: Working Inside and Outside Composition Studies October 1996 Charles Bazerman, Charles Cooper, Richard Lloyd-Jones, and Lee Odell

Randy Cauthen, interviewer
edited by Pamela Takayoshi

Randy Cauthen: There has been an argument about the professionalization of the discipline as a whole that it was better being on the outside looking in as far as intellectual purity and so on. Would any of you care to comment on that?

Lee Odell: I think maybe the price composition studies and rhetoric has paid to get in has been too high. I have reservations about how far post-structuralism or critical theories are going to take us. There is a kind of comfort in saying "Oh, well we are doing some of the same things that the literature people, the big boys, are doing," and this may be taking away from the sorts of things that composition studies and rhetoric should really be doing. You're more likely to see studies that involve critical theory now rather than studies of the composing process, but there is also an awful lot we don't know about writing outside of school. I hate to see us give that up just to get on the inside.

Charles Bazerman: There is an awful lot that people in other fields are learning about discursive practices that should be of great interest to people who are concerned with writing. Linguistics have changed, at least in some quarters, a great deal, and there is a return to some of the issues that were excluded by Chomsky-ism. So part of the question is—inside and outside of what. There were enormous motivations for some of us while we are on the outside (and we're still in many ways on the outside) to get inside and to do things we thought were important. There are many benefits for being on various kinds of inside. The one place that composition and rhetoric hasn't cracked yet at all is elite institutions—these are places of privilege, and these are places where composition and rhetoric could enter into a variety of conversations that are intellectually and socially very important. Getting inside of that is important, although I have very mixed feelings about the prices to be paid. On the other hand, maybe now that we are comfortably in, we can get more courage to assert where our own work leads us.

Charles Cooper: Of course, once you are brought in with tenure at an elite university, as both Chuck and I were, then you really can do anything you want and nobody seems to mind. I was very comfortable for nearly 20 years in the UCSD literature department, but I actually had very little interaction with most of my colleagues, and yet they were entirely supportive of what I was doing. I'm sure it struck most of them as a little weird, but I was productive and professionally involved and carried out my administrative assignment responsibly. My work was accepted and credited for what it was, including a textbook and a long period of consulting with the state Department of Education to develop a writing assessment. I don't know where we would go if not to English departments. We could go back to schools of education. That's where I started out, and I was very comfortable there. My interests, research, graduate courses—they were all encouraged. I don't know where the outside is. It must be different places at different campuses. The fundamental problem in research universities is bringing assistant professors of composition studies into English departments and getting them tenured.

Richard Lloyd-Jones: What characterizes English departments is the isolation of specialists in the programs. Medievalists barely talk to the Renaissance people, and so on. Furthermore, only people over 50 distinguish themselves as being Victorian or Romantic; others distinguish themselves by the kind of criticism they do, and they stand in isolation. When we stand in isolation, we are just like them. We are not an isolated subgroup. Noncomposition people pay us the courtesy of noninvolvement. They treat us the same way they would treat someone in chemistry or political science. We have our place, but it is not their place. They are only vaguely interested in what we are doing. We have a cadre of people who train the graduate students and supervise them to teach the freshmen and sophomores. But the regular English faculty don't really want to know anything about it because they are pretty sure it involves more work than they want to do. Mutual toleration is what I would say rather than really having a heart.

LO: How long can English departments flourish as English departments with that kind of isolation and with being able to say "I am sticking out this tiny little bit of turf and I am not going to have it include anything larger"? That seems to me deadly.

RLJ: I think it is deadly, but I think it applies to the whole institution. I don't think it applies to just English. I think it applies to almost all the big institutions in one way or another.

RC: What do you think can be done, or is there anything that can be done? I see it as part of the increasing atomization of the modern world. There is a huge degree of overspecialization of society as a whole.

RLJ: It's not going to be solved by English departments alone. The specialization is seen most dramatically in English, math, and foreign languages, where at the big schools you have two or three tiers of faculty. You have the TA, who is malleable and supervisible. You have the adjunct, who is very temporary, often a semester at a time, quite unsupervised, and often given very little support. Then you have the tenured faculty. Those three tiers are all labeled with an institutional name, and they are like the two worlds that Disraeli talks about—the rich and the poor. They never talk to each other. If the graduate faculty talks to grad students, they talk about dissertations, they don't talk about teaching titles. We have created this monster, which seems to be the lighter view of mass education at the post-secondary level. But it is headed for collapse. We have made a compromise with the schools. We haven't figured out how to deal with the problems yet, and I think somewhere in the next decade or decade and a half, there is going to be a big national explosion deciding how higher institutions are going to operate.

RC: The CCCC declaration on students' rights about language came out of the large social movements of the '60s. I wonder about the place of the profession now, given the fact that the country seems to be lurching fairly consistently toward the right.

RLJ: I think that the lurching to the right is a temporary situation, such as censorship. You always have it—we have a periodical battle about books. What we teach about language is always potentially subversive. As soon as you start saying that language adapts to different situations, it defines the audience, it defines reality, you're bound to get at our real human differences and therefore, it is always potentially going to irritate one group or another—right, left, middle, whatever.

CB: No matter the politics or configurations of a society, literacy is at the heart of the organization of society, and it is something that needs to be understood, needs to be supported to make the society work well, to give people the ability to change and participate. So that's a permanent charge we have, no matter what the politics are of instruction, scholarship, or research. Literacy is an enormous aspect of human life. English departments have historically varying rationales, which they have been willing to articulate or not articulate and which the public either supports or not supports. For a long time, that rationale was the maintenance of a cultural heritage. With the separation of church and state, it took on many of the values and traditions that might have been done with religion. In recent years, it's taken on several different functions, and it has rejected that role. One of those functions has been as an agent of cultural change. This is a role which has not made it popular with the public in the way that the maintenance of the heritage and the great books was a popular role. English departments were also places where oppositional and leftist forces could flourish. That works a little bit with cultural change, but it is slightly different. Given the political moves of the country and the fads and interests coming out of English departments, it may or may not be possible to find a rationale that would maintain large public funding and large interest in majors. That is a very complicated issue. *Their* maintenance is different from *our* maintenance unless we attach ourselves to their issues. I'm very much for those issues which the English department becomes a depository for—cultural concerns, justice, and contemplation. If we perceive composition only in terms of cultural change and cultural critique issues, though, I think we are missing the boat of our larger charge.

LO: I think we do miss that boat, and I understand the larger charge to be an understanding of literacy and the development of literacy so that people cannot simply adapt to our society but flourish in it, change it, work with it. I see that as our charge. But increasingly, composition studies is moving away from that charge. A couple of years ago at MLA, I argued that college English department faculty ought to have a view of literacy that would let them think about what happens in second grade classrooms, and people in the audience said: "I don't know what happens in a second grade classroom. Who am *I* to presume or tell second grade teachers?" They are no one to presume, and the reason they cannot presume is they don't have a comprehensive view of literacy that includes second graders, that includes people outside the academy. We are moving away from a comprehensive view toward a more narrow view that defines us and establishes a platform of ourselves in a scholarly way. Whatever we may think of the larger society, if we cannot develop any of the literacy in the larger society and make it coherent, then those platforms are worthless. I see us moving away from that charge...and I think that's terrible.

RLJ: The things that you were talking about this morning—the emphasis on an alternate language for visual rhetoric—indicates the degree to which some people in the field are immediately concerned with how you shape and embody knowledge for a larger public. But the other side is...when you commit yourself to academic language, you have already made a statement about who's in and who's out. Seeking a sort of professional identity status is a way of isolating ourselves. The very movement toward professionalization is a movement which draws from the larger responsibilities of society.

LO: It's going to take courage to think in some very different ways. We are being pressed to get into distance language at my university, and I'm going to teach a satellite writing course next fall. I have no idea how I am going to do it, and I certainly don't share my president's view that this is the panacea that this is going to save higher education. But it is clear that we cannot live in the 1950s. I think English departments are peculiarly likely to want to live in the 1950s.

RLJ: The nature of their studies is to look backward.

CC: My son-in-law consults with a state university system in getting the process of distance education moving along. And there will be no turning back, I'm sure of that. The focus is on developing courses that stand on their own, bringing together into a neat package whatever e-mail, Web, video, or text resources are required. You can do your coursework at home, in your car, or wherever you can plug in. You can complete a degree from Peoria—or Paraguay—if you can pay for the courses.

LO: But the irony is that this technological advance is an intellectual retreat. Once again, people are talking about delivery content as a synonym for education. A couple of friends are teaching a satellite course to 80 people. Because they are trying not to just deliver content, the work load is staggering for them. Eighty papers just came in the other day...80 papers...long papers...hypertext papers!

CB: In a competitive market, the possibility of serious interactivity is becoming very technologically supported and in ways that make it less of a burden...not just the papers that get mailed and you have to grade more papers, but there are more possibilities. It seems to me that any institution with the technical know-how, working together with faculty, can develop more interesting products than canned lectures. That may be too hard to do, too much of an up-front commitment.

LO: The technology exists so that classrooms can be expanded. People in this classroom can see people in other classrooms 1,000 miles away. But try interacting among not 30 people, but 80 or 100 people, and you can no longer think of it as a system for delivery content. But what people want most to see is the expansion of the delivery of content. The people who see the technology as solutions oversimplify the conceptual problems—it is going to be an enormous amount of work to bring that off and there still has to be a human being who does a lot to the conceptual work.

RC: Well, we have switched gears a little bit. What is your perspective on the internal conflicts within the field of composition—current traditional to expressionist to cognitivist to social movement? Do you think that those kinds of conflicts, which have occasionally gotten extraordinarily heated, are inevitable as part of professionalization?

LO: A little conflict can heighten or clarify in some way, but finally, I think it is very sad because we lose something in these battles. In looking vigorously at what this will do and what it won't do, we simply reject this as positivist or as expressivist. In place of thinking where that expressive element might fit in some larger scheme, we deny it, and I think that is just destructive to the profession. But we try to act as though things are wholly included or excluded.

CB: I agree very much with what Lee is saying about the range of validity and intersections. Situating cognitive studies and the relationship between cognition and social practices is very big right now. I know several projects that are at that intersection now. So that's to the good. But certain publications get more cited and more read than others—for example, those things of mine that are clearly identifiable within some category get read and cited. The work I've been doing, which is trying to create integrations, by and large goes unnoticed. The disparity has been quite amazing to me about the difference, and in fact, I don't see issues I could pursue in isolation—I have to move to these integrated accounts of what I want to grasp. But, the integrative accounts are just not of interest...are hard for people to read....

RLJ: They're hard for people to quote.

CC: I think these camps or divisions produced a lot of posturing, meanness, and friction, but I think we have to live with that. As literacy specialists especially, we have to embrace any new theory of language at least to figure out what it has to offer, no matter how outlying or threatening it may be. I have always believed that the more theories and methods you know, the greater number of choices you have as a mentor and researcher and curriculum specialist.

Author Index

Subject Index